Trademark Acknowledgments

glasshaus has endeavored to provide trademark information about all the companies and products mentioned in this book by the appropriate use of capitals. However, glasshaus cannot guarantee the accuracy of this information.

Credits

Authors
Michael Bordash
Peter Fletcher
Alan Foley
Robert Goodyear
Alex Homer
Peter-Paul Koch
Bill Mason
Bob Regan
Adrian Roselli
Cliff Wootton

Contributing Author
Dave Gibbons

Technical Reviewers
Martin Honnen
Mark Horner
Mid Jamie
Jody Kerr
Shefali Kulkarn
Tim Luoma
David Schultz
Jon Stephens
Rick Stones

Proofreader
Agnes Wiggers

Commissioning Editor
Chris Mills

Lead Technical Editor
Amanda Kay

Technical Editors
Daniel Walker
Mark Waterhouse
Alessandro Ansa

Publisher
Viv Emery

Brand Visionary
Bruce Lawson

Project Manager
Sophie Edwards
Helen Cuthill

Graphic Editors
Rachel Taylor
Pip Wonson

Graphic Designer
Dawn Chellingworth

Indexer
Bill Johncocks

About the Authors

Michael Bordash

Michael Bordash found his addiction to the Internet in 1996 when he constructed "InternetDJ.com" from his dorm room at New York University, a collaborative of underground and signed DJs and music producers. Mr. Bordash recently merged his successful Internet business consulting practice with IP-Soft.net, a managed network and application development services organization based in downtown New York City. Mr. Bordash continues creating music and managing InternetDJ.com trying to break the first "Internet" artist in his spare time.

Peter Fletcher

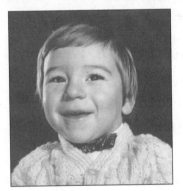

Peter Fletcher has been working in web development since 1997, for most of that time with UK-based publisher Peer Information, via a degree in Philosophy and Theatre Studies and an MSc in Cognitive Science. Interests, professional and recreational, include using the Web as a distributed communications medium, analyzing web traffic data, and working with experimental performance group Stan's Cafe. His personal projects are documented at http://www.joyfeed.com. He is now a freelance web consultant and writer, dividing his time between Birmingham and Barcelona.

Alan Foley

Alan Foley is an assistant professor of Instructional Technology at North Carolina State University in Raleigh, North Carolina, where he teaches graduate classes in the College of Education. Alan holds a Ph.D. in Educational Technology from the University of Wisconsin, Madison. His current research interests include web accessibility and pedagogy, and accessible multimedia production.

Prior to completing his Ph.D., Alan was a high school English teacher. While teaching he was introduced to the world of instructional technology and web design. He has taught web design in a variety of educational and corporate settings and consults schools and universities on accessibility and usability issues.

Robert Goodyear

Unlike most *normal* Florida natives, Robert Goodyear spent the better part of his early years developing unmatched fly-tying skills (it's a fishing thing – although oddly not found in Florida either) and playing concert piano – that is, when he wasn't being roughed up by the other kids in his neighborhood. As the scars from this checkered past faded with time, Rob has been able to develop an impressive professional resume, beginning his career as a photojournalist for the Associated Press, New York Times News Group and UPI, as well as through a variety of state and federal work-release programs throughout the United States and former Soviet Union, eventually winding up with advertising giant Young & Rubicam in Chicago.

Beyond his ten-plus years of expertise in design, branding, creative direction, copywriting, commercial photography, and client wrangling, Rob also has an innate good sense that prompted him to recently flee the sub-zero Chicago winters in search of a new and warmer life in sunny Southern California.

These days, Rob serves as US Production Director of The Global Beach Group, a privately held software development and professional services company with offices in London, Geneva, and Southern California. Rob currently lives near LA with his wife Beth, daughter Lilly, and their dogs Bosco, Tess, and Daisy, where he spends his free time changing diapers, chasing his dogs at the beach, and changing diapers. (Did we mention the diapers?)

Alex Homer

Alex Homer is a computer geek and web developer with a passion for ASP.NET. Although he has to spend some time doing real work (a bit of consultancy and training, and the occasional conference session), most of his days are absorbed in playing with the latest Microsoft web technology and then writing about it. Living in the picturesque wilderness of the Derbyshire Dales in England, he is well away from the demands of the real world – with only an Internet connection to maintain some distant representation of normality. But, hey, what else could you want from life?

Peter-Paul Koch

Peter-Paul Koch is a freelance web developer in Amsterdam, the Netherlands. He specializes in JavaScript, writes and maintains the JavaScript Section, http://www.xs4all.nl/~ppk/js/, and is a columnist at Digital Web (http://www.digital-web.com/).

Bill Mason

Bill Mason has been building web sites since 1996, first to fuel his love for "Star Trek," then later as a career. Most recently he was employed at the United States cable network Oxygen Media. Currently he works freelance, focusing on front-end development and accessibility. When not working, "Star Trek" continues to fuel his fire. Visit him at http://www.accessibleinter.net/.

This could only be dedicated to my wife, Miriam. She stood by me when things were at their worst, and reminded me that I am a valued person in times when I sincerely doubted it. I love you.

Bob Regan

Bob Regan is the product manager for accessibility at Macromedia. In that role, he works with designers, developers, and engineers from around the world to communicate existing strategies for accessibility as well as develop new strategies. He works with engineers and designers within Macromedia to develop new techniques and improve the accessibility of Macromedia tools.

Bob has a Masters degree from Columbia University in Education. He is currently a doctoral student in Education at the University of Wisconsin – Madison. His dissertation research looks at accessibility policy implementation strategies.

Bob spent six years as a teacher and technology leader in Chicago and New York City. Working with teachers and students across a range of ages and subject matter, he has extensive knowledge of elementary and secondary education. Bob spent two years teaching web design and accessibility at the University of Wisconsin – Madison.

Adrian Roselli

Photo by Rhea Anna

Adrian Roselli is a founder and partner at Algonquin Studios, located in Buffalo, New York, and also holds the moderately confusing title Vice President of Interactive Media.

Adrian has almost 10 years of experience in graphic design, web design, and multimedia development, as well as extensive experience in interface design and usability. He has been developing for the World Wide Web since its inception, when he should have been falling asleep in a video-editing suite. Adrian is also a board member of the American Advertising Federation affiliate in Buffalo (Brainstorm). One of the founders of evolt.org, Adrian has even found time to send scathing site critiques to some of the regulars on the evolt.org mailing list, which is where he spends much of his free time.

Adrian is known as "aardvark" in the wild jungles of the Internet, although if you ask him how he got that nickname, he'll just change the subject and try to steal your sandwich.

I need to thank my family and friends for being genuinely concerned that I had been kidnapped for the duration of this writing. I thank the kind folks over at evolt.org who let me babble from a soapbox on a nearly daily basis. I thank my partners and staff at Algonquin Studios for putting up with me instead of locking me in my office. And I thank Stimulance for feeding me caffeine before I'd doze off in front of my laptop.

Cliff Wootton

Cliff Wootton is a freelance technical consultant in the Internet and Broadcast/Interactive TV industries. Client work has ranged from dynamic web content services and special projects within BBC News Online and architectural design of the BBC News Interactive TV loops service, which has recently won an RTS award for technical innovation. Cliff is married with three daughters and pursues interests in music production and multimedia research outside of work.

I'd like to dedicate this book project to my colleague Russell Merryman who constantly inspires me with his insights into the editorial aspects of our Interactive TV collaborations and his deep knowledge of all topics related to the Doctor Who TV series.

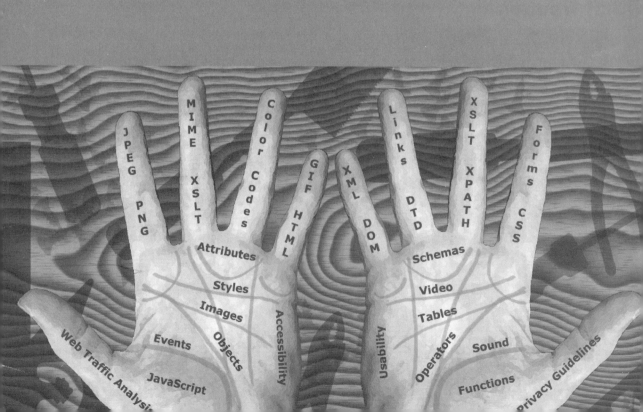

Table of Contents

Table of Contents

Table of Contents

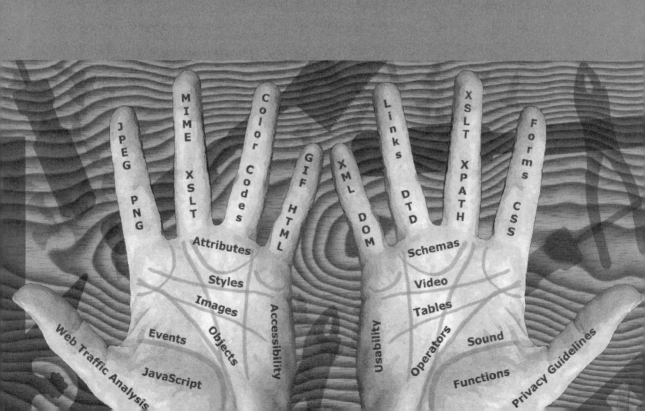

Introduction

So you're good enough to call yourself a web professional, but can you remember everything you need for every occasion? Indeed, should you have to? After all, wouldn't you rather be creating new ideas than remembering some small snippet of JavaScript syntax?

With the help of this book, you'll not need to keep all the syntax and good design rules in your head. It provides a far-reaching reference for client-side technologies and design principles, aiming to answer questions you'll come up against every day. As you'll see from the size, it's not going to be exhaustive; we don't cover topics that you'll only see perhaps once in your career. Neither is it an in-depth tutorial; you should have seen most of these concepts before. However, for those few subjects you haven't had time to read up on yet and need answers about now, it will provide the help you need.

What's It All About?

This should be the one book you buy to carry everywhere you go as a web designer and developer interested in using client-side technologies. From XHTML, CSS, and JavaScript, to Graphics, Usability, and Accessibility, this book has it all, even a look at analyzing your site traffic. If something you know how to do slips your mind as you're building your latest site, reach for the answers: reach for this book.

Who's This Book for?

We assume that you already know a bit about web design and development, and don't need to be led by the hand through the basic tasks. Instead, it's all about being a practical reference for your work.

If you are looking for a more tutorial-style book about the whole web design world, check out *Fundamental Skills of Web Design and Development*, (glasshaus, by Rachel Andrew, Chris Ullman, and Crystal Waters, ISBN: 1-904151-17-5).

What Do I Need to Begin?

To use this book you need a reasonable degree of competence with the technologies covered. You should have a working knowledge of HTML, or XHTML, CSS, and JavaScript. We'll cover the basics of XML, image formats, multimedia, and usability and accessibility practices as well, so you don't need to know all about these. Other than this basic knowledge (and you might be surprised how much you do know), you'll probably want a web browser or two, and a text editor or other web software package such as Dreamweaver but, since you're a web professional, you'll almost certainly have these anyway.

What's Inside?

References, references, and more references. Each chapter is packed with the most frequently encountered elements, objects, methods, uses, practices, and problems associated with the topic it covers.

Chapter 1 quickly refreshes your memory of XHTML. For those who have only used HTML 4.01 before, it introduces the differences, which are small. It includes the elements for tables, forms, styles, links, objects, and images, together with attributes for them all.

In *Chapter 2*, we cover CSS, the best way to style your XHTML documents. After some discussion of how it works, there are property and selector references, so you don't need to carry the whole standard around in your head.

Chapter 3 dives straight into JavaScript, with a brief recap of how and when to use scripting. After that, it's all references: common events, common operators, common objects, and common functions.

In *Chapter 4* we run through those objects that browsers make available to scripting with JavaScript. We'll look at the properties and methods they have, and how to manipulate them.

Chapter 5 examines XML: it reminds you of what it is and the basic rules to follow. As well as providing a reference for using XML, the differences between Schemas and DTDs and when to use which, there is a summary of XSLT and XPath, along with a big XML DOM reference.

In *Chapter 6*, we go over the DOM objects, properties, and methods. We cover Level 0 DOM (the equivalent of the functionality in Netscape 3), the intermediate DOMs of Netscape 4 and IE 4, and finally the W3C DOM for the latest browsers.

Chapter 7 covers the issue of which graphics format to use for what situation: GIF, JPEG, or PNG. You'll never get the wrong one again with this book to hand.

In *Chapter 8*, we take you back to your multimedia options. What there is, how to get it on your page, and where it will and won't work. For those of you who are interested in a more detailed reference to the various multimedia formats and players (QuickTime, Real, Windows Media, and MPEG), there is a *Supplement* to this chapter available to download from *http://www.glasshaus.com*.

In *Chapter 9*, we revisit making your site usable. It's no longer enough that your site looks good, it now has to be easy to use by your target audience too.

In *Chapter 10*, accessibility is the topic up for revision. We look at what it is, how it relates to usability, what you have to do to be compliant with the WCAG guidelines, and who can help.

Finally, *Chapter 11* fills us in on how we can find out if any of our work is being noticed with a quick round-up of web traffic analysis techniques. There's also a refresher on important privacy guidelines.

There are three appendices, consisting of lists of useful values.

Appendix A lists HTML color codes, in name and RGB values, for both the Web Safe Palette of colors, and a much broader range that is supported by most browsers.

Appendix B lists characters you have to escape to use in your web pages, as well as those you may want to but don't always have to.

Appendix C covers those MIME types you're most likely to want to use.

Support and Feedback

Although we aim for perfection, the sad fact of book publication is that a few errors will slip through. We would like to apologize for any that have reached this book despite our efforts. If you spot an error, please let us know about it using the e-mail address *support@glasshaus.com*. If it's something that will help other readers then we'll put it up on the errata page at *http://www.glasshaus.com*.

This e-mail address can also be used to access our support network. If you have trouble running any of the code in this book, or have a related question that you feel that the book didn't answer, please mail your problem to the above address quoting the book title (*The Web Professional's Handbook*), the last 4 digits of its ISBN (**1221**), and the relevant chapter and page number.

Web Support

You'll want to go and visit our web site, at *http://www.glasshaus.com*. It features a freely downloadable compressed version of the full code for this book, in both .sit and .zip formats, for Mac and Windows users, as well as the *Supplement* for *Chapter 8*. You'll also find a copious links to sites covering all topics in this book. For your convenience, we've collected these together so they're only a click away, to save you typing in complex and lengthy URLs. You can also find details of all our other published books, author interviews, and more.

1

- The rules of XML and XHTML

- Element references by type, with their attributes

Author: Michael Bordash

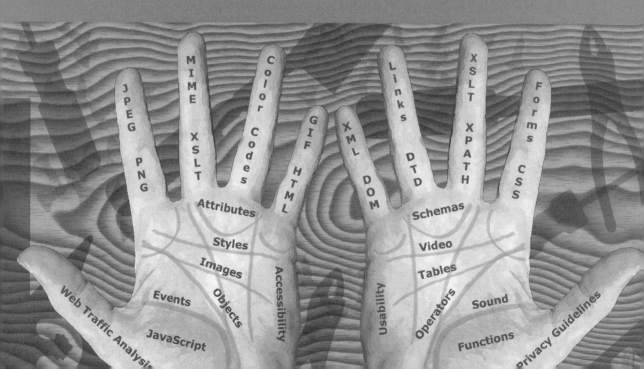

XHTML/HTML

HTML (Hypertext Markup Language) is an application of SGML (Standard Generalized Markup Language). It is the collection of tags and their attributes that is used to create documents on the World Wide Web. HTML documents are plain-text files that can be stored on a web server and made available to the public. Web browsers like Internet Explorer, Netscape Navigator, Opera, or Lynx interpret tags within HTML documents and display the contents (text, images, or objects) of those tags on your computer screen.

Markup languages use **tag containers** to describe the content of a document. In HTML, the tags are enclosed within angle brackets (< >) and are case-insensitive:

```
<h1>Sample Title Text</h1>
```

This tells the parser that the text contained within the tags is a heading, and the browser will display it accordingly. Note that the closing tag is distinguished from the opening tag by a forward slash (/). The opening and closing tags, together with the data contained within them, form what is known in markup terminology as an **element**.

This seemingly simple paradigm of describing content in a logical fashion has caused countless headaches for web technologists and presentation designers. HTML is not a layout tool like Photoshop or even Microsoft Word. Instead, HTML defines the structure of a set of information contained within the HTML file.

This is where a common misuse of HTML comes into play. The intention of HTML is to present data in a non-platform specific way by using tags (like <strong>, <hn>, and <em>) that describe the logic of the document itself. A common misuse of HTML is to use certain tags for setting presentation instead of describing the content. For example, <font> tags are commonly used to describe the formatting of content within web pages. But if describing the format of content was never the intention of HTML, where did the <font> tag come from anyway? To explaining this matter in the clearest possible way, a brief history of HTML is in order.

Brief History Of HTML

1992 – Definition of HTML 1.0
Tim Berners-Lee, a computer scientist at CERN (the European Center for Nuclear Research), defined HTML for the purpose of sharing technical data between universities. The language is an application of SGML (Standard Generalized Markup Language) that allows content within documents to be structured logically using specific elements and attributes. SGML defines the DTD (Document Type Definition) and syntax for HTML. HTML1+ was introduced a year later and added further tags such as tables and forms.

1993 – HTML 2.0
HTML 2.0 became the standard until 1997. HTML 2.0 conforms to the HTML DTD as defined by SGML. It contains everything from the 1.0 specification, and added several new elements.

1994-1996 – HTML 3.0 / 3.2
At this time, the Web was expanding dramatically and Netscape was the clear browser winner. Netscape, responding to popular demand of webmasters worldwide, added several of their own tags into the mix, the `<font>` tag to name one. These tags came to be known as Netscape Extension Tags and the HTML standard as an SGML application began to skew. As mentioned before, HTML was never intended to describe the presentation of content and this lack of standards conformance caused headaches for HTML writers worldwide.

In 1994, the World Wide Web Consortium (W3C) was founded to maintain the logical evolution of HTML and to prevent browser manufacturers from developing proprietary tags. HTML 3.2 was the first standard recommended which left out several of Netscape's and Microsoft's Extension Tags. HTML 3.2 was officially approved as an HTML standard in 1997.

1997-1999 – HTML 4.0 / 4.01
HTML 4 became the official HTML specification in 1998. A major goal of HTML 4 was to deprecate presentation tags introduced by HTML 3, namely `<font>`, `<center>`, `<strike>`, and `<u>`. One of the major goals of HTML 4.0 was to facilitate the **separation of an HTML document's structure from its presentation**, making it possible to control the way the document is presented independently of the content. This allowed, for example, developers to make global changes to the look and feel of the site, without having to go into each individual HTML document to change the colors and fonts of each element. CSS (**Cascading Style Sheets**) was introduced within the HTML 4.0 specification to define the presentational information, leaving the HTML document to describe the structure of the content only, and not things like background colors and font faces. HTML 4.01 was introduced in 1999 to clean up minor elements. HTML 4.01 is the current and final release of HTML.

However, even with the addition of CSS to the HTML specification, the popular browsers will still display badly written and incorrect markup reasonably well. For example, if you happen to forget to close a `<font>` tag in your document or forget to end your table cell definition (`</td>`) most web browsers will let you get away with it. The result may not look pretty, but the browser will parse the document nevertheless.

The W3C set up a committee under John Bosak and Tim Bray to come up with a solution to this problem, and they developed a new markup language called XML (**Extensible Markup Language**).

2000-2002 – XHTML 1.0 / XHTML 1.1
XHTML is the reformation of HTML 4 in XML 1.0. XML 1.0 was developed as a restricted form of SGML, retaining much of its power and losing much of its complexity. Major benefits to XHTML included easy integration of new markup capabilities through the benefits of XML, and easier interoperability among distinct user agents.

Before stepping into XHTML, let's take a look at XML and how it relates to the application of XHTML.

XML

We will be looking at XML in more detail in *Chapter 5*, but now we'll just see how it relates to what we know already. XML allows data to be self-describing and is not concerned about how it appears in a browser. XML is a facility through which information can be exchanged or stored across different operating systems, applications, and data sources. An XML document must conform to a specific set of rules, it must be both **well-formed** and **valid**. We will see what this means in more detail soon, but in short a well-formed document must satisfy the following rules:

- ♦ All elements must have opening and closing tags
- ♦ Empty elements must be of a special form
- ♦ All elements must be nested properly
- ♦ There must be a single root element containing all the other elements
- ♦ XML is case-sensitive

Closing All Elements

In XML all elements, including single elements, must be closed properly . For example the following markup is completely valid in HTML:

```
<ul>
<li>Item One
<li>Item Two
</ul>
```

To conform to the rules of XML, however, you would have to close all the <li> tags:

```
<ul>
<li>Item One</li>
<li>Item Two</li>
</ul>
```

Empty Elements

In HTML there are certain elements that do not have any content, for example <br>, which inserts a line break, or <hr>, which outputs a horizontal line. As we've seen in the rule above, XML insists that all open tags must be closed, so when we have empty elements, the correct way to handle them is with a forward slash like this:

```
This is a sentence.<br />
```

Note the whitespace before the slash. Here is another example of an empty element, this time an image tag that defines certain properties of the image, such as its location, alternative text, and dimensions:

```
<img src="image.gif" alt="My Image" width="2" height="10" />
```

Nesting Elements

Your tags must be nested properly and you must ensure that you close your tags in the correct order, one element must be completely contained in another, for example, the following line of markup is not well-formed:

```
<strong>This markup <em> is not</strong> well-formed.<em>
```

To correct this line of code, you would have to close the `<em>` element before closing the `<strong>` element:

```
<strong>This markup <em> is</em> well-formed.</strong>
```

Root Element

There must be a single element that contains the entire document. This is what the parser uses to determine if it has reached the end of the document or not:

```
<rootelement>
other tags and data go in here
</rootelement>
```

Case-Sensitivity

Within the prior HTML specification, it was possible to mix cases within your tag declarations. For example, this would be completely legal in HTML:

```
<H1>Web page title goes here</h1>
```

In XML this wouldn't be well-formed. XML would consider the `<H1>` tag to be completely different from the `<h1>` tag.

XHTML

We can use the vocabulary of HTML with the syntax of XML; this reformulation of HTML as an XML application is called **XHTML (Extensible Hypertext Markup Language)**. XHTML has the same tags as HTML, but follows the XML grammar; it combines the benefits of HTML with those of XML. In fact, since it is nearly identical to HTML, all modern browsers can parse XHTML documents. Additionally, because XHTML is an XML application, XHTML documents can be displayed in XML-enabled devices (such as certain PDAs, mobile phones, and web browsers) by applying distinct stylesheets appropriate to the user agent rendering the XHTML document.

This is accomplished by utilizing the XSLT language. XSLT is a part of XSL, the stylesheet language for XML. XSLT allows you to translate conforming XML documents, like XHTML, into other XML documents. It is in this specific application where document interoperability exists. Please refer to *Chapter 5* for more information about XSLT translations.

Adherence to the XHTML standard will force developers and HTML hacks alike to create well-formed documents that can be platform- and device-independent. Whether you currently maintain a web site or are just getting started on your first web page, XHTML is the best choice for creating web documents and will be the focus for the tag reference section in this chapter.

HTML will no longer be developed by the W3C, so for the rest of the chapter we will only refer to current XHTML1.0 tag definitions. There are several rules you must adhere to in order to develop a well-formed, accessible and portable web document. All the rules we mentioned earlier about XML documents also apply to XHTML documents; so marking up in XHTML has to be done a little more carefully than it was in HTML. We will now look at some of the differences between HTML and XHTML.

Including an XML Declaration

As XHTML is an application of XML, the following line should appear first in your document:

```
<?xml version="1.0" encoding="UTF-8"?>
```

An XML declaration is not required in all XML documents, but document authors are strongly encouraged to include the declaration at the outset. The XML declaration is, however, required when using encoding other than the standard UTF-8.

> *This line may cause errors in certain browsers (like IE 5.5 Mac) and may cause the browser to render the page as XML and not XHTML. Attribute this sporadic behavior to growing pains of browser conformity to the XHTML specification. You may want to leave this out until all browsers conform to the standard.*

Including a DTD

All XHTML documents must begin with a Document Type Declaration, which names the Document Type Definition (DTD). The declaration will tell the browser which DTD it should parse the document against. There are three types of DTD available for XHTML. **DTD Strict** is used when you want to pay strict adherence to XHTML 1.0 specifications. DTD **Transitional** ("Loose") is used when you want to be able to use some deprecated HTML tags and attributes along with certain elements of XML. This DTD will allow you to write backwards-compatible markup. You should use this when you need to design web pages that are accessible to older browsers that cannot parse XHTML correctly. DTD **Frameset** is used when you want to incorporate frames in your web application. Here are the three DTDs as they would appear on the first line of your web document**:**

```
<!DOCTYPE html PUBLIC "-//W3C//DTD XHTML 1.0 Strict//EN"
          "http://www.w3.org/TR/xhtml1/DTD/xhtml1-transitional.dtd">
```

```
<!DOCTYPE html PUBLIC "-//W3C//DTD XHTML 1.0 Transitional//EN"
        "http://www.w3.org/TR/xhtml1/DTD/xhtml1-strict.dtd">
```

```
<!DOCTYPE html PUBLIC "-//W3C//DTD XHTML 1.0 Frameset//EN" "
        http://www.w3.org/TR/xhtml1/DTD/xhtml1-frameset.dtd">
```

Including the XML Namespace

XHTML documents must include the specific XML namespace to be used when parsing the document. Within the <html> element, you must specify which XML namespace is to be used with the xmlns attribute, thus:

```
<html xmlns="http://www.w3.org/1999/xhtml"></html>
```

An XML namespace is a collection of specific elements and attributes used for a specific application. In the instance of XHTML, we use the namespace definition URI http://www.w3.org/1999/xhtml, which is the unique name given to the collection of elements and attributes used in an XHTML document.

Including head and body Tags

You must use the <head> and <body> tags in your document, and the first element in the head must be the <title> element much like the following skeleton:

```
<!DOCTYPE html PUBLIC "-//W3C//DTD XHTML 1.0 Strict//EN"
        "http://www.w3.org/TR/xhtml1/DTD/xhtml1-strict.dtd">
<html xmlns="http://www.w3.org/1999/xhtml">
  <head>
    <title>Document Title</title>
  </head>
  <body>
  </body>
</html>
```

The <head> and <body> elements define and separate the distinct sections of an XHTML document. The <head> section contains the title, metadata such as keywords, and a description (useful for search engine indexing) and other information that is not considered actual document data. The <body> section contains the document data rendered by the browser.

Quoting All Tag Attributes

Whenever you want to include an attribute for a tag, you must always use quotation marks around the value. The XML specification indicates that both single and double quotes are allowed for quoting attribute values. For example the following line of code is valid in HTML, but not in XHTML:

```
<img src=image.gif height=150 width=23>
```

In XHTML we would have to add quotation marks around the attribute values:

```
<img src="image.gif" height="150" width="23" />
```

Also HTML allowed attribute minimization, where you could omit the value of the attribute and the parser would set it to a default value, for example:

```
<input checked>
```

is equivalent to:

```
<input checked="checked">
```

This shortcut is not allowed in XHTML; you have to write out the attribute value in full.

Commenting XHTML Markup

It is good practice to add comments in your markup to help others understand your code quickly; it also makes it more understandable for you when you look at it again at some later date. To add comments within XHTML documents you use <!-- -->. This comment section will prevent browsers from parsing text between the start and end tags. For example:

```
<!-- This won't appear in your browser -->
```

There is a caveat with this however; HTML developers enclose JavaScript within comment tags to stop old browsers without JavaScript interpreters displaying the code as plain text in the browser. With XHTML, XML parsers are not required to include any data between <!-- --> tags which means your JavaScript may not be parsed at all. The way around this is by using CDATA sections. CDATA is an XML section that tells the parser to ignore any markup tags between <![CDATA[and]]>. For example:

This may not work:

```
<script language="Javascript">
<!--
while(j<=2) { }
//-->
</script>
```

This definitely works using CDATA in XHTML:

```
<script language="Javascript">
//<![CDATA[
while(j<=2) { }
//]]>
</script>
```

Using Lowercase

We mentioned previously that XML is case-sensitive; this rule also applies to XHTML. In XHTML, all tag names and attribute names must be lowercase. In addition, event attributes must all be lowercase, so it is `onload` not `onLoad`. If you use certain WYSIWYG editors (or that nifty Adobe Photoshop PSD to HTML exporter), you may want to reconsider using a plain old text editor, TopStyle, Dreamweaver MX, or CSE HTML Validator to ensure strict XHTML adherence. Also, it is recommended that all CSS style declarations be lowercase.

No More <font>

The `<font>` tag is now obsolete and is not supported in XHTML 1.0 Strict DTD. If you are updating your HTML pages to XHTML, it is wise to kill your `<font>` tags and define all presentational and formatting information in Cascading Style Sheets. As discussed earlier in this chapter, CSS allows for the complete separation of document style from content layout. For the complete CSS reference see *Chapter 2*.

Reference Section: XHTML1.0

The following section has been provided to serve as a quick reference for all XHTML tags. The reference has been split into several subsections to make it easier to find what you are looking for.

The *Standard Element Attributes* section is where you will find those attributes that are common to nearly all XHTML elements. Look within the optional attributes of any element to see which standard elements are available.

Similar elements have been organized into groups to make it easier to pinpoint the element reference you're looking for. These groups include:

- ◆ Structural Elements – elements that set forth the initial creation of an XHTML document

- ◆ Presentational Elements – elements that describe character, paragraph, block, and linking format

- ◆ Table Elements – elements that are used to create tables within XHTML documents

- ◆ Form Elements – elements that are used to create forms for data entry within XHTML documents

- ◆ Image Elements – elements that are used to display images and image maps within documents

- ◆ Frame Elements – elements that are used to create sub-windows within an XHTML document

- ◆ Listing Elements – elements that are used to create ordered or unordered lists of data within an XHTML document

- ◆ Object elements – elements that are used to embed external media objects and applications within an XHTML document

Standard Element Attributes

Here are the standard attributes for XHTML elements. These attributes are available for nearly all XHTML elements. Available attributes are indicated beneath the optional attributes for each element.

Core Attributes

The following core attributes allow you to define various presentational aspects of content within most XHTML elements. For example, the `class` attribute is used to define the specific CSS class to use for presenting the content tagged by an element. For more information on defining CSS classes for use with XHTML tags, see *Chapter 2*.

Core Attribute	Comments
class	Specifies the class or style of the element defined in the web document or in a stylesheet.
id	Specifies the unique identification for an element. An ID is sometimes necessary when using client-side scripts that interact with inline elements, or elements that interact with each other.
style	Deprecated.
title	Specifies text to display in a "Tool-Tip" which pops up in Internet Explorer when you hover your pointer over a specific object. Also used by some screen readers in place of the URL for a link.

Internationalization Attributes

Internationalization attributes allow you to specify the language to use for presenting content. Use the `lang` attribute to specify the language code and the `dir` attribute to specify in which direction the text should be displayed.

Internationalization Attribute	Comments
dir	Specifies the direction to output text, either left to right (default) or right to left. This is useful for languages that read from right to left.
lang	Specifies in what default language code to output text.

For more information on international language codes please visit the following web page: http://www.w3.org/International/O-HTML-tags.html.

XHTML/HTML

13

Event Attributes

Event Attributes allow you to associate scripts with certain HTML actions. For example, you can write a JavaScript function to check the validity of an e-mail address. You would use the `onsubmit` attribute in the `<form>` element to associate the form with the e-mail validation script. When the user submits the form, the script is then called.

Event attribute	Comments
onload	Specifies script to load when web document loads in browser
onunload	Specifies script to load when browser leaves or unloads web document
onchange	Specifies script to load when specific element attribute value changes
onsubmit	Specifies script to load when specific form is submitted
onreset	Specifies script to load when reset button in specific form is pressed
onselect	Specifies script to load when specific element is selected
onblur	Specifies script to load when specific element loses the cursor focus
onfocus	Specifies script to load when specific element gains the cursor focus
onkeydown	Specifies script to load when specific key is pushed down
onkeyup	Specifies script to load when specific key is released
onkeypress	Specifies script to load when specific key is pushed down and released
onclick	Specifies script to load when primary mouse button is clicked
ondblclick	Specifies script to load when primary mouse button is double-clicked
onmousedown	Specifies script to load when primary mouse button is held
onmousemove	Specifies script to load when primary mouse cursor moves

Event attribute	Comments
onmouseover	Specifies script to load when primary mouse cursor moves over a specific element
onmouseout	Specifies script to load when primary mouse cursor moves off a specific element
onmouseup	Specifies script to load when primary mouse button is released

Special Characters

Certain characters can only be rendered in a web browser by using escape codes. Here are the most common escape characters in use:

Special Character	Comments
	Specifies a blank non-breaking space to be inserted.
&amp;	Specifies an ampersand ("&") to be inserted.
&lt;	Specifies a less-than sign ("<") to be inserted.
&gt;	Specifies a greater-than sign (">") to be inserted.
&trade;	Specifies a trademark symbol (" ™") to be inserted.
&copy;	Specifies a copyright symbol (" ©") to be inserted.
&reg;	Specifies a registered symbol (" ®") to be inserted.

For further lists of escape characters see http://www.w3.org/TR/REC-html40/sgml/entities.html, or Appendix B.

Deprecated Elements

The following elements were deprecated and not supported in XHTML 1.0 Strict DTD:

- ♦ <applet> – Use <object> instead.
- ♦ <font> – Define your presentation attributes within a stylesheet.
- ♦ <s>, <strike> – Define this style within a stylesheet.
- ♦ <u> – Define this style within a stylesheet.

Structural Elements

Structural elements allow you to define the overall structure of an XHTML document.

Comments

The comment element is used when you want to include text within the source XHTML document without having it displayed in the web browser. The syntax is as follows:

```
<!-- Text to be commented -->
```

Doctype Declaration

The `<!DOCTYPE>` declaration tells the browser which specification should be used to load the web document. Please note that this is not an XHTML tag and does not require the closing slash. XHTML1.0 requires the use of one of the following document types:

XHTML Strict DTD (adheres strictly to the XHTML specification):

```
<!DOCTYPE html PUBLIC "-//W3C//DTD XHTML 1.0 Strict//EN"
          "http://www.w3.org/TR/xhtml1/DTD/xhtml1-strict.dtd">
```

XHTML Transitional DTD (combines elements of HTML 4.01 and XHTML 1.0):

```
<!DOCTYPE html PUBLIC "-//W3C//DTD XHTML 1.0 Transitional//EN"
          "http://www.w3.org/TR/xhtml1/DTD/xhtml1-transitional.dtd">
```

XHTML Frameset DTD (combines the XHTML Transitional DTD with frame capabilities)

```
<!DOCTYPE html PUBLIC "-//W3C//DTD XHTML 1.0 Frameset//EN"
          "http://www.w3.org/TR/xhtml1/DTD/xhtml1-frameset.dtd">
```

HTML

The `<html>` element must appear exactly once. It tells the user agent that it will be parsing an HTML document:

```
<html xmlns="http://www.w3.org/1999/xhtml"></html>
```

Attribute	Comments
xmlns	The xmlns attribute defines the XML namespace and is required for valid XHTML documents
dir	Optional core attribute
lang	Optional core attribute

Note that the `version` attribute has been deprecated.

head

The `<head>` section contains information about the web document that is not displayed in the web browser. Content contained in the `<head>` section can include metadata such as keywords and a page description (relevant to search engines and browser add-ons), the document title, a stylesheet link reference, and any scripts that may be used in the document. It takes the following optional attributes:

Attribute	Comments
profile	The `profile` attribute is optional; it contains a URL to a document containing meta-information about the current document. If you are using multiple URLs, separate them with a space. This may be useful if you want to separate metadata from the document itself.
class, id, title	Optional core attributes.
dir, lang	Optional internationalization attributes.
onclick, ondblclick, onmousedown, onmouseup, onmouseover, onmousemove, onmouseout, onkeypress, onkeydown, onkeyup	Optional event attributes.

title

The `<title>` element allows you to enter the title of your document. The content between the tags appears in the title bar of the web browser and serves as the title within your Bookmarks/Favorites. It takes the following optional attributes:

Attribute	Comments
class, id	Optional core attributes
dir, lang	Optional internationalization attributes

base

The `<base>` element allows you to specify a base URL for all subsequent links within your web document. It is an empty element, so remember the forward slash `<base />`. The `href` attribute contains the URL to be used as the base for all links in your web document:

```
<base href="http://www.mydomain.com/" />
```

link

The `<link>` element allows you to create a relationship between your web document and other distinct documents. You will most commonly encounter `<link>` when defining your stylesheet. It is an empty element, so remember the forward slash: `<link />`. It takes the following optional attributes:

Attribute	Comments
charset	Used for internationalization; it specifies the character encoding of target URL.
href	Specifies destination URL for link.
hreflang	Used for internationalization; it specifies the language of target URL.
media	Specifies the type of device the related document will be shown upon. Possible values are `all`, `braille`, `print`, `projection`, `screen`, and `speech`.
rel	Specifies relationship between current document and target URL. Certain user agents use this to build proprietary navigation elements. Possible link-type values are: `alternate`, `designates`, `stylesheet`, `start`, `next`, `prev`, `contents`, `index`, `glossary`, `copyright`, `chapter`, `section`, `subsection`, `appendix`, `help`, and `bookmark`. Custom link-type value conventions must be cited within a profile. See the `profile` attribute of the `<head>` tag for more information.
rev	Specifies relationship between target URL and current document. Possible link-type values are as for `rel` above. Custom link-type value conventions must be cited within a profile. See the `profile` attribute of the `<head>` tag for more information.
target	Specifies target link destination window or frame. `_blank` will open new window with default local user window attributes. `_parent` will open link in parent frameset of framed window. `_self` will open link within same frame as it was clicked. `_top` will open link within the current full window.

Attribute	Comments
type	Specifies the type of content the user agent expects to find when loading target URL (for list of valid MIME types current at the time of writing, see *Appendix C*).
class, id, and title	Optional core attributes.
dir, lang	Optional internationalization attributes.
accesskey, tabindex	Keyboard attributes.
onfocus, onblur, onclick, ondblclick, onmousedown, onmouseup, onmouseover, onmousemove, onmouseout, onkeypress, onkeydown, onkeyup	Event attributes.

meta

The <meta> element allows you to enter specific key words describing the content of your web document. Some search engines and web browsers use this. The <meta> element also allows you to control data in the HTTP header. Again, this is an empty element, so you need to use the forward slash for well-formed XHTML. It takes the following optional attributes:

Attribute	Comments
name	This names the variable that the metadata specified in the content attribute will be associated to. Its most commonly used values are author, description, keywords, generator, and revised. The description and keyword meta-name are most commonly used to describe your web document for proper search engine listing.
content	This contains all the meta-information we want to register. It is good to supply this information in a form that fits with the name attribute, so a list of comma-delimited values if name is set to keywords.
http-equiv	The metadata specified in the content attribute will be associated with the header-type entered here. Its possible values are: content-type, expires, refresh, and set-cookie.
scheme	Specifies the formatting of the value specified in the content attribute.
dir, lang	Internationalization attributes.

script

The `<script>` element contains any client-side scripting (for example JavaScript or VBScript). You can also specify a remote file for the browser to parse and execute instead of containing it in your current web document. It takes the following optional attributes:

Attribute	Comments
type	This attribute is required, its most common values are: `text/javascript`, `text/jscript`, and `text/vbscript`. It specifies the type of scripting language the browser will parse.
charset	Used for internationalization; it specifies the character encoding of the target URL.
defer	With this attribute present, the browser will defer execution of the script and continue to parse the web document.
src	Specifies an external URL where the browser will find the script to process. It is easier to maintain and update your code by storing your client-side scripting in a separate file. Use the `src` attribute to specify the file location of your scripts.
xml:space	This is a core attribute, it tells the browser how to handle whitespace. Its value can be `preserve` or `default`.

Note that `language` is deprecated. You must use `type` to specify what scripting language you are using.

noscript

The `<noscript>` element specifies content for browsers that do not support the script language specified in the `<script>` tag, or if the user has turned script support off. Its core attributes are `class`, `id`, and `title`, and its internationalization attributes are `dir` and `lang`. It takes the following optional attributes:

Attribute	Comments
class, id, and title	Optional core attributes
dir, lang	Optional internationalization attributes

style

The `<style>` element is used to define a stylesheet for your web document. You should avoid using this element declaration; instead use the `<link>` tag to associate an external CSS file to your web document. It takes the following optional attributes:

Attribute	Comments
type	The `type` attribute is mandatory; it is used to specify the language of the stylesheet you are using. The most common value is `text/css`.
media	This specifies the type of device the stylesheet will be used upon. The values it takes are `screen`, `tty`, `tv`, `projection`, `handheld`, `print`, `braille`, `aural`, and `all`.
title, dir, lang, xml:space	Optional core attributes.
dir, lang	Optional internationalization attributes.

For the complete CSS reference, see *Chapter 2*.

body

The `<body>` section contains all the information you want to display to the user within the browser window. Take note that the presentational attributes (such as `alink`, `background`, and `bgcolor`) are deprecated and are not available in the XHTML Strict DTD. Presentation attributes need to be defined within a stylesheet. The `<body>` element takes the following optional attributes:

Attribute	Comments
alink	This attribute is deprecated. It takes a hexadecimal color value: #RRGGBB.
background	This attribute is deprecated. It takes the filename of the background image.
bgcolor	This attribute is deprecated. It takes a hexadecimal color value: #RRGGBB.
link	This attribute is deprecated. It takes a hexadecimal color value: #RRGGBB.
text	This attribute is deprecated. It takes a hexadecimal color value: #RRGGBB.
vlink	This attribute is deprecated. It takes a hexadecimal color value: #RRGGBB.
class, id, title	Core attributes.
dir, lang	Internationalization attributes.

Table continued on following page

Attribute	Comments
onload, onunload, onclick, ondblclick, onmousedown, onmouseup, onmouseover, onmousemove, onmouseout, onkeypress, onkeydown, onkeyup	Event attributes.

General Presentational Elements

The following elements are used for basic document presentation. Keep in mind that CSS is where the bulk of detailed presentation attributes are defined.

Anchor

The <a> tag is used to define links to specific XHTML documents, or within a document. The <a> tag is also used to define anchor bookmarks within an HTML document. The default window target is the current page. It takes the following optional attributes:

Attribute	Comments
charset	Used for internationalization; it specifies the character encoding of the target URL.
coords	Specifies coordinates for regions within images and image maps. It takes a coordinate value schematic based on required shape attribute value (see below in this table). For example, if shape="rect" then you would use coords="left,top,right,bottom". If instead shape="poly" then you would use: coords="x1,y1,x2,y2,...,xn,yn".
href	This specifies the destination URL
hreflang	Used for internationalization; it specifies the language of the target URL. It takes the language code as a value.
rel	Specifies relationship between current document and target URL. Certain user agents use this to build proprietary navigation elements. Possible values are: alternate, designates, stylesheet, start, next, prev, contents, index, glossary, copyright, chapter, section, subsection, appendix, help, and bookmark. Custom link-type value conventions must be cited within a profile. See the profile attribute of the head tag for more information.

Attribute	Comments
rev	Specifies relationship between target URL and current document. Possible values are as for rel. Custom link-type value conventions must be cited within a profile. See the profile attribute of the head tag for more information.
shape	Specifies shape type for mapping tagged area; used with the coords attribute above. Possible values are: default, rect, circle, poly.
target	Specifies target link destination window or frame for URL. _blank will open new window with default local user window attributes. _parent will open link in parent frameset of framed window. _self will open link within same frame as it was clicked. _top will open link within the current full window.
type	Specifies the type of content the user agent expects to find when loading target URL (For a list of valid MIME types current at the time of writing, see *Appendix C*).
name	This attribute is deprecated and replaced by the id attribute in XHTML.
class, id, title	Core Attributes.
dir, lang	Internationalization Attributes.
accesskey, tabindex	Keyboard Attributes.
onfocus, onblur, onclick, ondblclick, onmousedown, onmouseup, onmouseover, onmousemove, onmouseout, onkeypress, onkeydown, onkeyup	Event Attributes.

Abbreviations

The <abbr> element specifies that you are using an abbreviated form of a word or phrase in your web document. The <abbr> element is useful for certain search engine indexing and screen readers. It takes the following optional attributes:

Attribute	Comments
`class`, `id`, `title`	Core attributes
`dir`, `lang`	Internationalization attributes
`onclick`, `ondblclick`, `onmousedown`, `onmouseup`, `onmouseover`, `onmousemove`, `onmouseout`, `onkeypress`, `onkeydown`, `onkeyup`	Event attributes

Acronyms

The `<acronym>` element specifies that you are using an acronym for a phrase in your web document. The `<acronym>` element is useful for certain search engine indexing. It takes the same optional attributes as the `<abbr>` element above.

Line Breaks

The `<br />` element specifies a line break in your web document. Note that it is an empty element so you need the closing forward slash. It takes the same optional attributes as the `<abbr>` element above.

Emphasized Text

The `<em>` element specifies emphasized text that most browsers will display as italic. Use `<em>` rather than the `<i>` element as certain screen readers will not interpret `<i>` as emphasized text. It takes the same optional attributes as the `<abbr>` element above.

Strong Text

The `<strong>` element specifies text that browsers usually display as bold. Use `<strong>` rather than the `<b>` element as certain screen readers will not interpret `<b>` as strong text. It takes the same optional attributes as the `<abbr>` element above.

Definitions

The `<dfn>` element specifies text in the form similar to a dictionary definition. Most browsers will display this text as italic. It takes the same optional attributes as the `<abbr>` element above.

Code Text

The `<code>` element specifies sourcecode text that most browsers will display in a mono-spaced font. It takes the same optional attributes as the `<abbr>` element above.

Sample Characters

The `<samp>` element specifies literal characters that most browsers will display in mono-spaced font. It takes the same optional attributes as the `<abbr>` element above.

Keyboard Text

The `<kbd>` element specifies sample keyboard entry text that most browsers will display in mono-spaced font. The tag can be used to indicate to the user specific text to type in the keyboard. It takes the same optional attributes as the `<abbr>` element above.

Variable Text

The `<var>` element specifies sample keyboard entry variable text that most browsers will display as italic. The tag can be used to indicate that the text is a variable name. It takes the same optional attributes as the `<abbr>` element above.

Headings (1-6)

The `<hn>` tags are used to create heading text. `<h1>` is the largest while `<h6>` is the smallest. You can include any combination of text and inline elements within these tags. More importantly, they create an outline of the document, for example, `<h1>` = heading of page, `<h2>` = subheading, etc. It takes the following optional attributes:

Attributes	Comments
align	This attribute is deprecated. It positions the heading. Possible values are: left, right, center, justify.
class, id, title	Core attributes.
dir, lang	Internationalization attributes.
onclick, ondblclick, onmousedown, onmouseup, onmouseover, onmousemove, onmouseout, onkeypress, onkeydown, onkeyup	Event attributes.

Quotation Text

The `<q>` element specifies text that is considered a quotation. Most browsers should display the text surrounded by double quotes. Unlike the `<blockquote>` tag, the `<q>` tag will not output paragraph breaks before and after the quotation. It takes the following optional attributes:

Attributes	Comments
cite	Contains URL to a separate web document containing the `<q>` content

Table continued on following page

Attributes	Comments
class, id, title	Core attributes
dir, lang	Internationalization attributes
onclick, ondblclick, onmousedown, onmouseup, onmouseover, onmousemove, onmouseout, onkeypress, onkeydown, onkeyup	Event attributes

Address

The `<address>` element can be used for indicating addresses and ownership information of your web document including your name and mailing address. Text contained within the `<address>` tags will appear italic in most browsers. It takes the same optional attributes as the `<abbr>` element above.

Block Quotes

The `<blockquote>` element is used to indicate a long block of text or quotation. The text appears with indentations on either side and paragraph breaks before and after the quote in most browsers. It takes the same optional attributes as the `<q>` element above.

Deleting

The `<del>` element can be used to specify text that has been deleted from a web document. Text within the `<del>` tags usually appears with a line through it. This may be useful with the `<ins>` tag for indicating a price discount in an e-commerce application. It takes the following optional attributes:

Attributes	Comments
cite	Contains URL to a separate web document containing the `<del>` content
datetime	Contains the exact date and time the delete occurred in the format: `YYYY-MM-DDThh:mm:ssTZD`
class, id, title	Core attributes
dir, lang	Internationalization attributes

Attributes	Comments
onclick, ondblclick, onmousedown, onmouseup, onmouseover, onmousemove, onmouseout, onkeypress, onkeydown, onkeyup	Event attributes

Inserting

The `<ins>` element can be used to specify editorial additions in a web document. Text within the `<ins>` tags usually appears with a line underneath it. It takes the same optional attributes as the `<del>` element above.

Divisions

The `<div>` section is used for defining blocks of content within web documents. The `<div>` tag allows you to apply attributes using a stylesheet class to content found within the element. The tag causes a line break to appear before and after the tags. Use the `<span>` tag when you want to apply attributes without the line breaks. It takes the following optional attributes:

Attributes	Comments
align	This attribute is deprecated, it positions the `div`. Possible values are: `left`, `right`, `center`, `justify`.
class, id, title	Core attributes.
dir, lang	Internationalization attributes.
onclick, ondblclick, onmousedown, onmouseup, onmouseover, onmousemove, onmouseout, onkeypress, onkeydown, onkeyup	Event attributes.

Horizontal Rule

The `<hr />` element will create a visible line wherever we place it. All presentation layer attributes have been deprecated since HTML 4.01 and are not available in XHTML 1.0 Strict DTD. It takes the following optional attributes:

Attributes	Comments
align	This attribute is deprecated. It positions the horizontal rule. Possible values are: left, right, center.
noshade	This attribute is deprecated. It controls the appearance of the horizontal rule and takes the values True and False.
size	This attribute is deprecated. It formats the size of the horizontal rule and takes the size in pixels or a percentage.
width	This attribute is deprecated. It formats the width of the horizontal rule and takes the size in pixels or a percentage.
class, id, title	Core attributes.
dir, lang	Internationalization attributes.
onclick, ondblclick, onmousedown, onmouseup, onmouseover, onmousemove, onmouseout, onkeypress, onkeydown, onkeyup	Event attributes.

Paragraphs

The `<p>` element specifies a block of content as a paragraph. Most web browsers insert a line break before the `<p>` tag. All presentation layer attributes have been deprecated since HTML 4.01 and will no longer be available. It takes the following optional attributes:

Attributes	Comments
align	This attribute is deprecated. It positions the paragraph. Possible values are: left, right, center.
class, id, title	Core attributes.

Attributes	Comments
dir, lang	Internationalization attributes.
onclick, ondblclick, onmousedown, onmouseup, onmouseover, onmousemove, onmouseout, onkeypress, onkeydown, onkeyup	Event attributes.

Pre-formatted Text

The `<pre>` element lets the browser know that text found between the `<pre>` tags is pre-formatted and that it should not alter the spacing or line breaks. It takes the following optional attributes:

Attributes	Comments
width	This attribute is deprecated. It specifies the number of characters per line.
class, id, title	Core attributes.
dir, lang	Internationalization attributes.
onclick, ondblclick, onmousedown, onmouseup, onmouseover, onmousemove, onmouseout, onkeypress, onkeydown, onkeyup	Event attributes.

Span

The `<span>` section is used for defining inline content within web documents. The `<span>` tag allows you to apply attributes using a stylesheet class to content found within the element. Unlike the `<div>` tag, `<span>` does not output a line break before and after the tag. It takes the same optional attributes as the `<abbr>` element above.

Bold Text

The `<b>` element specifies text that browsers usually display as bold. Use `<strong>` rather than the `<b>` element as certain screen readers will not interpret `<b>` as emphasized text. It takes the same optional attributes as the `<abbr>` element.

Italic Text

The `<i>` element specifies text that browsers usually display as italic. Use `<em>` rather than the `<i>` element as certain screen readers will not interpret `<i>` as emphasized text. It takes the same optional attributes as the `<abbr>` element.

Big Text

The `<big>` element specifies that text be displayed larger than the default font size in the web browser. How much larger is determined by the web browser. It takes the same optional attributes as the `<abbr>` element.

Small Text

The `<small>` element specifies that text be displayed smaller than the default font size in the web browser. How small is determined by the browser. It takes the same optional attributes as the `<abbr>` element.

Teletype Text

The `<tt>` element specifies that text be displayed in a Teletype of mono-spaced font in the web browser. It takes the same optional attributes as the `<abbr>` element.

Subscript Text

The `<sub>` element specifies that text be displayed as subscript. Most browsers display the text smaller and lower in position than the current font. It takes the same optional attributes as the `<abbr>` element.

Superscript Text

The `<sup>` element specifies that text be displayed as superscript. Most browsers display the text smaller and higher in position than the current font. It takes the same optional attributes as the `<abbr>` element.

Bi-Directional Override Text

The `<bdo>` element specifies that text be displayed as right-to-left or left-to-right. The default is left to right. This is useful when used with internationalization features, as certain languages read from right to left. It takes the following optional attributes:

Attributes	Comments
dir	This attribute is mandatory. It specifies the direction of the text, left-to-right or right-to-left. Its possible values are ltr and rtl.
class, id, title	Core attributes.
lang	Internationalization attribute.

Table Structure Elements

Table elements allow you to organize content in rows and columns within an XHTML document. It is not good practice to utilize tables for presentation purposes. In the case of document presentation, CSS is to be used always.

Table

The <table> element allows you to construct a table within a web document. The most common elements within the <table> tags include <thead>, <tbody>, <td>, <th>, and <tr>. See the *Example Table Application* section later in this chapter. The <table> element takes the following optional attributes:

Attributes	Comments
align	This attribute is deprecated. It positions the table, with the values: left, right, and center.
bgcolor	This attribute is deprecated. It sets the background color of the table. It takes a hexadecimal color value: #RRGGBB.
border	Specifies the width of the border surrounding the table, in pixels.
cellpadding	Specifies the width, in pixels or percentage values, between the content and it's binding data cell specified by the <td> tag.
cellspacing	Specifies the width, in pixels or percentage values, between the data cells specified by the <td> tag within its binding row specified by the <tr> tag.
frame	Specifies in what manner the border attribute should be applied to the table. Possible values are above, below, hsides, lhs, rhs, vsides, box, border.
rules	Specifies in what manner the border attribute should be applied to the data cell divider borders within the table. Possible values are none, groups, rows, cols, all.

Table continued on following page

Attributes	Comments
summary	This accessibility attribute specifies the purpose of the table. Content within this attribute will be used in conjunction with certain text-to-speech browsers.
width	Specifies the width in pixels or percentage values of the entire table.
class, id, title	Core attributes.
dir, lang	Internationalization attributes.
onclick, ondblclick, onmousedown, onmouseup, onmouseover, onmousemove, onmouseout, onkeypress, onkeydown, onkeyup	Event attributes.

Captions

The optional <caption> element must appear directly after the <table> tag. The <caption> element allows you to add a short description of its binding table. Text found with the <caption> tags will appear above the table. It takes the following optional attributes:

Attributes	Comments
align	This attribute is deprecated. It positions the caption. Possible values are: left, right, and center.
class, id, title	Core attributes.
dir, lang	Internationalization attributes.
onclick, ondblclick, onmousedown, onmouseup, onmouseover, onmousemove, onmouseout, onkeypress, onkeydown, onkeyup	Event attributes.

Column Layout Attributes

The optional `<col>` element must be used in conjunction with a `<colgroup>` element within a `<table>`. The `<col>` element specifies layout attributes for all data cells found within its column. Attributes used here will override the same attributes found within its binding `<colgroup>`. It takes the following optional attributes:

Attributes	Comments
align	Specifies the justification position for content within the data cells of the column. Possible values are `right`, `center`, `justify`, and `char`.
char	Specifies the character (like a *$* when displaying a column of monetary values) to align the content within the data cells of the column.
charoff	Specifies the pixel width between the content and its alignment character specified by the `char` attribute.
span	Specifies the number of additional columns the `<col>` element should apply its formatting within the `<table>`.
valign	Specifies vertical alignment of content within the data cells of the column. Possible values are `top`, `middle`, `bottom`, and `baseline`.
width	Specifies the width, in pixels or percentage values, of the column.
class, id, title	Core attributes.
dir, lang	Internationalization attributes.
onclick, ondblclick, onmousedown, onmouseup, onmouseover, onmousemove, onmouseout, onkeypress, onkeydown, onkeyup	Event attributes.

Column Group Layout Attributes

The optional `<colgroup>` element specifies layout attributes for all data cells found within its column span. You may also further specify distinct column attributes by using the `<col>` element with the `<colgroup>` tags. It takes the same optional attributes as the `<col>` element above.

Table Header

The `<thead>` must be used in conjunction with the `<tbody>` and `<tfoot>` elements. These three tags allow you to break up your table data into distinct sections. The `<thead>` specifies rows that are considered headers and may contain column titles. Dividing tables into `<thead>`, `<tbody>`, and `<tfoot>` allows scrolling of the `<tbody>` portion while keeping visible the `<thead>` and `<tfoot>` content. It takes the following optional attributes:

Attributes	Comments
`align`	Specifies the justification position for content within the data cells of the column. Possible values are `left`, `right`, `center`, `justify`, and `char`.
`char`	Specifies the character (like a *$* when displaying a column of monetary values) to align the content within the data cells of the column.
`charoff`	Specifies the pixel width between the content and its alignment character specified by the `char` attribute.
`valign`	Specifies vertical alignment of content within the data cells of the column. Possible values are `top`, `middle`, `bottom`, and `baseline`.
`class`, `id`, `title`	Core attributes.
`dir`, `lang`	Internationalization attributes.
`onclick`, `ondblclick`, `onmousedown`, `onmouseup`, `onmouseover`, `onmousemove`, `onmouseout`, `onkeypress`, `onkeydown`, `onkeyup`	Event attributes.

Table Body

The `<tbody>` must be used in conjunction with the `<thead>` and `<tfoot>` elements. See *Table Header* for more details. It takes the same optional attributes as the `<thead>` element above.

Table Foot

The `<tfoot>` must be used in conjunction with the `<thead>` and `<tbody>` elements. See *Table Header* for more details. It takes the same optional attributes as the `<thead>` element above.

Table Row

The `<tr>` element specifies a row within a table. It takes the same optional attributes as the `<thead>` element above.

Table Data

The `<td>` element specifies a piece of data within a table. The `<td>` tags must be contained within the `<tr>` tags. It takes the following optional attributes:

Attributes	Comments
abbr	Specifies an abbreviated version of the full data contained within the `<td>` tags
align	Specifies the justification position for content within the data cells of the column. Possible values are `left`, `right`, `center`, `justify`, and `char`.
axis	Specifies a name for data contained within the `<td>` tags.
bgcolor	This attribute is deprecated. It sets the background color of the cell. It takes a hexadecimal color value.
char	Specifies the character (like a $ when displaying a column of monetary values) to align the content within the data cells of the column.
charoff	Specifies the pixel width between the content and its alignment character specified by the `char` attribute.
colspan	Specifies the number of data cell columns this data cell should span.
headers	Specifies the header reference id to which the data cell corresponds.
height	This attribute is deprecated. It sets the height of the cell in pixels.
nowrap	This attribute is deprecated.
rowspan	Specifies the number of rows this particular data cell should span.
scope	Species to which scope this particular data cell contains layout information for. There are four possible values: `col`, `colscope`, `row`, and `rowgroup`. The `col` scope applies to all further data cells within the current cell's column. The `colgroup` scope applies to all further data cells within the current cell's column group. The `row` scope applies to all further data cells within the current cell's row. The `rowgroup` scope applies to all further data cells within the current cell's row.

Table continued on following page

Attributes	Comments
`valign`	Specifies vertical alignment of content within the data cells of the column. Possible values are `top`, `middle`, `bottom`, and `baseline`.
`width`	This attribute is deprecated. It sets the width of the cell in pixels or percentage values.
`class`, `id`, `title`	Core attributes.
`dir`, `lang`	Internationalization attributes.
`onclick`, `ondblclick`, `onmousedown`, `onmouseup`, `onmouseover`, `onmousemove`, `onmouseout`, `onkeypress`, `onkeydown`, `onkeyup`	Event attributes.

Table Data Header

The `<th>` element specifies a piece of header data within a table. The `<th>` tags must be contained within the `<tr>` tags. This tag should be contained within the first `<tr>` of a table and, in most browsers, text within the `<th>` tags will appear in bold. It takes the same optional attributes as the `<td>` element above.

Using Tables

For beginners, tables are one of the hardest tasks to grasp and master. Once you hold a firm understanding of table construction, you will be able to structure the presentation of data using rows and columns. Before we take a look at an example of a proper table design, keep these general rules in mind when constructing your table:

♦ Always indent nested table rows and data cells. As your tables grow complex, it will be easier to spot errors when your tags are indented properly.

♦ Keep it simple. Try to avoid lots of nested tables, as older browsers and slower computers may have a hard time rendering them all.

♦ Always use stylesheets to define the presentational attributes of a table.

♦ Remember to close your `<td>` and `<tr>` tags. Closing of these elements is now a requirement of the XHTML specification.

♦ It is highly recommended to always include a `<caption>` within your table, as this will allow you to provide the purpose of your table. The `summary` attribute of `<table>` allows you to specify information about your table for text to speech browsers.

Example Table Application

The following code displays a three-column table with one header row, two data rows, and a caption. No style has been applied to any content. Should you want to include a border around an empty cell be sure to use the special character for a blank space: .

```
<?xml version="1.0" encoding="iso-8859-1" ?>
<!DOCTYPE html PUBLIC "-//W3C//DTD XHTML 1.0 Strict//EN"
          "http://www.w3.org/TR/xhtml1/DTD/xhtml1-strict.dtd">
<html xmlns="http://www.w3.org/1999/xhtml">
<head>
  <title>Table Example</title>
</head>
<body>
  <table  border="1"  cellpadding="2"  cellspacing="2"  summary="Sample  XHTML
Table">
    <caption>Sample XHTML Table</caption>
    <tr>
      <th>Column One</th>
      <th colspan="2">Column Two &amp; Column Three</th>
    </tr>
    <tr>
      <td>Column One Row A</td>
      <td>Column Two Row A</td>
      <td>Column Three Row A</td>
    </tr>
    <tr>
      <td>Column One Row B</td>
      <td>Column Two Row B</td>
      <td>Column Three Row B</td>
    </tr>
  </table>
</body>
</html>
```

In Opera 6.01 it looks like this:

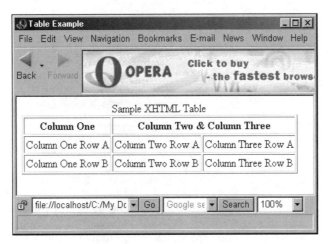

Form Structure Elements

Form elements are most commonly used to pass information from a user to a server-side processing script where it may be, for example, stored in a database or mailed to an administrator. Text entry elements in a form can include <input>, <option>, and <textarea>. See the *Example Form Application* section later in this chapter.

form

The <form> element is used to define fill-in forms. This element contains information on how the form should be processed and in what manner data should be sent to the URL specified in the action attribute. It takes the following optional attributes:

Attributes	Comments
action	This attribute is mandatory. It specifies the URL to which the form is submitted.
accept	This contains a comma-separated list of the allowable content types of the server receiving submitted data.
accept-charset	Defines a comma-separated list of valid character encodings for the form.
enctype	Defines the MIME type the browser should use when transferring the form data to the server.
method	Defines the method the browser should use when transferring the form data to the server. method can be set to either GET or POST. The GET method passes form variables and their values in the form of a URL querystring. For example: `process.pl?key1=value1&key2=value2` There is almost always a limitation on the size of a querystring as it depends on the server(s) hosting the processing script. A better option is the POST method, which uses the HTTP POST transaction. In theory there is no limit to the amount of data passed via the POST method, plus unlike the GET method, data will not be visible in the web browser's location input box.
name	Specifies a unique name for a form.
target	Specifies target destination window or frame indicated by the action attribute. Setting it to _blank will open new window with default local user window attributes. Setting it to _parent will open link in parent frameset of framed window. Setting it to _self will open link within same frame as it was clicked. Setting it to _top will open link within the current full window.

Attributes	Comments
class, id, title	Core attributes.
dir, lang	Internationalization attributes.
onclick, ondblclick, onmousedown, onmouseup, onmouseover, onmousemove, onmouseout, onkeypress, onkeydown, onkeyup	Event attributes.

fieldset

The `<fieldset>` element is used to group `<input>` elements. Most web browsers will draw a line around the elements. It takes the following optional attributes:

Attributes	Comments
class, id, title	Core attributes
dir, lang	Internationalization attributes
onclick, ondblclick, onmousedown, onmouseup, onmouseover, onmousemove, onmouseout, onkeypress, onkeydown, onkeyup	Event attributes

legend

The optional `<legend>` element specifies text to include within the border defined by the `<fieldset>` element. This element must be used within the `<fieldset>` tags. It takes the following optional attributes:

Attributes	Comments
align	This attribute is deprecated. Possible values are left, right, center.
class, id, title	Core attributes.
dir, lang	Internationalization attributes.

Table continued on following page

Attributes	Comments
onclick, ondblclick, onmousedown, onmouseup, onmouseover, onmousemove, onmouseout, onkeypress, onkeydown, onkeyup	Event attributes.

Input Field

The `<input>` element specifies a control that gathers information within a `<form>`. When `<input>` attribute `type="hidden"`, the element can also be used to hide variables and values from the user to be passed to a processor script in a `<form>`. Note that this is an empty tag so you need to add a forward slash `<input />`. It takes the following optional attributes:

Attributes	Comments
accept	Specifies a comma-separated list of MIME types the browser should allow, but only when the `type` attribute is set to `file`.
align	Specifies the justification position for text after an image only when the `type` attribute is set to `image`. Possible values are `left`, `right`, `center`, `justify`, and `char`.
alt	When the `<input>` attribute `type` is set to `image`, this attribute specifies alternative text for the browser to display when image rendering is turned off.
checked	When the `type` attribute is set to `checkbox`, you can set `checked="checked"` to specify that the input box should be checked. If the attribute `checked="checked"` is not present, the checkbox will be unchecked.
disabled	Specifies that the `<input>` field be disabled for user entry. The browser will display the input control as grayed out, and the user may not interact with it. Not used when the `type` attribute is set to `hidden`.
maxlength	Specifies the maximum number of characters to be allowed when `<input>` attribute `type="text"`.
name	Specifies a unique name for the current `<input>` field.
readonly	When the `type` attribute is set to `text`, this attribute specifies that the value of the `<input>` element is read-only and cannot be modified by the user.
size	Specifies the initial size in characters of the `<input>` element.
src	Specifies the URL of the image to load when the `type` attribute is set to `image`.

Attributes	Comments
type	Specifies the type of `<input>` field that should be displayed. Possible values are `button`, `checkbox`, `file`, `hidden`, `image`, `password`, `radio`, `reset`, `submit`, `text` (default)
value	Specifies the value of the `<input>` field depending on the value of the `type` attribute. If `type` is set to `text`, `password`, `hidden`, `image`, `radio`, or `checkbox`, the value is assigned to the element only. If the `type` attribute is set to `button`, `reset`, or `submit`, the value is assigned to the element and displayed on the button control in most web browsers. This attribute is not used when the `type` attribute is set to `file`.
usemap	Specifies the map ID to use in an image map when `type` is set to `image`.
class, id, title	Core attributes.
dir, lang	Internationalization attributes.
onclick, ondblclick, onmousedown, onmouseup, onmouseover, onmousemove, onmouseout, onkeypress, onkeydown, onkeyup	Event attributes.

Input Label

The `<label>` element is used to specify the content used to define a form element. When content between the `<label>` tags is clicked, the input focus is switched to the form element defined by the `<label>` tags for attribute. You must specify an `id` attribute within the form element you want to use. It takes the following optional attributes:

Attributes	Comments
for	Specifies the `id` of the form element you want to associate the label with
class, id, title	Core attributes
dir, lang	Internationalization attributes
onclick, ondblclick, onmousedown, onmouseup, onmouseover, onmousemove, onmouseout, onkeypress, onkeydown, onkeyup	Event attributes

Select Box

The `<select>` element allows you to display a select box with a list of options for the user to choose from within a `<form>`. The `<option>` element, along with the optional `<optgroup>` element, is used within the `<select>` tags to define option values. It takes the following optional attributes:

Attributes	Comments
disabled	Specifies that the select box and all `<option>` and `<optgroup>` elements bound by the `<select>` element are disabled for user interaction. Most browsers will display the control as grayed out.
multiple	Specifies whether the user can select more that one option in the list. Multiple select values are sent as an array to the script processor URL attribute defined by the `<form>` element. It takes a Boolean True or False.
name	Specifies a unique name for the current `<select>` box.
size	Specifies the number of options to be displayed by the web browser without using the drop-down control.
class, id, title	Core attributes
dir, lang	Internationalization attributes
onclick, ondblclick, onmousedown, onmouseup, onmouseover, onmousemove, onmouseout, onkeypress, onkeydown, onkeyup	Event attributes

Multi-line Text Input Fields

The `<textarea>` element specifies a multi-line text input field usually used within a `<form>` element. You need to specify the number of rows and columns using the rows and cols attributes. It takes the following optional attributes:

Attributes	Comments
rows	Specifies the number of default visible rows for text entry. This attribute is required.
cols	Specifies the number of default visible columns for text entry. This attribute is required.

Attributes	Comments
disabled	Specifies that the `<textarea>` element is disabled for user interaction.
name	Specifies a unique name for the current `<textarea>` box.
readonly	Specifies that the value of the `<textarea>` element is read-only and cannot be modified by the user.
class, id, title	Core attributes.
dir, lang	Internationalization attributes.
onclick, ondblclick, onmousedown, onmouseup, onmouseover, onmousemove, onmouseout, onkeypress, onkeydown, onkeyup	Event attributes.

Option Group

The `<optgroup>` element allows you to group several `<option>` elements contained within a `<select>` element. The text contained within the `<optgroup>` attribute label is not available to be selected by the user and forces text contained within bound `<option>` tags to be indented. It takes the following optional attributes:

Attributes	Comments
label	Specifies the text to display as a label in the `<select>` box. The text is usually displayed as bold or italics in most web browsers. This attribute is required.
disabled	Specifies that all `<option>` elements bound by the `<optgroup>` element be disabled for user selection.
class, id, title	Core attributes.
dir, lang	Internationalization attributes.
onclick, ondblclick, onmousedown, onmouseup, onmouseover, onmousemove, onmouseout, onkeypress, onkeydown, onkeyup	Event attributes.

Option

The `<option>` element specifies an option contained within a `<select>` element. It takes the following optional attributes:

Attributes	Comments
disabled	Specifies that the current `<option>` field is disabled for user entry
label	Specifies the text to display as a label in the `<select>` box when contained within the `<optgroup>` element.
selected	Specifies that the `<option>` element should be initially selected.
value	Specifies the value of the `<select>` field name attribute to be sent to the processing script URL attribute of the binding `<form>`.
class, id, title	Core attributes
dir, lang	Internationalization attributes
onclick, ondblclick, onmousedown, onmouseup, onmouseover, onmousemove, onmouseout, onkeypress, onkeydown, onkeyup	Event attributes

Button

The `<button>` element specifies a push-button that can be used with a `<form>` element. It takes the following optional attributes:

Attributes	Comments
disabled	Specifies that the `<button>` element is disabled for user entry.
name	Specifies a unique name for the current `<button>` element.
type	Specifies the type of `<button>` that should be displayed. Possible values are button, reset, and submit.
value	Specifies the initial value assigned to the `<button>` element.
class, id, title	Core attributes.

Attributes	Comments
`dir`, `lang`	Internationalization attributes.
`onclick`, `ondblclick`, `onmousedown`, `onmouseup`, `onmouseover`, `onmousemove`, `onmouseout`, `onkeypress`, `onkeydown`, `onkeyup`	Event attributes.

Using Forms

Forms are the means for users to submit information into your web server. With forms, you can create a server-side processing script that stores user-submitted data in a database, sends an e-mail to the administrator containing the submitted information, or manipulate information and HTML attributes within the web browser. Here are a few simple rules to follow when creating a form:

♦ Always include a form `action` and use the `POST` method for sending any data. The `POST` method uses the HTTP `POST` transaction, which has, in theory, no limit to the amount of data passed. Unlike the `GET` method, `POST` data will not be visible in the web browser's location input box.

♦ Always label your input fields clearly and succinctly.

♦ Make sure your input field `label` corresponds correctly to the `<input>` name.

♦ Incorporate HTML tables with your form, as it will be easier to lay out input fields, buttons, and their associated labels.

♦ Use `maxlength` carefully. Make sure the data you are expecting from the input field can be entered within the `maxlength` specified under all circumstances. In my experience, it's never a good idea to use `maxlength` as data validation and processing should always be kept separate from user-interface design.

♦ If you must include a *Reset* button, make sure it's on the right of the *Submit* button when designing interfaces for visual browsers. Most web users are used to this presentation, and will prevent them from accidentally clearing a form they just filled out. This will save you time responding to hate mail, take it from me.

Example Form Application

In this sample application, we will incorporate all the common form elements within a well-structured table:

```
<?xml version="1.0" encoding="iso-8859-1" ?>
<!DOCTYPE html PUBLIC "-//W3C//DTD XHTML 1.0 Strict//EN"
         "http://www.w3.org/TR/xhtml1/DTD/xhtml1-strict.dtd">
<html xmlns="http://www.w3.org/1999/xhtml">
<head>
  <title>Form Example</title>
```

```
</head>
<body>
  <form method="post" action="script.php">
    <table  border="1"  cellpadding="2"  cellspacing="2"  summary="Sample  XHTML
Form">
      <caption>Sample XHTML FORM</caption>
      <tr>
        <th>Input Labels</th>
        <th>Input Fields</th>
      </tr>
      <tr>
        <td>Your Name</td>
        <td><input type="text" size="30" maxlength="100" /></td>
      </tr>
      <tr>
        <td>What color are your eyes?</td>
        <td>
          <select name="eyecolor">
            <option value="green">Green</option>
            <option value="blue">Blue</option>
            <option value="brown">Brown</option>
          </select>
        </td>
      </tr>
      <tr>
        <td>What gender are you?</td>
        <td>
          <input type="radio" name="gender" value="Male" /> Male
          <input type="radio" name="gender" value="Female" /> Female
        </td>
      </tr>
      <tr>
        <td></td>
        <td>
          <input type="hidden" name="source" value="Web Pro Handbook" />
          <input type="submit" name="submit" value="Submit" />
          <input type="reset" name="reset" value="Reset" />
        </td>
      </tr>
    </table>
  </form>
</body>
</html>
```

This is what it looks like in Mozilla 1.0:

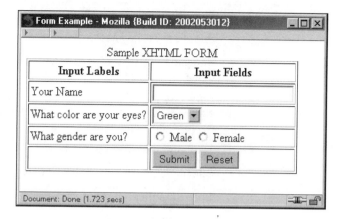

Image Elements

Image elements allow you to load images and image maps within an XHTML document. Images are useful for designing an effective user experience only when the browser allows for image rendering. Therefore, the `alt` attribute is required in order to provide a text description (up to 50 characters) of the image that may not render. For images requiring a description longer than 50 characters, use the `longdesc` attribute to provide a link to a distinct URL for the full text description. See also *Chapter 10* for guidelines on making images accessible.

Images

The `<img>` element specifies an image to load in the web browser at the current position. Note that it is an empty element, so the forward slash is required for well-formed XHTML. It takes the following optional attributes:

Attributes	Comments
alt	This attribute is required in XHTML. It specifies up to 50 characters of alternative text for the browser to display when image rendering is turned off or the image is not available.
src	This attribute is required. It specifies the URL of the image to display.
align	This attribute is deprecated. It positions the image. Possible values are: top, bottom, middle, left, right.
border	This attribute is deprecated. It specifies a border for the image.
height	Specifies the height in pixels or percent of the image.

Table continued on following page

Attributes	Comments
hspace	This attribute is deprecated.
ismap	Specifies that the image will use a server-side image map.
longdesc	Specifies the URL of a document that contains a long description of the current image.
usemap	Specifies the URL of a file or an image map ID that contains image-mapping information. Used in conjunction with separate `<map>` and `<area>` tags.
vspace	This attribute is deprecated.
width	Specifies the width in pixels or percent of the image.
class, id, title	Core attributes.
dir, lang	Internationalization attributes.
onclick, ondblclick, onmousedown, onmouseup, onmouseover, onmousemove, onmouseout, onkeypress, onkeydown, onkeyup	Event attributes.

Image Map Definition

The `<map>` element allows you to create a client-side image map that will allow the user to click on distinct regions within an image and open distinct URLs. Use the `<area>` element to define regions and URLs within an image. The map definition can be saved in a separate file or included within the same document as the associated `<image>` element. The `<image>` element's `usemap` attribute specifies the `id` attribute value of the `<map>` element. The `<map>` element takes the following optional attributes:

Attributes	Comments
id	This attribute is required. It specifies the unique name for the current image map.
name	This attribute is deprecated.
class, title	Core attributes.
dir, lang	Internationalization attributes.
onclick, ondblclick, onmousedown, onmouseup, onmouseover, onmousemove, onmouseout, onkeypress, onkeydown, onkeyup	Event attributes.

Image Map Area Definition

The `<area>` element specifies a region using coordinates and associates the region with a clickable URL in an image. Note that this is an empty `<area />` element. The `<area>` element takes the following optional attributes:

Attributes	Comments
alt	This attribute is required. It specifies text the browser should alternatively display for the region when image rendering is turned off or not available.
coords	Specifies coordinates for regions within images and image maps. The coordinate value schematic is based on the shape attribute value. For example, if shape were set to rect then you would use the coords values left, top, right, bottom. If instead shape is set to poly use x1, y1,x2, y2,..., xn, yn.
href	Specifies destination URL for clickable region.
nohref	Specifies whether or not region is clickable. It takes the logical values True or False.
shape	Specifies shape type for mapping area. Possible values are rect (default), circle, and poly.
target	Specifies target link destination window or frame for URL. _blank will open new window with default local user window attributes. _parent will open link in parent frameset of framed window. _self will open link within same frame as it was clicked. _top will open link within the current full window.
class, id, title	Core attributes.
dir, lang	Internationalization attributes.
onclick, ondblclick, onmousedown, onmouseup, onmouseover, onmousemove, onmouseout, onkeypress, onkeydown, onkeyup	Event attributes.

Data Listing Elements

List elements are used when you want to create a structured list of data within an XHTML document. Applications of lists include unordered information, ordered information, definitions, and navigation information. For example, when you want to create a step-by-step how-to guide, you would want to use an ordered list so sequential numbers would precede each step. In contrast, you would use an unordered list when you just want a bulleted list of items.

Definition Lists

The `<dl>` element specifies a definition list. This tag is useful when you want to state a series of definitions after a term. Elements contained with in the `<dl>` tags include the definition term, `<dt>`, and the definition data, `<dd>`. The `<dl>` element takes the following optional attributes:

Attributes	Comments
class, id, title	Core attributes
dir, lang	Internationalization attributes
onclick, ondblclick, onmousedown, onmouseup, onmouseover, onmousemove, onmouseout, onkeypress, onkeydown, onkeyup	Event attributes

Definition Term

The `<dt>` element specifies a definition term. Elements contained within the `<dt>` tag include definition data, `<dd>`. The `<dt>` element takes the same optional attributes as the `<dl>` element above.

Definition Description

The `<dd>` element specifies a definition of the `<dt>` element. Text is displayed as indented below the `<dt>` value in most browsers. The `<dd>` element takes the same optional attributes as the `<dl>` element above.

Ordered Lists

The `<ol>` element specifies an ordered list. Use the `<li>` element to specify individual list items. Sequential integers will appear before the list items. The `<ol>` element takes the following optional attributes:

Attributes	Comments
compact	This attribute is deprecated.
start	This attribute is deprecated.
type	This attribute is deprecated. It defines the way the list is numbered. Possible values are a, A, i, I, 1.
class, id, title	Core attributes.
dir, lang	Internationalization attributes.
onclick, ondblclick, onmousedown, onmouseup, onmouseover, onmousemove, onmouseout, onkeypress, onkeydown, onkeyup	Event attributes.

Unordered Lists

The `<ul>` element specifies an unordered list. An unordered list is a list of terms or phrases without a specific order. A bullet commonly precedes items in the `<ul>` list. Use the `<li>` element to specify individual list items. The `<ul>` element takes the following optional attributes:

Attributes	Comments
compact	This attribute is deprecated.
type	This attribute is deprecated. It defines the bullet type. Possible values are disc, square, and circle. Use CSS to define the style of preceding object.
class, id, title	Core attributes.
dir, lang	Internationalization attributes.
onclick, ondblclick, onmousedown, onmouseup, onmouseover, onmousemove, onmouseout, onkeypress, onkeydown, onkeyup	Event attributes.

List Items

The `<li>` element specifies a list item used within both the `<ol>` and `<ul>` elements. The `<li>` element takes the following optional attributes:

Attributes	Comments
type	This attribute is deprecated. It defines the bullet type. Use CSS to define the style of preceding object.
value	This attribute is deprecated.
class, id, title	Core attributes.
dir, lang	Internationalization attributes.
onclick, ondblclick, onmousedown, onmouseup, onmouseover, onmousemove, onmouseout, onkeypress, onkeydown, onkeyup	Event attributes.

Object Elements

Object elements have become an increasingly popular tool for embedding external applications and files within XHTML documents. Object elements allow you to specify a piece of media and the application used to process it external to the document browser. The `<object>` element specifies the object and other attributes used to process it, while the `<param>` element specifies any runtime parameters necessary for executing the object. Music, movies, Flash, Java applets, and ActiveX are common objects embedded within XHTML documents.

Object

The `<object>` element is used to embed an external file in a web document. The `<object>` attributes allow you to specify the applications required to render the object. For browsers that cannot render the `<object>`, you may include text between the `<object>` tags for the browser to display instead. The `<object>` element takes the following optional attributes:

Attributes	Comments
align	This attribute is deprecated. It positions the object. Possible values are top, bottom, left, right.
archive	Specifies a comma-separated list of URLs that are necessary for rendering the object.
border	This attribute is deprecated.
classid	Specifies the URL or ActiveX Control Class ID that is necessary for rendering the object. Possible values are URL and CLSID.
codebase	Specifies a base URL where the object's various application files are located which are necessary for rendering the object.
codetype	Specifies the MIME type of the object.
data	Specifies URL that contains data information that may be required for rendering the object.
declare	Specifies that the object should be declared and not be loaded or utilized until directed.
height	Specifies the height in pixels of the object.
hspace	This attribute is deprecated.
name	Specifies unique name for object.
standby	Specifies text to display in browser while object is rendered.
type	Specifies the MIME type of the data defined by the data attribute.

Attributes	Comments
usemap	Specifies the URL of a file or an image map ID that contains image-mapping information.
vspace	This attribute is deprecated.
width	Specifies the width in pixels of the object.
class, id, title	Core attributes.
dir, lang	Internationalization attributes.
onclick, ondblclick, onmousedown, onmouseup, onmouseover, onmousemove, onmouseout, onkeypress, onkeydown, onkeyup	Event attributes.

Object Parameters

The `<param>` element is used in conjunction with the `<object>` element. It allows you to pass run-time parameter values to the rendering object. This is an empty tag, so you need the forward slash. The `<param>` element takes the following optional attributes:

Attributes	Comments
name	Specifies a unique name for the parameter. This attribute is required.
type	`"mime-type"` Specifies the MIME type of the parameter.
value	`"text"` Specifies the value of the parameter.
valuetype	`"pixels"` Specifies the width in pixels of the object.
id	Core attribute.

Frame Elements

Frame elements allow you to load subwindows within a single XHTML document. Frames are more commonly used for navigation purposes. You may create one narrow frame to load navigation elements while keeping a larger frame for content. In addition, the `<iframe>` element allows you to create a free-floating window within an XHTML document. Frame elements are only available if you use the XHTML 1.0 Frameset DTD.

frame

The `<frame>` element used in conjunction with the `<frameset>` element specifies an independently controlled sub-window that may contain distinct web documents. Note that `<frame>` is an empty element. It takes the following optional attributes:

Attributes	Comments
frameborder	Specifies whether or not to display a border around the frame. It takes a logical value of 1 or 0.
longdesc	Specifies the URL of a document that contains a long description of the frame.
marginheight	Species the height in pixels of the top and bottom margins of the frame.
marginwidth	Species the width in pixels of the left and right margins of the frame.
name	Specifies the unique name of the frame.
noresize	Specifies whether or not to allow the user the ability to resize the frame window.
scrolling	Specifies whether to display scrollbars in the frame, or let the browser automatically display them. It takes the values yes, no, or auto.
src	Specifies the URL of the document to display within the frame window.
class, id, title	Core attributes.

frameset

The `<frameset>` element specifies a framed browser window. Use the `<frame>` elements within the `<frameset>` tags to define the sub-window frame to display in the browser. If you are using a `<frameset>` in your web document make sure to not include the `<body>` tag. See the *Example Frames Application* section later in this chapter for more information.

Attributes	Comments
cols	Comma-separated list of column widths, in pixels or percentage values, for each `<frame>` defined within the `<frameset>` tags.
rows	Comma-separated list of row widths, in pixels or percentage values, for each `<frame>` defined within the `<frameset>` tags.
class, id, title	Core attributes

iframe

The `<iframe>` element specifies a region within a web document that contains another web document. The `<iframe>` element is commonly used for loading remote advertisements in web documents. The `<iframe>` element is also available in the Transitional DTD. The `<iframe>` element takes the following optional attributes:

Attributes	Comments
align	Specifies the alignment of the frame in the web document. Possible values are top, bottom, middle, left, or right.
frameborder	Specifies whether or not to display a border around the iframe. It takes a logical value of 1 or 0.
height	Specifies the height in pixels or percent relative to the web document of the iframe.
longdesc	Specifies the URL of a document that contains a long description of the iframe.
marginheight	Species the height in pixels of the top and bottom margins of the iframe.
marginwidth	Species the width in pixels of the left and right margins of the iframe.
name	Specifies the unique name of the iframe.
scrolling	Specifies whether to display scrollbars in the frame, or let the browser automatically display them. It takes the values yes, no, or auto.
src	Specifies the URL of the document to display within the iframe.
width	Specifies the width in pixels or percent relative to the web document of the iframe.
class, id, title	Core attributes.

noframes

The `<noframes>` element specifies the content to display when a page loads in a browser that doesn't support the `<frame>` and `<frameset>` elements. The `<noframes>` element must be nested within the `<frameset>` element. It takes the following optional attributes:

Attributes	Comments
class, id, title	Core attributes
dir, lang	Internationalization attributes

Using Frames

XHTML1.0 allows for creating sub windows within a main (parent) widow within the web browser. You must make sure to use the Frameset DTD as your DOCTYPE as it is within this specification that the data type definitions for frames exist. Frames can be useful within certain web applications, however there are a few rules to follow when created a framed site:

♦ As there are several navigation, bookmark, and printing issues when individual sub window frames are built into the web browser, you may want to think twice about incorporating frames into your user interface.

♦ If you really must use frames, remember `rows` are horizontal and `cols` are vertical.

♦ It's a good idea not to use the `<body>` element within the frameset document. In some browsers, the frameset will not work properly with the `<body>` tag present.

♦ The value of the `name` attribute must not contain any spaces. It must be a single word.

♦ Always include a `<noframes>` section when using `<frameset>` and be sure to include explanatory information for users with browsers that do not support framed windows.

Example Frame Application

In this sample application, we will incorporate common frame elements creating two horizontal sub window frames. The top frame will be our HTML table example page and the bottom frame will be our HTML form example page:

```
<?xml version="1.0" encoding="iso-8859-1" ?>
<!DOCTYPE html PUBLIC "-//W3C//DTD XHTML 1.0 Frameset//EN"
          "http://www.w3.org/TR/xhtml1/DTD/xhtml1-frameset.dtd">
<html xmlns="http://www.w3.org/1999/xhtml">
<head>
  <title>Frameset Example</title>
</head>

<frameset rows="50%,50%">
  <noframes>
    <body><p>Please    view    this    page    with    a    browser    that    supports
frames.</p></body>
  </noframes>
  <frame name="TableSample" src="TableCodeSample.html" noresize="noresize"
         scrolling="auto" />
  <frame name="FormSample" src="FormCodeSample.html" noresize="noresize"
         scrolling="auto" />
</frameset>

</html>
```

In Internet Explorer we get:

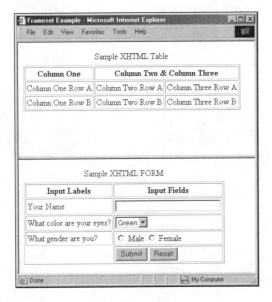

Summary

With new user agents surfacing every day, XHTML is the logical evolution of HTML and XML. XHTML allows for web designers to separate the structural layout of the document from the design elements used in its presentation. By adhering to the strict guidelines of XHTML, your web page will be accessible on practically all user agents on every platform, including PDAs and WAP-enabled mobile phones with XHTML-ready browsers.

After mastering the structural elements required to lay out a web page, you must now understand the concepts of designing the presentation layer with Cascading Style Sheets, which we will look at in the next chapter.

Other Books

- *Usable Forms for the Web*, glasshaus, ISBN 1-904151-09-4

- *Constructing Usable Web Menus*, glasshaus, ISBN 1-904151-02-7

- *Constructing Accessible Web Sites*, glasshaus, ISBN 1-904151-00-0

- *Beginning XHTML*, Wrox Press, ISBN 1-861003-43-9

- *HTML & XHTML: The Definitive Guide*, Fifth Edition, O'Reilly, ISBN 0-596003-82-X

- *XHTML Black Book: A Complete Guide to Mastering XHTML*, Paraglyph Publihsing, ISBN 1-932111-40-9

2

- Using CSS with HTML
- CSS property reference

Author: Bill Mason

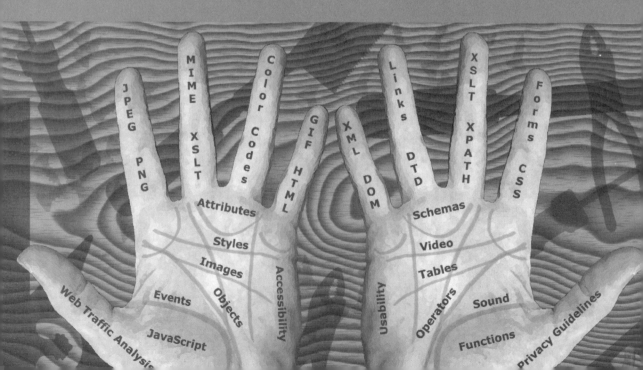

Cascading Style Sheets

Stylesheets are templates containing rules that describe how a browser should display documents on screen, in print, or in other media. Cascading Style Sheets (CSS) are the major tool for controlling the presentation of XHTML and XML documents. Clearly, without some control of presentation, the World Wide Web would be much less robust and visually pleasing an experience than it is today. There are other presentational tools besides CSS, but they have disadvantages.

XSL (Extensible Stylesheet Language) is an XML-style language that can transform XML into XHTML/CSS, but cannot be used directly in an XHTML document. For more details, see *Chapter 5*.

CSS was introduced in August 1996, when Microsoft released the first commercial browser with CSS support, Internet Explorer 3. IE 3 actually predates the designation of CSS Level 1 (CSS1) as a World Wide Web Consortium (W3C) recommendation by several months – CSS1 became a Recommendation in December 1996 and is the first of several versions of CSS that exist today. Netscape released its first CSS1 browser, Navigator 4.0, in June 1997. Opera followed with support in version 3.5 in November 1998.

CSS1 includes the basic presentation tools: control of font, color, text, and the "box model" of content/padding/border/margin. Browser support has been slow in following, however, and it is only in the last few years that the main browsers have approached a full, robust implementation of support for CSS1. Adoption of CSS by developers has expanded as browser support has increased. As that has happened, the ability to properly present CSS style has become nearly as important as presenting XHTML content correctly.

In May 1998 the W3C released CSS Level 2 (CSS2) as a Recommendation (*http://www.w3.org/TR/REC-CSS2/*). CSS2 builds upon CSS1 and adds more functionality, such as media types (including print stylesheets), additional positioning control, more internationalization features, generated content, and cursor controls. It also corrects errors in the CSS1 specification. In general, browser support for CSS2 is less than for CSS1, but the core of CSS2 is supported in the modern, mainstream browsers such as Internet Explorer 6, browsers based on the Gecko rendering engine (chiefly Netscape 6+), and Opera 6+.

At the time of writing, CSS2 Revision 1 (CSS2.1) is in development as a Last Call Working Draft of the W3C (*http://www.w3.org/TR/CSS21/*). Its purpose is to correct errors in CSS2 and to be "*a 'snapshot' of CSS usage: it consists of all CSS features that were implemented interoperably at the date of publication*". To that end, it removes some functions from CSS2 that had found no implementation to speak of in commercial browsers.

Some of those functions have been moved into CSS Level 3 (CSS3). CSS3 is currently in development as a group of 28 modules. The modules are in varying stages of completion at the time of writing, from having no public Working Draft yet produced to having achieved Candidate Recommendation status. The current status of CSS3 can be found at *http://www.w3.org/Style/CSS/current-work/*. In this chapter, discussion of CSS will refer to CSS2.1, as it is very similar to CSS2. Where appropriate, differences between versions 2 and 2.1 will be noted.

Using CSS in Documents

The aim of using CSS is to separate the content of a page from its presentation. Ideally, the CSS will contain all the style rules for a web site: fonts, colors, layout, etc. The XHTML will be strictly for tagging the content: marking up headings, paragraphs, etc. The advantage is that we can easily alter the entire presentation by changing the CSS, rather than having to change presentational elements buried in each individual XHTML page of a given site.

There are three primary ways to use CSS in your document. Your CSS rules can be:

- ◆ Stored in an external CSS file and called via the `<link>` element
- ◆ Placed within a `<style>` tag
- ◆ Inline within the `style` attribute of a HTML element

Additionally, the `@import` method can involve using both an external CSS file, and calling that file via a `<style>` element.

External CSS Called Via <link>

The most powerful feature of CSS is in its use for site-wide presentational management. One CSS file can contain all the styles for a web site. Changing just that one CSS file can make sweeping changes across the entire site. This is generally the best way to implement CSS on a site.

The file is called in the XHTML page via a `<link>` element located in the `<head>`, whose typical format is:

```
<link href="path_to_css_file" type="text/css" rel="stylesheet" />
```

The CSS file contains the CSS rules typically formatted as:

```
selector { property_name : property_value; }
```

An example would be:

```
p { font-size : small; }
```

Alternative Stylesheets and Switching Styles Called Via <link>

It is possible to designate alternative stylesheets in XHTML, so that in theory a user can switch between styles according to their personal preferences or accessibility needs (such as setting a larger default font size, or forcing all hyperlinks to appear underlined for easy identification). To tag the alternative stylesheet as such, the `rel` attribute in the `<link>` tag is changed to read `"alternate stylesheet"`. The `title` attribute is also set to give a name to the alternative stylesheet. For example:

```
<link href="path_to_alternate_css" type="text/css" rel="alternate stylesheet"
    title="My other style sheet" />
```

Browsers that currently have a built-in mechanism in the user interface for switching between stylesheets include Netscape 6+ (*View > Use Style*) and Opera 7 (*View > Style*).

Thus web sites wanting to offer this feature to their visitors will often include a scripted widget to make style changes and maintain the selected style while moving from page to page within the site. Such scripts can either run client-side or server-side. For good examples, read "*Alternative Style: Working with Alternate Style Sheets*" on *A List Apart* (*http://www.alistapart.com/issues/126/*) for a client-side (JavaScript/DHTML) program, or visit *http://alterior.net/archives/000021.php* for an example of a server-side script (PHP in this instance).

Placed within a <style> Tag

CSS rules can be embedded in the `<head>` of an XHTML page via the `<style>` tag. The format is:

```
<style type="text/css">
selector { property_name : property_value; }
</style>
```

Generally, the rules here will apply only to the particular page that the `<style>` tag appears on. See the `@import` section below for an exception to this. Since the rules will only apply to the given page, this is a less powerful implementation of CSS. You lose the ability to change all your pages by changing one CSS file; again `@import` excepted, see that section for more.

Commenting Out <style> Blocks

In HTML 4, it is a common practice to wrap an HTML comment around the content of a `<style>` tag, as follows:

```
<style type="text/css">
  <!--
  CSS rules here
  -->
</style>
```

The purpose of this is to hide the CSS rules from older browsers that did not support the `<style>` tag. The `<style>` tag was first supported in Internet Explorer 3, Netscape 4, and Opera 3.5. Older browsers might attempt to render the CSS rules right onto the web page as plain text.

In XHTML, this type of commenting is not permitted unless you wrap all the `<style>` tag content (including the comment tags) in a CDATA section marker, such as:

```
<style type="text/css">
<![CDATA[
  <!--
  CSS rules here
  -->
]]>
</style>
```

Leaving out the CDATA marker can be dangerous, depending on your server's configuration. An XHTML file can be served with an `application/xhtml+xml` MIME type, instead of the `text/html` MIME type typically used today for backward compatibility with older browsers. With an XML MIME type an XML parser, if it finds the comment tags without CDATA around them, will dutifully obey the comment tags and ignore all the CSS in between.

Some browsers, however, will not support and recognize the CDATA marker, and wind up ignoring the CSS rules entirely. At this point in web development and browser history, it is best to simply leave the comment tags out. Any browser old enough to choke on the `<style>` tag is going to be one that infrequently, if ever, visits your web site anyway.

Within the style Attribute

Almost any XHTML element can take the `style` attribute (exceptions: `<base>`, `<basefont>`, `<head>`, `<html>`, `<meta>`, `<param>`, `<script>`, `<style>`, and `<title>`). CSS rules can be written in the attribute in this format:

```
<element style="property_name: property_value;">
```

The CSS rules only apply to that specific element. So if, for example, you have this piece of code:

```
<p style="color: red;">CSS is very helpful.</p>
```

only this paragraph will have red text and other paragraphs would not.

Inline styles as a whole are reminiscent of embedding presentational markup such as `<font>` directly into a document, and probably just as undesirable. In fact, the `style` attribute is deprecated in XHTML 1.1 and is completely gone from the current Working Draft of XHTML 2.0, so using inline styles is definitely not a future-proof practice.

@import

The `@import` rule is used to import CSS from other external stylesheets. In that regard it is similar to the "link to an external stylesheet" method in that both access an external CSS file. `@import` uses a different syntax, and is easier to use when an XHTML page is linked to multiple stylesheets.

`@import` has two equivalent syntaxes:

```
@import "path_to_css_file";
```

```
@import url("path_to_css_file");
```

The choice of syntax can be important as older browsers either do not support both syntaxes (most notably, Internet Explorer will ignore CSS imported via the `@import "path_to_css_file";` method), or do not support `@import` at all. See the next section *Hiding CSS from older browsers* for details.

The `@import` rule can either be inside an external CSS file, or inside a `<style>` tag. In both cases, the `@import` rule **must** be the first CSS rule that appears. Other CSS rules can follow afterwards in the CSS file or in the `<style>` tag.

Hiding CSS From Older Browsers

With CSS implementation being incomplete and buggy in earlier browsers, it is often necessary to hide advanced CSS from these older browsers, so they don't act on CSS code that they would only implement incorrectly or break the page.

There are a number of ways to do this, but one of the most common is the use of `@import`. The `@import` rule is completely unsupported by Internet Explorer 3 and Netscape 4, both of which will ignore the CSS to be imported. The `@import "path_to_css_file";` syntax will also be ignored by Internet Explorer 4, whose CSS support is better than version 3 but still spotty.

Another common technique is to `<link>` to a "safe CSS" so that the older browsers can see and act upon it. The `<link>` is followed by an `@import`, usually via a `<style>` tag, of the more advanced CSS. For example:

```
<link href="safe_css_file" type="text/css" rel="stylesheet" />
<style type="text/css">
  @import "advanced_css_file";
</style>
```

This technique works well to segregate the more current browsers with good CSS support from the older ones that lack it. Internet Explorer 4.5 on the Macintosh can be an interesting exception. It understands `@import` but is old enough to sometimes have problems with the CSS you would typically be trying to hide by using `@import`. You should take that into account if this browser makes up a significant portion of your site traffic. Do thorough testing of your imported CSS in IE 4.5 on Macintosh.

Another common method of hiding CSS is by defining a media attribute on the `<link>` tag.

CSS for Different Media

CSS files can be specified as only to be used with certain media. The most common media types in use are `screen`, meaning computer screens, and `print`, for printed pages and print previews within browsers. Other types include:

- `all` (any device/user agent)

- `aural` (speech synthesizers)

- `braille` (devices that convert the page's text into a raised Braille readout for the visually impaired)

- `embossed` (Braille printers)

- `handheld` (PDA or smaller type devices, typically with a small screen and only able to handle limited bandwidth)

- `projection` (projecting pages on a screen, wall, etc., with a projector)

- `tty` (teletype machines and the like)

- `tv` (television)

By adding a media designation, you can hide your CSS from browsers that don't understand the designation. The syntax on a `<link>` tag would be as follows:

```
<link href="path_to_css_file" type="text/css" rel="stylesheet" media="all" />
```

This will cause Netscape 4 to ignore the CSS file. If a media attribute is set, Netscape 4 will only act on the CSS if the media is set to "screen".

There are other methods of hiding CSS from browsers. Some depend on browser bugs. Others use advanced CSS2 syntax that less compliant browsers will not understand. For a good list of additional methods and a breakdown of what browsers they are effective against, visit *http://pixels.pixelpark.com/~koch/hide_css_from_browsers/*.

CSS in Internet Explorer 3 and MSN TV

Two other browsers can provide CSS compatibility issues: Internet Explorer 3 and MSN TV (formerly WebTV). Both have limited CSS abilities and a number of bugs. It is generally best to hide CSS from these browsers unless you have a specific need to support them. Neither browser supports the `@import` technique so CSS can be hidden in this way.

If you do need to support these browsers, the following are good references:

- CSS1 Support in Microsoft Internet Explorer 3.0: *http://www.endoframe.com/css/ie3.html*

- MSN TV Server Developer Support Site: *http://developer.msntv.com/Develop/CSS.asp*

The Basics

To illustrate some basic CSS, we will walk through an annotated stylesheet. It is a template that can be used as a starting point for building a CSS file for a web site. It sets a number of default styles that an author would almost always change as the site developed, but the default styles provide a baseline from which to start.

This CSS is written for current browsers with good CSS support: Internet Explorer 5+, the Gecko family of browsers (chiefly Netscape 6+), and Opera 6+. Some of the code here will not work in older browsers or will break undesirably, most typically in Netscape 4. Notes about some of the potential problems are included in the annotation.

Please also refer to the *CSS Property Reference* section later in this chapter for details of any CSS properties listed here, and to the CSS Selector Reference for details about the syntax.

```
html {
  background : #FFFFFF;
  color : #000000;
  display : block;
  margin : 0;
  padding : 0;
}
```

Here we set the background color of the page as white, and the text color to black. It is preferable to do this on <html> and not on <body>. This is because if you have a small page where the <body> content is smaller than the canvas, and the colors are on <body>, then <body> will have your defined background color and the rest of the canvas (the <html>) will have whatever the browser default background color happens to be. The display : block; rule is set throughout on block-level HTML elements, simply to define the default. Margin and padding are set to zero as a basic default as well. Notice that the properties appear on separate lines for ease of reading.

```
body {
  display : block;
  font-family : Verdana, Geneva, Arial, Helvetica, sans-serif;
  line-height : 1.33;
  margin : 0;
  padding : 0;
  font-size : medium;
}
```

Here we have set the suggested fonts for use on the page using the font-family property. Verdana is a popular Windows screen font, Geneva a good Macintosh font, Arial another screen font prevalent on Windows and Macintosh systems, and Helvetica a common Unix font. sans-serif is at the end to suggest that if the user's system has none of these fonts, the browser's default sans-serif font should be used.

Line-height is a measure of the whitespace between lines. In print, this is commonly called "leading". The 1.33 tells the browser to set the line-height to 1.33 times the height of the font in use. Note that line-height should not be applied here if the CSS is for use with Netscape 4. Bugs it has with line-height will cause images on the page to be moved from their correct position, including on top of the page text. The font size is set to a basic default, medium.

```
a:link {
  background : transparent;
  color : #0000FF;
  text-decoration : underline;
}
```

The `color` of unvisited hyperlinks is set to blue, and the `background` is set to `transparent`. It is desirable to always set `background` and `color` together, even if just to set `background` to `transparent`. If `background` is not set, there is a potential for a display problem if a visitor has configured their browser to change the page background to something besides what you have defined. The `text-decoration` rule declares that the link should be underlined, which most browsers will do anyway.

```
a:visited {
  background : transparent;
  color : #990099;
  font-variant : small-caps;
  text-decoration : underline;
}
```

This section is for visited hyperlinks. As a visual aid, the rule suggests that the text of visited links be rendered in small capital letters (`small-caps`). This gives the visitor another cue (besides the color change) as to which links are visited and which are not. This rule would not work in Netscape 4 or Opera 6; those browsers would just ignore it.

```
a:hover {
  background : transparent;
  color : #000000;
  text-decoration : underline overline;
}
```

This section sets styles for when a link is being hovered over with the mouse. Here the rule says that besides the typical underline, we will add an overline (a line on top of the text) during a hover. Netscape 4 does not support hover and will just ignore these rules. This is a good reason to avoid the trick of setting `text-decoration` to none on `a:link` and `a:visited` and then setting `a:hover` to underline. Since Netscape 4 cannot do hover, the links will never appear underlined and can be harder to identify.

```
a:active {
  background : transparent;
  color : #FF0000;
  text-decoration : none;
}
```

This section defines styles for when a link is active, that is, being clicked on. Note that Netscape 4 does not support and simply ignores `a:active`.

```
address {
  display : block;
  margin : 0;
  padding : 0;
}

/*applet { display : inline-block; }*/
```

The above rule illustrates the syntax of CSS comments: `/* Commented material here. */`. In this case (and some others to follow) rules using `display : inline-block` are commented out because `inline-block` is new in CSS2.1 and does not exist in CSS2. Note also that rules with single properties tend to appear on one line, as here.

```
blockquote {
  display : block;
  margin : 0;
  padding : 0;
}

caption {
  display : table-caption;
  text-align : center;
}
```

For `<caption>`, we have set the clear default of displaying the content as `table-caption` (since the `<caption>` tag is for captioning a `<table>`). As the name implies, `text-align` defines how to align the text. Here we have chosen to center it. Other default display settings for table elements are scattered throughout the CSS.

```
cite { font-style : italic; }
```

The `<cite>` tag is typically used for tagging the names of works, such as book or movie titles. In print those are usually italicized, so the CSS uses the `font-style` property to suggest the same effect.

```
code { font-family : monospace; }
```

For the `<code>` tag (typically for marking computer code), we have used `font-family` again to change the font to a `monospace` font.

```
col { display : table-column; }

colgroup { display : table-column-group; }

dd {
  display : block;
  margin : 0;
  padding : 0;
}

del { text-decoration : line-through; }
```

As `<del>` is for marking a deleted item, `text-decoration` here requests a `line-through` effect: a horizontal line through the middle of the tagged text.

```
dfn { font-style : italic; }

dir {
  display : block;
  margin : 0;
```

```
    padding : 0;
}

div {
  display : block;
  margin : 0;
  padding : 0;
}

dl {
  display : block;
  margin : 0;
  padding : 0;
}

dt {
  display : block;
  margin : 0;
  padding : 0;
}

em { font-style : italic; }

fieldset {
  display : block;
  margin : 0;
  padding : 0;
}

form {
  display : block;
  margin : 0;
  padding : 0;
}

frame {
  display : block;
  margin : 0;
  padding : 0;
}

frameset {
  display : block;
  margin : 0;
  padding : 0;
}

h1 {
  display : block;
  font-size : xx-large;
  font-weight: bolder;
  line-height : 1;
  margin : 0;
  padding : 0;
}
```

For <h1> and the other heading tags to follow, we vary the font-size and line-height, and use font-weight to request a bolder text. Netscape 4 does not support bolder; for that browser, the absolute value bold should be used instead.

```
h2 {
  display : block;
  font-size : x-large;
  font-weight: bolder;
  line-height : 1;
  margin : 0;
  padding : 0;
}

h3 {
  display : block;
  font-size : large;
  font-weight: bolder;
  line-height : 1;
  margin : 0;
  padding : 0;
}

h4 {
  display : block;
  font-size : medium;
  font-weight: bolder;
  line-height : 1;
  margin : 0;
  padding : 0;
}

h5 {
  display : block;
  font-size : small;
  font-weight: bolder;
  line-height : 1;
  margin : 0;
  padding : 0;
}

h6 {
  display : block;
  font-size : xx-small;
  font-weight: bolder;
  line-height : 1;
  margin : 0;
  padding : 0;
}

head { display : none; }
```

It is somewhat pedantic to specify that none of the contents of `<head>` be displayed, as no browser will do that by default, although it is possible in an advanced CSS browser (like the Gecko family) to use CSS to force the contents of `<head>` to display.

```
hr {
   border : 1px inset;
   display : block;
   margin : 0;
   padding : 0;
}
```

For horizontal rules, the `border` property sets an inset style of border 1px wide. This basically mimics the typical default display of `<hr>` in browsers.

```
/*img { display : inline-block; }*/

/*input { display : inline-block; }*/

ins { text-decoration : underline; }

li { display : list-item; }
```

Again as a default, `<li>` tags are styled to display as list items. Note that you should never apply styles directly to `<li>` for Netscape 4. It has a bug where the styles will only be applied to the list item bullet and not to the list item text.

```
noframes {
   display : block;
   margin : 0;
   padding : 0;
}

/*object { display : inline-block; }*/

ol {
   display : block;
   list-style-type : decimal;
   margin : 0;
   padding : 0;
}
```

With `list-style-type`, we declare that `<ol>` tags (ordered lists/numbered list) will be displayed with each item in the list marked decimal (*1.*, *2.*, etc.). This is simply another default setting.

```
p {
   display : block;
   margin : 0;
   padding : 0;
}
```

```
pre {
  display : block;
  font-family : monospace;
  margin : 0;
  padding : 0;
  white-space : pre;
}
```

The white-space : pre rule defines how to treat whitespace in the `<pre>` tag. As a default, it preserves whitespace in the same fashion as browsers typically do with `<pre>`.

```
script { display : none; }

/*select { display : inline-block; }*/

strong { font-weight : bolder; }

sub {
  font-size : smaller;
  vertical-align : sub;
}

sup {
  font-size : smaller;
  vertical-align : super;
}
```

The sub and super values for vertical-align create the subscript and superscript effect typical of these two tags.

```
table { display : table; }

tbody { display : table-row-group; }

td { display : table-cell; }

textarea {
  cursor : text;
/*  display : inline-block;*/
}
```

The cursor property defines what type of cursor should be rendered when the pointer is over the `<textarea>`, in this case the default vertical text input bar familiar on PC screens.

```
tfoot { display : table-footer-group; }

th {
  display : table-cell;
  font-weight : bolder;
  text-align : center;
}
```

```
thead { display : table-header-group; }

tr { display : table-row; }

ul {
  display : block;
  list-style-type : square;
  margin : 0;
  padding : 0;
}

var { font-style : italic; }
```

Inheritance and the Cascade

An element on an XHTML page can inherit CSS values from its parent element. For example, one does not typically define a color for every element on a page. Color is usually defined in the `<body>`. From there other tags inherit it, and only on elements where you want a different color do you specify it in the CSS.

In the case of a property value being defined as a percentage of another element's value, the percentage itself does not inherit. Instead, the computed value of the percentage inherits. For example, given these CSS rules:

```
body { font-size : 10px;}
p {font-size : 130%;}
```

in this XHTML fragment:

```
<p>Here is a test of <span>font sizes.</span></p>
```

the `<p>` tag would be 13px (130% of 10px) in size. The `<span>` within the `<p>` does not become 17px (130% of 13px) in size; it simply inherits the computed value of 13px from the `<p>`.

A CSS property can be assigned the value `inherit` specifically. This can be used to force inheritance in situations where a value would not normally inherit. For example (not that you probably want to do this):

```
body { background : url(path_to_an_image_here) no-repeat;
p { background : inherit;}
```

In this case, whatever background image was assigned to `<body>` would also repeat in the background of every `<p>` tag on the page! You can also override inheritance by specifically assigning a value to the property in question on a given element.

Cascading Style Sheets get the "cascading" part of their name from the rules on how stylesheets from different origins interact. Cascade here means that a document can have styles from multiple sources linked to it. The multiple stylesheets have a cascading effect: each one in turn affects the display of the document according to rules that define a hierarchy for which stylesheet rules get priority over competing/conflicting rules from another stylesheet.

Stylesheets can have three origins:

- The author of the web page will include styles via `<link>`, `<style>`, and `@import`.

- The user of the browser may have a personal user stylesheet defined (see the *User Stylesheets* section, which follows).

- The browser itself will have default styles defined to use in the absence of any other instruction.

If these different stylesheets have conflicting rules on what styles to set for a given element or elements, the CSS cascade rules define how to "break the tie" and decide what rule to apply. The basic hierarchy, in order of which gets the most weight (that is, takes precedence), is:

1. User stylesheets

2. Author stylesheets

3. Browser default styles

A noteworthy exception is rules tagged as `!important`, in both author and user stylesheets, to give them more weight than a normally defined rule. However, user `!important` rules always outweigh author `!important` rules.

The full set of rules for determining the cascade is:

1. Take all rules for the element and property that fall in the desired media type.

2. Sort by weight and origin as discussed above:

- User styles tagged "`!important`" (see below)

- Author styles tagged "`!important`" (see below)

- Author styles

- User styles

- Browser styles

Any rule definition in an author or user stylesheet can have `!important` placed after it to indicate that this rule should be given more weight than a normal rule. Example: `p {font-size : 16px !important;}`.

3. Sort by specificity. Specificity is used to resolve conflict when two properties in separate rules, which apply to the same element, contradict each other. Rules that are more specific outweigh rules that are less specific. Specificity is calculated to a four-digit number ABCD (higher = more specific), determined as follows:

- A equals 1 if the rule is in the `style` attribute of an XHTML element (`<p style="font-size : 14px;">`. Such rules never have other selectors, so B, C, and D equal zero and the specificity of this type of rule is always 1000.

- B equals the number of ID attributes in the selector. For example, given the rule `#idname li a:hover {}`, there is one ID attribute, `#idname`, so B equals one.

- C equals the number of non-ID attributes plus the number of pseudo-classes in the selector. In the previous example, `#idname li a:hover {}` would have a C value of one for the one pseudo-class, `:hover`.

- D equals the number of elements in the selector. So `#idname li a:hover {}` has a D value of two for the two elements `li` and `a`. Thus this entire rule has a specificity of 112. (Pseudo-elements are ignored in calculating specificity.)

4. Finally, if there still is a tie, the order the rules are specified in becomes important. The last rule specified wins. (Rules that are `@import`-ed in always come before rules in the stylesheet itself.)

Presentation that comes from the XHTML itself, such as a `<font>` tag or an `align` attribute is considered as having the same weight as if it had come from the browser's stylesheet. Note that this is a change in CSS2.1. CSS2 gives presentational XHTML a specificity of zero and assumes the XHTML to be positioned is at the start of the author stylesheet. CSS1 gives presentational XHTML a specificity of 1 and assumes the XHTML to be positioned at the start of the author stylesheet.

User Stylesheets

Browsers today allow the user to pre-define their own stylesheet. A user can set styles that they always want to have, such as having the font set to a certain size. This goes beyond the normal preferences options present in a browser's interface, such as setting default fonts or whether to use the author's defined colors. A user stylesheet can contain CSS rules of any sort.

User stylesheets are stored on the user's computer and can be set as follows in these major browsers:

- Internet Explorer 6/PC: under *Tools > Internet Options > Accessibility*, *Format documents using my style sheet* should be checked, then browse your filesystem to where your stylesheet is stored.

- Internet Explorer 5.1/Mac: under *Explorer > Preferences > Web Content*, check *Use my style sheet* then click *Select Style Sheet* and browse to where the sheet is stored.

- Mozilla and Netscape 7/PC and Mac: name your user stylesheet `userContent.css` and place it in the `/chrome/` subdirectory located below your `/profile/` directory.

- Opera 6 and 7/PC: under *File > Preferences > Page Style* click *Choose* under *My style sheet* and browse to where your file is stored.

- Opera 5/Mac OS 9: under *Edit > Preferences > Page Style* click the button with the folder icon on it under *My style sheet* and browse to where your file is stored.

Absolute and Relative Positioning

Absolute and relative positioning are the major layout tools of CSS.

Absolute Positioning

With absolute positioning, an element is removed completely from the normal flow of the document. Its position is defined by the use of the properties `top`, `bottom`, `right`, and/or `left`. The element is positioned with respect to its containing block.

Absolute positioning has of late become a tool of choice for creating pages that do not use `<table>` elements to control layout. A typical example is shown at *http://www.accessibleinter.net/*, a basic two-column layout. The template relies on absolute positioning to move the left column content (which is actually below the main text of the page in the XHTML code and thus would normally render below the main page copy) up into what becomes the left navigation bar.

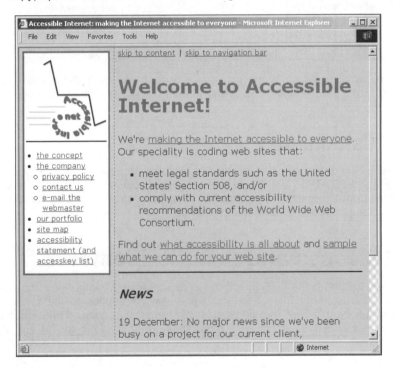

Another layout of note for its not using `<table>` elements is located at *Wired* (*http://www.wired.com*). Again, the left column is placed via CSS when it actually appears near the bottom of the XHTML code.

Also note fixed positioning, which is the same as absolute except that instead of positioning the element with respect to its containing block, the element is positioned with respect to the viewport (the browser window).

Relative Positioning

Relative positioning sets the position of an element relative to where it would have been statically positioned in the normal XHTML flow. Again, the same four positioning properties are used to define where the element will render. See *http://cita.rehab.uiuc.edu/courses/2002-09-REHAB711NC/lec10/slide13.html* for a basic example of this technique.

Pseudo-Classes and Pseudo-Elements

Pseudo-classes are defined in the CSS specification as classifying "elements on characteristics other than their name, attributes, or content" so that styles can be applied to them. Generally they are classified in ways outside that which would be possible from their positions in the document, such as styling a `<p>` tag or all `<em>` tags within `<h1>` tags. They are best known for the link pseudo-classes, though there are others.

Link Pseudo-Classes

We saw these two earlier in the annotated stylesheet:

♦ `:link` sets styles for all unvisited links.

♦ `:visited` sets styles for all visited links.

Dynamic Pseudo-Classes

These classes are typically associated with hyperlinks, but can actually apply to any element. At the time of writing, only the Gecko family of browsers and Opera 7 support using pseudo-classes in this fashion. They are dynamic in that an element may move into and out of the pseudo-class depending on the user interaction (a hyperlink is hovered over and takes on the `hover` rules, then the mouse moves away and the `hover` rules no longer apply).

♦ `:hover` sets a style while an element is hovered over but not clicked on (typically meaning hovered over with a mouse).

♦ `:active` is the style applied while activating an element (while clicking on a hyperlink).

♦ `:focus` is the style applied while an element has focus (cursor placed in a text field, or tabbing onto a hyperlink).

Proper Order of Pseudo-Classes on Hyperlinks

Since the dynamic pseudo-classes are not mutually exclusive – an element can be in multiple dynamic states simultaneously – the order the pseudo-classes appear in is important. Recall in the discussion of the cascade that when all else is equal, the last rule defined wins. So the pseudo-classes should be set in a specific order to work correctly.

The traditional school of thought in writing hyperlink pseudo-class styles recommends defining them in this manner:

♦ `a:link`

♦ `a:visited`

♦ `a:hover`

♦ `a:active`

The `:focus` pseudo-class has generally been omitted since browser support is poor. It is, however, a useful tool, particularly for helping keyboard users determine where on the page their cursor is (by using the focus styles to draw attention to it). As of this writing, only Netscape 6+ and Internet Explorer 5 for the Mac support `:focus`.

As browser support improves, however, this system can inadvertently create problems. Since `:hover` and `:active` can apply to any element, these rules will give those effects to `<a>` elements that are target anchors, not hyperlinks, such as:

```
<a name="theanchor" id="theanchor">I am an anchor.</a>
```

Less-compliant browsers would not apply any `:hover` or `:active` styles to what would otherwise be plain text. So to solve the problem, we would have to write another rule for those `<a>` elements. Or, the rules can be written in this revised format:

Cascading Style Sheets

- ◆ `:link:focus, :visited:focus`

- ◆ `:link`

- ◆ `:visited`

- ◆ `:link:hover, :visited:hover`

- ◆ `:link:active, :visited:active`

In this method, `:hover` and `:active`, as well as `:focus`, can only match hyperlinks since they are tied to `:link` instead of to an `<a>` element. This has the advantage of being forward-compatible with XHTML 2.0 as well, since XHTML 2.0 allows any element to be a hyperlink, not just an `<a>` element. Even `:focus` has found a home in the rules as well – its odd location is to circumvent browser bugs in Internet Explorer 5.0/PC. The only disadvantages noted at the time of writing come in two browsers. Internet Explorer 3 will apply the `:focus` styles to the body of the page's text. Opera 6/PC and 5/Mac will not apply any `:hover` or `:active` styles, as the browser has a bug where it does not understand this combining of pseudo-classes.

(Note: This guide to ordering pseudo-classes is adapted from an original article by the author which first appeared on *evolt.org, http://www.evolt.org/*).

Other Pseudo-Classes

`:lang` matches elements that are in a particular language. Language is defined by the `lang` attribute in XHTML, and by the `xml:lang` attribute in XML. So for example:

```
span:lang(fr)
```

would match against any `<span>` tag that had a `lang` attribute equal to `fr` (French).

Different languages have different conventions for such things as quotation marks, when to bold/italic, etc. With this pseudo-class one stylesheet can contain different rules for different languages, rather than having separate sheets for each language.

`:first-child` matches any element that is the first child of the parent element.

Pseudo-Elements

Pseudo-elements "*create abstractions about the document tree beyond those specified by the document language*" (*http://www.w3.org/TR/CSS21/selector.html#x22*). They enable the developer to apply styles to abstract structures that are otherwise indefinable.

- ◆ `:first-line` applies styles to the first line of a `block` element, such as a paragraph.

- ◆ `:first-letter` applies styles to the first letter of a block element. These two pseudo-elements are useful for creating effects typically found in print, such as having a large styled letter as the first letter of a paragraph.

- ◆ `:before` and `:after` insert content specified in the CSS rule before or after a particular element. See the next section for an example of how this can be used.

Revealing The accesskey Via Pseudo-Elements

XHTML has the `accesskey` attribute, where a key can be assigned to a hyperlink or a form field. This key, in combination with a modifier key on the keyboard (typically the *Ctrl* key in Windows or the *Command* key on a Mac) will enable the browser to jump into that form field or activate the hyperlink.

In the typical browser, though, the `accesskey` is invisible unless the page specifically lists or shows what `accesskey`s exist and what they're assigned to. With a little help from pseudo-elements, though, you can have the page's CSS display this information.

The CSS rule looks like this:

```
*[accesskey]:after {
  content : " <" attr(accesskey) ">";
}
```

`*` is the universal selector. It means this rule applies to any element. `[accesskey]` means "*if the accesskey attribute exists*". So the rule so far is "*For any element, if the* `accesskey` *attribute has been defined....*" `:after` means that the generated content will appear after the element. The `content` property defines what the generated content will be. First we print a space and a <, then `attr(accesskey)` means "*print the value of the* `accesskey` *attribute for this element*". We then close by printing >.

So for an example, this hyperlink:

```
<a href="somewhere.html" accesskey="s">A link to somewhere</a>
```

would look like this in the browser with the CSS applied:

A link to somewhere <s>

This does require some strong browser support. Currently this technique would only work in the Gecko browser family, and in Opera 7. Other browsers would just ignore the CSS and do nothing. But since it does degrade safely in browsers that don't support it, it's a useful trick.

CSS Property Reference

Key		
property-name	Description of shorthand property	
	property-value	Description of default value.
	property-value	Description of other possible value. Text in <angle brackets> indicates a user-specified value.
[property-name]	Property that can be defined within the above shorthand property.	
	property-value	Description of default value.
	property-value	Description of other possible value. Text in <angle brackets> indicates a user-specified value.

All properties take the value of "inherit", meaning, "inherit the value of the parent element". Many values are set as a given amount of a specific unit of length, or as a percentage. See the *Choosing the right unit of measurement* section that follows for more details on the types of units available.

background	Shorthand for the background properties.	
[background-color]	Set background color.	
	transparent	The background of the parent element shows through
	<color name>	The background color is set to the named color
	<RGB code>	The background color is set to the specified color
[background-image]	Sets a background image.	
	none	No background image
	<URL>	Background image taken from the supplied URL.
[background-repeat]	Whether/how a background should tile.	
	repeat	Tiles the background horizontally and vertically
	repeat-x	Tiles horizontally (on the x-axis)
	repeat-y	Tiles vertically (on the y-axis)
	no-repeat	No repeating/tiling

[background-attachment]	Does background image scroll?	
	scroll	Image scrolls as the document is scrolled
	fixed	Image is fixed in place
[background-position]	Position of background image right and down the element box.	
	You can combine two of the keywords, as in top left or center right	
	0%	0%is the default value
	top	Background is positioned at the top
	center	Background is positioned at the center
	bottom	Background is positioned at the bottom
	left	Background is positioned at the left
	right	Background is positioned at the right
	\<length unit\>	Background is \<length unit\> from top, can specify as em, px, or pt.
	\<percentage\> \<percentage\>	0% 0% is top-left corner, 100% 100% is bottom-right corner

border	Shorthand for the border properties	
[border-width]	Width of all four borders around an element.	
	medium	Border is of medium width
	thin	Border is thin
	thick	Border is thick
	\<length unit\>	Border will be of \<length unit\> width, in px.
[border-style]	Styling of all four borders around an element	
	none	No styling applied
	hidden	Border is hidden
	dotted	Border is dotted
	dashed	Border is dashed
	solid	Border is solid
	double	Border is double
	groove	Border is a groove
	ridge	Border is a ridge

	inset	Border is inset to the boundary
	outset	Border is outset to the boundary
[border-collapse]	Selects table-cell border model to use. *Note: the default was "collapse" in CSS2. It was changed in CSS2.1 since most browsers use "separate" or have built-in behavior that more resembles "separate".*	
	separate	Use the separate border model (one continuous border around tables, table cells, etc.)
	collapse	Use the collapsing border model (borders around cells, rows, columns, etc. can be controlled as with the rules attribute of the XHTML <table> tag)
[border-color]	Colors of all four borders around an element. *Default value is the color set for each side* *Note: In CSS2 "color" was used instead of "border-top-color"*	
	<color name>	Border is set to specified <color name>
	<RGB code>	Border is set to specified <RGB code>
	transparent	Allows underlying color through
[border-spacing]	Distance between adjacent table cell borders. Value is set as a length unit	
	0	No space between adjacent cell borders
	<length unit>	Adjacent cell borders <length unit> spaced, in px.

border-top, border-right, border-bottom, border-left	Shorthand for width, style, and color of borders
[border-top-color], [border-right-color], [border-bottom-color], [border-left-color]	Colors for each border. Set individually as **[border-color]** above Default value is the color set for each side

[border-top-style], [border-right-style], [border-bottom-style], [border-left-style]	Styles for each border. Set individually as **[border-style]** above	
[border-top-width], [border-right-width], [border-bottom-width], [border-left-width]	Width of each border. Set individually as **[border-width]** above.	

bottom	Positioning of an element.	
	`auto`	Position is calculated by browser's default
	`<length unit>`	The element is the specified length from the bottom, in `px`
	`<percentage>`	The element is the specified percentage of its parent element from the bottom
top	Positioning of an element. Set as **[bottom]** above	
left	Positioning of an element. Set as **[bottom]** above	
right	Positioning of an element. Set as **[bottom]** above	

caption-side	Position of a table caption	
	Note: CSS2 also has the values of "left" and "right", which have been removed in CSS2.1.	
	`top`	Caption is above the table box
	`bottom`	Caption is below the table box

clear	Which sides of element box should clear (not be adjacent to) an earlier float? (equivalent to `<br clear="..." />` in XHTML)	
	`none`	No attempt to clear a float
	`left`	Render this box clear of left-floated boxes
	`right`	Render this box clear of right-floated boxes
	`both`	Render this box clear of all floated boxes

clip	What part of an absolutely positioned box should be visible?	
	`auto`	Visible region is calculated as the normal size and location of the element box
	`rect`	The syntax `rect([top], [right], [bottom], [left]` defines how much to offset the clipped region from the normal visible box borders.

color	Foreground color of textual content	
		Default value is browser-dependent
	`<color name>`	Text is set to specified `<color name>`
	`<RGB code>`	Text is set to specified `<RGB code>`

content	Used to generate content (render content that is not in the XHTML code) with the `:before` and `:after` pseudo-elements. *Note: CSS2 had the additional values of [counter] and [uri],which have been dropped in CSS2.1.*	
		Default value is an empty string
	`string`	A string of text
	`attr[X]`	Returns the value of attribute `X` for whatever selector the CSS rule applies to
	`open-quote,` `close-quote`	Returns an appropriate set of quotation marks
	`no-open-quote,` `no-close-quote`	Returns an empty string for quotation marks

cursor	Define what type of cursor to display	
	Note: "progress" is new in CSS2.1 and does not exist in CSS2. Also note that the value [uri] existed in CSS2 and has been dropped in CSS2.1.	
	`auto`	Browser picks the appropriate cursor
	`crosshair`	A "+" shaped cursor
	`default`	OS/platform default, typically an arrow
	`pointer`	Arrow that indicates a hyperlink below the cursor
	`move`	Shows that some object is to be moved

	`e-resize,`
	`ne-resize,`
	`n-resize,`
	`nw-resize,`
	`w-resize,`
	`sw-resize,`
	`s-resize,`
	`se-resize`
		Shows that an edge of an object can be moved

	`text`	The text below the cursor is selectable, usually rendered as an I-bar
	`wait`	Hourglass or watch symbol that a program is doing something and the user should wait
	`progress`	Indicator that the program is doing something but that the user can still interact. The indicator is often a "spinning beach ball" symbol, or an arrow with an hourglass.
	`help`	Some sort of help is available for the object under the cursor. Can be a "?" symbol or a "help balloon"

direction	Direction of the flow of text	
	`ltr`	Text runs left to right
	`rtl`	Text runs right to left

display	Defines how an element will display	
	`inline`	Element displays inline
		Note: while the default is inline, browser stylesheets will change the default of many elements (such as paragraphs) to block

Table continued on following page

Cascading Style Sheets

2

	block	Element displays as block-level
	inline-block	Element internally acts as block-level, but flows in the document as an inline box *Note: This value did not exist in CSS2. CSS2 had the value "compact", which has been dropped in CSS2.1. The value of "marker" has also been dropped in CSS2.1.*
	list-item	Element displays like a list item, generating an overall block box and a list-item inline box
	none	Element is not displayed on the page
	run-in	Can be inline or block, depending on the context
	table, inline-table, table-row-group, table-column, table-column-group, table-header-group, table-footer-group, table-row, table-cell, table-caption	Element displays as the appropriate type of table element

empty-cells	Whether or not borders and background should be rendered for empty table cells	
	show	Render borders and backgrounds
	hide	Do not render borders and backgrounds

float	Whether and how a box should be floated	
	none	Box does not float
	left	Box floats left, content flows to its right
	right	Box floats right, content flows to its left

font	Shorthand for font properties	
	caption	Font for captioned controls (such as form buttons)
	icon	Font used on icon labels
	menu	Font used in menus (such as a drop-down menu)

	message-box	Font used in dialog boxes
	small-caption	Font used for labeling small controls
	status-bar	Font used for window status bar text
[font-style]	Font face	
	normal	Normal face for the font
	italic	Italic face
	oblique	Oblique face
[font-variant]	Font variation to apply	
	normal	Display the font normally
	small-caps	Render a small-caps font
[font-weight]	Boldness to apply to a font	
	normal	No boldness (equivalent to 400 on the following scale)
	[100, 200, 300, 400, 500, 600, 700, 800, 900]	Sequence/scale of font boldness to apply
	bold	Bold (equal to 700 on the above scale)
	bolder	Bolder than the parent element (one step up the scale)
	lighter	Less bold than the parent element (one step down the scale)
[font-size]	Sizing of fonts	
	medium	Roughly equivalent to `<font size="3">`
	xx-small	
	x-small	
	small	
	large	
	x-large	
	xx-large	
	larger	Makes the font one size larger than its parent
	smaller	Makes the font one size smaller than its parent
	<length unit>	Specify font size in px, pt, or em
	<percentage>	Makes the font a percentage of its parent

[font-family]	Specifies a font	
		The default is browser-dependent
	`<family-name>`	The name of a particular font (such as Verdana)
	`<generic-family>`	A generic font family name (`serif`, `sans-serif`, `cursive`, `fantasy`, `monospace`)
[line-height]	Leading between lines of text	
	`normal`	Browser chooses a reasonable value based on the font
	`<length unit>`	Line will be the specified height in `px`
	`<number>`	Line height will be the font size of the element multiplied by the supplied number
	`<percentage>`	Line height will be a percentage of the font size of the element

height	Height of an element	
	`auto`	Height is automatically determined by the browser, based on the content of the element and the surrounding elements
	`<length unit>`	Element is the specified height, in `px` or `em`
	`<percentage>`	Element is a percentage of the height of its parent
width	Width of an element. Set as **[height]** above	

letter-spacing	Spacing between characters of text	
	`normal`	Standard spacing for the given font
	`<length unit>`	Characters are spaced the specified distance, in `px`, or `em`, in addition to the standard spacing

list-style	Shorthand for the list-style properties	
[list-style-type]	Appearance of the list item bullet/marker	
	`disc`	Marker is a disc
	`circle`	Marker is a circle
	`square`	Marker is a square

	decimal	Marker is numeric, starting at 1
	decimal-leading-zero	Numeric with leading zero (01, 02, etc.)
	lower-roman, upper-roman	Lowercase Roman numerals (i, ii, iii) Uppercase Roman numerals (I, II, III)
	lower-greek	Lowercase classical Greek: (, ,)
	lower-alpha, lower-latin	Lowercase ASCII letters
	upper-alpha, upper-latin	Uppercase ASCII letters
	hebrew	Traditional Hebrew numbering
	armenian	Traditional Armenian numbering
	georgian	Traditional Georgian numbering
	cjk-ideographic	Plain ideographic numbers
	hiragana	a, i, u, e, o, ka, ki, etc.
	katakana	A, I, U, E, O, KA, KI, etc.
	hiragana-iroha	i, ro, ha, ni, ho, he, to, etc.
	katakana-iroha	I, RO, HA, NI, HO, HE, TO, etc.
	none	No marker is displayed
[list-style-position]	Location of bullet in the overall block box	
	outside	Bullet falls outside the box
	inside	Bullet falls inside the box
[list-style-image]	Image to use as the "bullet" for list items	
	none	No image for list item bullets
	<URI>	URI to the image to be used

margin	Shorthand for the margin properties	
[margin-right]	Right margin width of most elements	
	0	No margin
	auto	Margin is set as browser default
	<length unit>	Margin is set to specified length, in px or em
	<percentage>	Margin is set to specified percentage of parent element's margin

[margin-left]	Left margin width of most elements, set as **[margin-right]** above
[margin-top]	Top margin width of most elements, set as **[margin-right]** above
[margin-bottom]	Bottom margin width of most elements, set as **[margin-right]** above

max-height	Maximum height on all but non-replaced inline elements and table elements	
	`0`	No limit on the element's height
	`<length unit>`	Element is limited to specified height, in `px` or `em`
	`<percentage>`	Element is limited to specified percentage of parent element's height
max-width	Maximum width on all but non-replaced inline elements and table elements. Set as **[max-height]** above.	

min-height	Minimum height on most elements	
	`0`	No minimum to the element's height
	`<length unit>`	Element is limited to specified height, in `px` or `em`, as a minimum
	`<percentage>`	Element is limited to specified percentage of parent element's height, as a minimum
min-width	Minimum width on most elements, set as **[min-height]** above	

outline	Shorthand for the outline properties	
[outline-color]	Color of outlines (the lines that appear around a hyperlink if you tab-keyboard the cursor onto it)	
	`invert`	Performs a "color inversion" on the pixels on the screen
	`<color name>`	Outline color is set to specified color name
	`<RGB code>`	Outline color is set to specified RGB code
[outline-style]	Style of the outline	
	`none`	No outline
	`dotted`	Outline is dotted
	`dashed`	Outline is dashed

		solid	Outline is solid
		double	Outline is double
		groove	Outline is a groove
		ridge	Outline is a ridge
		inset	Outline is inset to the boundary
		outset	Outline is outset to the boundary
[outline-width]		Width of the outline	
		medium	Outline is of medium width
		thin	Outline is thin
		thick	Outline is thick
		<length unit>	Outline is the specified width, in px

overflow	How to display content that flows outside the confines of the element's box	
	visible	Render the overflow content
	hidden	Hide the overflow content
	scroll	Provide scrollbars for viewing overflow content, regardless of whether an overflow has actually occurred or not
	auto	Browser-dependent response

padding	Shorthand for the padding properties	
[padding-top]' **[padding-right],** **[padding-bottom],** **[padding-left]**	Padding around each of the four sides of an element	
	0	No padding
	<length unit>	Element has specified padding, in px or em
	<percentage>	Element has specified percentage of parent element's padding

page-break-after	Page break rules for after an element box	
	auto	Page break is neither forced nor forbidden
	always	Always page break
	avoid	Avoid a page break

	left	Force one or two page breaks as required to make the next page a "left" page
	right	Force one or two page breaks as required to make the next page a "right" page
page-break-before	Page break rules for before an element box. Set as **[page-break-after]** above.	
page-break-inside	Page break rules inside an element box. Set as **[page-break-after]** above.	

position	Positioning of an element box	
	static	Box is laid out by normal positioning rules
	relative	Box will be offset by a given amount relative to its normal position
	absolute	Box is positioned by top, right, bottom, and left properties
	fixed	As absolute, except that the box is fixed in position

quotes	Designates quotation marks to be used	
		The default value is locale- and browser-dependent
	none	The content property open-quote and close-quote values will produce no quote marks
	<string string>	The quote symbols specified in string will be used. Multiple strings for quotes within quotes can be specified

table-layout	How to lay out table contents in table and inline-table elements	
	auto	Use an automatic table layout
	fixed	Use a fixed layout independent of the actual contents of the table cells

text-align	How to align block content	
		The default value depends on browser and on normal flow of text (left to right or right to left)
	left	Left-justify the text

	right	Right-justify the text
	center	Center the text
	justify	Justify the text
	\<string\>	Applies only to table cells; sets a string on which cells will align

text-decoration	Decoration to apply to text	
	none	No decoration
	underline	Text is underlined
	overline	Text has a line above it
	line-through	Text has a line through its middle, horizontally
	blink	Text blinks on and off

text-indent	How much to indent the first line of a block of text	
	0	No indent
	\<length unit\>	Indent measured as a length unit
	\<percentage\>	Indent measured as a percentage

text-transform	Capitalization transformation effect	
	none	No special effect
	capitalize	Capitalize the first character of each word
	uppercase	Uppercase all characters
	lowercase	Lowercase all characters

unicode-bidi	Part of defining how text is properly bi-directional rendered	
	normal	No special rules/embedding apply
	embed	For inline-level elements, a new level of embedded is opened in the bi-directional algorithm
	bidi-override	Depending on the type of element, creates an override of the normal algorithm

vertical-align	Vertical positioning rules, relative to parent element.	
	Note that these rules are not meant to be used to "center" an element between the top/bottom of the page, though users often try to do that)	
	`baseline`	Baseline aligned with baseline of parent box
	`sub`	Lowers baseline to create "subscript" effect. Doesn't change font size.
	`super`	Raises baseline to create "superscript" effect. Doesn't change font size.
	`top`	Align top with the top of the line box.
	`text-top`	Align top with the top of parent element's font.
	`middle`	Align vertical midpoint with the baseline of parent plus half the x-height of parent.
	`bottom`	Align bottom with the bottom of the line box.
	`text-bottom`	Align bottom with the bottom of parent element's font.
	`<length unit>, <percentage>`	Positive numbers raise the positioning, negative lower it.

visibility	Whether or not a box's element is rendered	
	`inherit`	Box inherits its visibility from its parent element
	`visible`	Box is visible
	`hidden`	Box is hidden
		Note: a hidden box still affects the overall page layout (it takes up space on the page though the content is hidden from view, other elements will interact with it in terms of float, applying margin, etc.).
	`collapse`	Causes table rows or columns to be removed; in non-table situations, the same as hidden

white-space	How to handle whitespace within an element	
	`normal`	Browser collapses whitespace sequences, and line breaks as needed
	`pre`	No collapsing of whitespace sequences, line breaks at new lines in the code
	`nowrap`	As normal, but line breaks are suppressed

word-spacing	Space between words	
	normal	Normal as defined by the font and/or the browser
	`<length unit>`	In addition to the default, specified in px, em

z-index	Stacking of positioned boxes (which element box should be on top of the others, when boxes overlap)	
	auto	Stacking level as from the parent
	`<number>`	A number that equals the stack level (highest number is at the top of the stack, lower numbers follow in order)

The following properties are in CSS2, but have been dropped from CSS2.1: counter-increment, counter-reset, font-size-adjust, font-stretch, marker-offset, marks, orphans, size, text-shadow, and widows.

Additionally, all the aural stylesheet properties (stylesheets for speech synthesizers and speech browsers) have been removed from CSS2.1, since in CSS2.1 aural stylesheets are not a part of the normative specification (they still exist as an informative appendix to the specification): azimuth, cue, cue-after, cue-before, elevation, pause, pause-after, pause-before, pitch, pitch-range, play-during, richness, speak, speak-header, speak-numeral, speak-punctuation, speech-rate, stress, voice-family, and volume.

Choosing the Right Unit of Measurement

CSS offers a number of ways to define what units of measure your CSS properties will be in. Units of length can be absolute in size, or relative to some other property.

Absolute lengths include:

♦   cm (centimeters)

♦   in (inches)

♦   mm (millimeters)

♦   pc (picas, where 1 pica equals 12 points)

♦   pt (points, where 1 point equals 1/72 inch)

Relative units include:

♦   em (ems, a unit relative to the height of the font)

♦   ex (x-height, relative to the height of the letter "x" in a given font)

♦   px (pixels, which are relative to the screen resolution)

Also relative is defining the measurement of a given property as a percentage of another value.

Note: since aural stylesheets are not part of the normative CSS2.1 specification as they were in CSS2, the following aural units are also no longer normative in CSS2.1: deg (degrees), grad (grads), rad (radians), ms (milliseconds), s (seconds), Hz (Hertz), and kHz (kilo Hertz).

Choosing the correct means of measurement can be crucial, particularly when defining font sizes. A poor choice can impact on the accessibility and usability of the web page in question.

Absolute units are generally of least value, with the exception of points. Points are a unit of measurement in print and thus are perfectly acceptable and suited for print stylesheets. Points should **not** be used for a screen stylesheet, as they will render at varying sizes depending on the user's platform and screen resolution. Often a font in points that simply looks small on a Windows machine will become illegible on a Macintosh.

Relative units are better to use, but browser bugs make most of them (including percentages) useless unless you use techniques to hide CSS from specific browsers (see the earlier section in this chapter). Netscape 4 has problems with ems, exs, and percentages. Internet Explorer 3 renders ems as pixels, and has issues with percentages. Without techniques to hide CSS from certain browsers, only the pixel is considered a safe cross-browser, cross-platform unit. Its major drawback is that Internet Explorer on the PC will not allow you to resize fonts measured in pixels, as other browsers will. This is a major accessibility issue as users lose the ability to resize text to their comfort level if the pixel size is too small.

Also note that font size can be defined using keywords (xx-small, x-small, small, medium, large, x-large, xx-large). Again, browser bugs make this method useless unless you hide the CSS from browsers that have problems with it. But if you are doing that, this method can be one of the best ways to define font sizes. For more on this technique, "*Using Relative Font Sizes*" on Dive into Accessibility at *http://diveintoaccessibility.org/day_26_using_relative_font_sizes.html* is recommended reading.

CSS Selector Reference

Selector	Definition	Example
*	Universal selector, matches any element	*[lang] { font-style : italic; }
X	Matches any element of type X	p { font-size : 14px; }
X Y	Matches any element Y that is a descendant of an element X	h1 strong { color : red; }
X>Y	Matches any element Y that is a child of an element X	html>body { font-size : medium; }
X:first-child	Matches any element X that is the first child of its parent element	p:first-child { font-weight : bold; }

Selector	Definition	Example
X:link, X:visited	Matches element X if X is an unvisited or visited hyperlink	a:link { text-decoration : underline; }
X:active, X:hover, X:focus	Matches element X during certain user actions (X is active, hovered over, or has the focus)	a:hover { text-decoration : none; }
X:lang(y)	Matches element X if X is in language Y	abbr:lang(fr) { font-style : italic; }
X+Y	Matches any element Y that is immediately preceded by an element X	h1+p { margin-top : 0;}
X[attribute]	Matches any element X that has the named attribute set (regardless of the attribute's value)	acronym[title] { cursor : help; }
X[attribute="y"]	Matches any element X that has the named attribute set and equal to y in value	a[accesskey="0"] { font-weight : bold; }
X[attribute~="y"]	Matches any element X with the named attribute, where the value of the attribute is a list of space-separated values, one of which equals Y	p[class~="summary"] { color : green; }
X[attribute|="y"	Matches any element X with the named attribute that has a hyphen-separated list of values beginning with y	label[for|="required"] { font-weight : bold; }
X.y	Matches any element X with a class attribute that is a list of space-separated values, one of which equals y	ul.mainlist { list-style-type : disc; }
X#y	Matches any element X with an id attribute that equals y.	p#intro { line-height : 1.3; }

Summary

CSS is an integral piece of today's web development. With it, the classic separation of content from presentation is possible. While the latest browsers have strong CSS1 support, CSS2 support is not quite complete. Older browsers remaining on the market in substantial numbers that bugs even in their CSS1 support. This makes the techniques of hiding advanced CSS from older browsers an important part of CSS development.

Another integral part of CSS development is its power in creating accessible web pages. CSS's ability to handle presentation, coupled with the user's ability to write their own user stylesheet and introduce it into the cascade, give the end-user strong tools in controlling a web page's presentation to suit his/her needs. As with any tool, there are right and wrong ways to use CSS to enhance usability and accessibility.

CSS offers a vast array of tools to the front-end developer. This broad range is a must-have for today's web development.

Other References

The most obvious book to go to next is *Cascading Style Sheets: Separating Content from Presentation*, from glasshaus, ISBN 1-904151-04-3. As with all the other chapters in the book, a wide selection of links are available from our web site.

3

- JavaScript syntax reference and tutorial
- Native JavaScript object references

Author: Cliff Wootton

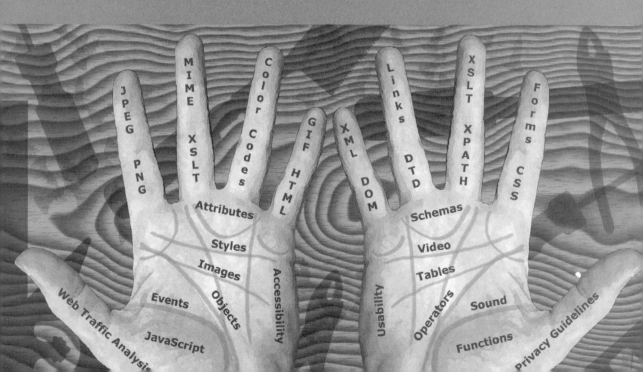

Core JavaScript

In this chapter we will explore JavaScript from top to bottom. To start with, we shall explore the origins of the JavaScript language, before going over the language from first principles until we arrive at object-based concepts. By then, we shall have learned enough to build some quite sophisticated scripts and run them in a browser. We will cover browser extensions in *Chapter 4*.

JavaScript Origins

Version 2.0 of the Netscape browser appeared in late 1996 and provided a primitive but interesting new technology: **LiveScript**. Over the next few releases of Netscape this evolved into JavaScript. Here is a summary of the different versions of JavaScript and the browsers they were implemented in:

Version	ECMA	Notes
LiveScript 1.0	No	The original precursor to JavaScript.
JavaScript 1.0	No	Netscape Navigator 2 implemented this. Now mostly obsolete.
JavaScript 1.1	Yes	Supported in Netscape Navigator 3 and Netscape Enterprise Server 2. Also supported in Opera version 3. More robust and better support for arrays. Image replacement and access to plugin properties. Scroll control.
JavaScript 1.2	No	Netscape Navigator 4.0 to 4.05 added RegExp, `switch` and `delete`, `Screen` object and interval timer, window `move` and `resize`, object and array literals.
JavaScript 1.3	Yes	Version 4.06 to 4.76 of Netscape Navigator added better exception handling. Also supported by Netscape Enterprise Server 3.
JavaScript 1.4	Yes	Netscape Navigator version 5 (not widely released).
JavaScript 1.5	Yes (v3)	Netscape Navigator 6 introduced exception handling. This version was compliant with ECMA standard 3rd edition.

Once the Netscape browser introduced scripting capabilities, it immediately gave them an advantage over the Microsoft Internet Explorer (IE) browser. Microsoft was quick to spot this and upgrade their browser, so it had similar functionality, using their own similar scripting language called **JScript**. The following table summarizes the different versions of JScript support:

Interpreter	ECMA	Notes
JScript 1.0	No	Equivalent to JavaScript 1.0 and released with IE 3.0.
JScript 1.1	No	Never released.
JScript 1.2	No	Evidence of its existence, but status unknown.
JScript 2.0	No	Released with IIS 1.0. Also implemented in later versions of IE 3.
JScript 3.0	Yes	Equivalent to JavaScript 1.2 and released with IE 4.0, IIS 4.0, and WSH 1.0 (some features are in IE 3.02)
JScript 4.0	Yes	Released with Visual Studio 6.0 but not provided with browser installs. Might affect browser operation since JScript components might overwrite those provided by a browser install.
JScript 5.0	Yes	Equivalent to JavaScript 1.5 and supported on all 32-bit Windows operating systems with IE.
JScript 5.1	Yes	Released with IIS 5.0 on Windows 2000.
JScript 5.5	Yes (v3)	Released with IE 5.5.
JScript 5.6	Yes (v3)	Released with IE 6.

This period of rapid, competitive, and destructive evolution of the language was referred to as the **browser wars**. It led to a great deal of angst for webmasters, who found it difficult to code their JavaScript and mark up their pages with HTML so that their content was on both Netscape and IE browsers.

Most web content is standardized by the W3C (World Wide Web Consortium) organization, but the standard relating to the JavaScript language itself is published by **ECMA** (European Computer Manufacturers' Association, *http://www.ecma.ch/*). They have evolved a standard referred to as **ECMA-262**, but also known as **ECMAScript**, that describes the core scripting language. Work on this standard commenced in 1996 and was initiated by Netscape. The first edition was released in June 1997. The standard has been revised twice since. The standard describes the core language but does not cover the document object model, which defines how scripts written in the language interact with the pages that contain them. The document- and client-based extensions to the language are the main cause of differences between one implementation and another.

Although the Edition 3 standard is the latest revision, the 2nd edition is also relevant. Versions of Netscape Navigator prior to release 6 are based on the 2nd edition. IE 5.5 and later, as well as Netscape version 6/7 upwards, aim for compliance with the 3rd edition of the ECMAScript standard.

Adding JavaScript to Your HTML Pages

JavaScript code can be added to the HTML content of your page in two ways:

♦ Within or referenced by the `<script>` element, which we'll discuss below.

♦ As the value of event handler attributes to HTML elements, which we'll cover later in this chapter.

The <script> Tag

The `<script>` tag is used to contain JavaScript. It has the following, commonly-used, attributes:

Attribute	Status	Description	Example Values
language	Deprecated (HTML 4)	Specifies the language and version of the script. This provides a means of hiding JavaScript written according to newer syntax conventions from older browsers that cannot cope with it. In general, you should always try to specify the lowest version of JavaScript to achieve maximum portability.	JavaScript JavaScript1.0 JavaScript1.6
Type	Mandatory (HTML 4+)	Defines the MIME type of a script block and is preferred over the `language` attribute.	text/javascript
Src	Optional	Includes a script source file. This enables you to share one source file between various pages. Also used with the archive attribute.	include.js
archive	Not standardized	Extracts script code from a Zip archive. Rarely used, but is supported by IE and Netscape version 4 browsers.	test1.zip
for ... event	IE only and not standardized	Associates a script block with an event as a handler. This is discussed later on when we look at event handling.	FOR="Xbutton" EVENT="Click()"
Defer	Optional	Allows execution of code in this script block to be deferred until some code that creates some output is encountered. Designed to improve throughput and performance.	n/a

Core JavaScript

type attribute

HTML 4 compliant `<script>` tags should include a `type` attribute and be formed like this:

```
<script type="text/javascript">
```

This is preferred because it describes the MIME type of the content within the <script> block. The older technique, is to use the `language` attribute, but this can lead to portability problems.

Placing Scripts

Usually, you place the `<script>` tag in the `<head>` or `<body>` section of the page.

The <head>

In the `<head>` context, the script is expected to provide some support to the rest of the page, so you might place useful functions and event-handler code here. You can also put some global code here, for example initializing global variables. You won't be able to access any objects that belong to the `<body>` of your page, since they won't yet exist.

If you place a `document.write()` instruction in the `<head>` block (outside of a function, of course), then you should make sure it writes something that is relevant to the header of an HTML or XHTML page. For example, you could write the document title, or an embedded stylesheet, here. However, if you just write textual output, or markup tags which should be in the body, such as `<P>`, then you will, strictly, be writing these in the header of your document. Netscape and IE browsers may still be smart enough to place them in the page body (as you probably intended). However, at best, you are simply adding to the processing time for the page (and assuming that the client has this functionality; many slimmer browsers, such as those used on mobile phones, won't). At worst, your pages won't validate as standards-compliant (X)HTML.

The <body>

You can place `<script>` tags within the `<body>` of the document. These scripts may also contain functions, but are more likely to contain inline code to be executed as the page is loading. If your inline script code is going to do any `document.write()` calls to modify the HTML as the page is loaded, then this is the best place to put the code.

When the browser encounters a `<script>` tag, it pauses the processing of the HTML page and executes the code contained within it. This may affect subsequent HTML output or generate some HTML of its own to be placed in the page at the point where the `<script>` block appears. Any lengthy script evaluation is going to slow down the display of your page, so you should defer any such extended processing until the page has loaded. For example, you can include `<script>` tags within an `onload` event handler in the `<body>` tag. This code will not execute until the closing `</body>` tag is encountered and the page has loaded. This may still cause a performance hit if you are using included `.js` files within the script, however, since they will need to be requested from the web server.

Note that during page loading, until you have reached the closing `</body>` tag, the page exists in an intermediate state, where objects and memory locations are not locked down. This may cause problems in writing to the document or changing the content of HTML elements, such as `<div>` or `<span>` blocks. In particular, until the page is completed the `<object>` element is not properly linked into a structure in which it can be accessed, so you cannot `document.write()` into its content. Some browsers may be more forgiving than others over this problem, but it's best avoided for reasons of portability.

Elsewhere

In some situations, the `<script>` tags can appear outside the `<head>` and `<body>` tags. For example, if you are using a frameset, you can put the `<script>` block after the `<head>` tag but before the `<frameset>` tag.

The </script> Pitfall

You cannot use the string "`</script>`" within an inline JavaScript fragment. Even if it is enclosed inside quotation marks, it will still be seen by the parser and interpreted as a closure to the `<script>` tag. You will need to hide it by escaping the terminating slash.

So, if you need to say this:

```
var myScriptTag = "</script>";
```

Then you should do this:

```
var myScriptTag = "<\/script>";
```

which will hide the tag from the parser. This is generally applicable to all markup generated by script code, so you might also use "`<\/td>`" and "`<\/p>`" for example.

The <noscript> Tag

Browsers that support the `<script>` tag should also support the `<noscript>` tag. This allows you to provide some alternative content for when the user has turned off scripting support. Browsers that don't support the `<noscript>` tag will likely also not support the `<script>` tag either and will default to displaying the content inside both tags as if it were HTML. The content of the `<noscript>` tag is likely to be fine but the content inside the `<script>` tag should be enclosed within some HTML comment delimiters to prevent it being displayed.

```
<html>
<head>
<meta http-equiv="content-type" content="text/html; charset=UTF-8" />
<title>Noscript example</title>
</head>
<body>
This is processed as HTML content
<script type="text/javascript">
<!-- //Place an HTML comment here
document.write("This is the active script content which must be hidden");
//close the HTML comment here
-->
</script>
<noscript>
This HTML content is only visible if the browser understands scripting but
cannot honor the script tag or if the browser knows nothing about scripting
support.
</noscript>
This is some trailing HTML content.
</body>
</html>
```

Try viewing this example in your browser, then disable JavaScript on the browser and reload the page. Although this is often considered necessary only for very old browsers that don't recognize the `<script>` tag, as you can see, modern browsers will also make use of `<noscript>` tagged content if:

♦ They have JavaScript disabled.

♦ The type of script that is indicated in the opening `<script>` tag is unsupported by that browser.

♦ They are of a type that cannot support client-side scripting, such as those used on smartphones and PDAs.

Variables

Variables are containers into which you can store a primitive value or a reference to an object. They must have unique names within their scope within the document. These names are called **identifiers**. Here are some rules governing how identifiers are used in JavaScript:

♦ Identifiers are case-sensitive

♦ Identifiers cannot contain any of the characters +, -, *, %, !, <, >, =, ?, ~, &, and /.

♦ Identifiers can contain numbers, but must not start with a number.

♦ Identifiers cannot consist of the JavaScript reserved words (listed below). If you do use these words, in certain contexts, the interpreter will completely misunderstand your intent and may parse them as legitimate statements or function names.

Here is a list of reserved words in the JavaScript environment:

abstract	alert	arguments	Array
blur	Boolean	Boolean	break
byte	callee	caller	captureEvents
case	catch	char	class
clearInterval	clearTimeout	close	closed
confirm	const	constructor	continue
Date	debugger	default	defaultStatus
delete	do	document	double
else	enum	escape	eval
export	extends	false	final
finally	find	float	focus
for	frames	function	Function

Table continued on following page

goto	history	home	if
implements	import	in	Infinity
innerHeight	innerWidth	instanceof	int
interface	isFinite	isNaN	java
length	location	locationbar	long
Math	menubar	moveBy	moveTo
name	NaN	native	netscape
new	null	Number	Object
open	opener	outerHeight	outerWidth
package	Packages	pageXOffset	pageYOffset
parent	parseFloat	parseInt	personalbar
print	private	prompt	protected
prototype	public	RegExp	releaseEvents
resizeBy	resizeTo	return	routeEvent
scroll	scrollbars	scrollBy	scrollTo
self	setInterval	setTimeout	short
static	status	statusbar	stop
String	super	switch	synchronized
this	throw	throws	toolbar
top	toString	transient	true
try	typeof	unescape	unwatch
valueOf	var	void	volatile
watch	while	window	with

Declaring Your Variables

It is good practice to declare all variables before you use them, like this:

```
var newVariable;
```

An uninitialized variable has the value undefined, but it is good practice to store an initial value in the variable when it is first created. This requires the assignment operator (=). The a value to the right of the assignment operator is read from, and assigned to the identifier on the left of the assignment operator. You cannot assign values to constants, of course:

```
var firstValue = 10;
var secondValue = firstValue;
//The next line is illegal, and will not work...
10 = secondValue;
```

You can declare and initialize several variables in one line, as shown below. Although this saves on space, it makes the script a little more difficult to read, so on the whole it is better to put variable declarations on separate lines:

```
var varOne = 1, varTwo = 2, varThree = 10;
```

Variable Scope

The **scope** of a variable is the area over which it is accessible.

♦   When declared using the `var` keyword and placed in any `<script>` block but outside a function declaration, a variable is deemed to be **global** in scope, meaning it will be accessible both inside and outside functions. Changing the value of such a variable when inside a function alters the value for all subsequent references to that variable, wherever they are. It is good practice to place `var` declarators for global variables inside a `<script>` block within the `<head>` of the document.

♦   Variables declared using the `var` keyword inside a function are **local** within that function or any nested function declarations thereof. Outside that function, the variable is no longer accessible.

♦   Not using the `var` keyword to declare a variable deems a variable to be **global** in scope regardless of where it is declared.

JavaScript allows variable names in local contexts to override those in the global context. This means that when a variable name is reused within a function, the local value will be used in place of the global one. Moreover, changing the local value within the function body will not affect the global value.

```html
<html>
<head>
<meta http-equiv="content-type" content="text/html; charset=UTF-8" />
<title>Variable scope example</title>
</head>
<body>
<script type="text/javascript">
// Declare a global value
var myVariable = "Global Value";

// Declare a local value inside a function body
function local_scope()
{
  var myVariable = "Local Value";
  document.write(myVariable + "<br />");
}
```

```
// Demonstrate the scope: local value overriding the global one
document.write(myVariable + "<br />");
local_scope();
document.write(myVariable);
</script>
</body>
</html>
```

This generates the output:

Global Value
Local Value
Global Value

Data Types

JavaScript variables are loosely typed: they are not declared with any type and they can take on any type during their lifetime.

Primitive data types simply hold a value. There are three straightforward data types and two special types in core JavaScript. We will see how to use these different data types in the next few pages:

♦   Boolean

♦   Number

♦   String

♦   Null

♦   Undefined

Primitive data simply holds a value and yields it when asked for it, nothing more. All of the core primitive data types other than `Null` and `Undefined` have object-wrapped counterparts. JavaScript cleverly coerces primitives into objects whenever necessary. Placing an object wrapper around a primitive value provides additional capabilities to the storage container.

For example, although a `String` primitive can be added to (via concatenation), a string *object* can also be split into individual elements because it supports the `split()` method.

Furthermore, you can augment these behaviors with your own methods by modifying each object's prototype. For instance, you could create a special-purpose method that takes the data type into account when you call it, and yet has the same name for all supported data types. This allows for your code to be unaware of the underlying primitive data types.

Say you want the last two characters of any given value to be returned. For a string, you would do this via the existing substring extraction methods. If you wanted to do the same thing on a `Number` object (to get the last two digits of any number), you could do the same thing, of course – by coercing the value into a string first. However, a more elegant solution might be to perform a modulo 100 expression on the value, to obtain the same two characters, but in the form of a number.

You could now write two separate methods, one for the `String` object and one for the `Number` object, each of which uses the functionality best suited to that data type, but each with the same name – say `lastTwoChars()`. A call such as:

```
inputValue.lastTwoChars()
```

would go to the `lastTwoChars()` method of either the `String` or `Number` object, depending on whether `inputValue` was a string or a number, but it would not be apparent to the programmer using them that two completely separate pieces of code were involved.

The next tables summarize the effects of conversion between primitive and object-wrapped values.

From primitive type	Resulting object		From Object class	Resulting primitive
Boolean	Create a new `Boolean` object whose default value is the input value.		Boolean	The value is returned unchanged.
Number	Create a new `Number` object whose default value is the input value.		Number	The value is returned unchanged.
String	Create a new `String` object whose default value is the input value.		String	The value is returned unchanged.
			Object	The default value defined by the object's internal `DefaultValue()` method is returned. Coercion to the preferred type happens and is context dependant on where the result is being assigned.

Converting from an object to some other type generally goes smoothly, but some implementations have exhibited strange behavior when converting to a Boolean value from an object. The value `false` should result if the `object` has the value `false`, `zero`, `NaN`, `Null`, `Undefined`, or is an empty string. However, bugs have been reported that suggest that, in some early interpreters, if the object had any value other than `Null` or `Undefined`, `true` was returned. This is something of a legacy issue, however, so these days it may be of no consequence.

Type conversion between primitives is also possible, but the values may be changed along the way. Clearly a `Number` object and `Number` primitive should be able to hold the same value. However, a `String` object being converted to a `Number` primitive may lose some precision.

Literals are constant values used in assignments or as arguments to functions or expressions. They describe some fundamental source value which can be assigned to a variable or used to instantiate an object. This should not be confused with primitives which are simple data types. Primitives values can be described with a literal value but so can objects. A literal is considered to be a primary expression when it is being evaluated, meaning that it cannot be degenerated to any smaller sub-expression.

There are several kinds of literals. Four are based on the primitive types: `Boolean`, `Numeric`, `String`, and `Null`. Others allow objects to be defined in a literal manner. These are objects that can also be manufactured from literals: `Array`, `RegExp` (Regular expression), and `Object`. Host environments may define additional object types and syntax for specifying them in a literal form as dictated by their own needs.

Booleans

Boolean primitives (and literals) can define the value `true` or `false`.

Boolean Conversion to Number

The `false` value is coerced to zero when a Boolean value is converted to a number. Zero is not actually the same as `false`, but for most practical purposes this won't cause any problems. The Boolean value `true` is a non-zero number, although it often becomes `1` in numeric terms. You should not rely on its value though.

Type Conversion to Boolean

You can convert any value to a Boolean like this:

```
var myBoolean = Boolean(oldValue);
```

This table summarizes the values you get when converting from another type to a Boolean value:

From Value	Resulting Boolean
No value	false
undefined	false
Null	false
Boolean false	false
Boolean true	true
NaN	false
0	false
Non zero number	true
Zero length string ""	false
Non zero length string	true
Object	true

Boolean Object

The Boolean object supports the methods shown in the next table, for converting to other kinds of values. However the Boolean object provides very little additional functionality over that already provided by the Boolean primitive.

Method	Description
toString()	Returns a string version of the Boolean object's value.
valueOf()	Yields a Boolean primitive version of the object.

Numbers

Number primitives can define a positive or negative number. The value is represented as a 64-bit quantity and is a **floating point** value. **Integers** are considered to be floating point values with zero decimal places after the point. The ECMA 262 standard mandates the range of possible values as follows:

- ♦ Max numeric value $1.7976931348623157 * 10^{308.}$

- ♦ Min numeric value $5 * 10^{-324}$

Type Conversion to Number

You can convert any value to a Number like this:

```
var myNumber = Number(oldValue);
```

Using an arithmetic operator you can force a type conversion by subtracting zero from a value to yield a numeric result.

```
document.write(typeof(true - 0));
```

This table summarizes the values you get when converting from another type to a number:

From value	Numeric result
No value	0.
Undefined	Returns NaN.
Null	0.
Boolean false	0.
Boolean true	1.
Number	No conversion, the input value is returned unchanged.
Non numeric string	NaN.

From value	Numeric result
Numeric string	The numeric value rounded down if the number of digits exceeds the numeric accuracy specified by `Number.MAX_VALUE`.
`Object`	Internally, a conversion to one of the primitive types happens followed by a conversion from that type to a number. Some objects will return a number that is readily usable; others will return something that cannot be converted and `NaN` will result.

Number Literals

Number literals are constant numeric values expressed in Decimal, Hexadecimal, or Octal notation. The numeric values can be formatted as integer or floating point presentation.

```
var newFloatValue = 1.96;
```

For very large or small value floating point numbers you can use exponential notation. The following expression assigns the value 1.08×10^{23} to the variable called `floatingResult`.

```
floatingResult = 1.08e+23;
```

Hexadecimal values must always be integers and can be uppercase or lowercase. Furthermore, they must always begin with 0x and can contain the characters 0-9 and A-F:

```
myHexValue = 0xFF;
```

Octal values must always be integers, start with a zero, and contain only the characters 0–7. This can lead to some strange errors if you place leading zeros in front of your numeric values, on the assumption that they will still be considered decimal values by your code.

```
myOctalValue = 0377;
```

Not a Number

`NaN`, standing for 'Not-a-Number', means the result of an expression has been evaluated, but does not generate a meaningful numeric value. You can evaluate an expression and test for this value with the `isNaN()` function without crashing your script. A constant that represents this value is available as a property of the `Global` object.

Infinity

The values positive and negative `Infinity` can also be represented in a Number primitive (or object) as `Number.POSITIVE_INFINITY` and `Number.NEGATIVE_INFINITY`. These could be the result of an expression where some value was divided by zero. You can use the `isFinite()` function to test for the presence of this value. This value is also reflected as a property of the Global object.

Number Object

The `Number()` constructor is invoked by the `new` operator, for example:

```
new Number(1000);
```

This will create a new object of the `Number` type. You can invoke the constructor without the `new` operator like this:

```
Number(1000);
```

However, you would get a primitive number as a result of this and not a `Number` object. JavaScript is somewhat forgiving and you may not notice this happening until later on when it becomes important that you have a `Number` object and not a number primitive.

These are the methods supported by `Number` objects. (Some methods are deprecated and have been omitted from this list.) However, the `Number` object provides only marginal functionality over that already provided by the `Number` primitive. The useful additions principally allow for some reformatting of values.

Method	Description
`toExponential(digits)`	Converts the number to an exponential format representation. The argument specifies the number of decimal digits.
`toFixed(digits)`	Converts the number to a fixed-format representation. The argument specifies the number of decimal digits.
`toLocaleString()`	Converts a number to a string taking locale specific settings into account. This might affect punctuation and delimiter characters which can be defined within the client environment.
`toPrecision(digits)`	Convert a number to a string, automatically selecting fixed or exponential notation in an implementation-defined manner. The argument specifies the number of decimal digits and can be a value from 1 to 21. If the precision is omitted, the value 10 is assumed.
`toString(radix)`	The result of this method is a string primitive representation of the numeric value of the receiving object, rendered according to the passed-in radix value. Useful for converting between one base and another. The default radix is assumed to be 10. If you specify a radix of 8, you get an Octal value. A radix of 2 yields a binary value and a radix of 16 will generate a hexadecimal value. The range of possible values is from 2 to 36.
`valueOf()`	A `Number` object is converted to a simple number primitive. You probably won't need to do this very often yourself, because JavaScript is smart enough to convert number primitives to `Number` objects and vice versa whenever it needs to.

Strings

String primitives are designed to hold a Unicode-based string. Unicode is a double-byte character set allowing the full 65536 different and unique glyphs to be represented. This means that you can include ligatures, currency symbols, and international special characters within a web page. However, there are some caveats, mostly to do with the underlying support in the platform that the web browser is running on. The safest course is to only rely on the bottom-most 256 characters of the Unicode character set.

Including some characters within a string primitive might be tricky since there are not always keyboard equivalents for them. You can generate a special escape sequence to insert them instead: see *Appendix B*.

Type Conversion to String

You can convert any value to a string like this:

```
var myString = String(oldValue);
```

Concatenating a zero-length string to a value will also convert it to a string data type:

```
document.write(typeof(1000 + ""));
```

Converting other data types to strings goes according to these rules:

From Value	Resulting String
Undefined	"undefined"
Null	"null"
Boolean	If the argument is true, then the result is "true", otherwise the result is "false".
Number	Special cases are provided for NaN and Infinity where "NaN" and "Infinity" will be returned. Otherwise the string is a textual representation of the value.
String	No conversion, the input value is returned unchanged.
Object	An internal conversion to a primitive takes place followed by a conversion from that primitive to a string. Some objects will return a string value that is immediately useful; others might not have a meaningful string representation.

String Literal

A string literal is zero or more characters enclosed in matching single or double quotes. String values can use double quotes or single quotes, but they must be balanced:

```
myString1 = "A string goes here.";
myString2 = 'single quoted';
```

You can also embed single quotes inside double quotes and vice versa:

```
myString3 = 'A string with double " quotes';
myString4 = "He's got lot's of single quotes";
```

Special characters can be inserted with escape sequences. Be aware that these sequences are not presented in the same way as HTML character entities. Values are represented in a different number base in each of these contexts.

You can escape any character and specify it by its octal, hexadecimal, or Unicode equivalent code point. Note that the octal values will be in the range 0 to 377 and the hexadecimal values will be in the range 0 to FF. The octal and hexadecimal escapes can only cover the first 256 character codes, some of which are control codes and should not be used anyway. The Unicode escape gives access to the full 65536 character codes in the Unicode character set.

```
myString5 = "double quote \" inside double quotes";
myString6 = 'A backslash done as an escape \134';
```

Any numeric values that they use will *not* appear to be the same as those used in an HTML character entity. This is an octal-based JavaScript escaped character:

♦   \134

This is a decimal-based HTML character entity:

♦   &134;

Here is an example that illustrates the two forms. Run it and you should see two different character glyphs presented:

```
<html>
<head>
<meta http-equiv="content-type" content="text/html; charset=UTF-8" />
<title>Escaping differences example</title>
</head>
<body>
JavaScript escape (
<script type="text/javascript">
document.write("\134")
</script>
)<BR />
HTML escape (&#134;)
</body>
</html>
```

This next example generates a table showing decimal, binary, octal, and hex values up to 255 with their special character equivalents. Note that, here, we are using a `String.fromCharCode()` method to convert the numeric value into a character glyph:

```
<html>
<head>
<meta http-equiv="content-type" content="text/html; charset=UTF-8" />
```

```
<title>Look-up table generator</title>
</head>
<body>
<script type="text/javascript">
// Create a 0-255 lookup table
document.write("<table border=1>");
document.write("<tr><th>Index</th>");
document.write("<th>Binary</th>");
document.write("<th>Octal</th>");
document.write("<th>Hex</th>");
document.write("<th>fromCharCode</th>");
document.write("<th>JS escaped</th>");
document.write("<th>HTML entity</th></tr>");

for(ii=0; ii<256; ii++)
{
    // Generate a binary representation
    myBinary            = ii.toString(2);
    myBinaryPadding     = "00000000".substr(1,(8-myBinary.length));


    // Generate an octal representation
    myOctal             = ii.toString(8);
    myOctalPadding      = "0000".substr(1,(4-myOctal.length));


    // Generate a hexadecimal representation
    myHex               = ii.toString(16);
    myHexPadding        = "00".substr(1,(2-myHex.length));


    // Convert the decimal value to a character glyph
    myStringFromCharCode = String.fromCharCode(ii);


    // Make a glyph using JS backslash escape (uses eval)
    myEval = "myJavaScriptEscape = '\134" + myOctal + "'";
    eval(myEval);


    // Make a glyph with an HTML character entity
    myEntity = "&#" + ii + ";";

    document.write("<tr align=right><td>");
    document.write(ii);
    document.write("</td><td>");
    document.write(myBinaryPadding+myBinary);
    document.write("</td><td>");
    document.write(myOctalPadding+myOctal);
    document.write("</td><td>");
    document.write(myHexPadding+myHex.toUpperCase());
    document.write("</td><td>");
    document.write(" "+myStringFromCharCode);
    document.write("</td><td>");
```

117

```
        document.write(" "+myJavaScriptEscape);
        document.write("</td><td>");
        document.write(" "+myEntity);
        document.write("</td></tr>");
    }
    document.write("</table>");
    </script>
    </body>
    </html>
```

Unicode

The version 3.0 Unicode standard is now available. However, most JavaScript implementations will be compliant with the earlier Unicode version 2.0 standard that has been in existence for some years. You can find out more about Unicode at the web site *http://www.unicode.org/*, but you will have to purchase the specification in book form if you want the complete standard.

String Escape Characters

Here are some common string primitive escape sequences:

Escape sequence	Meaning	8-bit ASCII
\"	Double Quote	"
\'	Single Quote (Apostrophe)	'
\\	Backslash	\
\a	Audible alert (IE displays the letter a)	<BEL>
\b	Backspace (ignored silently in IE)	<BS>
\f	Form Feed (ignored silently in IE)	<FF>
\n	Line Feed (Newline – IE inserts a space)	<LF>
\r	Carriage Return (IE inserts a space)	<CR>
\t	Horizontal Tab (IE inserts a space)	<HT>
\v	Vertical tab (IE displays the letter v)	<VT>
\0nn	Octal escape	-
\042	Double Quote	"
\047	Single Quote (Apostrophe)	'
\134	Backslash	\
\xnn	Hexadecimal escape	-
\x22	Double Quote	"

Escape sequence	Meaning	8-bit ASCII
\x27	Single Quote (Apostrophe)	'
\x5C	Backslash	\
\unnnn	Unicode escape	-
\u0022	Double Quote	"
\u0027	Single Quote (Apostrophe)	'
\u005C	Backslash	\
\uFFFE	A special Unicode sentinel character for flagging byte-reversed text	
\uFFFF	A special Unicode sentinel character	

String Object

The `String()` constructor is invoked by the `new` operator, for example:

```
new String("Some Text");
```

This will create a new object of the `String` type. You can invoke the constructor without the `new` operator like this:

```
String("Some Text");
```

However, you would get a primitive string as a result from this and not a `String` object. JavaScript is somewhat forgiving and you may not notice this happening until later on when it becomes important that you have a `String` object and not a primitive string.

String Object properties

Aside from the constructor and prototype, the only other property of a `String` object of interest is the `length` property. This reflects the number of characters in a string.

```
myLength = myString.length;
```

String Object methods

These are the methods supported by `String` objects. Some methods are deprecated and have been omitted from this list:

Method	Description
`charAt(position)`	The character at the position in the string indicated by the argument value is returned by this method.
`charCodeAt(position)`	This method returns the Unicode code point of the character at the indicated position.
`concat(string2)`	A method for concatenating as opposed to the concatenate operator. The argument string is appended to the `String` object receiving the `concat(string2)` method call.
`fromCharCode(arg0, arg1, …)`	Constructs a new string from a sequence of Unicode character code point values each passed as a separate argument. Note that this is a static (or class) method and therefore must be used with the `String` object and not your user-created instances of it. Thus: `String.fromCharCode(65,66,67)`.
`indexOf(key, pos)`	Returns a value indicating the location of the search string within the receiving string object. The first argument is taken as the search key and the second (optional) argument indicates the starting position to begin searching at. Omitting the second argument implies the whole string should be searched.
`lastIndexOf(key, pos)`	Locate the rightmost occurrence of the search string within the receiving string object. This is a search that proceeds in the reverse direction to that of the `indexOf()` method. The second argument is also optional.
`localeCompare(string2)`	The locale-sensitive comparison takes special international characters and locale-specific text issues into account and properly matches the strings. The receiving string object is matched against the string that is passed as an argument.
`match(regexp)`	This is one of the additions to the String object to support regular expressions. The matches are returned in an array with each match in a separate element. The regular expression pattern is passed as an argument.
`replace(regexp, newString)`	The search pattern locates matches, which are then replaced by the string value in the second argument. The regexp argument is used to match a source string.

Method	Description
search(regexp)	The character location where the match occurred is returned. If there is no match then the value -1 is returned instead. The search pattern is passed in the form of a regular expression in the argument.
slice(start, end)	Returns a substring sliced out of the original. See the join() method of array objects. The beginning of the substring is indicated by the start parameter. The right-hand side is indicated by the end parameter. The end parameter can be omitted which will imply that the substring continues to the end of the source string.
split(pattern, count)	Split a string and store the components in an array. The patterns can be a simple sequence of characters or a regular expression. The optional count value can indicate a limited number of times that the splitting will occur.
substr(start, length)	This is a variation of the String.substring() method. The difference is that the substring length is passed as the second argument rather than the substring ending character index. The length parameter is optional.
substring(start, end)	If only one argument is provided, this method returns a substring starting at the indicated character position and proceeding to the end of the string. Where two arguments are provided the start and endpoints of the string are used to slice out a portion and return just that part. This is functionally identical to the slice() method.
toLocaleLowerCase()	Converts a string to all lowercase using a locale-sensitive character mapping.
toLocaleUpperCase()	Converts a string to all uppercase using a locale-sensitive character mapping.
toLowerCase()	This method returns a string primitive containing the value of the object with all characters converted to lowercase.
toString()	Returns a string primitive version of an object.
toUpperCase()	The result of this method is a string primitive containing the value of the object with all characters converted to uppercase.
valueOf()	The numeric equivalent of the string value is returned.

Null

The Null data type (and literal) can contain just one value – null. It is used as a default value for some function results and you may get this back as the result of a method or property request. It isn't quite the same as the undefined value; a null value is a meaningful result – it is the quantity 'nothing'. That is not the same as not getting a result at all.

Undefined

The Undefined data type has exactly one value – undefined. It is also often used as a default value. It isn't the same as Null. In this case it is the total absence of a value, whereas null is the presence of a value which signifies 'nothing'. Because there is a literal value that means undefined, you could assign that value to a variable which would then return the value undefined. But then that variable would have been defined to contain the value undefined. From the point of view your script code has, it cannot tell the difference between a genuinely undefined value and a variable whose value has been set to the value undefined.

A constant that represents this value is available as a property of the Global object.

Array Objects

If you think of a variable as being a container for a single data item of one particular type, then an array is a set of containers arranged in a collection. They are ordered so that they can be referred to by their position in the set. These items can be accessed by name or by index position in the array. Because they are collected and accessible as a set, they may be sorted into sequenced patterns.

The generic data type of these storage containers is Array. This is simply an object container that maintains a length property according to how elements are added to the set. There are variations on this theme in the web browsers and one example is a Collection, which we shall look at later, when we discuss the specific capabilities of the browser-based implementations of JavaScript.

Accessing the individual elements of the array can be accomplished in two ways. Either in a bracket-delimited form or by means of the dot notation:

♦   myArray['one']

♦   myArray.one

There are also some finer points to these indexing schemes which we shall look at shortly.

Constructing Arrays

Creating an array is straightforward: you must use the new operator. The arguments passed to the constructor affect the way that the array is initialized.

If no arguments are passed, then an empty array is created whose length is zero.

```
myArray = new Array();
```

If the call to the constructor has a single numeric argument, then it is taken as a `length` value (the number of containers or elements in the array you expect to need):

```
myArray = new Array(12);
```

The array declared above has 12 elements, with positions numbered 0 to 11 (since array indexes are zero-based). A single argument of non-numeric type results in an array containing one element and having a `length` value of `1`. The non-numeric value will be stored in that element.

```
myArray = new Array("One-string");
```

If there is more than one argument, then each argument is placed into the array in the order of presentation, and the `length` value is set according to the number of arguments provided.

```
var day_names = new Array("Su","Mo","Tu","We","Th","Fr","Sa");
```

Numeric Indexes

Array elements can be retrieved or set by selecting them numerically within the set of elements contained in the array, remembering that indexes are zero-based.

```
myArray = new Array(2);
myArray[0] = "First Element Value";
myArray[1] = "Second Element Value";
```

The number of elements available within the array is stored in the `length` property of the array. Storing values into indexes that are the same as or higher than the current value of the `length` property will automatically extend the array and reset the `length` property. An array with only one entry in the 100th element (index value 99) is very sparsely populated, but still would report a `length` value of 100.

The range of numeric index values is from 0 to $2^{32}-1$.

Named Indexes and Dot Notation

Accessing and setting elements of an array by name rather than index number simply requires the name to be added to the array reference with a dot separator between them.

These are all valid array element references:

```
// store an element name in a variable
myIndex = "three";

// Assign some array element values
var myArray = new Array();
myArray["one"] = "C";
myArray['two'] = "D";
myArray[myIndex] = "E";
myArray.three = "F";
```

Note that adding named elements to an array will not modify the `length` property. However, you can process all elements in the array by using a `for(... in ...)` enumerator loop.

Multi-Dimensional Arrays

Multi-dimensional arrays are not supported directly in JavaScript, but you can construct them with arrays of arrays. This could be useful for working out 3D transformations, for example if you want to operate on a Scalable Vector Graphic (SVG) data set.

```
var matrix = new Array(2);

matrix[0] = new Array(2);
matrix[0][0] = 1;
matrix[0][1] = 0;

matrix[1] = new Array(2);
matrix[1][0] = 0;
matrix[1][1] = 1;
```

Array Object Methods

An array object supports the following methods:

Method	Description
concat(val1, val2, ...)	Concatenates the values passed as arguments onto the end of the array. Creates new indexed elements as required. The result is returned as a new array instance leaving the original array object that received the concat() method call unchanged.
join(separator)	Assembles all the array elements in sequence, placing the joining string between each one and turns the result into a String value. The joining string is passed as an argument to this method. See the split() method of String objects.
pop()	Removes the element at the end of the array and returns it as the result of this method. The array is shortened by one item.
push(val1, val2, ...)	The values passed as arguments are added to the end of the array. This is the complement of the pop() method which together provide a rudimentary stacking facility.
reverse()	Reverses the sequence order of all array elements. The first shall be last and the last shall be first.
shift()	Removes the front-most item from the array and returns it to the caller. The push(), pop(), shift(), and unshift() methods provide a way to build FILO stacks and FIFO buffers.

Method	Description
`slice(start, end)`	Given a range of elements in the arguments to this method, the result is a smaller array containing just the required subset. The end parameter is optional and will indicate that the range extends to the end of the array if it is omitted.
`sort(comparator)`	Arranges the array elements into order. You can optionally pass a reference to a function object to be called to compare two array items. That comparator can then make a decision on the ordering. This technique allows you to sort collections of very complex items such as objects. Without a comparator, the `sort()` method will sort using a string conversion before comparing the elements. Sorting numerics correctly requires a comparator function otherwise 2800 will be sorted earlier than 290.
`splice(start, qty, elems)`	Given a start position, a range, and a set of new items, you can insert or replace part of the array collection with this method.
`toLocaleString()`	Returns a string primitive version of the array with the characters normalized according to the current international language settings of your browser.
`toString()`	Returns simple string-based version of the array. All elements will be concatenated in a string-wise fashion. Joined elements will be separated by a comma character.
`unshift(val1, val2, ...)`	Adds items to the head of the stack. Such items as are passed as arguments will be added to the front of the array.

Array.sort() with Comparator Function

Sorting an array without using a comparator function that you have written will simply organize the array elements in alphabetical order. This example shows how to organize the elements according to the length of the string they contain. It does this by calling back to a function object that we provide in our script source:

```html
<html>
<meta http-equiv="content-type" content="text/html; charset=UTF-8" />
<head>
<title> Array sort with comparator demo</title>
<script type="text/javascript">
// Comparator function
function compare(aValue1, aValue2)
{
   if(aValue1.length < aValue2.length)
   {
      return -1;
   }
   if(aValue1.length > aValue2.length)
   {
```

```
         return 1;
      }
      return 0;
   }
   // Optimized comparator function
   // Provided to indicate a functionally identical but
   // more compact comparator albeit less easy to understand
   function optimalCompare(aValue1, aValue2)
   {
      return (aValue1.length - aValue2.length);
   }

   // Display an array in a table
   function displayArrayAsTable(anArray)
   {
      var myLength = anArray.length;
      document.write("<table border='1'>");
      for(var myIndex = 0; myIndex < myLength; myIndex++)
      {
         document.write("<tr><td>");
         document.write(myIndex);
         document.write("</td><td>");
         document.write(anArray[myIndex]);
         document.write("</td><td>");
         document.write(anArray[myIndex].length);
         document.write("</td></tr>");
      }
      document.write("</table>")
   }
</script>
</head>
<body>
<script type="text/javascript">
myString1 = "This is a sentence made of words.";
document.write("Original input string<br />")
document.write(myString1)

myArray = myString1.split(" ");
document.write("<br /><br />String split into an array<br />")
displayArrayAsTable(myArray);

myArray.sort(compare);
document.write("<br /><br />Array sorted<br />")
displayArrayAsTable(myArray);

myString2 = myArray.join(" ");
document.write("<br /><br />Array joined up as a string<br />")
document.write(myString2)

</script>
</body>
</html>
```

126

Array Literals

JavaScript version 1.2 introduced the capability of creating arrays from a literal expression without first using a constructor and then assigning individual elements. Such array construction can also be nested to create multi-dimensional arrays.

```
// Create a simple array with a literal
var myArray = [ 100, 1.34, 100 ];

// Create a simple array with more complex elements
var myArray = [ 100, 1.34, "String text", true, { prop:100 } ];

// Create a nested multi-dimensional array
var matarray = [ [1,0], [0,1]];

// JavaScript expression in arrays
var exprarray = [ Math.random()*10, Math.random()*100 ];

// Sparse array
var sparse = [100, , , , , 1000];
```

Expressions and Operators

An expression is a combination of values and identifiers, and can contain operators that act on them. Operators come in three basic physical forms based on the number of values or identifiers they act on:

♦ Unary operators (`<value><operator>` or `<operator><value>`)

♦ Binary operators (`<value_1><operator><value_2>`)

♦ Ternary operators (`<value_1><operator_1><value_2><operator_2><value_3>`)

Most operators are binary. There are a few unary operators and only one ternary, which is a special form of the conditional flow control (`if(…) … else …`).

The **associativity** of an operator indicates the order of evaluation of its operands. An operator with an associativity of **left to right** evaluates the expression in the operand to its left and then the one to the right. The alternative is **right to left** associativity. Most operators have left to right associativity but this can be controlled by overriding the precedence rules with grouping operators (parentheses).

LValues and RValues

LValues and RValues are a way that programmers conceive the operands that are placed either side of an assignment operator. The L and R stand for Left and Right and refer to the side of an assignment operator they can be placed without the interpreter complaining.

An LValue is something that can be written to. An RValue is something that is read from.

Literal values are constants. They cannot have a value stored in them because they are constant. That means they cannot be placed on the left-hand side of an assignment expression. Your interpreter will generate an error message if you try to do this. Therefore a literal can only be used as an RValue.

Variables can be used as LValues or RValues. Before assigning anything to them, they will contain an undefined value and therefore they should be used as an LValue at least once before they are ever used as an RValue.

Prefix Operators

Prefix operators are unary operators placed immediately before their operands.

Operator	Description
++	Increment the operand by 1.
--	Decrement the operand by 1
-	Unary minus. Negates the current value. (Multiply by −1.)
+	Unary plus. A cast operator that performs a type conversion to number. Used to change the data type of a value before it is used in a subsequent expression evaluation.
typeof	This unary operator returns a string describing the data type of a value or expression. The typeof operator is also available in a format that is presented as a function call (typeof()). The result is similar to using the unary operator but places grouping parentheses around the operand.
void	Used in special cases where an expression needs to be evaluated because its side-effects are required, but any resulting value is not required, and therefore does not need to be assigned to a variable. Basically the expression is evaluated but the result discarded.
new	Invokes a constructor to create a new instance of an object.
delete	Provides a way to delete an object property.
fn()	Function calls resemble a unary operator and can be used amongst the other operators in an expression.

The meanings of some of these operators may vary when they are used in other contexts. For example, the plus sign will concatenate or add when used as a binary operator.

The typeof Operator

This operator produces a string that contains the operand's type. When you use it, it looks like a function due to its parentheses. However, it can be used with and without its grouping parenthesis, which is why it qualifies as an operator.

```
// Testing a string value
var aString = 'String text';
document.write(typeof(aString));      // Yields "string"

// Testing variables that exist but not yet assigned
var aVar1;
document.write(typeof aVar1);         // Yields "undefined"

// Testing variables that do not yet exist
document.write(typeof aVar2 );        // Yields "undefined"
```

Note that the expression contained in the operand is evaluated, but only its type is extracted. There are times when this is advantageous and can avoid a runtime error. For example, because it will return the Undefined value without causing a script error, you can use it to check for the existence of a variable before using it in another expression. This kind of defensive coding leads to far more robust script designs.

The typeof operator is one of few ways in which you can use a variable that is not yet defined by assigning a value to it. It will yield the undefined type for variables that have not been initialized. Thus you can determine if it is safe to use them as RValues in an assignment expression.

You can distinguish between function objects and other kinds of objects with the typeof operator. However, typeof will not tell you any more than that. To find out any more specific information about object types, you can compare the object constructor property with one of the built-in types. You can examine the constructor property of the target object and in some implementations ask for its name property (this is not standardized though and not available on IE on the Windows platform). Some built-in objects don't allow this and some implementations may hide constructors or several of their properties. There are some DOM-related techniques that can tell you which HTML tag was used as the source data for creating the object. Sometimes a toString() conversion on the object will yield a function name and occasionally you may need to check prototype values or test for the existence of specific properties. If all else fails, you have to assume that it is just an object of arbitrary type.

void Operator

The void operator is used to allow the operand to be evaluated in the normal way (perhaps it is an expression or function call), but to force an undefined value to be returned in its place. A very useful place for this is when you create javascript: URLs, such as that shown here:

```
<a href="javascript:void(callHandler('testString'));">
```

Making sure the result of the expression is void helps the browser cope with the fact you are calling a script and not fetching a document. This technique is useful if you want to evaluate an expression merely for the benefit of its side-effects and without any interest in the value it returns. However, don't use void if you want the result of the JavaScript execution to be used as the content of a window.

You can also use the void operator to manufacture an undefined value in older browsers that have no keyword already defined. Here is an example:

```
myUndefinedValue = (void 0);
```

This is unnecessary now that JScript 5.5 supports an `undefined` value in compliance with ECMA edition 2. Other implementations will also support this, in order to be standards-compliant.

Object Operators

The `new` and `delete` keywords are classed as operators since they are used in an expression-like syntax.

The new Operator

The new operator yields a freshly created instance of its operand object. In this sense it behaves like a function that returns an object as a result. To make a new object of any kind with the `new` operator, you need a constructor. You can use one of the built-in constructors, or use the `new` operator on an object that you are holding a reference to in a variable. This is the general form:

```
var myObject = new objectConstructor(initialData);
```

The delete Operator

The `delete` operator is used to delete a property from an object or delete a reference to an object (simply assigning a `null` value to an object property will not remove it; nor will assigning the `undefined` value). It can also be used to delete an element from an array.

This example will remove the `prop` property from this instance of `myObject`.

```
myResult = delete myObject.prop;
```

If you check for the existence of the property, it should now return the value `undefined`.

The in Operator

The `in` operator is also useful when examining objects for the presence of a property since it provides a Boolean value indicating whether a property exists in an object. Here is a short example code fragment that demonstrates how:

```
// Create an object with a name property
var obj = { name: 'Tom' };

// Display the test result, delete the property and test again
alert('name' in obj);
delete obj.name;
alert('name' in obj);
```

Note that this technique is not currently portable across all browsers and versions.

The instanceof Operator

The object referred to by the left operand is examined and its type compared with the type of the object on the right. The object on the right should be an object with a constructor.

130

This operator yields the Boolean `true` value if both objects are of the same type.

The test also yields `true` when you take inheritance into account. For example, a `Date` object is a member of the `Date()` class as well as the `Object()` class.

Postfix Operators

Postfix operators are unary operators placed immediately after their operands.

Operator	Description	Example
++	Increment the operand by 1 after use.	`document.write(myIndex++)`
--	Decrement the operand by 1 after use.	`myCounter--`

Arithmetic Operators

These operators include the additive and multiplicative operators. They also include the prefix and postfix operators that increment and decrement the operands before and after use.

The result of an expression using these operations will be a numeric value. However, you can also generate the `NaN` (Not a Number) value and `Infinity` by performing inappropriate evaluations – dividing by zero, for example.

You may experience some variance between the various implementations of JavaScript when using these operators. Rounding of values is of special concern and some IE browsers will round a floating-point value to an integer before evaluating an expression that uses the modulo (`%`) operator.

Additive Operators

Here is a table summarizing all operators that can be classified as additive, even those which can be classified in other categories:

Value	Meaning	Example
+	Add	`sum = a + b;`
-	Subtract	`difference = b - a;`
+=	Add and assign	`a = a + b;`
		`a += b;`
-=	Subtract and assign	`a = a - b;`
		`a -= b;`
++	Increment	`++myValue;`
--	Decrement	`--myValue;`

Additive operators perform numeric addition and subtraction or string concatenation depending on the native type of the operands.

Multiplicative Operators

The following table lists all operators are multiplicative and those that are classified under other categories, which are also multiplicative by implication:

Operator	Description	Example
%	Remainder or Modulo	`remainder = a % 100;`
*	Multiply	`products = a * b;`
/	Divide	`dividend = a / b;`
*=	Multiply and assign to an LValue	`a = a * b;`
		`a *= b;`
/=	Divide and assign to an LValue	`a = a / b;`
		`a /= b;`
%=	Remainder and assign to an LValue	`a = a % b;`
		`a %= b;`

Operands that are used with multiplicative operators must have values than can be converted to a meaningful numeric quantity.

Concatenation Operator

The addition operator (+) is overloaded such that, when one of the arguments is a string value, the result will be concatenated rather than added. Some ambiguity arises when both values can be coerced into a numeric form. This could lead to a numeric addition (although in almost all recent browsers, concatenation results). If there is a risk of ambiguity, then a defensive coding technique is to provide a string type as well, forcing a concatenation. This also clarifies your intent to anyone doing maintenance on the code later on:

```
// This is ambiguous when examining the code.
a = "1" + "2";

// The intent of this is quite clear.
a = "" + "1" + "2";
```

The original strings are not modified since the result of a concatenation is a new string. However, you might assign that to one of the source variables, thus destroying the original value. Here are some more examples where the code might look ambiguous:

```
// Add two numeric strings together with a string to number conversion.
// The result of this expression is 3. The Number() constructors change
// the strings to numeric values.
var a = Number("1") + Number("2");


// Convert the string to a number by subtracting 0 then add 2.
// The result is 3 because the content of b is a numeric value
// after the first line.
var b = "1" - 0;
b = b + 2;


// Shortening the script to eliminate one line for the sake
// of efficiency does not yield the same result. The result
// of this line is not 3 as you might expect but "12",
// because the numeric conversion does not now take place.
var b = "1" + 2;

// Here we have a numeric to string conversion which yields
// the result "12" because the "2" forces the conversion.
var b = 1;
b = b + "2";

// In this example, we convert a Boolean value to a Number. The true value
// converts to 1. We add another 1, so the result is 2. Boolean false
// converts upwards to 0.
b = true;
b = b + 1;

// Converting a Boolean value to a string yields the result "true1"
b = true;
b = b + "1";
```

Large amounts of string concatenation within a web browser can lead to memory leaks in some versions of IE and it is a good idea to avoid putting string concatenators in a loop, which is fired in an interval timer, for example. The only time the lost memory is freed up, is when the page is reloaded. This is a fairly common bug and shows up in many applications. String creation and destruction on a large scale should always be avoided to enhance your application's reliability in IE browsers.

Bitwise Operators

Bitwise operators convert all operands to 32-bit integers and apply the operator to them on a bit by bit basis.

Here is a table of the operators in the bitwise category (aside from the shift operators). Some are members of the assignment operator category, but perform bitwise operations before assigning the result:

Operator	Description	Example
~	Unary bitwise complement (NOT)	`a = ~b;`
&	Bitwise AND	`a = a & b;`
|	Bitwise inclusive OR	`a = a | b;`
^	Bitwise XOR (exclusive OR)	`a = a ^ b;`
&=	Bitwise AND and assign to an LValue	`a = a & b;` `a &= b;`
|=	Bitwise inclusive OR and assign to an LValue	`a = a | b;` `a |= b;`
^=	Bitwise exclusive XOR and assign to an LValue	`a = a ^ b;` `a ^= b;`

Here is an example of what happens when you use a bitwise AND operator. Here we only illustrate a shortened 8-bit version of the operator being used.

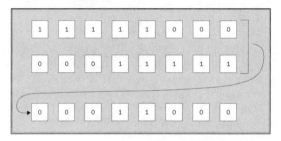

Shift Operators

These operators are a special case of the bitwise operators since they shift the bit pattern in the operand. The bits are shifted either left or right. These are descended from classic assembler language operations. Some of these are compound operators, which also assign their result to an LValue.

Op	Description	Example
<<	Bitwise left shift	`a = b << 3;`
>>	Bitwise right shift	`a = b >> 3;`
>>>	Bitwise right shift (unsigned)	`a = b >>> 3;`
<<=	Bitwise shift left and assign to an LValue	`a = a << 3;` `a <<= 3`
>>=	Bitwise shift right and assign to an LValue	`a = a >> 3;` `a >>= 3;`
>>>=	Bitwise shift right (unsigned) and assign to an LValue	`a = a >>> 3;` `a >>>= 3;`

Here is an illustration of the left shift operator. We only show what happens with an 8-bit value but this shift could be applied to a 32-bit data value with similar effect.

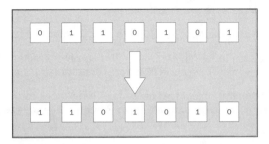

Relational Operators

These binary operators test the relationship between two values and always yield a Boolean result. Although generally considered to be members of the relational operator set, equality and non-equality tests are classified specifically as equality operators in the ECMA standard.

Type conversion may be required if two operands of different types are compared. If necessary, either of the operands will be promoted into the higher form if they are not of the same type. This means that `Booleans` become `Numbers` and `Numbers` become `Strings`, as necessary.

Operator	Description	Example
==	Equal to	if(a == b) …
===	Identically equal to	if(anObject1 === anObject2) …
!=	NOT equal to	a = (one != two);
!==	NOT identically equal to	result = item1 !== item2;
<	Less than	if(a < 100) …
<=	Less than or equal to	while(b <= 50) …
>	Greater than	if(thread > 3) …
>=	Greater than or equal to	status = count >= 50;

Equality operators

Equality operators deal exclusively with the test for the operands being equal to one another. They yield a value of `true` or `false`. Testing two operands for equality follows these basic rules:

♦ If the native types of the two operands are not the same, then the values are not equal unless a numeric coercion yields equal values or the operands both yield `null`/`undefined` values.

♦ If the type of the left operand is `undefined` or `null`, it is assumed to be equal to the right operand.

- If either of the operands is NaN then they are assumed to be not equal.

- Positive and negative zero are equal values.

- Boolean values must be identical values to be considered equal.

- Two strings of the same length containing the same character sequence (identical copies of one another in terms of Unicode character code points) are assumed to be equal.

- References to the same object test as equal. References to two different objects containing the same property values, even though they may be copies of one another, are not equal.

- When comparing different types of operands, coercion techniques may be used to force the comparison to be conducted according to string, numeric, or Boolean rules.

- If one of the operands is an object and the other is not, then the object is converted to a primitive.

String comparisons can be forced by concatenating values of other types to an empty string. It may help to use parentheses to guarantee that precedence is established as you intend it to be.

```
("" + a) == ("" + b)
```

Numeric comparisons can be forced by subtracting zero. Again, grouping operators using parentheses helps to establish the desired precedence:

```
(a - 0) == (b - 0)
```

Testing for equality of numbers may be done with a precision finer than you really care about. To avoid this, you can set a precision value in a variable, and then subtract from one another the absolute values of the operands you are comparing. If the difference between the operands is smaller than your precision value, then the two values are close enough to yield a match.

Boolean comparisons can be forced by performing a logical NOT on both operands. In this case, precedence control with grouping operators may not be as necessary as it is with the addition and concatenation operators:

```
!a == !b
```

The values null and undefined are generally considered to be equal although they are distinctly different values. This is because early implementations did not support an explicit undefined value and allowed for it to have the same meaning as the null value.

Two string objects may represent the same string value. Comparing the objects for equality will yield false because the references to the objects are being compared and not the object values themselves. However forcing a primitive string comparison may in fact yield a true value when testing for equality. Do this by converting the objects as part of the comparison process by type conversion or valueOf() methods.

Identity Operators

The `===` and `!==` operators test not just for equality but for identity being the same. When testing with the identical operator (`===`), the two operands are compared and the `true` value is returned if they are equal **and** of the same type. In other words, both operands must be of the same type and value, otherwise `false` is returned.

When performing a test with the NOT identical operator (`!==`), the two operands are compared and `false` is returned if both values are equal and of the same type; otherwise `true` is returned.

Logical Operators

Logical operators (sometimes called conditional operators) perform an operation on the Boolean value(s) of the operand(s).

- ♦ AND (`&&`) is a binary operator

- ♦ OR (`||`) is a binary operator

- ♦ NOT (`!`) is a unary operator

Operand 1	Operand 2	AND result
true	true	true
true	false	false
false	true	false
false	false	false

Operand 1	Operand 2	OR result
true	true	true
true	false	true
false	true	true
false	false	false

Operand	NOT result
true	false
false	true

The input value(s) may not be Boolean, but will be converted to Booleans using the rules for that type. This conversion happens automatically, but may not always be what you expect. Refer to the earlier discussion on Boolean primitives for a list of the results of the type conversion.

The JavaScript interpreter is also quite smart, because for some operator and value combinations it can perform a lazy evaluation. For example, if an expression like this is presented:

```
A && B
```

then if `A` is false, `B` does not need to be evaluated to know that the result will be `false`. This can significantly speed up interpretation because evaluating `B` might have involved an object reference or perhaps an expression evaluation. This suggests you may effect some performance gains by placing the more complex expressions in the right-hand operand.

You can also exploit lazy evaluation by checking for the existence of an object before operating on it. The interpreter will not attempt to operate on the right-hand side if the left is `false`, so a potential error is avoided. If the lazy evaluation mechanism were not present, the interpreter would evaluate both halves of this expression and throw an error if the object did not exist:

```
if (document.images && document.images.imageName)
{
    document.images.imageName.src = …
}
```

Assignment Operators

Here is a table summarizing the assignment operators, most of which can be secondarily classified as members of other operator categories:

Value	Equivalent	Meaning
=	a = b	Simple assignment to an LValue
+=	a = a + b	Add and assign to an LValue
-=	a = a - b	Subtract and assign to an LValue
*=	a = a * b	Multiply and assign to an LValue
/=	a = a / b	Divide and assign to an LValue
%=	a = a % b	Remainder and assign to an LValue
&=	a = a & b	Bitwise AND and assign to an LValue
|=	a = a | b	Bitwise inclusive OR and assign to an LValue
^=	a = a ^ b	Bitwise exclusive XOR and assign to an LValue
<<=	a = a << b	Bitwise shift left and assign to an LValue
>>=	a = a >> b	Bitwise shift right and assign to an LValue
>>>=	a = a >>> b	Bitwise shift right (unsigned) and assign to an LValue
++	a = a + 1	Increment LValue
--	a = 1 - 1	Decrement LValue

Parenthesis Grouping Operator

The grouping operator is a pair of parentheses placed around an expression or expressions to control the precedence of evaluation in expressions so that the sub-expressions are evaluated in the correct order. It is also used to enclose the arguments to a function or method.

Placing parentheses around expressions controls the order in which they are evaluated and can override the normal precedence that operators assume. This allows `delete` and `typeof` operations to be applied to expressions in parentheses for example.

Controlling the precedence of expressions allows operators with lower precedence to be evaluated ahead of the higher priority expression operators. For example:

```
A + B * C
```

By implication, the above equation is executed like this:

```
A + (B * C)
```

However, A and B can be added before the multiplication like this:

```
(A + B) * C
```

This forces the addition to occur before the multiplication and is functionally equivalent to:

```
A * C + B * C
```

Coding Structure

Scripts are executed one source statement at a time. Because individual statements are separated by semi-colons, you can place several on one line or give each one a line of its own with no ill effects. The interpreter makes two passes over the script source. In the first pass, all the top-level function declarations are processed. On the second pass, statements that are in the top level (that is, outside a function body) are executed.

However, certain control structures can alter the flow and redirect the execution to another part of the script source, as we'll see later in this section.

Comments

Good coding style suggests that you should place sufficient comments in the code to allow subsequent developers to understand your intent. Single-line comments are written like this:

```
// This is a whole line of comment
var myVariable;  // The rest of this line is a comment
```

A multiple line comment is written like this:

```
/* This is a
Multiple line
comment block */
```

Statements

A statement is a discrete instruction in a script that causes something to happen. The statements in JavaScript can be classified into several categories. Here is the basic set of classifications:

- ◆ Variable statement – A declaration of a local or global variable.

- ◆ Empty statement – A semicolon on its own.

- ◆ Expression statement – A combination of variables, identifiers, and possibly operands.

- ◆ If statement – Conditional execution of a block of code with an optional alternative block of code.

- ◆ Iterative statement – A means of executing a block of code repetitively until a test condition is satisfied.

- ◆ Switch selector – A means of executing one of a variety of possible code blocks selecting the best according to an input value.

- ◆ Continue statement – A way of canceling iteration and commencing the next.

- ◆ Break statement – Means of breaking out of an iteration or a switch selector.

- ◆ Return statement – A way to unconditionally leave a function and return to its caller, optionally handing back a value.

- ◆ With statement – A means of adding an object to a scope chain. This is not used very often.

Statements are executed in the order in which they appear in the script source text except when the flow of control is redirected by a conditional switching expression, function call, iterator, or jump statement.

Statement Labels

From JavaScript version 1.2, any statement can be labeled with an identifier. The identifier can be any legal JavaScript name that does not match a reserved keyword.

The namespace that labels exist in is separate from that of variables and function names. This means you can use the same identifier names over again, although it is probably not good practice to do so.

Code Blocks

Blocks of code are delimited by placing opening and closing braces around them. A block is a list of statements that form one syntactic unit. This is particularly useful in conditional execution and iterative execution, both of which are expected to operate on a single syntactic unit. A block allows that single syntactic unit to be composed of multiple lines of source script text.

Braces must be used in pairs. Although the JavaScript interpreters may forgive you when you miss out some language elements, errors can occur which are very subtle and difficult to diagnose if you misplace a brace character. Modern text editors give you a lot of help when balancing pairs of braces.

From version 1.2 of JavaScript, you can name the code block and use the labeled form of the `break` and `continue` keywords to exit the block prematurely, as we'll see shortly.

Controlling the Execution Flow

There are several ways of controlling the execution flow of a script. The most likely example is when a function is called. A function declaration allows a fragment of code to be reused many times without needing to repeat it. Functions can call other functions and a nested execution flow is quite commonplace.

An additional flow control technique is to use the operator precedence rules to determine the order in which operands are evaluated within an expression.

Operator Precedence Rules

Precedence is that order in which operators and operands are evaluated when they are assembled into an expression. A simple expression, with two operands on either side of a single operator, clearly has a very simple precedence structure. But what if another operator and operand is added? For example:

```
A + B * C
```

Previous experience tells us that B is multiplied by C before adding A to the result, but a novice might assume that A is added to B before multiplying the sum by C. A quite different value would be obtained.

The operator precedence rules are best illustrated in a tabular form. These JavaScript operators are listed in order of precedence. Expressions may be nested within the operators and the precedence rules determine how that nesting is worked out. The associativity column indicates the direction in which items are evaluated when several items are placed adjacent to one another at the same precedence level:

Operator	Description	Associativity
( )	Grouping operator.	L-R
[]	Array index delimiter.	L-R
.	Property accessor.	L-R
++	Postfix increment.	L-R
--	Postfix decrement.	L-R
!	Logical NOT.	R-L
~	Bitwise NOT.	R-L
++	Prefix increment.	R-L

Table continued on following page

Operator	Description	Associativity
`--`	Prefix decrement.	R-L
`-`	Negate operand.	L-R
`delete`	Deletes a property from an object.	R-L
`new`	Invokes an object constructor.	R-L
`typeof`	Determines the type of a value.	R-L
`void`	Always yields the undefined value.	R-L
`*`	Multiplies.	L-R
`/`	Divides.	L-R
`%`	Remainder.	L-R
`+`	Converts the operand to a numeric value.	L-R
`+`	Adds.	L-R
`-`	Subtract.	L-R
`+`	Concatenate string.	L-R
`<<`	Bitwise shift left.	L-R
`>>`	Bitwise shift right.	L-R
`>>>`	Bitwise shift right (unsigned).	L-R
`<`	Compares less than.	L-R
`<=`	Compares less than or equal to.	L-R
`>`	Compares greater than.	L-R
`>=`	Compares greater than or equal to.	L-R
`in`	Property is in object.	L-R
`instanceof`	Object is instance of another object.	L-R
`==`	Compares equal to.	L-R
`!=`	Compares NOT equal to.	L-R
`===`	Compares identically equal to.	L-R
`!==`	Compares identically NOT equal to.	L-R
`&`	Bitwise AND.	L-R
`^`	Bitwise XOR.	L-R
`|`	Bitwise OR.	L-R

Operator	Description	Associativity
&&	Logical AND.	L-R
||	Logical OR.	L-R
? :	Conditional execution.	R-L
=	Assigns.	R-L
*=	Multiplies and assigns.	R-L
/=	Divides and assigns.	R-L
%=	Remainder and assign.	R-L
+=	Adds and assigns.	R-L
-=	Subtracts and assigns.	R-L
<<=	Bitwise shift left and assign.	R-L
>>=	Bitwise shift right and assign.	R-L
>>>=	Bitwise shift right (unsigned) and assign.	R-L
&=	Bitwise AND and assign.	R-L
|=	Bitwise inclusive OR and assign.	R-L
^=	Bitwise XOR and assign.	R-L
,	Argument delimiter.	L-R
;	Empty statement.	L-R
{ }	Delimits code block.	L-R

To see how the precedence rules affect your expression and whether one operator will be evaluated before another, compare the relative positions in the table. The one that is higher up the table will be evaluated first. If you use the same operator several times at the same precedence level in the evaluation, look at the associativity column to see the order of evaluation within that precedence level. The grouping operator can be applied wherever necessary to ensure the evaluation occurs in the order that you require.

Functions

A function declaration is a description of a function within the script source text. A function is declared with the `function` keyword, parentheses enclosing the formal arguments, and a block of executable code enclosed in curly braces. The formal arguments are those which are enumerated in the function declaration and must be passed in by any calling script.

```
function aFunctionName(aFormalArgument, anotherFormalArgument)
{
   // Some code goes here in the function body
   return(myResultValue);
}
```

Functions will always return a result, but a function call can be cast to a `void` type, which discards the resulting value. If you don't indicate a result to return yourself, the function will return the value `undefined`.

return

A `return` keyword is used to unconditionally exit from a function, and pass back a result (specified following the `return` keyword) and execution flow to the caller of the function.

Function Objects

Many built-in objects are functions. They can be invoked with arguments. Some of these are constructors. They are functions that are intended to be used with the new operator.

`Function` objects come in four varieties according to how they are implemented. They may be built-in to the interpreter or may be provided as extensions in the script itself. The four types of functions are:

- ♦ Declared functions in script source text.
- ♦ Anonymous functions built with the `function` object constructor from your script.
- ♦ Implementation-supplied functions built into the host environment.
- ♦ Internal functions built into the JavaScript language.

Because a function is an object, you can associate it with your own objects by means of a reference to the `Function` object from a property. Those properties become methods by virtue of being a function reference.

These are the important properties of a `Function` object:

Property	Description
arguments	An array containing all the arguments passed to the function as it is called.
length	The number of arguments passed when the function was called.

Here is a summary of the important methods belonging to a `Function` object:

144

Method	Description
`apply(anObject,args)`	The `Function` object is applied to the object passed in the first argument. The value of the `'this'` keyword in the function body will refer to the passed object and any arguments to the function will be transferred from the array passed in the `args` parameter to the formal parameters of the function being called.
`call(anObject,arg1, arg2, ...)`	The `Function` object is applied to the object passed in the first argument. The value of the `'this'` keyword in the function body will refer to the passed object and any arguments to the function will be transferred from the arguments to the formal parameters of the function being called.
`toString()`	Returns a string representing the `Function` object.

Conditional execution

It is sometimes necessary to be able to alter the route of execution through the script, based on the outcome of a conditional (usually logical) expression. There are various conditional flow structures that can be used.

if(...)

The `if(...)` statement is used to conditionally execute a code block, depending on the outcome of an expression. This mechanism is called **branching**. The expression within the parentheses (the condition) is evaluated and cast to a Boolean value. If it yields a `true` value, then the code in the block following it is executed. Otherwise, the code is ignored and execution continues at the statement following that code block.

```
if(condition)
{
    code to be executed if condition is true
}
```

if (...) else

The `if(...) else` statement extends the capability of the previous `if(...)` control structure. Adding the `else` keyword enables us to specify an alternative block of code to be executed if the outcome of the condition yields the `false` value. Again, the expression in the parentheses (the condition) is evaluated and cast to a Boolean value. If it yields a `true` value as a result, then the code in the first associated code block is executed. Otherwise, the code in the first block is ignored and the code in the block following the `else` keyword is executed.

```
if(condition)
{
    code to be executed if condition is true
}
else
```

```
{
  code to be executed if condition is false
}
```

for(...)...

A `for(...)` loop allows a code block to be repeatedly run while a condition holds true. The control construct in a `for(...)` loop has three semicolon-separated expressions. They are all optional. However, the semicolons must all be present to indicate the placement of any expressions in the heading. The three expressions are used as follows:

♦ Initialization of the enumerator. This can also declare *and* initialize a variable to be used as an enumerator if one has not already been created.

♦ Condition to test for. The `for(...)` loop exits when this condition becomes `false`. While it is `true`, the loop will continue to cycle.

♦ The incrementor or decrementor. This allows you to alter the enumerator in some way at the end of each loop of the code.

The loop can be completed early, using the `break`, `continue`, or `return` statements – although `return` is only valid within a function body, and actually breaks out of the function as a whole.

```
for(initialization; condition; incrementor)
{
  code to be run while condition is true
}
```

For example:

```
for(i=0; i<5; i++)
{
  document.write(i + " ");
}
```

Result:*01234*

Adding a label in front of an iterator allows you to associate a label name with a break or continue statement. This means that you can break or continue nested iterators from deep inside them. This can greatly simplify the logic of a looping system.

```
// An example break to a labeled line
outerLoop:
for (var i=0; i <= max; i++)
{
  for (var j=0; j <= max2; j++)
  {
    if (i== someNum && j ==someNum2)
    {
      break outerLoop;
    }
  }
}
```

for(... in ...)

There is an alternative `for(...)` loop structure called the `for(... in ...)` loop which is for operating on objects: it enumerates through the properties of an object. The first item in the control construct is a container that a value can be assigned to (an LValue expression). The item following the `in` keyword is the object whose properties are to be enumerated. Each time round the loop, the name of an object property will be assigned to the LValue.

```
for(LValue in Object)
{
   code to be executed while properties of the object are looped over
}
```

Object properties that have the `DontEnum` attribute set will not be enumerated in this iteration statement.

Note that the range of properties for a particular object may vary between one JavaScript implementation and another. Nor are they always listed in the same order.

During each iteration, the property name can be used as a key to extract the property value from the object. Dot notation or bracket notation are appropriate. However, empirical evidence suggests that interpreters occasionally have difficulty in substituting variable names into the dot notation form. So square-bracketed indexing by member name is shown here. This looks like an array reference but is in fact a generic way of accessing member properties of objects.

```
// Loop through the properties of an object, only printing
// properties that have the string data type

for(myProperty in myObject)
{
   if(typeof(myObject[myProperty]) == "string")
   {
      document.write(myProperty, + ": " + myObject[myProperty] + "<br \/>");
   }
}
```

while(...)

Although the `while(...)` statement is an iterator, it is functionally related to the `if(...)` statement since it will execute the statement block only as long as the condition enclosed in parentheses evaluates to `true`. The difference between `if(...)` and `while(...)` is that `if(...)` only processes the statement block once, whereas `while(...)` processes the statement block repeatedly until something causes the condition to evaluate to `false`.

```
while(condition)
{
   code to execute while condition is true
}
```

A `while(...)` loop tests the condition *before* execution of each pass through the loop. If a `do(...)` loop is supported by the implementation, it would test the condition *after* each pass through the loop.

A `break` statement can be used to terminate a `while` iterator prematurely – perhaps within a conditional test that is supplementary to the one in the `while(...)` heading. A `continue` statement can be used to initiate the next cycle of the `while(...)` iterator early, without completing the current iteration – again, probably in a supplementary conditional test. If a labeled `continue` is used, the condition is tested again, and the loop will cycle if necessary.

```
// An enumerator built with a while statement
var a = 10;
while(a > 0)
{
  document.write("*");
  a--;
}
```

Result:

****

```
// A labeled while loop
a = 0;
head: while(a < 20)
{
  document.write(a);
  a++;
  if(a > 10)
  {
      continue head;
  }
  document.write("*<br />");
}
```

Result:
*0**
*1**
*2**
*3**
*4**
*5**
*6**
*7**
*8**
*9**
10111213141516171819

do ... while(...)

A `do ... while(...)` loop is a variation on the `while(...)` iterator.

148

A `while(...)` iterator checks the condition and only executes the code block if it is `true`. This means that a `while(...)` loop may never execute even once. In contrast, a `do ... while(...)` iterator checks the condition once the code has been executed. This ensures that a `do ... while(...)` iterator will always perform at least one execution of the code block, even if the condition proves `false` the first time it is tested.

```
do
{
    code to execute on first iteration and thereafter if condition is true
}
while(condition)
```

If a labeled `continue` is used (available from version 1.2 of JavaScript), it is intended that execution should drop to the bottom of the loop and test the condition again before cycling or falling out.

In the example below, note carefully the line that increments the counter. If you leave it out, you create an endless loop and the browser locks you out. You must make sure your loop exit condition can evaluate to `false` eventually unless you intend for it to run forever.

```
// Looping counter demo
myCounter = 10;
do
{
  document.write(myCounter + "<br />");
  myCounter++;
}
while(myCounter < 15);
```

Result:

10
11
12
13
14

switch(...)

The `switch(...)` statement evaluates the expression between parentheses and then selects a labeled statement block for execution according to the value resulting from the expression. If there is no match, then a `default:` code block is used.

Usually, each labeled `case` should be terminated by a `break` keyword to avoid the execution dropping down through into the handler for the next case in the script source. On the other hand, this may be what you intend – omitting the `break` keyword allows several cases to be matched and handled with a common fragment of code.

```
switch(expression)
{
  case value1: code to execute if value1 equals expression
  case value2: code to execute if value2 equals expression,
               or if the value1 case code did not use break
  default:     code to execute if neither value1 or value2 matched expression,
               or if the value2 case code did not use break
}
```

ECMAScript version 2 compliant JavaScript implementations will match strings as well as integers. The version 3 of the standard and more recent versions of the browsers (NNav 6, IE 5.5, Opera 6) allow any data type to be used. Netscape 4 will throw an error if anything other than a primitive (Boolean, Number, String) is used, however.

```
// An example switch statement
switch(myValue)
{
  case 1:     document.write("one");
              break;
  case 'too': document.write("two");
              break;
  default:    document.write("unknown");
              break;
}
```

Note that the matching is carried out using the identically equal operator so placing a string value in the switch() statement will not match an integer value placed in the case label unless the case label is quoted. So, this doesn't work:

```
var a = "2";
switch(a)
{
  case 2: …
}
```

… but this should be fine:

```
var a = "2";
switch(a)
{
  case "2": …
}
```

You need to be careful when nesting switch(…) statements. The case labels will be subordinate to the closest enclosing switch(…) given the rules of precedence and block structuring of the code. The case labels must be unique within a single switch(…) structure, but can duplicate case values in other switch(…) structures within the same or an enclosing code block.

break

The break keyword is a jump statement used within an iterator statement to abort the current cycle and exit from the smallest enclosing iteration immediately. Execution continues at the line following the statement block associated with the iterator. A break can only legally exist inside:

- A while(...) loop

- A for(...) loop

- A case branch for a switch statement

The break should be executed conditionally; otherwise it would cause the remaining lines to be redundant because no execution flow would ever reach them. JavaScript will not warn you about this.

At version 1.2 of JavaScript, the break statement was enhanced to support a label as a breaking destination.

```
label1: code block or statement
...
break: label1;
```

When the break is processed, it will jump to the end of the statement that has been labeled.

continue

The continue keyword is used in an iterator loop to proceed to the next cycle without executing the remaining lines in the statement block. A continue statement can only legally exist inside a while(...) or for(...) loop.

Like break, the continue statement would normally be executed conditionally, otherwise it would cause the remaining lines in the code block to be redundant since no execution flow would ever reach them. JavaScript will not warn you about this.

At version 1.2 of JavaScript, the continue statement was also enhanced to support a label as a continuing destination.

```
label2: code block or statement
...
continue: label2;
```

When the continue is processed, it will jump to the start of the statement that has been labeled. If an iterator is labeled, then the continue is associated with that iterator. Note that break and continue behave slightly differently.

Exception Handling

An exception occurs when an expression yields a result that was not expected or wanted. In numerical expressions, the NaN value is provided for just such a circumstance. NaN represents a numeric quantity that cannot be resolved within the range of meaningful values. The interpreter knows it is numeric, but the value is indeterminate. The null, undefined, and infinity values also help in the management of such exceptions.

In JavaScript, the exception functionality is provided by the try ... catch ... finally ... and throw(...) statements. The error that is being caught is passed back in an Error object container.

try ... catch ... finally ...

This statement provides a way to execute a section of script; if it has a problem, some recovery action can trap the error and handle it gracefully. Unfortunately, this mechanism is not supported by the version 4 browsers and will cause a syntax error when executed in one of these older browsers.

There are three basic parts to this mechanism.

- ◆ The try statement is followed by a block of code that you think may be problematic.

- ◆ If an exception of any kind happens in the try code block, execution is immediately passed to the catch(...) code block that follows it. The catch code block is passed an Error object containing details of the kind of exception that has occurred.

- ◆ When the catch(...) code block completes, the execution drops into the block of code associated with the finally statement. In the case of the try code block not having any exceptional behavior, execution also drops into the finally code block, bypassing the catch code block altogether. So, the finally code block always gets executed after the try block whether the catch code is executed or not. You might use the finally code block to tidy up or discard some unwanted objects.

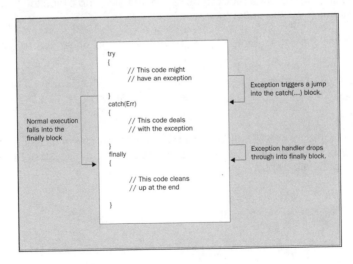

152

In the example below, the `try` code block makes sure two values are presented in the correct order. If they are not in the right order, an exception is thrown and during the exception handling they are swapped over. We put up an alert and set a flag that is presented in the output just to flag that the exception happened when we test the code.

```
// Example of using the throw statement to trigger an exception
function testThrow(arg1, arg2)
{
  var switched = "NO";

  // Force an error condition
  try
  {
     if(arg1 < arg2)
     {
        throw "Wrong order";
     }
  }
  catch(myErr)
  {
     alert(myErr);

     var temp = arg1;
     arg1 = arg2;
     arg2 = temp;

     switched = "YES"
  }
  finally
  {
     document.write("Biggest : "  + arg1 + "<br />");
     document.write("Smallest : " + arg2 + "<br />");
     document.write("Switched : " + switched + "<br />");
     document.write("<br />");
  }
}

testThrow(100, 200);
testThrow(300, 100);
```

Result:

Biggest : 200
Smallest : 100
Switched : YES

Biggest : 300
Smallest : 100
Switched : NO

throw

The `throw` statement provides a way to create an exception, which will be passed to an associated `catch` handler in a `try` … `catch` structure. The real advantage of `throw` comes from enclosing a body of script within an exception handler and dealing with all of the incipient problems with a single 'catch-all' mechanism. Typically you might use it within a function body that is called from within the `try` … `catch` structure, like this:

```
// This script could potentially fail in many different ways
try
{
    risky_code_1();
    risky_code_2();
    risky_code_3();
    risky_code_4();
}
catch (errorCode)
{
    // Recover from all error conditions
}

// Only one of the risky code blocks shown, the others have
// similar condition tests and throw clauses.
function risky_code_1()
{
    if(someErrorHappens)
    {
        throw(errorCode1);
    }
    return;
}
```

Each of the error-prone functions could throw an exception. Execution will immediately jump to the `catch(…)` block neatly skipping over the intervening problem code.

You can throw complex values such as objects, which can convey a large amount of information about the problem so that the error handler can do a really good recovery job. In this example, an object literal manufactures an object to throw back:

```
// How to throw a temporary object to the handler
throw {
      errString:"An error has occurred",
      errNumber: 3
      };
```

A more standards-compliant approach is to use the `Error()` object constructor to manufacture an ECMAScript version 3 compliant object to hand back.

```
throw new Error("error message")
```

Throwing to onError Handlers

The `throw(...)` mechanism is really intended to be used in the context of `try` ... `catch` ... but you can use it to trap the error with the client-side `onerror` event-handling support.

Placing a `throw(...)` statement into your code will force the error handling to be invoked. However if you use it outside a `try` ... `catch` block, the browser error handling will generate an error due to there being no way of catching the thrown event. It forces an event handler to be called instead of the `catch(...)` block.

You can handle this by assigning an error-handler function to the `onerror` property and making sure that the error handler returns a `true` value to signify that the error does not require further processing. Note that you get some contextual information as well so you can make the response context-sensitive.

```
// Define an error handler function
function myErrHandler(anException, aURL, aLineNumber)
{
  alert("An error happened and was caught by this handler.");
  return true;
}

// Register the error handler
onerror = myErrHandler;

// Throw an exception
throw "ERR";
```

Error Objects

This object is provided to create custom error codes for your application. The ECMA standard (edition 3) describes them as objects that are thrown as exceptions when a runtime error occurs.

These objects are passed as the first argument of the `catch(...)` block in a `try` ... `catch` ... structure where you can inspect them and deal with the error. This example is commonly used but is not standards-compliant. It only works on IE browsers.

```
// Force an error condition
myError = new Error(100, "My user defined error text")

try
{
  throw myError;
}
catch(anErr)
{
  confirm(anErr.description);
}
finally
{
  alert("Sorted");
}
```

You can create your own error objects like this:

```
//Creating an Error object instance
myErrorObject = new Error(aNumber, aText);
```

The two arguments supplied to the `Error()` constructor describe the error number and give a textual description. They are both optional.

The ECMAScript standard-compliant approach only supports a single property containing the error text. The IE implementation places an additional error number property before that and incorrectly names the text message property.

The Global Object

When an interpreter is embedded into an application such as a web browser, the application creates a host object, which it binds to the interpreter. This host object becomes the Global object. In the case of a web browser, that Global object is the `window` object.

The global object is provided as a default place to attach properties and methods. Although you may not realize it, when you create a global variable it is implemented as a property of the Global object.

The ECMA standard specifies that implementations of JavaScript support a few utility functions. The globally accessible utility functions such as `parseInt()` and `isNaN()` are methods belonging to the Global object. Because they belong to the Global object, we don't need to specify the object as a prefix when we invoke them. This means they look just like utility functions that you might have made yourself.

These are the functions that are available:

Function	Description
parseFloat(string)	Used for converting strings containing floating-point values into a numeric primitive.
parseInt(string)	Used for converting strings into integer values. This form assumes base 10 or special prefix characters to signify octal and hex values.
parseInt(string, radix)	Used for converting strings into integer values. However, you can convert from a variety of different number bases by specifying a radix value.
isNaN(number)	Tests the argument to see if it is numeric and equivalent to 'Not a Number'.
isFinite(number)	Tests the argument to see if it is a finite value.
escape(string)	Converts the string argument to a URL-encoded version of the string. You will have seen this kind of conversions in the URL location bar of your browser. This is deprecated and has been superseded in the ECMA standard.

Function	Description
unescape(string)	Decodes a URL-encoded value. This has also been superseded.
eval(code)	Takes the string argument and interprets it and executes it as JavaScript.
encodeURI(uri)	A standards-compliant replacement for escape().
decodeURI(uri)	Supersedes unescape().
encodeURIComponent(string)	An encoder for a portion of a URI.
decodeURIComponent(string)	A decoder for a portion of a URI.

The parseFloat() Function

The parseFloat() function returns a numeric value, unless the string cannot be resolved to a meaningful value in which case NaN is returned instead. It produces a number value dictated by interpreting the contents of the string as if it were a decimal literal value. During conversion parseFloat() ignores leading whitespace characters so you don't have to remove them from the string before conversion takes place.

Note that parseFloat() will only process the leading portion of the string. As soon as it encounters an invalid floating point numeric character it will assume the scanning is complete. It will then silently ignore any remaining characters in the input argument. The parseFloat() function will not cope with leading currency symbols but does extract meaningful data from strings that have textual content following the number to be parsed.

Example	Result
myDistance = parseFloat("100.56 miles");	myDistance contains the value 100.56
myPrice = parseFloat("£10.35 per kilo");	myPrice contains the value NaN because the currency symbol "£" aborts the parseFloat() operation before it extracts any numeric value

The parseInt() Function

The result of this function call is an integer value, unless the string cannot be resolved to a meaningful value in which case NaN is returned instead. During conversion, parseInt() will remove any leading whitespace characters. You don't need to do that to the string before parsing it. Note also that parseInt() may only interpret the leading portion of a string. As soon as it encounters an invalid integer numeric character it will assume the scanning is complete. It will then silently ignore any remaining characters in the input argument.

Example	Result
`myInteger = parseInt("100 cubic feet");`	`myInteger` contains the value `100`.
`myPrice = parseInt("10.35 per kilo");`	`myPrice` contains the value `10` since the period is not a valid integer character.
`myValue = parseInt("0119");`	`myValue` contains 9. Because there is a leading zero, octal notation is assumed. 9 is an invalid octal character. So the octal value 11 is evaluated. In decimal, this is 9.
`myValue = parseInt("0119", 10);`	`myValue` contains 119. The radix value forces the evaluation to be decimal.

The `parseInt()` function produces an integer value dictated by interpreting the string argument according to the specified radix. By default, with only one parameter, that radix is assumed to be decimal with the caveat that preceding a value with 0 is treated as an octal value and 0x forces a hexadecimal conversion. The `parseInt()` function can happily cope with numbers in any base, provided the radix is specified in the second parameter. Typical radix values are:

◆ `2` – Binary

◆ `8` – Octal

◆ `10` – Decimal

◆ `16` – Hexadecimal

Example	Result
`fromBinaryValue = parseInt("1001010", 2);`	74
`fromOctalValue = parseInt("0377", 8);`	255
`fromDecimalValue = parseInt("1000", 10);`	1000
`fromHexValue = parseInt("AFCC", 16);`	45004

The isNaN() Function

This function checks for the `NaN` value. It applies the internal `ToNumber` operator to its argument and returns `true` or `false` depending on whether the value is a number or not.

Value	isNaN() result
"4"	false
"4A"	true
true	false
"true"	true
false	false
"false"	true
100.00	false
undefined	true
Infinity	false
null	false

The result is `true` for invalid numeric values and `false` for valid numeric ones. Note that some values are type converted during the test and the results are not always what might be expected. For example, Boolean values are considered to be valid numbers, as are `infinity` and `null`.

The isFinite() Function

This is a built-in function to check for the `Infinity` value. It applies the internal `ToNumber` operator to its argument, then returns `true` or `false` depending on whether the value is a finite number or not. The result is `true` for a valid and finite numeric value and `false` if the value is `NaN` or one of the `Infinity` values.

The escape() Function

The `escape()` function computes a new version of the string value it is passed. The new version has certain characters replaced with hexadecimal escape sequences.

- ♦ All character codes from zero to 32 (decimal) will be escaped.

- ♦ All character codes above 126 will be escaped.

```
<html>
<head>
<meta http-equiv="content-type" content="text/html; charset=UTF-8" />
<title> Create a 0-255 lookup table of escapes </title>
<body>
<script type="text/javascript">
document.write("<table border=1>");
document.write("<tr><th>Index</th>");
document.write("<th>Char</th>");
document.write("<th>Escape</th></tr>");
```

```
for(ii=0; ii<256; ii++)
{
  myChar          = String.fromCharCode(ii);

  document.write("<tr align=right><td>");
  document.write(ii);
  document.write("</td><td>");
  document.write(" "+myChar);
  document.write("</td><td>");
  document.write(escape(myChar));
  document.write("</td></td>");
}
document.write("</table>");
</script>
</body>
</html>
```

The unescape() Function

This function is the complement of the `escape()` function. A string that might have been escaped with the `escape()` function either locally or remotely in a web server can be converted back to a normal unescaped string with this function.

As far as ECMAScript is concerned, this is superseded in edition 3 with a new set of generalized URI-handling functions. The JScript 5.5 documentation refers to this as a deprecated feature.

The encodeURI() Function

This function replaces the `escape()` function in pre ECMAScript v3 implementations. All characters apart from the following will be encoded into a hexadecimal form. These are left as they are:

- ◆ ASCII equivalent letters and digits

- ◆ Tilde (~)

- ◆ Underscore (_)

- ◆ Period (.)

- ◆ Exclamation (!)

- ◆ Minus (-)

- ◆ Asterisk (*)

- ◆ Single quote (')

- ◆ Round brackets

- ◆ Semi-colon (;)

- ◆ Slash (/)

- ◆ Query (?)

- ◆ Colon (:)

- ◆ Commercial at sign (@)

- ◆ Ampersand (&)

- ◆ Equals (=)

- ◆ Plus (+)

- ◆ Dollar ($)

- ◆ Comma (,)

- ◆ Hash (#)

All characters up to the maximum Unicode code point above 126 will be encoded. The encoded output uses the UTF-8 scheme. This encodes single-byte characters from 0 to 7F in the form %XX. Unicode characters from 0080 to 07FF will be encoded in the form %XX%XX and characters from 0800 upwards will be in the three-byte %XX%XX%XX form. The selection of the appropriate 1,2, or 3 byte decoding frame depends on the value of the first character in the escape sequence.

Note that this encoding mechanism is different to, and therefore not compatible with, the escape() function. You must use the correct decoder for each encoding scheme.

If you need to encode only part of a URI, then encodeURIComponent() should be used. This will encode some of the characters that encodeURI() leaves intact. Those characters are the ones that have special meaning in a URI and would be used as delimiters for example. The encodeURIComponent() function leaves these characters intact:

- ◆ ASCII equivalent letters and digits

- ◆ Tilde (~)

- ◆ Underscore (_)

- ◆ Period (.)

- ◆ Exclamation (!)

- ◆ Minus (-)

- ◆ Asterisk (*)

- ◆ Single quote (')

- ◆ Round brackets

The decodeURI() Function

This is the complementary decoding mechanism for use with escape sequences generated by the encodeURI() function. This should be used to decode entire URI strings where the variant called decodeURIComponent() is appropriate when operating on parts of a URI.

The eval() Function

When the `eval()` function is called, it expects a string to be passed in its single argument value. The contents of that string should be a syntactically correct executable script source text. The script gets executed and the result generated is returned as the result of the `eval()` function. Your `eval()` code may also have side-effects and can modify objects outside the code being evaluated.

This example takes a fragment of JavaScript source that is contained in a form input element and then evaluates it. The result is placed in another form element:

```
<html>
<head>
<meta http-equiv="content-type" content="text/html; charset=UTF-8" />
<title>JavaScript eval example</title>
<script type="text/javascript">
function evalForm (form)
{
   form.output.value = eval(form.input.value);
}
</script>
</head>
<body>
<form>
<fieldset>
<legend>Enter JavaScript code to evaluate</legend>
<textarea name="input" cols="80" rows="10">
new Date()
</textarea>
<br />
<input type="button" value="evaluate JavaScript code"
        onclick="evalForm(this.form);" />
</fieldset>
<fieldset>
<legend>output</legend>
<textarea name="output" cols="80" rows="5"></textarea>
</fieldset>
</form>
</body>
</html>
```

This example uses `eval()` to generate a list of character glyphs by constructing an escape sequence in a string and then using `eval()` to render the backslash escape.

```
<html>
<head>
<meta http-equiv="content-type" content="text/html; charset=UTF-8" />
<title>Escaping via eval example</title>
</head>
<body>
<script type="text/javascript">

for(myCharCode=0; myCharCode<255; myCharCode++)
{
   myEval = "'\134" + myCharCode.toString(8) + "'";
   myJavaScriptEscape = eval(myEval);
```

162

```
document.write(myCharCode + " : " + myJavaScriptEscape + "<br/>");
}
</script>
</body>
</html>
```

JavaScript Objects

Until now we have mentioned objects in passing and as a means of wrapping the various primitive data types to enhance what we can do with them. Now we can delve into the finer points.

An object is simply a container for data and its power lies in its ability to also refer to the functional processing that can be carried out on that data. If you take two quite dissimilar objects, you can provide some functional code that applies to each one individually and by naming these functions identically, you can invoke consistent behavior across all the different types of objects you might encounter.

For example, a picture object and text paragraph object can both respond to a draw instruction but would implement that in a quite different fashion. If a document is a container for multiple paragraphs and pictures, its draw instruction would traverse its collection of child objects sending each one the draw instruction in turn.

Object Properties

A property consists of a name, a value, and a set of attributes. It belongs to an object.

You can create new properties belonging to the object itself or to its prototype if you want to share them among all instances of an object class. Here is an example:

```
// Create a new object
var myObject = new Object();

// Add some properties to it
myObject.property0 = 1;
myObject ['property1'] = "string";

// Retrieve a value from a property
extractedValue = myObject.property0;
```

Since a property belongs to an object, each instance of a particular object class can maintain its own properties independently of other objects. Properties belonging to a single object are called instance variables.

Properties are containers for values whereas methods are actions. Properties are read-only, write-only, or read and write. Some properties are internal and private to the object and are not therefore exposed as scriptable items. Accessing properties of an object by name simply requires the name to be added to the object reference with a dot separator between them or with the bracketed notation.

```
anObject.aProperty
anObject["aProperty"]
```

You can usually access all of the properties belonging to an object with a `for(…) in(…)` enumerator. The exception to this is any properties that have the `DontEnum` attribute set internally. Since you cannot access that property attribute from script, you also cannot override it. It doesn't mean the property is inaccessible, just that it won't be listed in the enumerable series.

The object properties are accessed by name but those names can be spelled with purely numeric digits. So item `4` is really accessed as item `"4"`. This gives rise to some problems with the dot notation.

```
// This works fine in both cases
myObject[4]
myObject["4"]

// This gives rise to a syntax error
myObject.4
```

The dot notation is easier to work with when a sequence of parent-child references is being traversed, but the bracketed notation is more versatile, in that you can use strings to name the properties to be accessed without the name being known in advance (for example, obtaining property names by computation as opposed to hardcoding). So the name of the identifier can be derived from an expression but it must yield a meaningful string value that corresponds to a genuine or potential property of the receiver.

The object to which the property access message is being directed can also be derived by evaluating an expression.

Setting the value of a property simply requires that you place the property reference on the left-hand side of an assignment expression. You may also set properties if special convenience methods have been provided. These might be implemented to check the value being passed for validity before assigning it to the property:

```
myObject.myProperty = newValue;
```

Reading the value from the property simply requires that the property reference be placed on the right:

```
presentValue = myObject.myProperty;
```

Generally speaking, you can use properties wherever you would use variables.

Object Methods

Functions are implemented in the script interpreter as function objects and are accessed as methods when they are themselves associated with an object by being attached to a property. Methods are owned by objects. They can also share methods they inherit from their prototype.

So a method is simply a function that is written in a particular way that means it works well when associated with an object. It is invoked as the "receiver of a message" rather than a function call.

As soon as you find yourself using the `this` variable, then it's likely your function is no longer useful as a standalone function and ought to really be recoded as a method.

```javascript
// Function to print an owner object property
function my_name()
{
  document.write(this.name);
}

// Create a new object instance
var myObject = new Object;

// Define the name property for the object
myObject.name = "Example";

// Associate the function so it can be used as a method,
// note that we omit the parentheses
myObject.my_name = my_name;

// Call the function via the method interface
myObject.my_name();

// Call the function normally
my_name();
```

Prototype-based Inheritance

When you define a new kind of object type for your own use, the functional behavior is maintained in a prototype object. Any methods you define for that new class will belong to the prototype.

You can also define shared properties which can be read from any instance object of that class, but will actually be provided indirectly by the prototype object through the instance. If, on the other hand, you assign a value to a property belonging to an instance, a value is stored in that instance object and will not be shared between all the instances of the class. To assign a value that can be shared, you can store a value in the instance object's prototype.

Prototypes can be referenced using the dot-separated object hierarchy notation. With an object called `myObject`, its prototype would be accessed like this:

```javascript
myPrototype = myObject.prototype;
```

If any properties are added to the prototype, they will be shared by, and be available to, all objects created by the constructor associated with that prototype. Such objects may override the inheritance by having identically named properties added to them directly.

```javascript
myObject.aPrivateProperty
myObject.prototype.aSharedProperty
```

JavaScript supports an inheritance chain based on prototypes. This is created by defining the parent class in the constructor. Not all implementations expose the prototype property of their objects. If the prototypes are accessible, you can walk this prototype chain by referring successively to each prototype's prototype. You know you have reached the top when you find an object whose prototype is `null`. That object is the master object. Here is an illustration of this linkage:

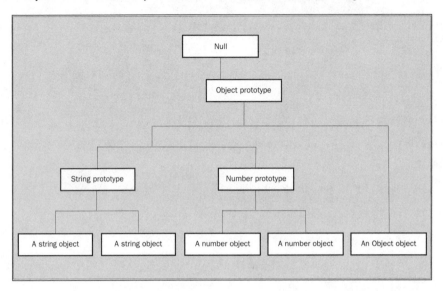

A prototype may have an implicit reference to its parent prototype. This provides inheritance through a Prototype Chain that is analogous to the Super-Class and Sub-Class mechanisms in a class-based object-oriented language. It is not quite the same however because the inheritance takes place at the object level and there are no true classes to instantiate.

Constructors

A `constructor` property is a function object that creates and initializes new objects. Each constructor has an associated prototype object that provides inheritance and shared properties. There are `constructor` properties belonging to the Global object for all the built-in (native) object prototypes. However, the host implementation may add others for you to use. New objects are created using the `new` operator.

Here is a very simple constructor:

```
function Square(aSize)
{
    this.size = aSize;
}
```

To use it to make a new `Square` object we simply do this:

```
mySquare = new Square(10);
```

This object doesn't do very much that is new or original but it does already inherit some capabilities from the master object which its prototype refers to. We can add some more specialized capabilities, as well. In this case it is a square so we can provide a method that returns its area.

```
function Square.prototype.area()
{
    return (this.size * this.size);
}
```

Note that we named the function using the dot notation. This allows us to create a new function and associate it with the constructor without polluting the global function namespace. Like this:

```
function area()
{
    return (this.size * this.size);
}

Square.prototype.area = area;
```

Object Literals

JavaScript version 1.2 introduced the ability to construct objects directly from object literals. The object is created and returned by an expression, which can then be assigned to a variable; regardless of what name you give the variable, the class of the newly created object is still `Object`.

First of all, let's create an object using a literal, but without adding any additional properties. It is basically an empty object container:

```
// Create an empty object
var empty = { };
```

Now we can make it a little more complex by adding a property. The strings prior to the colon symbols represent the names of the properties while the text following the colon describes the value placed in that property.

```
// Create a simple one-property object
var simple = {
              prop:100
             };
```

Expanding our concept, let's create an object with multiple properties, each one separated from the next by a comma:

```
// Create a three-property object
var moreProps = {
            propertyOne:23,
            propertyTwo:'a string',
            propertyThree:false
          };
```

Available Core Object Types

JavaScript version 1.x does not actually support object classes in the conventional sense that an object-oriented language implies. However, the different types of objects that it supports behave in many ways like a class-based system. We refer to the built-in `Object` class with a capitalized name. When referring generically to objects of other classes, the word object is all lowercase. Therefore we can have an `Object` object and a `String` object. There are several groups of object classes, organized according to how they are implemented.

- ♦ Native objects are built into the core language
- ♦ Host objects are also built-in, but created outside the JavaScript core functionality
- ♦ User-defined objects are created in the script source and don't exist until the script is executed.

These are core objects defined by ECMA and accessible as properties of the global object and do not include the host objects provided by the browser. The object versions of the primitive types provide a much richer interface than the primitive version can support. These are present in all standards-compliant JavaScript implementations whatever the context:

Object	Description
Global	A container for global properties, methods, and functions. There is no object type called "Global". It is just convenient to refer to the host object in that way.
Array()	A constructor for collections of objects in a sequence.
Boolean()	A constructor for the logical value container.
Date()	A constructor for the date value container.
Number()	A constructor for the numeric value container.
Object()	A constructor for the generic object.
String()	A constructor for the sequence of characters container.
RegExp()	A constructor for the regular expression evaluator.
Error()	A constructor for error objects.
Function()	A constructor for the function code container.
Arguments	A container for the arguments and other function attributes.
Math	A container for math functions.

These are special core objects that are based on the `Error()` constructor. They apply to specific errors and are created when an exception is thrown.

Object	Description
`EvalError()`	Instantiated for errors that occur during an `eval()` function.
`RangeError()`	Instantiated for errors due to a numeric range exception.
`ReferenceError()`	Instantiated for errors due to a non-existent variable reference.
`SyntaxError()`	Instantiated when a syntax error is encountered in the code.
`TypeError()`	Instantiated when a value of the wrong data type is encountered.
`URIError()`	Instantiated when errors are encountered during URI encode and decode operations.

The Math Object

This is a globally available object containing a library of mathematical functions. The `Math` object provides the following constant values:

Constant	Description
`E`	The value of e which is the base of natural logarithms.
`LN10`	The natural logarithm of 10.
`LN2`	The natural logarithm of 2.
`LOG10E`	The base-10 logarithm of e.
`LOG2E`	The base-2 logarithm of e.
`PI`	The value of .

These functions are provided as static members of the `Math` class object:

Function	Description
`abs(a)`	Returns the absolute value of the argument.
`acos(a)`	Returns the inverse Cosine of the value. The result is in radians.
`asin(a)`	Returns the inverse Sine of the value. The result is in radians.
`atan(a)`	Returns the inverse Tangent of the value. The result is in radians.

Function	Description
`atan2(y, x)`	Computes the inverse tangent of a slope. Note the position of the arguments. The result is in radians.
`ceil(a)`	Rounds up to the nearest integer value.
`cos(a)`	Returns the Cosine of the angle expressed in radians.
`exp(a)`	Computes the value of e raised to the power of the argument.
`floor(a)`	Rounds down to the nearest integer value.
`log(a)`	Computes the natural logarithm (to the base e) of the argument.
`max(a, b, ...)`	Returns the maximum value of a set of values.
`min(a, b, ...)`	Returns the minimum value of a set of values.
`pow(x, y)`	Computes the value of x raised to the power y.
`random()`	Returns a pseudo-random number.
`round(a)`	Rounds up or down to the nearest integer value.
`sin(a)`	Returns the Sine of the angle expressed in radians.
`sqrt(a)`	Computes the square root of the argument.
`tan(a)`	Returns the Tangent of the angle expressed in radians.

The Date Object

A `Date` object accesses a number that denotes a particular instant in time that is accurate to within a millisecond. With this object you can work out what the time is now or manufacture various time and date values using the constructor. The `Date` object provides a very rich interface.

The object has a very large number of methods available. They provide a way to operate with time values that are accurate to the millisecond. Dates can be expressed in milliseconds since 1-Jan-1970 or as component values in years, months, days, hours, minutes, seconds, and milliseconds. Relative time values can be computed by working out a value in milliseconds and then finding the difference between two date and time values.

New `Date` objects are constructed like this:

```
new Date()
new Date(millisecondsTime)
new Date(Date.UTC(y, m, d, hh, mm, ss, ms))
new Date(Date.parse(stringContainingDateAsText))
```

Here is a summary of the available methods. There are variants of these methods which use a UTC time value as well as local time based versions. UTC time is equivalent to GMT and the values are based on the equivalent time at the Greenwich Meridian. Note that deprecated functionality is not listed here:

Local time method	UTC method	Description
getDate()	getUTCDate()	Returns the day number of the month.
getDay()	getUTCDay()	Returns the day of the week (zero-based).
getFullYear()	getUTCFullYear()	Returns the year number in full.
getHours()	getUTCHours()	Returns the hours portion of the time value, zero-based and with respect to a 24-hour clock.
getMilliseconds()	getUTCMilliseconds()	Returns the milliseconds portion of a time value.
getMinutes()	getUTCMinutes()	Returns the minutes portion of a time value.
getMonth()	getUTCMonth()	Returns the month of the year (zero-based).
getSeconds()	getUTCSeconds()	Returns the seconds portion of a time value.
getTime()		Returns the current time in milliseconds since 1-Jan-1970. This result is also obtained with the valueOf() method.
getTimezoneOffset()		Returns the offset in minutes between local time and UTC (GMT).
setDate(day)	setUTCDate(day)	Sets the day number of the month.
setFullYear(y)	setUTCFullYear(y)	Sets the year value.
setFullYear(y,m)	setUTCFullYear(y,m)	Sets the year and month values.
setFullYear(y,m,d)	setUTCFullYear(y,m,d)	Sets the year, month, and day values.
setHours(hh)	setUTCHours(hh)	Sets the hours value.
setHours(hh,mm)	setUTCHours(hh,mm)	Sets the hours and minutes values.
setHours(hh,mm,ss)	setUTCHours(hh,mm,ss)	Setss the hours, minutes, and seconds values.

Table continued on following page

Core JavaScript

3

Local time method	UTC method	Description
setHours(hh,mm, ss,ms)	setUTCHours(hh,mm, ss,ms)	Sets the hours, minutes, seconds, and milliseconds values.
setMilliseconds (msec)	setUTCMilliseconds (msec)	Sets the milliseconds value.
setMinutes(mm)	setUTCMinutes(mm)	Sets the minutes value.
setMinutes(mm,ss)	setUTCMinutes(mm,ss)	Sets the minutes and seconds values.
setMinutes(mm, ss,ms)	setUTCMinutes(mm, ss,ms)	Sets the minutes, seconds, and milliseconds values.
setMonth(mon)	setUTCMonth(mon)	Sets the month value.
setMonth(mon,day)	setUTCMonth(mon,day)	Sets the month and day values.
setSeconds(ss)	setUTCSeconds(ss)	Sets the seconds value.
setSeconds(ss,ms)	setUTCSeconds(ss,ms)	Sets the seconds and milliseconds values.
toDateString()		Returns just the date portion of the date presented as a human-readable string in local time coordinates.
toLocaleDate String()		Returns just the date portion of the date presented as a human-readable string in local time coordinates and formatted according to the user preference settings.
toTimeString()		Returns just the time portion of the date presented as a human-readable string in local time coordinates.
toLocaleTime String()		Returns just the time portion of the date presented as a human-readable string in local time coordinates and formatted according to the user preference settings.
toLocaleString()		Returns a human-readable date and time string computed in local time coordinates and formatted according to the user preference settings.
toString()	toUTCString()	Returns a human-readable date and time string computed in local or UTC time coordinates.

These are class methods used as factories to create new `Date` objects or calculate time values without needing to manufacture an object.

Static method	Description
`Date.parse(string)`	Parses the string to compute the number of milliseconds between the passed date value and 1-Jan-1970. This avoids the need to create a `Date` object.
`Date.UTC(y,m,d,hh,mm,ss,ms)`	Converts a componentized date value into milliseconds since 1-Jan-1970 based on that being the time value at Greenwich.
`Date(milliseconds)`	Converts a milliseconds (since 1-Jan-1970) value into a date object.
`Date(y,m,d,hh,mm,ss,ms)`	Converts a componentized date value into a date object based on that being the time value in a locale-specified time zone.

Regular Expressions

Regular expressions are a way of describing a pattern match that can be used to select a group of characters from an input string. This usually then leads on to replacing them with some other set of characters. It is analogous to the find and replace capability in a word processor.

JavaScript version 1.2 introduces regular expression support by way of a specialized `RegExp` object. This is a utility that UNIX developers have long known about and used. It has migrated into many desktop applications now and has become a somewhat portable way of matching text strings with one another and performing edits on them.

The regular expression syntax adopted by JavaScript version 1.2 emulates that which was commonly used in Perl interpreters. Specifically the syntax that is supported is generally called Perl version 4. In JavaScript version 1.3, the regular expression syntax is expanded to support what is known as Perl 5 syntax.

Regular expressions are managed by creating a `RegExp` object with the `RegExp()` constructor. `RegExp` objects support a literal syntax and can be created on the fly without needing a constructor call, which makes them extremely convenient to deploy. That is accomplished using `RegExp` literals.

RegExp Reference

Character matching is accomplished with `RegExp` literal characters:

Pattern	Description
0 to 9	Itself
a to z	Itself
A to Z	Itself
\$	A single dollar sign ($)
*	A single asterisk (*)
\+	A single plus sign (+)
\,	A single comma (,)
\.	A single period (.)
\/	A single slash (/)
\?	A single question mark (?)
\\	A single backslash (\)
\^	A single circumflex (^)
\d	Any digit character as per [0-9]
\D	Any non-digit character as per [^0-9]
\f	A form feed
\n	A newline
\r	A carriage return
\S	A non-space character
\s	A space character
\t	A tab character
\v	A vertical tab
\w	An alphanumeric character and underscore as per [0-9a-zA-Z_]
\W	An non-alphanumeric character and underscore as per [^0-9a-zA-Z_]
|	A single vertical bar (|)
\(	A single opening parenthesis (()
\)	A single closing parenthesis ())

Pattern	Description
\ [	A single opening square bracket ([)
\ ]	A single closing square bracket (])
\ {	A single opening curly brace ({)
\ }	A single closing curly brace (})
\nnn	The ASCII character encoded by the octal value nnn
\onnn	The ASCII character encoded by the octal value nnn
\uhhhh	The Unicode character encoded by the hexadecimal value hhhh
\xhh	The ASCII character encoded by the hexadecimal value hh
\c•	The control character equivalent to ^•
\c@	(NUL) – Null character
\c[	(ESC) – Escape
\c\	(FS) – File separator (Form separator)
\c]	(GS) – Group separator
\c^	(RS) – Record separator
\c_	(US) – Unit separator
\cA	(SOH) – Start of header
\cB	(STX) – Start of text
\cC	(ETX) – End of text
\cD	(EOT) – End of transmission
\cE	(ENQ) – Enquiry
\cF	(ACK) – Positive acknowledge
\cG	(BEL) – Alert (bell)
\cH	(BS) – Backspace
\cI	(HT) – Horizontal tab
\cJ	(LF) – Line feed
\cK	(VT) – Vertical tab
\cL	(FF) – Form feed
\cM	(CR) – Carriage return

3

Core JavaScript

Table continued on following page

Pattern	Description
\cN	(SO) – Shift out
\cO	(SI) – Shift in
\cP	(DLE) – Data link escape
\cQ	(DC1) – Device control 1 (XON)
\cR	(DC2) – Device control 2 (tape on)
\cS	(DC3) – Device control 3 (XOFF)
\cT	(DC4) – Device control 4 (tape off)
\cU	(NAK) – Negative acknowledgement
\cV	(SYN) – Synchronous idle
\cW	(ETB) – End of transmission block
\cX	(CAN) – Cancel
\cY	(EM) – End of medium
\cZ	(SUB) – Substitute
\0 to \9	The last remembered substring as per the $n property.
[\b]	A literal backspace not to be confused with a word boundary match (using the \b outside square brackets)

The positional indicators control where in the line the pattern is being matched:

Pattern	Description
^	Indicates the start of the line.
$	Indicates the end of the line.
\b	Indicates a word boundary. Note that this cannot be used in a bracketed character class [\b] means backspace not word boundary.
\B	Indicates any non-word boundary location.
.$	The last character at the end of the line (the dot matches one character).
\b\d*\b	A complete word composed only of numeric digits.
\b\w*\b	A complete word.
\s*$	All of the trailing whitespace.
^$	A line with nothing between the start and end, an empty line.

Pattern	Description
`^.`	The first character at the beginning of the line (the dot matches one character).
`^.*$`	The entire line regardless of its contents.
`^\s`	A leading whitespace character.

The repetition operators control how many times the pattern match is applied:

Pattern	Description
`{a,b}`	Match the item to the left between <a> and <b> times.
`{a,}`	Match the item to the left at least <a> times or more.
`{a}`	Match the item to the left exactly <a> times, n more, no less.
`?`	Match the item to the left zero or one times.
`+`	Match the item to the left 1 or more times.
`+?`	Match the item to the left 1 or more times using a minimal matching technique.
`*`	Match the item to the left zero or more times.
`*?`	Match the item to the left zero or more times using a minimal matching technique.
`{0,1}`	Match the item to the left zero or one times (alternative form).
`{0,}`	Match the item to the left zero or more times (alternative form).
`{1,}`	Match the item to the left 1 or more times (alternative form).

These flags can be used in regular expressions to indicate how the expression is to be applied to the data:

Flag	Description
`i`	Ignore case
`g`	Match globally
`ig`	Ignore case and match globally
`m`	Multiple-line parsing

Regular expressions are too large a topic to cover comprehensively here. We only have space to show a few small examples of how to use them.

The Wrox book, *Beginning JavaScript*, Paul Wilton, ISBN 1-86100-406-0, devotes an entire chapter to the use of regular expressions.

```
<html>
<head>
<meta http-equiv="content-type" content="text/html; charset=UTF-8" />
<title>Regular expression example</title>
</head>
<body>
<script type="text/javascript">
// Make the RegExp from a literal
myRegExp = /[0-9]{2}-([a-zA-Z]{3})-[0-9]{4}/;

// Create the input search string
myString = "01-Jan-1954";

// Run the search
myArray = myRegExp.exec(myString);

// How many items are there in the array
document.write(myArray.length);
document.write("<BR>");

// Display the source string
document.write(myArray[0]);
document.write("<BR>");

// Display the month name sub-match
document.write(myArray[1]);
document.write("<BR>");
</script>
</body>
</html>
```

Regular Expression Literal

A `RegExp` literal is defined as some matching expression enclosed in slash characters.

```
// Create a RegExp object using a constructor
var myRegExp = new RegExp("sque[ea]ky", "g");

// Create the same RegExp object with a reg exp literal
var myRegExp = /sque[ea]ky/g;
```

The grammar for building regular expressions is somewhat complex. The rules are basically straightforward, with a sequence of individual matching rules assembled together and enclosed in slashes. There can be some modifier flags placed after the second slash delimiter.

Here are some example Regular Expression literals:

```
/^JavaScript/
/19[0-9][0-9]*/
/\binterpreter/i
/squeek/g
```

You can assign these expressions to variables, which will then contain a `RegExp` object.

```
// Declare a variable and assign a RegExp literal to it
var myPattern = /x$/;

// Now do the same thing with a RegExp constructor
var myPattern = new RegExp("x$");
```

Test a String with RegExp

This example tests a string and only yields `true` if the value is a four-digit numeric value. It's good for checking form content to see that a value has been entered in the correct format. The principal `RegExp` patterns used here are `\d` to indicate a digit followed by `{4}` to indicate a repetition count. The pattern is bounded by the beginning and end of line flags so that the form specifically mandates a four-digit value and no other additional text.

```
<html>
<head>
<meta http-equiv="content-type" content="text/html; charset=UTF-8" />
<title>Testing strings with RegExp</title>
</head>
<body>
<script type="text/javascript">
document.write("1 "     + testForFormValue("1")     + "<BR />");
document.write("12 "    + testForFormValue("12")    + "<BR />");
document.write("123 "   + testForFormValue("123")   + "<BR />");
document.write("1234 "  + testForFormValue("1234")  + "<BR />");
document.write("12345 " + testForFormValue("12345") + "<BR />");

function testForFormValue(aString)
{
    var myRegExp = /^\d{4}$/;
    return myRegExp.test(aString);
}
</script>
</body>
</html>
```

Summary

We have explored a very large territory in this chapter. We've gone from basic concepts of how an object-oriented language like JavaScript works, through to some fairly detailed discussion of regular expressions and data-type manipulation. Along the way, we've explored those various data types, operators, and language control flow constructs.

Now you are sufficiently well armed to explore JavaScript even more, with the help of *Chapter 2*, which covers CSS, *Chapter 4* on browser extensions, and *Chapter 6*, which talks about DOM. To make effective use of JavaScript and build modern and sophisticated dynamic content-driven web sites, a sound working knowledge of CSS and DOM is necessary.

4

- Top level browser object reference

Author: Cliff Wootton

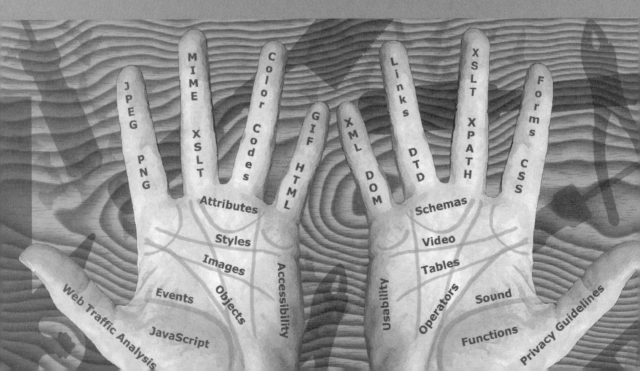

Client Browser Extensions

In the Netscape and IE web browsers, object models are provided as representations of the window, the document, the browser, event capturing mechanisms, and the stylesheet. Each of these object models interacts with the others and is a way of representing the tangible real-world objects.

Portability Issues

The browser manufacturers (principally Netscape and Microsoft) have introduced several useful objects for operating on the content of the window, the document, and the browser itself. A large proportion of these objects is not portable: that is, they are available in one or other of the popular browsers but not both. This means you cannot build scripts that use them unless you are prepared to deploy multiple versions of your content. Most organizations are not prepared to multiply the effort required to publish their web site and so they only make one version available. This approach tends to use IE special features if it goes beyond the basic portable browser-provided facilities.

The situation is further complicated by incompatibilities across different platforms, and a feature which you might make use of on Windows in IE may not be introduced until a later version on the Macintosh platform. Browser version detection is not sufficient. Some features never make the transition across platforms because they rely on operating system services that are simply not available.

The window Object

The `window` object is implemented as the `Global` object within the JavaScript environment. This means that the object has all of the properties and methods of the core `Global` object plus some additional capabilities to support the browser object model. Because the `window` object is the `Global` object, adding global properties (variables) during script execution attaches them to the `window` object. They are therefore always accessible without your needing to preface a reference to them with an object identifier.

The `window` object represents the browser container that the `document` object lives in and a new one is created for each window that the browser opens. The implications of this are that scripts running in one window operate in a separate context to scripts running in another. There is one unique Global object for each window in a web browser.

There is also one for each frame in a frameset. This means that you can have several Global objects that do not share their properties and methods with one another. Adding a global variable to one window does not make it available across the entire browser.

In a frameset, locating other adjacent windows is done by accessing the `parent` property of the `window` object. This will be the `window` object itself in a topmost window. In a frameset, it will point at the containing frame immediately outside the window.

Whether you can actually access objects in other windows or frames comes down to some basic security issues. Generally the security policy prevents access to code that arrives from different servers. You can legally get at values in pages served from the same host as your page. It is unreasonable to expect to be able to access variables in a page served from another host. This can lead to difficulties if you serve your site from multiple hosts. It isn't as limiting as all that though and there are ways to grant permission to access frames from the same domain via the security policy in the browser.

window Properties

These properties are provided by the `window` object in addition to those already described for the Global object in *Chapter 3*. The properties in this table are considered to be standard features and are available in all but the very earliest versions of browsers. Both Netscape and IE provide additional properties. Deploying pages that use those properties, however, will prevent your pages from being seen properly by all your users:

Property	Description
closed	This is a Boolean value that indicates the current disposition of the window. If the window is closed, the object that represented it is not destroyed. Instead, this property is set to the value `true`.
defaultStatus	This property contains a string that is displayed in the status bar when no other user action or script content is displaying a text there. It is commonplace to put a rollover script that updates the status bar; this value is used when the mouse rolls off the active element.
document	A reference to the `document` object that reflects the current content of the window. This is described in detail in *Chapter 6*.
frames[]	A collection of references to other `window` objects that are contained within individual frames within the current window.
history	A reference to the `history` object that contains a list of pages that have been visited recently.
length	Identical to the `frames.length` value.
location	A container for the current location (URL) of the window. You can change this object to go to a new page under script control.
name	A string containing the current window name.
navigator	A reference to the `Navigator` object. This contains properties that tell you about the browser application.

Property	Description
opener	A reference to another `window` object that contained a script that created this window. The value is only appropriate for top-level windows and is a handle from which you can access properties and methods in the window. This is useful for creating pop-up windows and passing values back from a dialog.
parent	A reference to the `window` object that contains this window when a frameset is being created. This value is equivalent to the `window` and `self` properties when we have arrived at the topmost `window` object.
screen	An object that represents the display surface the window is being presented on. All windows in a display share this object.
self	A reference to the `window` object that the property belongs to.
status	A string that is currently being presented in the status line of the window furniture.
top	A reference to a window as the top of a frameset tree. If the value here is the same as that in the `window` and `self` properties, we are in the topmost window.
window	Identical to the `self` property.

window Functions

The `window` object also provides these additional functions over and above those already available from the core Global object. Again, only those functions that are standardized and available widely are listed:

Method	Description
alert(string)	Presents an alert dialog box on the screen. The dialog contains the message string and a button to dismiss the alert.
blur()	Removes keyboard focus from the window. Keyboard control is passed to a containing top-level window if the window being blurred is a frame. If the window is a topmost window, that window is placed in the background and deactivated.
clearInterval(id)	Clear the interval timer defined by `setInterval()`.
clearTimeout(id)	Clear the timed event defined by `setTimeout()`.
close()	The window will be closed. If the window is in a frameset, this function is only meaningful in the topmost window.
confirm(string)	Presents a dialog with the message `string` and two buttons. Clicking the *OK* button returns `true` and clicking the *Cancel* button returns `false`.

Table continued on following page

Client Browser Extensions

4

Method	Description
`focus()`	This is the opposite of the `blur()` function and makes a window active and responsive to keyboard events.
`moveBy(x,y)`	Moves the window by the indicated distance in `x` and `y`.
`moveTo(x,y)`	Moves the window to the specific position indicated in `x` and `y`.
`open(url, name, features, replace)`	Opens a new top-level window, or locates an existing object that represents a named window. See the more detailed description below for a discussion of the arguments available with this function.
`print()`	The browser will behave as if the *Print* button had been clicked.
`prompt(string, default)`	A dialog for text entry is presented to the user. The message `string` is displayed and if a `default` string is provided, it will be placed in the editing area. Clicking *OK* will return the user entered input. The *Cancel* button returns a `null` value.
`resizeBy(x,y)`	Enlarge or reduce the window by the amount specified in the `x` and `y` parameters.
`resizeTo(x,y)`	Set the new window size to the value specified in the `x` and `y` parameters.
`scrollBy(x,y)`	Scroll the window content by the amount specified in the `x` and `y` parameters.
`scrollTo(x,y)`	Scroll the window content to the position indicated by the `x` and `y` parameters.
`setInterval(script, interval)`	The `script` code is executed periodically with a repeat time indicated in the `interval` parameter. The value is specified in milliseconds. An ID value is returned which you can use with the `clearInterval()` function to cancel this timer.
`setTimeout(script, timeout)`	The `script` code is executed just once with a delay time indicated in the `timeout` parameter. The value is specified in milliseconds. An ID value is returned which you can use with the `clearTimeout()` function to cancel this timer.

Events Supported by Window Objects

Event mechanisms are a good way to add functionality to the user interaction. Rather than let the browser handle the user's mouse clicks, you can intervene with JavaScript and add all kinds of sophisticated behavior to each user-driven trigger.

Most events that you will write scripts for will be based on content that resides under the `document` object, which is covered in *Chapter 6*. With the work being done on the DOM standard, it is hoped that browser manufacturers will deploy more robust and portable solutions, but we still have a long way to go on this issue.

Because of this, the `window` object best deals with a few useful events. The following event handlers are sufficiently portable to be used across the range of currently deployed browsers. They are defined by attaching some code in a `<body>`, `<frameset>`, or `<frame>` tag through the `tag` attribute named below. For example, `<body onload="alert('Hi there');">` displays an alert when the page has completed loading. Event handlers can also be attached by assigning a reference to a handler function to the named property of the `window` object:

Event handler	Description
onblur	This event is activated when a window loses focus, either manually or under script control.
onerror	If a script error occurs, this event handler can be used to catch and deal with it. There are some reliability issues with this in version 6 of Netscape Navigator.
onfocus	This event is activated when a window regains focus, either manually or under script control.
onload	When a page has completed loading, the event handler associated with this property will be called.
onresize	If a window is resized, you may want to reposition some of the content. This handler will be called at an appropriate time when the window size changes.
onunload	When a window is closed, you may want to dispose of some objects. This handler is called just before the window closure is completed.

In the timer example script presented shortly we see how the `onload` event handler is used to initiate some animation only when it is certain that the page has finished loading and therefore all the necessary assets are to hand.

Opening New Windows

It is quite common to want to open a new window. Perhaps you want the user to enter some details into a form and a simple prompting dialog is not sufficiently flexible. The `window.open()` function provides a way to open a new window, locate an existing one by name, or change the location URL for a window.

The `open()` function has four parameters and returns a reference to a new or existing `window` object:

Parameter	Description
url	An optional string to indicate the URL to be loaded into the new window. An empty string or missing argument value will cause the new window to be opened but no page to be loaded.

Table continued on following page

Parameter	Description
name	A name for the new window. This name can be used with the `target` attribute for an `<a>` or `<form>` tag. If a window already exists with the `name`, a reference to its `window` object is returned.
features	This string describes the window appearance and furniture that decorates it. The `features` string is ignored when an existing window is being referred to with the `name` argument.
replace	An optional Boolean value that indicates whether the window's `history` object should be appended to or the current entry replaced.

The features list can contain the following flags. Note only those that are available on a portable basis are listed here. IE and Netscape each support features that the other does not honour. The features are specified as a comma separated list of `name=value` pairs:

Feature	Description
height	The height of the new window in pixels measured in the Y-axis.
left	The position of the left edge of the window in pixels in the X-axis. Netscape Navigator does not support `left`, so you should use `screenX` instead.
location	The value `yes` or `no` to switch the visibility of the location bar.
menubar	The value `yes` or `no` to switch the visibility of the menu bar.
resizable	The value `yes` or `no` to control whether the window is resizable or not.
scrollbars	The value `yes` or `no` to switch the visibility of the scroll bars. This can affect whether window content is scrollable or not on Netscape Navigator. If the scroll bars are off, the window will not scroll. In version 4 of Navigator, you then have to use a `<layer>` to reposition the content. In subsequent versions, CSS positioning techniques may provide a more portable alternative.
status	The value `yes` or `no` to switch the visibility of the status bar.
toolbar	The value `yes` or `no` to switch the visibility of the tool bar.
top	The position of the top edge of the window in pixels in the Y-axis. Netscape Navigator does not support `top`, so you should use `screenY` instead.
width	The width of the new window in pixels measured in the X-axis.

Because the Netscape Navigator and IE browsers specify their default screen locations with different feature names, you need to specify both. Each browser, however, at least ignores the other's preferred naming convention so a portable solution could look like this:

```
<html>
<head>
<meta http-equiv="content-type" content="text/html; charset=UTF-8"
/><title>Window opening example</title>
</head>
<body>
<script type="text/javascript">
var myFeatures = "";

myFeatures += "left=100,";
myFeatures += "screenX=100,";
myFeatures += "top=100,";
myFeatures += "screenY=100,";
myFeatures += "width=500,";
myFeatures += "height=500,";
myFeatures += "location=yes,";
myFeatures += "toolbar=yes";

window.open("http://www.w3c.org/", "Example", myFeatures, false);
</script>
</body>
</html>
```

The placement of the commas is important and no whitespace is allowed in the feature string. If there is any whitespace or if commas are omitted, the parser will not see all the features in the list.

Timer Examples

Timer events are created by calling a timer setup function and giving it a delay value. You can also cancel timeouts. Be careful not to cancel a timeout that has already been processed because it is no longer in the queue. Managing timeouts is tricky and exposes you to an area where the browser is somewhat less reliable than mainstream functionality.

Nevertheless, timer events are useful for managing refreshes and animation. You can interlock a refresh with some animation or scrolling so that the refresh exhibits as few screen redrawing artifacts as possible.

window.setInterval()

The `setInterval` method establishes a periodically scheduled execution timer that runs the same fragment of script continuously with a delay timer between each cycle.

If you only want to delay the execution of some code and you want it to be executed just once, then use the `setTimeout` method instead. That will defer execution and clear its timer automatically when it executes.

This example demonstrates `setInterval`. Without this interval between value increments, the display would not update. The example runs in IE 5+ and Netscape 6+:

```
<html>
<head>
<meta http-equiv="content-type" content="text/html; charset=UTF-8" />
<title>Interval timer demo</title>
</head>
<body>
<div id="ABC">
</div>
<script type="text/javascript">
myTarget = document.getElementById("ABC");

myIndex = 0;

myIntervalId = setInterval("incrementor()", 100);

function incrementor()
{
   myTarget.innerHTML = myIndex++;
}
</script>
</body>
</html>
```

window.setTimeout()

The `setTimeout` method provides a way to defer the execution of a fragment of script. It is analogous to the `eval` method with a delay before execution. Although this method returns an ID value that can then be used with the `clearTimeout` method to cancel the execution, it is very likely that the deferred code will have executed already. You should set a flag accordingly so that you can avoid killing a deferred task that has already been completed.

Code executed by this deferred mechanism will only be executed once. If you want it to be executed continuously then `setInterval` is a better alternative. On the other hand, you may want to conditionally defer it again in which case you should call a handler function and before exiting it, make another call to `setTimeout` to activate another deferred task.

As is the case with `setInterval` and `eval`, you can execute multiple statements so long as they are separated by semi-colons.

This facility was popularly used to present a message in the status bar and then clear it again after some period of time has elapsed. It can be used to generate some animation in the status bar although many people consider this to be a design cliché and much overused. If you do animate the status bar, you should consider whether it is useful and not distracting. These days, more interesting animated effects are carried out in the window using CSS style controls.

These timed animations are generally best initiated by an `onLoad` event handler in the first place so that they don't commence until the page has completed loading.

The example is a cut-down version of the ticker script used in the BBC *News Online* web site. The display techniques are the same but the example only shows one story. To see the real ticker in operation, refer to *http://news.bbc.co.uk/* and view it with an IE browser.

In the News Online ticker, many coding compromises were necessary to work round object boundary bugs in the IE for Macintosh browser. Because the ticker is constantly being updated, the object boundary is changing all the time and although this was played in an `<IFRAME>`, the mouseover and mouseout events caused the IE browser to crash frequently. When you create and destroy an element, the mouse might have rolled over the old instance and the event handler still be processing some code associated with it. While that is going on, you have destroyed the object to which it is attached and then constructed a new one and placed it under the mouse. This implies that the mouse is now rolled over an object but did not trigger a rollover event for that new object. Understandably, the user interface mechanisms get very confused about this sort of thing. They expect objects to be stable and stay in existence while their UI appearance is being updated.

Earlier versions of the ticker also did a large amount of string creation/destruction, which caused somewhat massive memory leaks. You can alleviate this by using meta refresh tags to force the garbage collection to happen every so often.

```html
<html>
<head>
<meta http-equiv="content-type" content="text/html; charset=UTF-8" />
<title>Timeout demo</title>
<style type="text/css">
<!--
A { font-family: Verdana, Arial, Helvetica, sans-serif, "MS sans serif";
    font-size: 11px;
    line-height: 11px;
    text-decoration: none;
    color: #333366;
    font-weight: bold;
}

A.latest { color: #CC3300;}

A:hover { color: #CC3300; }
-->
</style>

<script type="text/javascript">
var theTickerText = "The ticker text goes here ";
theTickerText += "and plays out until it is finished before repeating again.";
var theCharacterTimeout = 45;
var theStoryTimeout      = 5000;
var theEnumerator        = 0;

// --- Run the ticker
function doTheTicker() {
  if((theEnumerator % 2) == 1) { writeTicker("_"); }
  else { writeTicker("*"); }

  theEnumerator++;

  if(theEnumerator == theTickerText.length+1) {
    writeTicker("");
```

```
      theEnumerator = 0;
      setTimeout("doTheTicker()", theStoryTimeout); }
   else {setTimeout("doTheTicker()", theCharacterTimeout); }
}

function writeTicker(aWidget){
   if (document.all) {
      document.all.hottext.innerHTML =
             theTickerText.substring(0,theEnumerator) + aWidget; }
   else if (document.getElementById) {
      document.getElementById('hottext').innerHTML =
             theTickerText.substring(0,theEnumerator) + aWidget;  }
}
</script>
</head>
<body onLoad="doTheTicker();">
<a id="latest" class="latest" href="/" target=_top>LATEST: </a>
<a id="hottext" href="/"></a>
<noscript>
Upgrade your browser or turn on JavaScript to see the ticker animation.<br>
</noscript>
</body>
</html>
```

The frames Collection

This is a collection of references to other `window` objects that are contained within individual frames within the current window. Only the immediate contents of the window are listed. Frames constrained within one of these child windows will not be listed in this collection but will be contained in a `frames` collection belonging to that child window. Clearly, this property is only of any use when a window contains a frameset. The number of frames in this collection is available in the `frames.length` property and is also reflected in the `window.length` property.

Here is a frameset layout on a page:

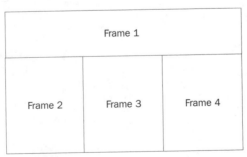

This is the minimal HTML that's required to generate the frameset layout above:

190

```
<html>
<head>
<meta http-equiv="content-type" content="text/html; charset=UTF-8" />
<title>Frameset demo</title>
</head>
<frameset rows="*,*" >
  <frame src="./frame.html" name="headerFrame">
  <frameset cols="*,*,*" >
    <frame src="./frame.html" name="subFrame2">
    <frame src="./frame.html" name="subFrame3">
    <frame src="./frame.html" name="subFrame4">
  </frameset>
</frameset>
</html>
```

And here is the organisation of the frames from a JavaScript point of view:

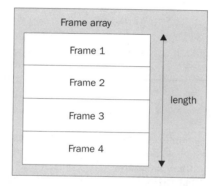

If we place some script into the frames that checks the `frames` array belonging to the parent window, we can use an identity test to match an object in the array with the `window` object in each frame. Having matched them, we can highlight the object in a listing. Note that exactly the same code is running in each frame, as shown below for `frame.html`:

```
<html>
<head>
<meta http-equiv="content-type" content="text/html; charset=UTF-8" />
<title>Frame content</title>
</head>
<body>
<script type="text/javascript">
var ii = 0;

for(ii=0; ii<parent.length; ii++) {
   if(parent.frames[ii] == self) {
      document.write("<strong>");
      showName(ii);
      document.write("</strong>"); }
   else { showName(ii); }
}
```

```
function showName(anIndex) {
    document.write(anIndex + ". ");
    document.write(parent.frames[anIndex].name);
    document.write("<br>");
}
</script>
</body>
</html>
```

And here is the output that you should see:

0. **headerFrame**		
1. subFrame2		
2. subFrame3		
3. subFrame4		

0. headerFrame	0. headerFrame	0. headerFrame
1. **subFrame2**	1. subFrame2	1. subFrame2
2. subFrame3	2. **subFrame3**	2. subFrame3
3. subFrame4	3. subFrame4	3. **subFrame4**

The history Object

The `history` object gives you very limited access to the list of URLs that have been visited with the current window. The length of this collection depends on how many places you have visited, and also whether you have disabled the collection of this information. Your preference settings for `history` also limit the length of your history. In practice the values you get back for the `length` property are inconsistent with the observed content of the history menu.

From the scripting point of view, most of what the `history` object holds is secured to prevent people from examining your browsing history and sending a list of what you have chosen back to their server. This almost completely negates its usefulness.

The `history` object supports the following methods:

Method	Description
`back()`	Go back to the previous URL. You might know what this page is by carefully tracking the session state but you cannot guarantee that every page the user visits has come from your site. They might have momentarily gone to look at something else and then resumed a session with you.
`forward()`	Go forward to the next URL in the list. How do you know what that is going to be in any user's browsing session?

Method	Description
`go(relativeIndex)`	The index controls whether to go forwards (positive), backwards (negative), or to reload the current page (zero). Calling `history.go(-1)` is equivalent to calling `history.back()`. Early versions of Netscape Navigator exhibited problems with `go(0)` as a reloading mechanism. The `location` object is probably a better means of accomplishing this. IE only supports the values `-1`, `0`, and `+1`.
`go(subString)`	JavaScript 1.1 added a means of searching the `history` collection using a matching string. This is only likely to be useful if you have a pretty good idea of what is in the `history` collection. That suggests your session management at the server end needs to be involved. The user may still prevent this from functioning usefully by having a history list that is very short or turning off history collection in the first place.

On the whole, the `history` object is so limited and the support is so patchy across all the browser versions and platforms that it is hardly of any use at all.

Persistent Storage of Session State

One small but potentially useful observation is that on IE 5.1 for Macintosh, 6 for Windows, and Mozilla 1.0, you can add a property to the `history` object and store a persistent value there. A subsequent page can then retrieve this value. It may not be very portable but in constrained environments such as intranet systems, you may be able to control the deployment of browsers sufficiently for it to be usable.

Here is the content of a scripting block on the first page to set this value up:

```
<script type="text/javascript">
history.myProperty = "Persistent value";
</script>
```

This script block can be placed in a subsequent page to retrieve the value:

```
<script type="text/javascript">
document.write(history.myProperty);
</script>
```

This kind of persistence can be useful because you can preserve some session state data in the client. Another more portable way to do that is to enclose the window in a frameset and store values in the parent frame. This is appropriate even for a single window application since the user does not need to know that a frameset exists at all. So long as the parent frame remains intact, the session state values will be accessible.

The location Object

The `location` object for a window provides an interface that allows you to examine or change the document `href` that is currently being displayed in the window. Changing any of these properties will reload the page except for the case of the `hash` property which will move to a different hash anchor within the current document and does not require a reload.

The `location` object supports the following properties:

Property	Description
href	This is the entire URL for the document. You can read it from this property and use it as a complete URL or extract portions of it. Any substrings you are likely to need will be available from the other properties supported by this object. Note that the `window.open()` function also provides a way to load the window with a new URL value. Modifying properties of the `location` object seems to be a more natural way to accomplish this. This technique affects the current contents of the `history` collection. An alternative is the `replace` method, which does not add a new history item.
protocol	This property contains the protocol that was used to load the page. It is most likely to be `"http:"`. You could look at the value and see if it is `"http:"` or `"https:"` and make some choices about what to do in the page depending on whether you have a secure or non-secure connection. Pages loaded from your local disk will have the value `"file:"` in this property.
host	The `hostname` and `port` properties concatenated together as a single string are accessible here. Changing this value forces a reload from the new host and port.
hostname	Just the hostname. Changing this value forces a reload from a different host. All other aspects of the request will be the same.
port	Just the port number. Changing this value will attempt to connect to a different port number on the same server from which the page was previously loaded.
pathname	The folder and document description within the host that served the page. Modifying this value will request a different document from the same server and port.
search	The part of a URL that is placed following a query (?) character. These strings are usually parameters that are passed to some dynamic page-generating process in the server. Modifying this value requests a new page from the same dynamic process but with a new search key.
hash	You can name anchors throughout a document so as to scroll immediately to a place partway through a page. Changing this value will move the viewing window to a different point but will not reload the document.

The `location` object supports the following methods:

Method	Description
`reload()`	This form of the `reload` method with no parameter attempts to reload the document from the server. The reload will be aborted if the document has not been modified in the meantime. This is functionally the same as using the `history.go(0)` method but is a more appropriate naming convention for what is being scripted.
`reload(forceFlag)`	If you want to force a reload of the document, the Boolean argument should be set to `true`. If the argument is `false`, it behaves as if the argument had been omitted.
`replace(urlString)`	This will load a new document into the window but differs from the technique where you just assign a new value to the `href` property. In this case, a new history table entry is not created whereas assigning an `href` value will add a new item to the `history` collection.

The navigator Object

The `navigator` object is named after Netscape Navigator but is also present in other browsers since it has become the de facto standard for finding the name and version of a browser. You can inspect the various properties belonging to the `navigator` object and establish the name and type of the browser, its version, and the platform it is running on.

The `navigator` object provides portable support sufficient to determine what sort of browser is being used. There are, however, additional capabilities that are only available in limited situations. Oddly, the capabilities provided by IE on the Macintosh platform exceed those on the Windows platform as far as what you can do with the `navigator` object.

This is in the area of plugin and MIME-type support and you can construct a more graceful degradation of your document content by detecting that a certain plugin or MIME type is not supported before you try to use it. This support is provided principally through the `mimeTypes` and `plugins` properties both of which yield an array.

These are the portable properties of the `navigator` object:

Property	Description
`appCodeName`	This is an identifier for the application. It is now used as a generic identifier for the application and in a web browser always yields the value `"Mozilla"`. You might as well hard code a string literal constant in your script since this property isn't going to tell you anything particularly useful.

Table continued on following page

4

Property	Description
appName	This string tells you which browser is in use. It contains the values "Netscape" or "Microsoft Internet Explorer". There are no standards for this property, but detecting one or other of these is probably sufficient.
appVersion	The first part of the string returned by this property is a version number. The remainder is rather implementation dependent. You can use the parseInt and parseFloat functions to extract the major and minor version values. The rest of the string will require specialized coding and prior knowledge of the browser you expect to be targeting to be useful.
cookieEnabled	This returns a Boolean flag that indicates whether cookies are enabled or not. Netscape supports it from version 6 onwards, although IE supports it from version 4 onwards.
language systemLanguage	This property yields a language code using the two- and five-letter abbreviations. The five-letter form is a two-letter language and a two-letter regional variant, separated by an underscore. On Navigator, the language property should be used; on IE, the systemLanguage property should be used. IE also provides the userLanguage property to determine the user's preferred language.
platform	The string returned by this property tells you what platform is being used. It may be important to know whether you are displaying the page on Windows, Linux, or MacOS. From a creative point of view, you could optionally select an appropriate graphic style that is sympathetic to the platform being used.
userAgent	The string returned by this property typically contains a concatenation of appCodeName, appVersion, and a more extensive descriptive string. You can actually determine quite a lot about the user from this string although there are no standards. Since the Netscape browser became open source, some very strange values are presented in this string so you should be quite defensive in your coding style.

Listing the Supported MIME Types and Plugins

Here are some examples of browser detection. Note that they do have limited portability but are still useful. The examples use the mimeTypes and plugins properties to extract lists in the form of an array. IE implements the properties but they are empty.

This first example uses the navigator object to list all the supported MIME types in the browser:

```
<html>
<head>
<meta http-equiv="content-type" content="text/html; charset=UTF-8" />
<title>Show all mime types installed</title>
</head>
```

```
<body>
<script type="text/javascript">
for (var myIndex=0; myIndex<navigator.mimeTypes.length; myIndex++) {
  for(var myProperty in navigator.mimeTypes[myIndex]) {
    document.write(myProperty);
    document.write(":");
    document.write(navigator.mimeTypes[myIndex][myProperty]);
    document.write("<br>"); }
  document.write("<hr>");
}
</script>
</body>
</html>
```

Note that this works in Netscape Navigator and on IE for Macintosh, but oddly it doesn't work in IE for Windows. Mozilla 1.0 works fine, being essentially the same as Netscape Navigator 6. Opera 6.01 gives the `navigator.mimeTypes.length` property, but doesn't print the contents of `navigator.mimeTypes[]` so you just get a number of horizontal lines.

This is a similar script to list all the currently installed plugins:

```
<html>
<head>
<meta http-equiv="content-type" content="text/html; charset=UTF-8" />
<title>Display all plug-in names</title>
<body>
<script type="text/javascript">
for (var myIndex=0; myIndex<navigator.plugins.length; myIndex++) {
    document.write(navigator.plugins[myIndex].name);
    document.write("<hr>"); }
</script>
</body>
</html>
```

This also works on Netscape and IE for Macintosh but not in IE on the Windows platform, although Mozilla 1.0 works fine. Opera 6.01 displays all the information as well.

The screen Object

The `screen` object is accessed via a reference from the `window.screen` property. The object returned supports properties that describe the display surface that the window is drawn on. There are no methods. The Netscape browser provides several additional but non-portable properties. The properties that are available on the Netscape and IE browsers are:

Property	Description
height	The physical height of the display surface in pixels.
width	The physical width of the display surface in pixels.

Table continued on following page

Property	Description
availHeight	The height after taking any taskbars, menus, and any other permanent screen furniture into account.
availWidth	The width after taking taskbars and other permanent screen furniture into account.
colorDepth	The depth of the color space in bits per pixel. For a physical mapping this is the bit depth of the display. For palette-driven displays, this may be fewer bits than the display is capable of rendering.

Summary

In this chapter we have looked briefly at six of the more useful and readily available objects and collections we can use to find out about and manipulate the user's browser.

♦ The `window` object allows us to create new browser windows, and locate and manipulate existing ones.

♦ The `frames` collection gives us references to other `window` objects that are contained within individual frames within the current window.

♦ The `history` object gives us very limited access to the list of URLs that have been visited with the current window, and allows us to traverse that history in a limited manner.

♦ The `location` object provides an interface that allows us to examine or change the document `href` that is currently being displayed in the window.

♦ The `navigator` object gives us some potentially useful information about the user agent we're dealing with. It also gives us the ability to check what MIME types it supports and what plugins it has available (but not for IE on Windows).

♦ The `screen` object has a number of properties that describe the display surface that the window is drawn on, but doesn't allow us to change them.

Client Browser Extensions

5

- The rules of XML

- Validation with DTD and XML Schema

- Transformation with XSLT and XPath

Author: Alex Homer

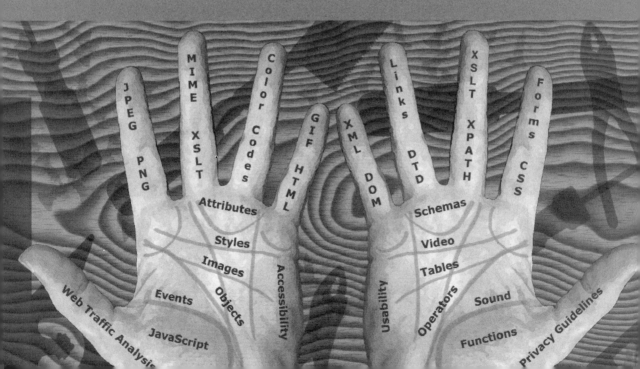

XML

This chapter discusses **Extensible Markup Language**, or XML. While XML has been around for a few years, so that most developers have had at least a taste of it, it's important to appreciate exactly how it is used, what it can do, and the rules that it imposes. In this chapter, we look at:

♦ A brief introduction to XML, and why and how you should consider using it

♦ The construction of an XML document; its elements, attributes and other nodes like processing instructions, document type declarations, and comments

♦ The rules of XML. What constitutes a well-formed and a valid XML document

♦ What XML namespaces are, and how they are used

♦ How XML can be validated, with either a DTD (Document Type Definition) or a Schema

♦ The core Document Object Model (DOM), including those aspects specifically related to XML

♦ Other XML-based standards that you may come across

We start with a look at the background and use of XML.

Introduction to XML

One problem that application developers have faced for a long time is how data can be passed from one platform to another, or one location to another, in a format that is non-proprietary. Most existing techniques (other than XML) depend on the recipient having special software installed, or at least running a compatible operating system and application. Examples of this type of data are "Office"-type documents such as word processor files or spreadsheets, or database files. On the Web, when using a browser to access data, technologies like Microsoft's Remote Data Service and other similar formats are application-specific. And even formats such as comma-delimited text (CSV or Comma-Separated-Values) require the recipient to know something about the format in use (for example, which values are numbers, and whether text values are enclosed in double quotes or not).

The Vision

Way back in 1995, Alan Cooper, designerof Microsoft Visual Basic, wrote the following in his book "*About Face*" (Wiley, ISBN 1-56884-322-4):

> "*SGML is an emerging standard that could provide a common format for exchanging data...*"

> "*In UNIX, any program can write and read an ASCII text file, regardless of the program that created it...*"

> "*Unfortunately, ASCII is a weak file format, lacking structure of any kind...*"

So it's clear that, even then, the problems we face today were well known. XML (which is based on SGML) attempts to solve all these problems by providing a way to persist and communicate data or information in a format that is:

- **Text-only**, limited to 7-bit and therefore able to be transported over the Web. And, by using specific encodings such as UTF-8 and UTF-16, any character can be represented within the 7-bit format.

- **Human-readable**, so that it is fast and easy to understand.

- **Standardized** across all operating systems and applications, so that it can be freely exchanged between any applications, and sent to any remote locations without requiring foreknowledge of the format requirements.

- **Self-describing**, with a means of specifying what the structure and content types should be.

- **Familiar** to developers, in that the syntax and structure are similar to HTML.

However, while XML looks like HTML, there are several fundamental differences:

- HTML is predominantly used to describe presentation (and layout) of documents, while XML allows you to describe both the structure *and* content. With XML, you decide what the element and attribute names are, and (within the rules for XML that we discuss shortly) how they are nested and located within the document.

- XML is a **self-describing language**, in that the element and attribute names can precisely describe the content rather than being predefined as they are in HTML.

- XML is a **subset** of SGML (Standard Generalized Markup Language), a language that is used to define other markup languages. On the other hand, HTML is a markup language that is an **application** of SGML because the meaning of the set of elements and attributes that are available is pre-defined.

In this chapter, we'll be looking at the structure of an XML document, and the way that elements and attributes are used to represent data within the document.

The Construction of an XML Document

Every XML document must conform to a set of rules that define the overall document construction and the way that elements and attributes make up the document. This is often referred to as the **grammar** of XML. In comparison, the actual element and attribute names, and the type of content they contain, are defined in a DTD or schema, which we'll come to shortly.

The overall construction of an XML document is:

- The **Document Prolog**, which can contain only:
    - Processing instructions <? ... ?>
    - The document type declaration <!DOCTYPE ...>
    - Comments <!-- ... -->.
- A **Single Root Element**, inside which all other content is contained.
- The **Document Epilog**, which can contain only:
    - Processing instructions
    - Comment elements.

In almost all cases, an XML document starts with the XML declaration, a special type of processing instruction, such as:

```
<?xml version="1.0"?>
```

This declaration can also contain information about the content of the document. The following defines the encoding of the document and specifies that there is no external DTD or schema for validation (we look at validation in general later in this chapter):

```
<?xml version="1.0" encoding="UTF-8" standalone="yes"?>
```

The Rules of XML

The actual content of an XML document looks very similar to the markup we use to create an HTML page. XML uses elements and attributes, with basically the same syntax and delimiters as HTML. However, the rules for XML are a lot stricter than those we usually find in HTML. This simplifies the parsing process for a document, and helps to avoid ambiguity when reading documents. Also this leaves less leeway for parsers to interpret the same markup differently.

Using the Correct Terminology

One important point is that we usually try to use the correct terminology when referring to XML documents, their content, and the way that they are processed. XML can be persisted to a **file** or a **document**, but there is no such thing as an XML **page**. Likewise, we do not load XML into a **browser**. We always load it into a **parser** or a **processor** (although some applications of XML, such as SVG and SMIL, which we briefly discuss later, can be loaded into a browser as they are designed to produce output from the specific elements that they contain).

When describing the contents of an XML document, be aware of the difference between **tags** and **elements**. In the following, the opening tag is `<elem type="this">` and the closing tag is `</elem>`. The tag name is just `elem`. The attribute is `type="this"`, made up of the attribute name `type` and the attribute value `this`. The **element**, however, is made up of the opening and closing tags with all the data between: `<elem type="this">the value</elem>`

Well-formedness and Validity

Two terms often applied to an XML document are:

♦ **Well-formedness**, which means that the document and all its contents conforms to all of the standard XML rules for structure (see below).

♦ **Validity**, which means that the document has a DTD (Document Type Definition) or Schema available that specifies a set of element and attribute names, how they may be structured relative to one another, and what values they can contain, and that the document conforms to all these specifications.

Remember, that well-formedness and validity are *not* the same thing. To be valid, an XML document must also be well-formed. However, a well-formed XML document may not necessarily be valid.

Standard XML Rules for Structure

To be **well-formed**, an XML document must only contain elements that:

Have a **closing tag**, or a closing "**slash**" that indicates an empty element, for example:

```
<elem-name>the value</elem-name>
```
or
```
<elem-name value="the value" />
```

Enclose all attribute values in either **single** or **double quotes**:

```
<elem-name value='the value' />
```
or
```
<elem-name value="the value" />
```

Nest properly without overlapping:

```
<i><b>my</b> value</i>
```
and not:
```
<b><i>my</b> value</i>
```

Use only **XML-legal characters** and **legal element names** (see section on element and attribute names below)

Must contain a **single root element** that contains all other content except the prolog and epilog

Element and Attribute Names

One of the most important differences between XML and HTML is that element and attribute names are always **case-sensitive**. The two elements `<MyElement>` and `<myelement>` are actually instances of two **different** elements.

Element and attribute names must start with an alphabetic character (which can be a Unicode letter character if required), an underscore '_', or a colon ':'. However, to avoid confusion when namespaces are used, it is better to avoid starting element or attribute names with a colon.

Element and attribute names **cannot contain spaces**. The W3C recommends using hyphens to separate words within an element or attribute name (for example `first-name`), or 'camel' notation (for example, `firstName`).

Legal Characters

Certain characters are not legal in XML documents. They must be replaced by the equivalent **entity reference**, or enclosed in a **CDATA section**.

Entity References

An entity reference is a way of specifying a character that is not legal within the content of a document (in other words, a character that is reserved for use as a delimiter or other special purpose). Most XML parsers recognize a set of standard entity replacements that are similar to HTML:

- less than (<) can be replaced by `&lt;`

- greater than (>) can be replaced by `&gt;`

- single quote (') can be replaced by `&apos;`

- double quote (") can be replaced by `&quot;`

- ampersand (&) can be replaced by `&amp;`

As an example, we might use the following to describe a kind of dessert made by "Bob & Joey's":

```
<ice>Bob &amp; Joey's</ice>
```

Any non-legal character can alternatively be replaced by the equivalent standard numeric entity reference. This has one of the following formats:

```
&#[decimal-unicode-character-value];
```

```
&#x[hexadecimal-unicode-character-value];
```

For example, the ampersand character can be replaced by `&#38;` or `&#x26;`. A useful list of decimal and hexadecimal character codes can be found at *http://www.unicode.org/*. See also *Appendix B*.

```
<ice>Bob &#x26; Joey's</ice>
```

Entity references cannot be used in element or attribute names, or in the value of an attribute. They can only be used within the text contained by an element.

CDATA Sections

For content that contains many non-legal characters (for example when the document contains script code), a CDATA section can be used to hide the content from the parser. Note that this is different from converting the characters into entity reference equivalents, where the content is visible to the parser:

```
<ice><![CDATA[Bob & Joey's]]></ice>
```

Whitespace Characters

Certain characters, such as spaces, tabs, and carriage returns (character codes #x20, #x9, #x0D, and #x0A) are defined in XML as being **whitespace**. These are not always processed as part of the document – they are commonly only used to make the visual representation of the document itself easier to read.

When they occur within element opening tags (between the element name and any attributes it contains) and outside of elements, they are considered to be **non-significant** whitespace characters.

Whitespace characters contained within the value of an element (between the opening and closing tags) are considered to be **significant**. They are part of the value of the element, and are processed as such.

Most XML parsers and processors can be configured to preserve (process) non-significant whitespace characters if required, while significant whitespace characters are always preserved.

An XML Document Example

The following shows an example XML document, booklist1.xml. Notice that the inherent freedom to define your own element and attribute names, and how the elements are nested, allows hierarchical data to be stored in an intuitively obvious and human-readable form:

```
<?xml version="1.0" encoding="UTF-8" standalone="yes"?>
<!-- a list of books created 2000-09-28T04:16:27 -->
<booklist>
  <book category="Dreamweaver">
    <title>Dreamweaver MX: PHP Web Development</title>
    <authors>
      <author>Bruno Mairlot</author>
      <author>Gareth Downes-Powell</author>
      <author>Tim Green</author>
    </authors>
    <publisher>glasshaus</publisher>
    <pages>320</pages>
    <isbn>1904151116</isbn>
    <price currency="USD">39.99</price>
```

```
      <price currency="GBP">28.99</price>
    </book>
    <book category="Accessibility">
      <title>Accessible Web Sites</title>
      <authors>
        <author>Jim Thatcher</author>
        <author>Sarah Swierenga</author>
        <author>Cynthia D. Waddell</author>
        <author>Bob Regan</author>
        <author>Shawn Lawton Henry</author>
        <author>Paul Bohman</author>
        <author>Michael Burks</author>
        <author>Mark D. Urban</author>
      </authors>
      <publisher>glasshaus</publisher>
      <pages>410</pages>
      <isbn>1904151000</isbn>
      <price currency="USD">49.99</price>
    </book>
  </booklist>
```

XML Namespaces

The freedom to design your own documents, and use whatever element and attribute names you like, can cause problems when your document is passed to someone else. They may need to combine documents, or carry out standardized processing. However, if the element or attribute names you have used are the same as those used in another document, but mean something different (for example a `<table>` element in one document might describe dining room furniture, while in another document it might describe a list of the high- and low-tide times at specific locations).

To avoid this, elements and attributes within an XML document can be defined as being within a specific **namespace** (in much the same way as program variables and objects are defined in a namespace when writing code).

Namespace URIs

The namespace URI (Uniform Resource Identifier) is a value that should be globally unique to your XML vocabulary. The most common value used for this is a domain name, since these are unique to your organization, and by adding something to the end of the domain name you can make it unique to a specific document or a set of documents.

> Note that the fact that it is a domain name does **not** mean that an application will access that URL. It is simply a unique identifier, and carries no connotations for access to any domain it might describe.

All elements and attributes written within an element that carries a namespace definition (using the `xmlns` attribute), as well as the element itself, are then assumed to be located within this namespace. A processor can tell that they are not the same as similarly named elements and attributes in another document that are in a different namespace.

```
<?xml version="1.0"?>
<table xmlns="http://mysite.com/defaultNamespace">
  <dimension measure="inches">
    <width>58</width>
    <height>34</height>
  </dimension>
  <number-of-legs>4</number-of-legs>
</table>
```

Namespace Prefixes

As well as specifying a namespace, it is also possible (and usually preferable for clarity) to use a prefix with each element (and sometimes with each attribute) to denote the namespace in which they reside. The prefix is declared in the namespace definition, and then used on any element or attribute that you wish to reside in that namespace.

```
<?xml version="1.0"?>
<table>
  <dimension measure="inches" xmlns:units="http://mysite.com/m-units">
    <units:width>58</units:width>
    <units:height>34</units:height>
  </dimension>
  <number-of-legs>4</number-of-legs>
</table>
```

Using Multiple Namespaces

Namespace prefixes are especially useful if there are elements from different namespaces within the document. The namespace specified using the xmlns attribute without a prefix is associated with any contained elements and attributes without a prefix.

```
<?xml version="1.0" ?>
<table xmlns="http://mysite.com/defaultNamespace"
       xmlns:number="http://mysite.com/m-number">>
  <dimension measure="inches" xmlns:units="http://mysite.com/m-units">
    <units:width>58</units:width>
    <units:height>34</units:height>
  </dimension>
  <number:number-of-legs>4</number:number-of-legs>
</table>
```

Using Namespaces with Attributes

The same rules apply to attributes within an element as to the nested elements within an element. Attributes live in the same namespace as their owning element, unless they are placed into a different namespace using a namespace prefix:

```
<?xml version="1.0"?>
<table xmlns="http://mysite.com/defaultNamespace"
       xmlns:units="http://mysite.com/m-units">
  <dimension units:measure="inches">
    <units:width>58</units:width>
    <units:height>34</units:height>
  </dimension>
  <number-of-legs>4</number-of-legs>
</glasshaus:table>
```

In this example, the `<table>`, `<dimension>`, and `<number-of-legs>` elements are in the namespace `"http://mysite.com/defaultNamespace"`, while the `measure` attribute and the `<width>` and `<height>` elements are in the namespace `"http://mysite.com/m-units"`.

Validating XML

In order to validate an XML document, there must be a definition available that denotes the structure and content that is considered to be valid. Because XML is a subset of SGML, the original and obvious technique for defining the structure and content of an XML document was to use SGML syntax. This type of definition is called a **Document Type Definition** (DTD).

However, DTDs are not the ideal answer, as they apply several serious limitations to the way that XML documents can be validated (we look at these later after describing what DTDs are). Consequently, DTDs are now generally being superseded by **XML Schemas**. We examine XML Schemas later in this chapter.

Document Type Definitions (DTDs)

A Document Type Definition or DTD is used to declare to the processor or parser exactly what "type" of document this is, in terms of the standards it complies with and the way it should be processed. The rules of SGML specify that a DTD is specified using a `<!DOCTYPE>` node. These nodes are not confined to XML documents, for example it's common for an HTML page to declare the HTML DTD that it conforms to (in this case the HTML 4.01 standard) using:

```
<!DOCTYPE HTML PUBLIC "-//W3C//DTD HTML 4.01 Transitional//EN"
          "http://www.w3.org/TR/html4/loose.dtd">
```

The values that can follow the `DOCTYPE` keyword in a declaration like this are:

♦ The document name. This is also the name of the root element in the document. In an HTML page, this will always be the value "`HTML`". This value is mandatory.

♦ The value "`PUBLIC`" or "`SYSTEM`" (in capital letters), followed by the identifier for the set of entity references used in the document. These values are optional.

- An optional specification of the DTD. This can either be:

    - **Inline**, enclosed in square brackets. This is not shown in the previous example, as it is not used with HTML documents.

    - **A URI** of the DTD. The URI `"http://www.w3.org/TR/html4/loose.dtd"` is given above.

DTD Syntax

A DTD consists of a series of SGML elements that define the elements and attributes that are used in the document. The available SGML elements are:

Name	Description	Example
ELEMENT	Defines an element and its content.	`<!ELEMENT tables (table+)>`
ATTLIST	Defines an attribute for an element, and optionally its default and permissible values.	`<!ATTLIST price currency (USD | GBP) "USD">`
ENTITY	Defines an entity that is used in the document, providing the name and the replacement text.	`<!ENTITY GBPoundSign "&#163;">`
NOTATION	Defines how the value of an element or attribute should be handled, usually describing the format or the application that should be used to handle the value.	`<!NOTATION jpeg SYSTEM "file:///C:/utils/Viewer2.exe">`

The DTD can also contain comments `<!-- ... -->` and processing instructions `<? ... ?>` if required.

A DTD Example

We'll look at the SGML elements in more detail shortly, but first here's an example of a DTD. We are using a modified version of the sample XML document you saw earlier in this chapter (without `category` attributes for the `<book>` elements), and are specifying the DTD **inline** (within the document, rather than in a separate file):

```
<?xml version="1.0"?>
<!DOCTYPE booklist [
  <!ELEMENT booklist (book*)>
  <!ELEMENT book (title,authors,publisher,pages?,isbn,price+)>
  <!ELEMENT authors (author+)>
  <!ELEMENT title (#PCDATA)>
  <!ELEMENT author (#PCDATA)>
  <!ELEMENT publisher (#PCDATA)>
  <!ELEMENT pages (#PCDATA)>
```

```
  <!ELEMENT isbn (#PCDATA)>
  <!ELEMENT price (#PCDATA)>
  <!ATTLIST price currency CDATA #REQUIRED>
]>
<booklist>
  <book>
    <title>Dreamweaver MX: PHP Web Development</title>
    <authors>
      <author>Bruno Mairlot</author>
      <author>Gareth Downes-Powell</author>
      <author>Tim Green</author>
    </authors>
    <publisher>glasshaus</publisher>
    <pages>320</pages>
    <isbn>1904151116</isbn>
    <price currency="USD">39.99</price>
    <price currency="GBP">28.99</price>
  </book>
</booklist>
```

This DTD specifies that:

- The document type is named `booklist`, and this is the root element name

- The `<booklist>` element consists of zero or more `<book>` elements

- Each `book` element contains a `<title>` element, an `<authors>` element, a `<publisher>` element, optionally a `<pages>` element, an `<isbn>` element, and one or more `<price>` elements in that order.

- Each `<authors>` element contains one or more `<author>` elements

- The `<title>`, `<author>`, `<publisher>`, `<pages>`, `<isbn>`, and `<price>` elements contain only text values and cannot contain other elements. The text values can contain **parsed character entities**, hence the term `#PCDATA`.

- The `<price>` element always has a `currency` attribute.

Element Definitions

When defining the content of an `ELEMENT`, the names of the child (nested) elements and any other content types are listed in parentheses together with special characters that define how these elements can appear. The special characters are:

Character	Description
,	A comma placed between element names defines the strict ordering of these elements within their parent element.
?	A question mark placed after an element name indicates that it is optional, and can only appear zero or one time.

Table continued on following page

211

Character	Description
+	A plus sign placed after an element name indicates that it can appear one or more times.
*	An asterisk placed after an element name indicates that it is optional and repeatable, and can appear zero or more times.
(..|..|..)	Specifies a list of valid elements or values, from which only one can appear.

Attribute Definitions

The DTD shown previously defines that the `<price>` element carries an attribute named `currency`. In the `ATTLIST` declaration, the first value is the element name and the second is the attribute name.

```
<!ATTLIST element_name attribute_name data_type appearance>
```

Attribute values can only contain text, and cannot contain parsed entities, so the `data_type` declaration for an attribute is usually `CDATA` (character data). However, it is also possible to specify a list of values that an attribute can take, and the default value if the attribute is optional and does not appear. For example, we can use the following to allow any one of four values, and specify that the default is `"USD"`:

```
<!ATTLIST price currency (USD|GBP|EURO|YEN) "USD">
```

At the end of the `ATTLIST` declaration is `appearance`: a definition of when and how the attribute can appear, and what values it can take:

- The value `#REQUIRED` means that the attribute must appear whenever this element is used in a document.

- The value `#IMPLIED` means that the attribute is optional.

- The value `#FIXED` specifies that an attribute will always have a fixed value, and is followed by what the value is: `<!ATTLIST price currency CDATA #FIXED "USD">`.

Finally, note that multiple attributes for an element can be defined in an `ATTLIST` element:

```
<!ATTLIST book name CDATA #REQUIRED
               topic CDATA #REQUIRED>
```

Entity Definitions

An entity is a key or token that specifies the actual content that will replace it in the document when it is parsed. Entities can be defined as being **internal** or **external**, which indicates where the value for the entity is found.

Internal entity definitions have the entity name and value defined within the `ENTITY` declaration:

```
<!ENTITY GBPoundSign "&#163;">
<!ENTITY copyright "Copyright glasshaus">
```

We could use these in an XML document like this:

```
<details>
  This book is priced at &GBPoundSign; 29.50 and is available now.
  &copyright;
</details>
```

External entities are used in the same way, but are defined in a separate document. This allows easier maintenance and reuse with other XML documents. The ENTITY element specifies the name of the entity, and the location of the file or resource containing the values:

```
<!ENTITY contents SYSTEM "http://mysite.com/contents/contents.xml">
```

Notation Definitions

A NOTATION element is used to "connect" a value in an XML document with a specific feature of the parser or processor, so that (usually) it can present that value in the appropriate way. However, notations can be used whenever it is necessary to pass instructions to the processor about how the values should be interpreted or formatted.

As an example, the following declares two NOTATION elements that provide specific meaning for "gif" and "jpeg" by indicating the applications that should be used to present the information. Then an ELEMENT named logo is defined with two attributes named "image-path" and "viewer" (which can only be "gif" or "jpeg"):

```
<!NOTATION gif  SYSTEM "file:///C:/utils/Viewer1.exe">
<!NOTATION jpeg SYSTEM "file:///C:/utils/Viewer2.exe">
<!ELEMENT logo #PCDATA>
<!ATTLIST logo image-path CDATA #REQUIRED
               viewer NOTATION (gif|jpeg)>
```

Within the XML document, we can then include an instance of this element:

```
<logo image-path="http://www.glasshaus.com/glasshaus.gif" viewer="gif">
  This is the alternative text for non-graphical clients
</logo>
```

Providing that the recipient has the appropriate application installed, the processor should be able to display the image.

Attaching a DTD to an XML Document

Our previous example included the DTD within the document. However, we can place it in a separate file and link to it. This allows markup declarations to be reused in multiple documents.

```
<?xml version="1.0" encoding="UTF-8" standalone="no"?>
<!DOCTYPE booklist SYSTEM "booklist.dtd">
<booklist>
  <book>
  ...
  </book>
</booklist>
```

The linked file (`booklist.dtd`) contains only the DTD:

```
<!ELEMENT booklist (book*)>
<!ELEMENT book (title,authors,publisher,pages?,isbn,price+)>
<!ELEMENT authors (author+)>
<!ELEMENT title (#PCDATA)>
<!ELEMENT author (#PCDATA)>
<!ELEMENT publisher (#PCDATA)>
<!ELEMENT pages (#PCDATA)>
<!ELEMENT isbn (#PCDATA)>
<!ELEMENT price (#PCDATA)>
<!ATTLIST price currency CDATA #REQUIRED>
```

What's Wrong with DTDs?

While DTDs are useful in defining the absolute structure (and to some extent the content) of an XML document, it's clear that they do have some severe shortcomings:

♦ They provide **poor semantic checking support**: for example, it's not possible to define exactly how many repeated elements are allowed. They also make it difficult to define the structure where content can be of mixed types.

♦ They provide **no way to define data types** for the values of elements or attributes. Everything is either parsed character data (`#PCDATA`) or plain text (`#CDATA`), though it is possible to define `ID` and `IDREF` types to provide links between elements.

♦ There is **no provision for defining the scope** in which elements or attributes are valid.

♦ There is **no support for inheritance**, so you can't easily reuse and adapt or extend complex element types for use in other documents.

♦ They use a **non-intuitive (SGML) syntax**.

XML Schemas

XML schemas overcome many of the shortcomings of DTDs:

♦ They have provision for **data typing**, including byte, date, integer, sequence, SQL & Java primitive data types, and others.

♦ They define a **type system** that is adequate for importing and exporting data from all kinds of database systems using native formats.

- They allow creation of **user-defined data types**, such as data types that are derived from existing data types and which may constrain certain of its properties (for example, range, precision, or length).

- They are **written in XML**, so they can be manipulated like any other XML document.

This last point is important, because it allows us to create, read, and process schemas in exactly the same way as we do XML documents (for example we can apply transformations using XSLT, or manipulate them using the XML DOM methods described later in this chapter).

The XML Schema standards are relatively new, and so other manufacturers have developed other standards purely to be able to implement something useful in their products while waiting for the final standards recommendation. For example, Microsoft has been using XML Data Reduced Schemas (XDR) for some time. However, now that the standards are available, they have switched to using the XML Schema (XSD) standards.

XML Schema Syntax

The rich and extensible nature of XML Schemas means that they are necessarily more complicated to explain and understand than DTDs. The W3C specifications detailing them fully run to several hundred pages. So, in this section, we confine ourselves to providing a concise overview of the syntax, structure, and workings of XML Schemas.

XML Schemas can be used to define two types of nodes and their content:

- **Simple types** are nodes that contain only parsed character data. They cannot contain other nested nodes or markup, and they cannot have any attributes.

- **Complex types** are everything else – nodes that can contain other nodes or markup and may have attributes.

It is also possible to define either of these types in two ways:

- As new **type definitions** (either simple or complex), which are then used elsewhere in the schema (or inherited into other schemas) to define concrete instances of that complex node type. In simple terms, we can use this type definition in the declaration of elements that actually appear in the document. It means that the types are reusable, making maintenance easier because changing the type definition changes all the instances that use the type.

- As concrete **instance declarations**, defining the elements (both simple and complex), attributes (complex types only), and markup content (complex types only) with specific names that appear in the document.

Defining a Schema for the Book List

To demonstrate the basic principles of XML Schemas, we describe the construction of a schema for the XML document containing a list of books that we saw earlier in this chapter, complete with `category` attribute for `<book>` elements. An abridged listing of that document is shown next:

```
<?xml version="1.0" encoding="UTF-8" standalone="yes"?>
<booklist>
  <book category="Dreamweaver">
    <title>Dreamweaver MX: PHP Web Development</title>
    <authors>
      <author>Bruno Mairlot</author>
      <author>Gareth Downes-Powell</author>
      <author>Tim Green</author>
    </authors>
    <publisher>glasshaus</publisher>
    <pages>320</pages>
    <isbn>1904151116</isbn>
    <price currency="USD">39.99</price>
    <price currency="GBP">28.99</price>
  </book>
  <!-- more books here -->
</booklist>
```

The complete XML Schema, `booklist_schema.xsd`, (which we discuss in the following sections) is:

```
<?xml version="1.0"?>

<xsd:schema xmlns:xsd="http://www.w3.org/2001/XMLSchema">

  <xsd:annotation>
    <xsd:documentation xml:lang="en">
     Schema for list of books.
    </xsd:documentation>
   </xsd:annotation>

  <xsd:element name="booklist" type="bookListType"/>

  <xsd:complexType name="bookListType">
    <xsd:element name="book" type="bookType" minOccurs="0"
                 maxOccurs="unbounded"/>
  </xsd:complexType>

  <xsd:complexType name="bookType">
    <xsd:sequence>
      <xsd:element name="title" type="xsd:string"/>
      <xsd:element name="authors" type="authorListType"/>
      <xsd:element name="publisher" type="xsd:string"/>
      <xsd:element name="pages" type="xsd:positiveInteger" minOccurs="0"/>
      <xsd:element name="isbn" type="xsd:string"/>
      <xsd:element ref="priceType"/>
     </xsd:sequence>
    <xsd:attribute name="category" type="xsd:string"/>
  </xsd:complexType>

  <xsd:complexType name="authorListType">
```

```
      <xsd:element name="author" type="xsd:string" maxOccurs="unbounded"/>
    </xsd:complexType>

    <xsd:complexType name="priceType">
      <xsd:element name="price" type="xsd:decimal"/>
      <xsd:attribute name="currency" type="currencyType" />
    </xsd:complexType>

    <xsd:simpleType name="currencyType">
      <xsd:restriction base="xsd:string">
        <xsd:enumeration value="USD"/>
        <xsd:enumeration value="GBP"/>
        <xsd:enumeration value="EURO"/>
        <xsd:enumeration value="YEN"/>
      </xsd:restriction>
    </xsd:simpleType>

</xsd:schema>
```

The Schema Declaration

The XML schema for the book list starts with the XML declaration, and contains the root element named xsd:schema:

```
<?xml version="1.0"?>

<xsd:schema xmlns:xsd="http://www.w3.org/2001/XMLSchema">
```

The namespace shown here is that for the May 2001 version 1.0 release of the XML Schema recommendations. Some parsers and processors may use a different namespace URI, as they may be built to use one of the previous releases of the specifications.

Annotations

Schemas can be annotated to allow human-readable information to be included, as well as allowing automated document handling or information systems to read the annotations. An <annotation> element can contain any number of <appinfo> and <documentation> elements, plus any other elements and attributes that are **not** in the XML Schema namespace (in our example here, these cannot use names starting with xsd:):

```
<xsd:annotation>
  <xsd:documentation xml:lang="en">
    Schema for list of books.
  </xsd:documentation>
</xsd:annotation>
```

Simple Element Instance Declarations

The XML document containing the list of books consists of a single root element <booklist>. In the schema, we can use a simple instance declaration of this element by naming it directly. The simple instance we're declaring here inherits its definition from a complex type named bookListType:

```
<xsd:element name="booklist" type="bookListType"/>
```

Alternatively, the type attribute can be one of the standard data types defined within XML Schema. The most commonly used data types are shown in the following table:

Character string types	string, normalizedString
Byte and binary data types	Boolean, unsignedByte, base64Binary, hexBinary
Integer number types	integer, int, unsignedInt, positiveInteger, negativeInteger, nonPositiveInteger, nonNegativeInteger, long, unsignedLong, short, unsignedShort
Non-integer number types	decimal, float, double
Date and time types, (including parts of a date)	time, date, dateTime, duration, gMonth, gYear, gYearMonth, gDay, gMonthDay

Simple Element Type Definitions – The currencyType Type

We also include a second simple declaration. However, this time it is a type definition that we'll use elsewhere in the schema, and not an instance declaration of an actual element (as shown in the previous code extract). The type is named `currencyType`, is of data type `string`, and it can only have one of the four values specified within the `<restriction>` element:

```
<xsd:simpleType name="currencyType">
  <xsd:restriction base="xsd:string">
    <xsd:enumeration value="USD"/>
    <xsd:enumeration value="GBP"/>
    <xsd:enumeration value="EURO"/>
    <xsd:enumeration value="YEN"/>
  </xsd:restriction>
</xsd:simpleType>
```

We can use this type elsewhere in the schema to declare and restrict the content of an element or an attribute.

Complex Type Definitions – The <booklist> Element

We've seen that a list of books is made up of a `<booklist>` element that is of type `bookListType`. This type is defined next. It is a complex type because it contains other elements, and not just parsed character data. This content is zero or more `<book>` elements:

```
<xsd:complexType name="bookListType">
  <xsd:element name="book" type="bookType" minOccurs="0"
               maxOccurs="unbounded"/>
</xsd:complexType>
```

There may be zero `<book>` elements (as defined by the `minOccurs="0"` attribute) in a `bookListType`, or any number greater than this (`maxOccurs="unbounded"`). If the `minOccurs` attribute is omitted, the default is 1 (the element or type must appear at least once). The default for `maxOccurs` is also 1 if omitted. So, if both are omitted, the element or type must appear only once.

Complex Type Definitions – The <book> Element

The `<book>` elements are defined as being of type `bookType`, and the definition of this type comes next. It consists of a sequence of elements and types, and so the content can only appear in the specified order.

Notice that the `<authors>` element consists of an `authorListType`, while the `<price>` element is defined as just a reference (`ref`) to a `priceType`. All the other elements are defined in terms of one of the basic XML Schema data types. The `<pages>` element is optional in our book list document, so it has a `minOccurs="0"` attribute in the schema.

```
<xsd:complexType name="bookType">
  <xsd:sequence>
    <xsd:element name="title" type="xsd:string"/>
    <xsd:element name="authors" type="authorListType"/>
    <xsd:element name="publisher" type="xsd:string"/>
    <xsd:element name="pages" type="xsd:positiveInteger" minOccurs="0"/>
    <xsd:element name="isbn" type="xsd:string"/>
    <xsd:element ref="priceType"/>
  </xsd:sequence>
  <xsd:attribute name="category" type="xsd:string"/>
</xsd:complexType>
```

Referencing Existing Types

The `<price>` element in the `bookType` definition shown previously is referenced with the attribute `ref="priceType"`, and without a `name` or a `type` attribute, while all the others are explicitly named using a `name` element and have the type definition or built-in data type specified.

Referencing a type without specifying a name (using a `ref` attribute instead of a `name` attribute) means that the element will inherit the name specified in the definition of the type. Any change to the `name` attribute for the element in the type definition will change the name of every element instance that inherits from that type.

Alternatively, when we include the `name` and `type` attributes, we can use a name for the element that is different from that specified in the type definition. This allows us where required (though not shown here) to use the same type definition to create instances of elements that have different names in the document.

Declaring Attributes – The category Attribute

The `bookType` definition also contains the declaration of an attribute named `category`. Any element that is declared using this type definition (in our case, a `<book>` element) will carry this attribute.

```
<xsd:attribute name="category" type="xsd:string"/>
```

An `<attribute>` declaration can also carry three other attributes:

Attribute	Description	Value(s)
use	The attribute being declared for this element or type can be optional, required, or prohibited. The default if omitted is `"required"`.	`use="required"` `use="prohibited"` `use="optional"`
default	The default value for an attribute that is optional.	`default="`*default-value*`"`
fixed	The value that the attribute must have when it appears.	`fixed="`*fixed-value*`"`

Attribute Groups

If there are several attributes that appear together, a complex type can be created that uses an **attribute group**. The attribute group is defined using `<attribute>` elements in the usual way:

```
<xsd:attributeGroup name="myAttrGroup">
  <xsd:attribute name="alignment" type="xsd:string"/>
  <xsd:attribute name="size " type="xsd:integer"/>
  <xsd:attribute name="color" type="xsd:string"/>
</xsd:attributeGroup>
```

Then the attribute group can be used in the definition of the element type:

```
<xsd:complexType name="myElementType">
  <element name="myElement" type="xsd:string"/>
  <xsd:attributeGroup ref="myAttrGroup"/>
</xsd:complexType>
```

Complex Type Definitions – The *<authors>* Element

The `<authors>` element in the XML book list can contain one or more `<author>` elements. In the definition of the `bookType`, it was defined as being of type `authorListType`. This is another complex type that defines the contained elements (`<author>` elements) as being of data type `string`. It can appear one or more times because there is no `minOccurs` attribute, and the `maxOccurs` attribute is set to `"unbounded"`:

```
<xsd:complexType name="authorListType">
  <xsd:element name="author" type="xsd:string" maxOccurs="unbounded"/>
</xsd:complexType>
```

Complex Type Definitions – The *<price>* Element

The final element used in the book list is the `<price>` element. In the definition of a `bookType`, we used:

```
       <xsd:element ref="priceType"/>
```

So the `priceType` definition must give the element a name (or inherit from another type definition that names the element). The data type is decimal:

```
    <xsd:complexType name="priceType">
      <xsd:element name="price" type="xsd:decimal"/>
      <xsd:attribute name="currency" type="currencyType"/>
    </xsd:complexType>
```

Note that the `<price>` element also has an attribute named `currency`. This uses the simple type definition of a `currencyType` type, which was shown earlier in this section of the chapter. So the `currency` attribute can only take one of the four specified string values shown in the definition.

Attaching a Schema to an XML Document

The XML schema specification defines two attributes `xsi:schemaLocation` and `xsi:noNamespaceSchemaLocation` in the namespace `http://www.w3.org/2001/XMLSchema-instance` to allow you to link an XML document to a schema. The latter is used when the XML Schema does not have a target namespace. For example:

```
    <?xml version="1.0" encoding="UTF-8" standalone="yes"?>
    <booklist xmlns:xsi="http://www.w3.org/2001/XMLSchema-instance"
              xsi:noNamespaceSchemaLocation="booklist_schema.xsd" />

    ...
    </booklist>
```

However, many applications, parsers, and processors provide a mechanism for validating an XML document against a specified schema without requiring that the schema be linked directly to the XML document. This approach provides for more freedom in using the appropriate schema, and only validates the document when required.

The XML Document Object Model

So far, this chapter has been concerned with the structure and validation of an XML document. However, XML was designed to allow documents to be manipulated using standard techniques that are common to all parsers and XML processors. The W3C recommendation (the XML DOM Level 2 Core Specification) defines the objects, methods, and properties that a compliant XML parser should make available for manipulating the content of a loaded XML document.

These objects, methods, and properties can be accessed in any language that the parser and operating system support. For client-side script using a parser that is installed on the client's machine, the usual language is JavaScript. Techniques for using JavaScript are contained in *Chapter 3*, with HTML DOM references in *Chapter 6*.

XML DOM Objects

The XML DOM specifies a series of object types (or interfaces) that can be used to access the various types of node (element, attribute, comment, processing instruction, and so on) in an XML document. These objects are listed in the following table. The final column indicates the numeric "node type" value. The first four objects in the table are base objects from which others inherit, and these do not have a "type" value:

Object	Description	Node Type Value
Node	A generic object that represents any type of node in a document. All specific node types inherit from `Node` and extend it to provide the required properties and methods.	–
NodeList	A collection or array of `Node` objects. Can be accessed by index only.	–
NamedNodemap	A collection or array of `Attr` nodes that can be accessed by name or index.	–
CharacterData	A generic object that represents nodes that contain text values, such as a `Comment` node or the `Text` node that contains the value of an `Element` node.	–
Document	Represents the entire XML document.	9
DocumentType	Represents the document type declaration, for example: `<!DOCTYPE booklist [ ... DTD here ... ]>`	10
DocumentFragment	Represents a section of XML (one or more nodes and their content) that have been created dynamically or loaded into the parser, but not yet inserted into the document "tree".	11
ProcessingInstruction	Represents a processing instruction node such as: `<?xml-stylesheet href="style.xsl"?>`	7
Element	Represents an element within the XML document.	1
Attr (attribute)	Represents an attribute of an element within the XML document.	2
Text	Represents the text content of an element within the XML document. The text content of an element is not a property of the element – it is the value of a `Text` node that is a child of the element.	3

Object	Description	Node Type Value
`Comment`	Represents a comment within the XML document, such as: `<!-- this is my document -->`	8
`Entity`	Represents an entity within the DTD of the XML document, for example: `<!ENTITY GBPoundSign "&#163;">`	6
`EntityReference`	Represents an entity reference within the XML document, for example: `&GBPoundSign;`	5
`CDATASection`	Represents a CDATA section within the XML document, for example: `<![CDATA[Bob & Joey's]]>`	4

`Notation`	Represents a notation within the DTD of the XML document, for example:
	
	`<!NOTATION jpeg SYSTEM`
	`            "file:///C:/View.exe">`
		12

Base XML DOM Objects and Object Hierarchy

The following diagram shows the inheritance hierarchy of the XML DOM objects. You can see that most of them inherit from `Node`, and so have all the properties and methods of the `Node` object. In two cases (`Comment` and `Text`), the objects inherit from the `CharacterData` object, which itself inherits from `Node`. The `CDATASection` object inherits from `Text` which itself inherits from `CharacterData`. Finally, `NodeList` and `NamedNodeMap` are separate – they do no inherit from `Node`:

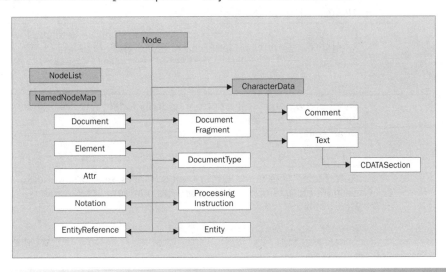

Next we'll take a look at the properties and methods of the four base objects (shown as shaded in the diagram): `Node`, `NodeList`, `NamedNodeMap`, and `CharacterData`. After this we look at the other specific objects in more detail. The tables indicate which properties and methods were added to the XML DOM Level 2, and are not available in Level 1.

Node Object

Property	Description and Syntax
`attributes`	Returns an `NamedNodeMap` object containing all the attributes of this node. Read-only. `NamedNodeMap = Node.attributes`
`childNodes`	Returns a `NodeList` containing all the child nodes of the node. Read-only. `NodeList = Node.childNodes`
`firstChild`	Returns a `Node` object representing the first child of the node. Read-only. `Node = Node.firstChild`
`lastChild`	Returns a `Node` object representing the last child of the node. Read-only. `Node = Node.lastChild`
`localName` *(added in Level 2)*	Returns the name of the current node without any namespace prefix that might be present. Read-only. *string* = `Node.localName`
`namespaceURI` *(added in Level 2)*	Returns the namespace URI for the node (not the namespace prefix). Read-only. *string* = `Node.namespaceURI`
`nextSibling`	Returns a `Node` object representing the node immediately following this node at the same level in the hierarchy of the document. Read-only. `Node = Node.nextSibling`
`nodeName`	Returns the name of the current node including any namespace prefix that might be present. Read-only. *string* = `Node.nodeName`
`nodeType`	Returns the type of the current node (that is, element, attribute, `CDATA` section, etc.) as one of the node type numbers listed earlier. Read-only. *integer* = `objXmlNode.nodeType`

Property	Description and Syntax
nodeValue	Sets or returns the value of the node. *string* = Node.nodeValue Node.nodeValue = *string*
ownerDocument	Returns a reference to the Document object for the document to which the node belongs. Read-only. Document = Node.ownerDocument
parentNode	Returns a Node object representing the parent of this node (for nodes that can have parents). Read-only. Node = Node.parentNode
prefix *(added in Level 2)*	Sets or returns the namespace prefix for the node. *string* = Node.prefix Node.prefix = *string*
previousSibling	Returns a Node object representing the node immediately preceding this node at the same level in the hierarchy of the document. Read-only. Node = Node.previousSibling

Method	Description and Syntax
appendChild()	Adds a specified node to the end of the list of the children of this node. Takes a Node object that represents the node or document fragment to be appended as its single parameter, and returns a reference to the node after it has been inserted. AppendedNode = ThisNode.appendChild(NodeToAppend)
cloneNode()	Returns a copy of the Node object. When the parameter is true, the method should also clone all descendant nodes of this node. NewNode = ThisNode.cloneNode(*Boolean*)
hasAttributes() *(added in Level 2)*	Returns a Boolean value indicating whether the node has any attributes. Read-only. *Boolean* = Node.hasAttributes()
hasChildNodes()	Returns a Boolean value indicating whether the node has any child nodes. Read-only. *Boolean* = Node.hasChildNodes()

5

XML

Method	Description and Syntax
insertBefore()	Inserts a specified `Node` immediately before another specified `Node`. A `Node` object representing the node to be inserted is passed as the first parameter, and a `Node` object representing an existing node in the document is passed as the second parameter. The method returns a reference to the inserted node. `InsertedNode = ThisNode.insertBefore(NodeToInsert, ExistingNode)` Note that if the `ExistingNode` parameter is `null`, `insertBefore()` behaves like the `appendChild()` method, in that the new node is placed at the end of the list of child nodes.
isSupported() *(added in Level 2)*	Tests whether the current DOM implementation (parser or processor) implements a specific feature, and if the current node supports that feature. The two parameters to the method are `String` types, and it returns `true` if the feature is supported. *Boolean* = `Node.isSupported(`*feature, version*`)`
normalize()	Puts all descendent `Text` nodes of this node into "normal" form, where only markup (tags, comments, processing instructions, `CDATA` sections, entity references, etc.) separates `Text` nodes. In other words, there are no adjacent `Text` nodes. There is no return value. `Node.normalize()`
removeChild()	Removes a specified child node. Accepts a `Node` object that represents the child node to be removed as the single parameter, and returns a reference to the removed node. `RemovedNode = ThisNode.removeChild(NodeToRemove)`
replaceChild()	Replaces the specified child node with a new node. Takes a `Node` object that represents the node or document fragment to replace the existing one as the first parameter, and a `Node` object that represents an existing node in the document as the second parameter. Returns a reference to the node that has been replaced (the existing node). `ReplacedNode = ThisNode.replaceChild(NewNode, NodeToReplace)` If the specified node does not exist, the new node is inserted after any existing child nodes.

NodeList Object

Property	Description and Syntax
`length`	Returns the number of nodes in the `NodeList`. Read-only (but will change as the `NodeList` changes). *integer* = `NodeList.length`

Method	Description and Syntax
`item()`	Returns a `Node` object based on the index position within the `NodeList` given as a parameter. `Node = NodeList.item(`*unsigned-long*`)`

NamedNodeMap Object

Property	Description and Syntax
`length`	Returns the number of nodes in the `NamedNodeMap`. Read-only (but will change as the `NamedNodeMap` changes). *integer* = `NamedNodeMap.length`

Method	Description and Syntax
`item()`	Returns a `Node` object based on the index position within the `NamedNodeMap` given as a parameter. `Node = NamedNodeMap.item(`*unsigned-long*`)`
`getNamedItem()`	Returns a `Node` object specified using the name of the node. `Node = NamedNodeMap.getNamedItem(`*node-name*`)`
`getNamedItemNS()` *(added in Level 2)*	Returns a `Node` object specified using the namespace URI (not the namespace prefix) and the local name of the node. `Node = NamedNodeMap.getNamedItemNS(`*namespace-uri*, *local-name*`)`
`removeNamedItem()`	Removes a `Node` object specified using the name of the node, and returns it. `RemovedNode = NamedNodeMap.removeNamedItem(`*string*`)`

Table continued on following page

Method	Description and Syntax

removeNamedItemNS()
 	
(added in Level 2)
	Removes a `Node` object specified using the namespace URI (not the prefix) and the local name of the node, and returns it.
	
	`RemovedNode = NamedNodeMap.removeNamedItemNS`
	`(`*namespace-uri*, *local-name*`)`

setNamedItem()	Adds a `Node` object that specifies the name of the node to the `NamedNodeMap` and returns `null` unless a `Node` with the same name already exists, in which case the new `Node` replaces the existing `Node` and the existing node is returned. `(Node | null) = NamedNodeMap.setNamedItem(Node)`
setNamedItemNS() *(added in Level 2)*	Adds a `Node` object that specifies the URI and local name of the node to the `NamedNodeMap` and returns `null` unless a `Node` with the same name already exists, in which case the new `Node` replaces the existing `Node` and this existing node is returned. `(Node | null) = NamedNodeMap.setNamedItemNS(Node)`

CharacterData Object

Property	Description and Syntax
length	Returns the number of characters contained within the value of the `Node`. Read-only. *unsigned-long* = `CharacterDataNode.length`
data	Sets or returns the character data that makes up the value of the `Node` as a `String`. *string* = `CharacterDataNode.data` `CharacterDataNode.data` = *string*

Method	Description and Syntax
appendData()	Appends the specified `String` to the end of the `Node` content. No return value. `CharacterDataNode.appendData(`*string*`)`
deleteData()	Deletes characters from the `Node` content. The start position and number of characters are provided as `unsigned long` parameters. No return value. `CharacterDataNode.deleteData(`*start-offset*, `                              `*character-count*`)`

Method	Description and Syntax
`insertData()`	Inserts the specified `String` into the `Node` content at the specified start position. No return value. `CharacterDataNode.insertData(`*start-offset*`, string)`
`replaceData()`	Replaces the specified characters within the `Node` content with a new `String`. The start position and number of characters are provided as `unsigned long` parameters. No return value. `CharacterDataNode.replaceData(`*start-offset*`,` *character-count, string*`)`
`substringData()`	Returns a string of characters from the value of the `Node`. The start position and number of characters are provided as `unsigned long` parameters. *string* `= CharacterDataNode.substringData(`*start-offset*`,` *character-count*`)`

Specific XML DOM Objects

Each of the objects or interfaces that represent a specific node type, such as `Element`, `Attr`, and `Comment`, inherits from `Node`. Hence they have all the methods and properties of the `Node` object. Some also inherit from other base objects such as `CharacterData` and `Text` (as shown in the earlier diagram), and so expose the properties and methods of these objects as well. Then, to these properties and methods they each add other properties and methods that are required to perform the manipulation of that type of `Node` in the document.

Document Object

The `Document` object represents the entire XML document. It adds methods to create new instances of `Node` objects (elements, attributes, comments, and so on), methods to import nodes from other documents, and methods to find nodes within a document:

Property	Description and Syntax
`doctype`	Returns the complete node containing the `DOCTYPE` declaration as a `DocumentType` node. Read-only. `DocumentType = Document.doctype`
`implementation`	Returns a `DOMImplementation` object that can be used to check what features the parser or processor supports. Read-only. `DOMImplementation = Document.implementation`
`documentElement`	Returns a reference to the root element for the document, as an `Element` node. Read-only. `Element = Document.documentElement`

Method	Description and Syntax
`createAttribute()`	Creates a new `Attr` node, using the specified name for the attribute (as a `String`). Returns a reference to the new `Attr` node. `Attr = Document.createAttribute(`*name*`)`

`createAttributeNS()`
 	
(added in Level 2)
	Creates a new `Attr` node, using the specified URI as a `String`, and qualified name as a `String` (that is, *prefix*:*local-name*). Returns a reference to the new `Attr` node.
	
	`Attr = Document.createAttributeNS`
	`(`*namespace-uri*`, `*qualified-name*`)`

`createCDATASection()`	Creates a new `CDATASection` node, using the specified `String` as the content. Returns a reference to the new `CDATASection` node.
	
	`CDATASection =`
	`Document.createCDATASection(`*string*`)`

`createComment()`	Creates a new `Comment` node, using the specified `String` as the content. Returns a reference to the new `Comment` node. `Comment = Document.createComment(`*string*`)`

`createDocumentFragment()`	Creates a new empty `DocumentFragment` node. Takes no parameters. Returns a reference to the new `DocumentFragment` node.
	
	`DocumentFragment =`
	`Document.createDocumentFragment()`

`createElement()`	Creates a new `Element` node, using the specified tag name as a `String` for the `Element` name. Returns a reference to the new `Element` node. `Element = Document.createElement(`*tag-name*`)`

`createElementNS()`
 	
(added in Level 2)
	Creates a new `Element` node, using the specified URI as a `String`, and qualified name as a `String` (that is, *prefix*:*local-name*). Returns a reference to the new `Element` node.
	
	`Element =`
	`Document.createElementNS(`*namespace-uri*`,`
	qualified-name`)`

Method	Description and Syntax

createEntityReference()	Creates a new `EntityReference` node, using the specified name as a `String`. Returns a reference to the new `EntityReference` node.
	
	`EntityReference =`
	`Document.createEntityReference(name)`

createProcessingInstruction()	Creates a new `ProcessingInstruction` node, using the specified *target-name* `String` as the name for the node, and a `String` that specifies the content of the node. Returns a reference to the new `ProcessingInstruction` node.
	
	`Processing Instruction =`
	`Document.createProcessingInstruction (target-name, data)`

createTextNode()	Creates a new `Text` node, using the specified `String` as the content of the node. Returns a reference to the new `Text` node. `TextNode = Document.createTextNode(string)`

getElementById()
(added in Level 2)
	Returns an `Element` node based on its `id` attribute (`String`) value. Requires the document to have an associated schema or DTD, which defines an attribute of the element as being of type `ID`. Returns `null` if the element is not located.
	
	`(Element | null) =`
	`Document.getElementById(id-string)`

getElementsByTagName()	Returns a `NodeList` object containing all the elements in the document that have the specified (`String`) element tag name. Use an asterisk as the parameter to get all elements. `NodeList = Document.getElementsByTagName(tag-name)`

getElementsByTagNameNS()
(added in Level 2)
	Returns a `NodeList` object containing all the elements in the document that have the specified (`String`) value for their namespace URI (not element prefix) and the specified (`String`) value for their local name.
	
	`NodeList =`
	`Document.getElementsByTagNameNS(namespace-uri, local-name)`

5

XML

Table continued on following page

Method	Description and Syntax
importNode *(added in Level 2)*	Imports a `Node` into the parser as an unattached `Node` or `DocumentFragment`, ready to be inserted into the document. Takes a reference to the `Node` to import and a `Boolean` value to indicate if all descendant nodes and content are to be imported as well as the specified node. Returns a reference to the imported node. `Node = Document.importNode(SourceNode, `*`Boolean`*`)`

Remember that after a new `Node` object of any type has been created or imported into the parser, it must be inserted into the document at the required position using the `insertBefore()`, `appendChild()`, or `replaceChild()` methods of another `Node` object already in the document.

DocumentType Object

The `DocumentType` object represents the document type declaration, for example:

```
<!DOCTYPE books [ ... DTD declarations here ... ]>
```

If this node contains an inline DTD, this is also contained within the `DocumentType` node.

Property	Description and Syntax
name	Returns the name of the DTD (the value immediately following the `DOCTYPE` keyword), as a `String`. This is also (generally) the tag-name of the root element. Read-only. *string* = `DocumentType.name`
entities	Returns a `NamedNodeMap` that references all `Entity` nodes defined within the `DOCTYPE` element. Read-only. `NamedNodeMap = DocumentType.entities`
notations	Returns a `NamedNodeMap` that references all `Notation` nodes defined within the `DOCTYPE` element. Read-only. `NamedNodeMap = DocumentType.notations`
publicId *(added in Level 2)*	Returns the `PUBLIC` (ID) value defined in the `DOCTYPE` element as a `String`. Read-only. *string* = `DocumentType.publicId`
systemId *(added in Level 2)*	Returns the `SYSTEM` (ID) value defined in the `DOCTYPE` element as a `String`. Read-only. *string* = `DocumentType.systemId`

Property	Description and Syntax
internalSubset *(added in Level 2)*	Returns the complete content of the `DOCTYPE` element as a `String`. Read-only. *string* = `DocumentType.internalSubset`

DocumentFragment Object

The `DocumentFragment` object represents a section of XML (one or more nodes and their content) that have been created dynamically or loaded into the parser, but not yet inserted into the document "tree". It inherits directly from `Node`, and has no properties and methods other than those of the `Node` object.

ProcessingInstruction Object

The `ProcessingInstruction` object represents a processing instruction node such as:

```
<?xml-stylesheet type="text/xsl" href="style.xsl"?>
```

Property	Description and Syntax
target	Returns the instruction name. In the code example above, the `target` property is the string: `xml-stylesheet`. Read-only. *string* = `ProcessingInstruction.target`
data	Sets or returns the complete content of the node except for the name of the instruction. In the code example above, the `data` property is the string: `type="text/xsl" href="style.xsl"`. *string* = `ProcessingInstruction.data` `ProcessingInstruction.data` = *string*

Element Object

The `Element` object represents an element within the XML document. It inherits directly from `Node`, so it exposes all the properties and methods of the `Node` object. It also adds a range of specific properties and methods appropriate for this type of node:

Property	Description and Syntax
tagName	Returns the name of the element, as in the opening tag. *string* = `Element.tagName`

Method	Description and Syntax
`getAttribute()`	Returns the value of an `Attr` node from the element as a `String`, using the name of the attribute (also specified as a `String`). *string* = `Element.getAttribute(`*name*`)`
`getAttributeNS()` *(added in Level 2)*	Returns the value of an `Attr` node from the element as a `String`, using the specified URI as a `String`, and local name (excluding the prefix) as a `String`. *string* = `Element.getAttributeNS(`*namespace-uri, local-name*`)`
`getAttributeNode()`	Returns an attribute from the element as an `Attr` object, using the name of the attribute (specified as a `String`). `Attr` = `Element.getAttributeNode(`*name*`)`
`getAttributeNodeNS()` *(added in Level 2)*	Returns an attribute from the element as an `Attr` object, using the specified URI as a `String`, and local name (excluding the prefix) as a `String`. `Attr` = `Element.getAttributeNodeNS(`*namespace-uri, local-name*`)`
`getElementsByTagName()`	Returns a `NodeList` object containing all the descendant elements of this element that have the specified (`String`) element tag name. Use an asterisk to represent all elements. `NodeList` = `Element.getElementsByTagName(`*tag-name*`)`
`getElementsByTagNameNS()` *(added in Level 2)*	Returns a `NodeList` object containing all the descendant elements of this element that have the specified (`String`) value for their namespace URI (not element prefix) and the specified (`String`) value for their local name. `NodeList` = `Element.getElementsByTagNameNS(`*namespace-uri, local-name*`)`
`hasAttribute()` *(added in Level 2)*	Returns a `Boolean` value indicating whether the element contains the specified attribute, using the name of the attribute (also specified as a `String`). *Boolean* = `Element.hasAttribute(`*name*`)`
`hasAttributeNS()` *(added in Level 2)*	Returns a `Boolean` value indicating whether the element contains the specified attribute, using the specified URI as a `String`, and the local name (excluding the prefix) as a `String`. *Boolean* = `Element.hasAttributeNS(`*namespace-uri, local-name*`)`

Method	Description and Syntax
removeAttribute()	Removes the specified attribute from the element using the name of the attribute (also specified as a `String`). No return value. `Element.removeAttribute(name)`

removeAttributeNode()	Removes the attribute (specified as an `Attr` object) from the element. Returns the attribute that was removed as an `Attr` object.
	
	`RemovedAttr =`
	`Element.removeAttributeNode(AttrToRemove)`

removeAttributeNS() *(added in Level 2)*	Removes the specified attribute from the element using the specified URI as a `String`, and the local name (excluding the prefix) as a `String`. No return value. `Element.removeAttributeNS(namespace-uri, local-name)`
setAttribute()	Adds an attribute to the element with the specified (`String`) name and (`String`) value, or sets the value of an existing attribute with that name. No return value. `Element.setAttribute(name, value)`
setAttributeNS() *(added in Level 2)*	Adds an attribute to the element with the specified namespace URI as a `String`, the qualified name as a `String` and value as a `String`, or sets the value of an existing attribute with that namespace URI and qualified name. No return value. `Element.setAttributeNS(namespace-uri, qualified-name, value)`
setAttributeNode()	Adds an attribute to the element using an `Attr` object that references an attribute with the required name. Returns the attribute that was added or set as an `Attr` object. `Attr = Element.setAttributeNode(Attr)`
setAttributeNodeNS() *(added in Level 2)*	Adds an attribute to the element using an `Attr` object that references an attribute with the required namespace URI, prefix, and local name. Returns the attribute that was added or set as an `Attr` object. `Attr = Element.setAttributeNode(Attr)`

Attr (attribute) Object

The `Attr` object represents an attribute of an element within the XML document. It inherits directly from `Node`, so it exposes all the properties and methods of the `Node` object – plus four other properties:

Property	Description and Syntax
name	Returns the name of the attribute. Read-only. *string* = Attr.name
ownerElement *(added in Level 2)*	Returns an Element object that references the element node that contains this attribute. Read-only. Element = Attr.ownerElement
specified	Returns a Boolean value that is true if this attribute exists and contains a value, or false if it appears only because a default value is specified in the schema or DTD. Read-only. *Boolean* = Attr.specified
value	Sets or returns the value of the attribute as a String. *string* = Attr.value Attr.value = *string*

Text Object

The Text object represents the text content of an element or elsewhere within the XML document. The text content of an element is not a property of the element – it is the value of a Text node that is a child of the element. It inherits from CharacterData, and so exposes all the properties of the Node object and the CharacterData object – plus one extra method:

Method	Description and Syntax
splitText()	Divides a Text node into two separate Text nodes at the offset specified by the unsigned long parameter. This is the opposite of the normalize() method, and useful if you want to insert other nodes within the content of the node at a specific point. Returns the specified characters from the end of the content as a new Text object. NewTextNode = TextNode.splitText(*offset*)

Comment Object

The Comment object represents a comment within the XML document, such as:

```
<!-- this is my document -->
```

It inherits from CharacterData, and so exposes all the properties of the Node object and the CharacterData object. It has no specific properties or methods of its own.

Entity Object

The `Entity` object represents an entity within the DTD of the XML document, for example:

```
<!ENTITY GBPoundSign "&#163;">
```

It inherits directly from `Node`, and so it exposes all the properties and methods of the `Node` object plus three properties that are specific to this type of node:

Property	Description and Syntax
`publicId`	Returns the `PUBLIC` (ID) value defined in the `Notation` node, as a `String`. Read-only. *string* = `Entity.publicId`
`systemId`	Returns the `SYSTEM` (ID) value defined in the `Notation` node, as a `String`. Read-only. *string* = `Entity.systemId`
`notationName`	Returns the name of the notation for the entity for unparsed entities. For parsed entities, this is `null`. *string* | `null` = `Entity.notationName`

EntityReference Object

The `EntityReference` object represents an entity reference within the XML document, for example: `&GBPoundSign;`. It has no properties and methods other than those of the `Node` object from which it inherits.

CDATASection Object

The `CDATASection` object represents a CDATA section within the XML document, for example:

```
<![CDATA[Bob & Joey's]]>
```

It inherits from `Text`, so exposes all the properties of the `Node` object, the `CharacterData` object, and the `Text` object. It has no properties and methods other than those of the objects from which it inherits.

Notation Object

The `Notation` object represents a notation within the DTD of the XML document, for example:

```
<!NOTATION jpeg SYSTEM "file:///C:/View.exe">
```

It inherits directly from `Node`, so it exposes all the properties and methods of the `Node` object, plus two properties that are specific to this type of node:

Property	Description and Syntax
publicId	Returns the PUBLIC (ID) value defined in the Notation node, as a String. Read-only. *string* = Notation.publicId
systemId	Returns the SYSTEM (ID) value defined in the Notation node, as a String. Read-only. *string* = Notation.systemId

Loading XML Documents into a Parser

While the XML DOM specifications are thorough in providing access to an XML document, they do not yet provide specifications for loading (and saving) XML documents with a parser or processor. Instead, each parser or processor manufacturer implements specific methods of their own for these tasks.

We'll now look at examples of **loading** a XML document for the Microsoft and Mozilla web browsers. In general, it is not possible to **save** the content of the parser locally because of the security restrictions of the browser.

Also bear in mind that the parsers installed on client machines may not support the full version 2.0 of the XML DOM. In this case, it is wise where possible to use only the version 1.0 methods and properties.

Loading XML Documents into IE

Internet Explorer version 5.0 and above installs the Microsoft MSXML parser, and this can be used to manipulate an XML document. There are two ways to load XML into the MSXML parser:

- ◆ As an **XML data island**, where the XML is specified along with the HTML sourcecode of the page.

- ◆ By loading it **synchronously** or **asynchronously** into an instance of the parser.

Loading XML as a Data Island

IE 5 and above allow use of the <xml> element within an HTML page to create an XML data island (note that this collides with the HTML 4 and XHTML 1.0 specifications):

```
<!-- HTML markup goes here-->
<xml id="myXMLDoc">
  <?xml version="1.0" ?>
  <booklist>
    <book>
      <!-- The rest of the XML goes here -->
```

```
      </book>
    </booklist>
  </xml>
  <!-- HTML markup goes here-->
```

Rather than specifying the XML directly in the source of the page, it can also be loaded directly from the server by specifying the URL of the XML document as the `src` property of the `<xml>` element:

```
  <!-- HTML markup goes here-->
  <xml id="myXMLDoc" src="books.xml"></xml>
  <!-- HTML markup goes here-->
```

In either case, the XML document is automatically loaded into an instance of the MSXML parser, which can then be referenced through the `id` of the `<xml>` element. Any loading or parsing errors are indicated by the `parseError` object's `errorCode` and `reason` properties. The `parseError` object is one of the specific objects included in the MSXML parser that allow documents to be loaded and saved:

```
  <script type="text/jscript">
    // get reference to data island
    oXMLData = document.all['myXMLDoc'];

    // check for a loading error
    if (oXMLData.parseError.errorCode != 0)
    {
      alert('Invalid XML file: ' + oXMLData.parseError.reason);
    }
    else
    {
      // now OK to access XML document
    }
  </script>
```

Synchronously Loading XML into the MSXML Parser

Using the MSXML parser directly is fundamentally the same as the previous example. The XML document instance is created using a `new ActiveXObject` statement, by specifying the class name string of the document object. To use the default version of MSXML, the class name is `MSXML.DOMDocument`. (Other versions can be used by specifying these directly, such as `MSXML2.DOMDocument.2.0` or `MSXML2.FreeThreadedDOMDocument`.)

After creating the XML document instance, the `async` property is set to `false` to indicate that loading should be synchronous (that is, the call to the `load()` method will not return until the document has finished loading). We also turn off validation of the document by setting the `validateOnParse` property to `false`. If required, and a schema or DTD is available and linked to the XML document, it can be validated by setting this property to `true`.

Then we call the `load()` method to load the XML document, and check for an error after loading has completed:

```
<script type="text/jscript">
  // create a new parser object instance
  oXMLData = new ActiveXObject('MSXML.DOMDocument');

  // set the other parser properties
  oXMLData.async = false;
  oXMLData.validateOnParse = false;

  // and load the document
  oXMLData.load('books.xml');

  // check for a loading error
  if (oXMLData.parseError.errorCode != 0)
  {
    alert('Error loading XML file: ' + oXMLData.parseError.reason);
  }
  else
  {
    // now OK to access XML document
    alert(oXMLData.documentElement.nodeName);
  }
</script>
```

XML can also be loaded into the MSXML parser as a `String` that contains the XML (instead of using the URL of the XML document). In this case, the `loadXml()` method is used:

```
oXMLData.loadXML('<?xml version="1.0" ?><booklist>... etc...</booklist>');
```

Asynchronously Loading XML into the MSXML Parser

XML documents can be loaded into MSXML asynchronously if required. This allows code in the page to continue executing while the XML is being loaded, giving a more responsive user experience. In this case, we have to create two separate functions that will look after loading the document and handling the event that occurs when the document is loaded.

The `async` property is set to `true` to indicate that the XML should be loaded asynchronously, and an extra property setting must be made to indicate to the parser the name of a function that it should call whenever the `readyState` property of the parser object changes:

```
<script type="text/jscript">
  function loadXMLDoc()
  {
    // create a new document object instance
    var oXMLData = new ActiveXObject('MSXML.DOMDocument');

    // set the other parser properties
    oXMLData.async = true;
    oXMLData.validateOnParse = false;

    // connect event with function to check when loading completes
    oXMLData.onreadystatechange = changeFunction;
```

```
    // and load the document
    oXMLData.load('books.xml');
}
```

As the parser loads the data, a regular series of `readystatechange` events are raised, and the **callback function** that is specified for the `onreadystatechange` property is executed. The value of the `readyState` property of the parser indicates what is happening as the loading progresses, with values from 1 (initializing), through 2 (loading) and 3 (parsing), to 4 (complete). At this point the callback function can check for an error, and start to process the XML document:

```
function changeFunction()
{
  // check value of readyState property of XML parser
  // value 4 indicates loading complete
  if (oXMLData.readyState == 4)
  {
    if (oXMLData.parseError.errorCode != 0)
    {
      // there was an error while loading
      alert('Error loading XML file: ' + oXMLData.parseError.reason);
    }
    else
    {
      // now OK to access XML document
      alert(oXMLData.documentElement.nodeName);
    }
  }
}

  loadXMLDoc();
</script>
```

Loading XML Documents into Netscape 6+ and Mozilla

Netscape 6.0 and Mozilla use the **Expat** parser, which allows asynchronous loading of XML documents by default, but the overall approach is similar to that in IE. However, in Mozilla, the parser is created as an `implementation` of the current document, which returns an XML document object. Then an event listener is added to the document that specifies the name of the callback function that will be called for the `load` event, after it is complete. Finally, the `load()` method is called:

```
<script type="text/javascript">
  function loadXMLDoc()
  {
    // create a parser instance
    var xmlDoc = document.implementation.createDocument('', '', null);

    // specify the event to listen far and the callback function name
    xmlDoc.addEventListener('load', documentLoaded, false);

    xmlDoc.load('books.xml');
  }
```

The callback function defined as the event listener (here named `documentLoaded`) is executed once loading is completed. In it we can check for an error, or use the XML document if there was no loading error:

```
function documentLoaded(e)
{
  if (!this.documentElement)
  {
    alert('Error loading XML file');
  }
  else if (this.documentElement.nodeName == 'parsererror')
  {
    alert('Error parsing XML document: ' +
          this.documentElement.firstChild.nodeValue);
  }
  else
  {
    // process document, for example:
    alert(this.documentElement.nodeName);
  }
}

loadXMLDoc();
</script>
```

To load an XML document synchronously, you can use the `XMLHttpRequest` object instead:

```
<script type="text/javascript">
  var xmlDocument;

  function loadXMLDocument (url)
  {
    if (typeof XMLHttpRequest != 'undefined')
    {
      var httpRequest = new XMLHttpRequest();
      httpRequest.open('GET', url, false);
      httpRequest.send(null);
      return httpRequest.responseXML;
    }
  }

  window.onload = function ()
  {
    xmlDocument = loadXMLDocument('books.xml');
    if (xmlDocument)
    {
      alert(xmlDocument.documentElement.nodeName);
      alert(new XMLSerializer().serializeToString(xmlDocument));
    }
  };
</script>
```

Note that Mozilla and Netscape do not ignore whitespace text nodes, unlike IE which does. In a document where whitespace is used to make the page more human-readable, this causes problems in cross-browser scripting. To get around this issue, use the `nodeType` property of the `Node` object to check for a value of 3 (meaning a text node) and if so, navigate the DOM tree as appropriate.

XML DOM Examples

This section contains three examples of how the DOM methods described earlier can be used to manipulate the contents of an XML document once it is loaded into the `xmlDoc` variable in an XML 1.0 and XML DOM 2.0 compliant parser.

Modifying an Existing Node

The first example uses the `firstChild` property of the root element of the document to get a reference to a `NamedNodeMap` containing the attributes of that node. Then it accesses the value of the attribute's child `Text` node, and inserts characters into it using the `insertData()` method:

```
//get the root element
theRoot = xmlDoc.documentElement;

//get the attributes for the first "book" node
mapBookAttrs = theRoot.firstChild.attributes;

// get the text node for the first attribute
attrBookText = mapBookAttrs[0].firstChild;

//insert the word 'Computer' in front of it
attrBookText.insertData(0, 'Computer ');
```

Building a NodeList and Removing Existing Nodes

The next example uses the `getElementsByTagName()` method of the `Document` object to get a `NodeList` of all elements with the name "author", and displays how many it found. Assume that the XML document that this script is working on has `<first-name>` and `<last-name>` elements within each `<author>` element. The script gets a reference to the `<first-name>` element for each `<author>` element in turn, and removes it from the document:

```
//get the root element
theRoot = xmlDoc.documentElement;

//get NodeList of <author> element nodes
listNodes = theRoot.getElementsByTagName('author');

//display the number found
alert('Found ' + listNodes.length + ' authors');

//loop through the list of authors
```

```
for (i = 0; i < listNodes.length; i++)
{
  //get a reference to this <first-name> node
  fNameNode = listNodes[i].childNodes(0);

  // ... and remove it from the document
  listNodes(i).removeChild(fNameNode);
}
```

Creating and Inserting New Nodes

The third example creates a new element named `"reviewed"`, and then gets a reference to the `firstChild` of the `firstChild` of the root element (in this example, we assume it is a `<book_title>` element). Next it inserts the new `<reviewed>` element into the document before the `<book_title>` element as a sibling (at the same level in the document hierarchy). Finally, it creates a new `Text` node with the value `"2002-10-28"` and appends that as a child of the new `<reviewed>` element – effectively setting the value of the `<reviewed>` element:

```
//get the root element
theRoot = xmlDoc.documentElement;

//create a new child element
newElem = xmlDoc.createElement("reviewed");

//get reference to first book_title element
titleElem = theRoot.firstChild.firstChild;

//insert reviewed element into document
newElem = theRoot.firstChild.insertBefore(newElem, titleElem);

//create a new text-type node
newText = xmlDoc.createTextNode("2002-10-28");

//append to reviewed element
newElem.appendChild(newText);
```

Other XML-Based Standards

This chapter is concerned with XML; other than XML Schemas, it avoids discussing other XML-based technologies or standards in depth. However, there are hundreds of applications of XML already available or under development. Remember that an **application of XML** is a set of rules that lays down a specific structure, and specific names for the elements and attributes in an XML document, so that it can be used by and for a specific application. The most important of these applications of XML are briefly discussed in the following sections.

Extensible Hypertext Markup Language (XHTML)

As we saw in *Chapter 1*, **XHTML 1.0** is a reformulation of HTML 4.0 into an XML-compatible syntax. XHTML pages are treated as valid XML documents, and handled in the same way as any other XML document. However, at the same time, an XHTML 1.0 document should also render without problems in an existing HTML-based browser (like IE 6 or Netscape 4). For this to work, the web page must be valid in XML terms, as well as containing appropriate content for rendering in a browser.

In fact, this is not difficult to achieve. The issue is that most web browsers are fairly relaxed about the validity of the HTML they can handle, and automatically make up for minor errors such as missing end tags and badly formed content. For a document to be considered as valid XHTML (and XML), it cannot contain this kind of invalid content.

XML Path Language (XPath)

XPath is a language for selecting sections of the content of any XML document. It provides features for pattern matching and filtering to select nodes, and functions to work with numbers, `String`, and `Boolean` values. It is also used in XSLT for matching templates and other processes. See the W3C site at *http://www.w3.org/TR/xpath* for more details. At the time of writing, XPath version 2.0 is a working draft. The latest recommendations are version 1.0, and this is the version that is described in this section of the chapter.

A Brief Guide to XPath

XPath supports two different approaches for pattern matching and filtering:

♦ The original proposal, now called the **Abbreviated Syntax**

♦ The new syntax, officially termed **Axes**

The following table compares the two syntaxes for the basic ways of specifying a node in an XML document:

Abbrev.	Axis	Meaning
/	`child`	Selects direct children of the current node
//	`descendant`	Selects nodes anywhere 'below' the current node
.	`self`	Selects the current node
..	`parent`	Selects the parent of the current node
@	`attribute`	Selects an attribute node from the current node
*	*	Selects all nodes irrespective of their name

The Axes syntax also adds several new selectors that can be used to specify the nodes that are matched (filtered) by XPath:

Axis	Meaning
ancestor	All direct ancestor nodes
following-sibling	The siblings of the current node (children of its parent) that follow the current node in the XML source.
preceding-sibling	The siblings of the current node (children of its parent) that precede the current node in the XML source.
descendant-or-self	The current node and all its descendants
ancestor-or-self	The current node and all its ancestors
following	All nodes following the current node in the order of the XML source
preceding	All nodes preceding the current node in the order of the XML source
namespace	The namespace node (for an element node only)

XPath Functions

XPath also includes several useful functions that can be used to specify the nodes that will be matched or selected:

String functions:	string() concat() starts-with() contains() substring() substring-before() substring-after() string-length() normalize-space() translate()
Numeric functions:	number() sum() floor() ceiling() round()
Boolean functions:	boolean() not() true() false() lang()

XPath Examples

The following table demonstrates some equivalent XPath expressions in both the abbreviated and the axes syntaxes:

XPath Axes Syntax	Abbreviated Syntax	Meaning
child::book	/book	All child elements of the current element that are named book.
descendant::book	//book	All descendant elements below the current element in the hierarchy of the document that are named book.

XPath Axes Syntax	Abbreviated Syntax	Meaning
`parent::book`	`../book`	The parent element of the current element, but only if it is named `book` (to get the parent element irrespective of the name use `parent::*` or `../*`).
`child::book[3]`	`/book[3]`	The third of the child elements of the current element that are named `book`.
`attribute::title`	`@title`	The attribute named `title` of the current element.
`attribute::dept="Sales"`	`@dept[.="Sales"]`	The attribute named `dept` of the current element, but only if it has the value `"Sales"`.
`attribute::width &gt; 10`	`@width[.&gt;10]`	The attribute named `width` of the current element, but only if it has a value that is greater that 10. Note the entity replacement for ">" that is required by the rules of XML document structure.

The next table shows some more complex examples of XPaths, using only the axes syntax:

XPath Axes syntax	Meaning
`child::*[attribute::status='OK']`	Any elements that are children of the current element, irrespective of the name of those elements, so long as they have an attribute named `status` that has the value `"OK"`.
`child::*[self::chapter or self::title]`	Any element that is a child of the current element, that is named `chapter` or `title`. The asterisk denotes an element with any name, but the condition part of the XPath (in square brackets) uses `self` to refer to the element being matched.
`child::para[position()=last()-1]`	The last but one of the child elements of the current element that have the element name `para`. The `position()` function is used to specify which element is matched in the list of child elements.

XPath Axes syntax	Meaning
`descendant::customer[starts-` `        with(child::customerID, 'A')]`	Any descendants of the current node that have the element name `customer`, where that `customer` element has a child element named `customerID`, and the value of that `customerID` element starts with the character "A".

Extensible Stylesheet Language (XSL)

XSL is a two-part technology designed to allow recursive processing of XML documents to add styling and presentation information, and to change their structure and/or content by applying a transformation. It has now evolved into:

- ♦ **XSL Transformations (XSLT)**. XSLT specifies how stylesheets written in an XML-compliant format can be used to transform one XML document into another XML document or even into documents in different formats. This is achieved through the use of templates that are matched via XPath expressions to specific elements or other parts of the document. These templates specify the content and structure of the output document at the points where the original document contains the matched elements or other content. This output can include nodes and values taken from the original document.

- ♦ **XSL Formatting Objects (XSL-FO)**. XSL-FO attempts to define a syntax for adding style to an XML document using a similar approach to CSS (Cascading Style Sheets), but in an XML-compliant syntax. At the present time, the standard is still under development, and there are few applications generally available that implement it.

See the W3C specifications at *http://www.w3.org/Style/XSL/* for more details.

A Brief Guide to XSLT

XSLT provides a recursive processing system: the stylesheet includes templates that are executed only when they match a specific node in the XML document. The match is defined using XPath, as defined in the previous section of this chapter. Each template specifies the actions that are to be carried out as it is executed. This could be generating output or executing another template.

An Example XML Document

To demonstrate how XSLT works, and the common elements, functions, and techniques, this section uses a simple XML document containing sales details of three computing books. Note the second line, which defines that the XML parser or processor should use the stylesheet named `book_report.xslt` to apply the presentation information to the document:

```
<?xml version="1.0"?>
<?xml-stylesheet type="text/xsl" href="book_report.xslt"?>
<booklist>
<item>
  <code>1043</code>
  <category>CSS</category>
```

```
   <release_date>2002-May</release_date>
   <title>Cascading Style Sheets: Separating Content from
     Presentation</title>
   <sales>127853</sales>
  </item>
  <item>
   <code>1051</code>
   <category>Scripting</category>
   <release_date>2002-Mar</release_date>
   <title>Practical JavaScript for the Usable Web</title>
   <sales>1375298</sales>
  </item>
  <item>
   <code>1086</code>
   <category>XML</category>
   <release_date>2002-Oct</release_date>
   <title>Practical XML for the Web</title>
   <sales>297311</sales>
  </item>
 </booklist>
```

An Example XSLT Stylesheet

The XSLT stylesheet named `book_report.xslt` applies several transformations to the content of the XML document. As well as generating HTML so that a normal web browser can display the content, it adds a heading, changes the ordering of the `<item>` elements, and displays information about the level of sales for each one – including adding an image when the sales are below a certain target level:

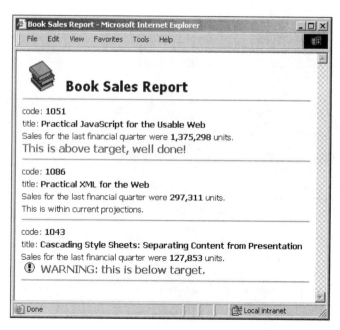

The Stylesheet Structure

An XSLT stylesheet is an XML document, so it consists of the XML declaration and a single root element. This root element is named `<xsl:stylesheet>` and must contain a namespace declaration that defines the XSLT standard that it conforms to. At the time of writing, XSLT version 2.0 is a working draft. The latest recommendation is version 1.0, and this is the version that is used in the example here.

```
<?xml version="1.0"?>
<xsl:stylesheet version="1.0"
                xmlns:xsl="http://www.w3.org/1999/XSL/Transform">
  <!-- Stylesheet Content -->
</xsl:stylesheet>
```

Inside the `<xsl:stylesheet>` root element are placed one or more `<xsl:template>` elements that define the way that the content of the XML document will be transformed. Other elements can be included as well, to define things like the output presentation (indenting, whitespace handling, parameters, and variables):

The Template for the Root Element

XSLT rules specify that the parser or processor should automatically look for a template that matches the root node of the document when it starts to process a stylesheet. This template carries the attribute `match="/"` to indicate that it matches the root node. This is the first template of the example stylesheet used to create the output shown earlier:

```
<xsl:template match="/">
  <html>
  <head>
  <title>Book Sales Report</title>
  <style type="text/css">
   body    {font-family:Tahoma,Arial,sans-serif;
             font-size:10pt; font-weight:normal;
             line-height:140%}
   .heading {font-family:Tahoma,Arial,sans-serif;
             font-size:16pt; font-weight:bold}
   .over    {font-family:Tahoma,Arial,sans-serif;
             font-size:12pt; color:green; font-weight:bold}
   .under   {font-family:Tahoma,Arial,sans-serif;
             font-size:12pt; color:red; font-weight:bold}
  </style>
  </head>
  <body>
  <div class="heading">
    <img src="books.gif" align="bottom" hspace="10" />
    Book Sales Report
  </div>
  <hr />
  <xsl:for-each select="descendant::item">
    <xsl:sort select="child::sales" order="descending" data-type="number" />
    <xsl:apply-templates select="child::code" />
    <xsl:apply-templates select="child::title" />
```

```
      <xsl:apply-templates select="child::sales" />
      <xsl:apply-templates select="child::release_date" />
      <hr />
    </xsl:for-each>
    </body>
    </html>
  </xsl:template>
```

In the example here, the template contains a mixture of content. Any elements in the `xsl` namespace (those with the prefix `"xsl:"`) are processed as instructions within the stylesheet. Any other content is output as text. So, as the template shown above is processed, the output will contain the opening `<html>` and `<head>` tags, the `<title>` element complete with the page title, the `<style>` element and its content, the closing `<head>` element, the opening `<body>` element, and a `<div>` with its content (an image and the page heading) followed by an `<hr />` element (note the space and closing slash required to make it valid in an XML document). This creates the visible section at the start of the page shown in the earlier screenshot.

Repeating Content

Next, the processor encounters the `<xsl:for-each>` element. This is a **repetition** instruction, and indicates that the processor should repeat the contained instructions for each node that matches the XPath expression specified in the `select` attribute. In the example stylesheet, the XPath selects all descendant elements that are named "`item`":

```
<xsl:for-each select="descendant::item">
```

Sorting the Results Set

Inside the `<xsl:for-each>` element is an `<xsl:sort>` element. This sorts the results set according to the value of the various attributes within this element. The example shown sorts the `<item>` elements into descending order of the value of their child element named `sales`. The `data-type` attribute indicates that these values are numeric, and should be sorted as such:

```
<xsl:sort select="child::sales" order="descending" data-type="number" />
```

Applying Other Templates

After the `<xsl:sort>` element come four `<xsl:apply-templates>` elements. These contain a `select` attribute that specifies (with an XPath expression) element(s) within the document. It instructs the processor to execute the template that best matches these elements.

```
<xsl:apply-templates select="child::code" />
<xsl:apply-templates select="child::title" />
<xsl:apply-templates select="child::sales" />
<xsl:apply-templates select="child::release_date" />
```

So, for the first of these instructions, the `select` attribute specifies that the template that best matches the `<code>` child elements of the current element should be executed.

Note that the nodes known as the **current context** change when the `<apply-templates>` instruction is processed. At the moment, in the template that contains the `<apply-templates>` element, the current context is one of the `<item>` elements selected by the `<xsl:for-each>` instruction. When the template that matches the `<code>` elements is executed, the current context is that `<code>` element. Once processing for that element is complete, execution returns to the template containing the `<xsl:for-each>` instruction and the current context returns to the `<item>` element. Then the next instruction in that template is executed. This is where the recursive nature of XSLT is demonstrated.

As we said earlier, the `<apply-templates>` instruction executes the template that **best matches** the selected node specified by the XPath in the `select` attribute. Often more than one template will match a node. In the example stylesheet there are three other templates:

```
<xsl:template match="sales">
  <!-- template content here -->
</xsl:template>

<xsl:template match="release_date">
  <!-- template content here -->
</xsl:template>

<xsl:template match="*">
  <!-- template content here -->
</xsl:template>
```

For the `<code>` elements, only the last of these templates matches, because it uses the XPath "*" expression that matches any element. However, when processing a `<sales>` element, there are two that match: the first and the last. In this case, only the first one, which specifies the element name, will be executed. The best match can depend on the element, its value, the attributes it carries, the value of these attributes, and the position within the document. The element that matches on most of the specified values for any of these factors is classed as the best match, and will be chosen for execution.

Outputting Element Names and Values

The last template in the stylesheet (match="*") is shown next. It contains two `<xsl:value-of>` instructions, separated by a semicolon and a space. The first `<xsl:value-of>` instruction carries a `select` attribute that uses the XPath function `name()` to output the name of the current element:

```
<xsl:template match="*">
  <xsl:value-of select="name()" />:
  <strong><xsl:value-of select="." /></strong><br />
</xsl:template>
```

The semicolon and a space are then output as literal text, followed by execution of the second `<xsl:value-of>` instruction that simply outputs the value of the current element using the XPath expression "." (that is, "current node"). So the output generated by this template is the name and value of the current element. This creates the first two lines for each item shown in the previous screenshot and repeated here:

```
code: 1051
title: Practical JavaScript for the Usable Web
```

Formatting Numbers and Conditional Execution

A template can contain **conditional** processing instructions. For example, the template that is executed for each `<sales>` element first outputs the value of that element, using the XSLT `format-number()` function against the current element (`"."`) and applying the format string `"#,###,##0"`.

Next comes an `<xsl:choose>` instruction. This can contain one or more `<xsl:when>` sections, and optionally an `<xsl:otherwise>` section that is processed only if *none* of the `<xsl:when>` sections are processed. The `<xsl:when>` instruction carries a `test` attribute that specifies the expression to evaluate. If it returns `true`, the content of that `<xsl:when>` section is processed or output:

```
<xsl:template match="sales">
  Sales for the last financial quarter were <strong>
  <xsl:value-of select="format-number(., '#,###,##0')" />
  </strong> units.<br />
  <xsl:choose>
    <xsl:when test=". &gt; 350000">
      <span class="over">This is above target, well done!</span><br />
    </xsl:when>
    <xsl:when test=". &lt; 150000">
      <span class="under">
        <xsl:element name="img">
          <xsl:attribute name="src">under.gif</xsl:attribute>
          <xsl:attribute name="align">bottom</xsl:attribute>
          <xsl:attribute name="hspace">5</xsl:attribute>
        </xsl:element>
        WARNING: this is below target.
      </span><br />
    </xsl:when>
    <xsl:otherwise>
      This is within current projections.<br />
    </xsl:otherwise>
  </xsl:choose>
</xsl:template>
```

The first `<xsl:when>` instruction in the example stylesheet is executed only when the value of the current element is greater than 350000 (note the use of "`&gt;`" for ">" here). The output generated is an HTML `<span>` element with the CSS style named "`over`", containing a congratulatory message.

The second `<xsl:when>` instruction is executed only when the value of the current element is less than 150000 (using "`&lt;`" for "<"). The output generated in this case is an HTML `<span>` element with the CSS style named "`under`". However, this time the content is an XSL instruction.

Creating Elements and Attributes

To create other HTML elements, the stylesheet has simply to output them as text. However, often the content of an element (or even the name) depends on values in the XML source document, so cannot be written in this way. The example stylesheet outputs an HTML `<img>` element from the second `<xsl:when>` section. While it could have been declared as literal text, like the one at the top of the page, it has been generated using stylesheet instructions to illustrate how to create elements that cannot be hardcoded.

The `<xsl:element>` instruction creates an element node in the output that has the name specified in the `name` attribute, in this case `img`. Inside the `<xsl:element>` element are a series of `<xsl:attribute>` elements that generate the attributes required for the new `<img>` element:

```
<xsl:element name="img">
  <xsl:attribute name="src">under.gif</xsl:attribute>
  <xsl:attribute name="align">bottom</xsl:attribute>
  <xsl:attribute name="hspace">5</xsl:attribute>
</xsl:element>
```

The output that this section of the stylesheet creates is:

```
<img src="under.gif" align="bottom" hspace="5"></img>
```

Together with the `<span>` element and literal text on this `<xsl:when>` section, the output looks like this:

Values from the XML document can also be included in an element or its attributes. For example, if the XML document contains a series of repeated `<image-url>` elements that hold the URL of an image, and `<description>` elements that hold a text description of each image, these values could be used to create the specific output for each image like this:

```
<xsl:element name="img">
  <xsl:attribute name="src">
    <xsl:value-of select="image-url" />
  </xsl:attribute>
  <xsl:attribute name="alt">
    <xsl:value-of select="description" />
  </xsl:attribute>
</xsl:element>
```

This might create HTML output like the following:

```
<img src="image1.gif" alt="This is image 1"></image>
<img src="image2.gif" alt="This is image 2"></image>
<img src="image3.gif" alt="This is image 3"></image>
```

Conditional Execution with an "If " Construct

XSLT also provides the equivalent to the `"If"` construct in traditional programming languages, but there is no `"Else"` section in XSLT. The `<xsl:if>` instruction carries a `test` attribute. Only if the expression in this attribute evaluates to `true` is the content of the `<xsl:if>` instruction executed.

In the template that is processed for each `<release_date>` element in the XML document, the XPath `substring-before()` function is used to test whether the first four characters of the value of this element (the year in our example) is a `String` that is less than (comes before in ANSI code terms) the `String` value `"2001"`. If so, it outputs some literal text. This can be seen in the last line of the output in the earlier screenshot of the complete page:

```
<xsl:template match="release_date">
  <xsl:if test="substring-before(., '-') &lt; '2001'" >
    Note that this is an old title, and is now out of print.
  </xsl:if>
</xsl:template>
```

There is a great deal more to XSLT than this chapter has room to cover, but what we have covered should provide a useful grounding and introduction to basic XSLT techniques.

XML Linking Language (XLink)

Elements of XML have no inherent 'meaning', so `<a>` outside an XHTML or HTML document means nothing. It certainly doesn't create a link between resources or documents. **XLink** is a rich syntax that uses XPath to select any sections of the target document as the "end point" of a link. It will eventually (once physical applications are available that use it) be able to provide 'Related Items' links and pop-up target lists. For more details see *http://www.w3.org/TR/xlink/*.

Resource Description Framework (RDF)

RDF is a way of defining metadata (data about data) for a document or resource, for example a description of a web page. This will lead in time to far better indexing and search capabilities, but depends on the source documents being XML-compliant (and most non-XHTML web pages today are not). RDF is not limited to indexing web pages, however, and can be used wherever metadata storage or distribution is required. See *http://www.w3.org/RDF/* for more details.

Simple Object Access Protocol (SOAP)

One fast-growing area of development on the Internet is **Web Services**. These provide a platform-independent and OS-independent way of sharing information, and (probably more importantly) implementing a programmatic interface that can be accessed over HTTP. In other words, a web server can expose programmatic methods that can be called from a remote client.

Web Services basically allow objects to communicate over HTTP, through proxy servers, using only standard protocol techniques. This is achieved by using XML as the data transport protocol, and SOAP is the basis for all this. It defines the way that parameters, return values, and messages are wrapped in XML for transmission. Other standards used in Web Services, such as the Web Service Description Language (WSDL), are also XML-based. For more details see *http://www.w3.org/2002/ws/*.

Scalable Vector Graphics (SVG)

SVG is an application of XML that provides a language for describing two-dimensional graphics. The main focus is on the creation of **vector graphic shapes**, which are basically just paths consisting of straight lines and curves. However, SVG can also be used to define images and text.

As well as being declaratively defined in the source file, SVG can be scripted using the standard methods of the XML DOM through a parser of choice. Each object within the rendered output also exposes events such as `onmouseover` and `onclick`, allowing the image or drawing to be interactive. SVG also incorporates SMIL elements to allow for declarative XML-based animations.

Bookmarks

Source Documentation

World Wide Web Consortium: *http://www.w3.org/*

Extensible Markup Language (XML) 1.0 (Second Edition) – W3C Recommendation 6 October 2000: *http://www.w3.org/TR/REC-xml*

Namespaces in XML – World Wide Web Consortium 14-January-1999: *http://www.w3.org/TR/1999/REC-xml-names-19990114/*

Document Object Model (DOM) Level 2 Core Specification Version 1.0 – W3C Recommendation 13 November 2000: *http://www.w3.org/TR/2000/REC-DOM-Level-2-Core-20001113/Overview.html*

W3C XML Path Language (XPath) Version 1.0: *http://www.w3.org/TR/xpath*

W3C XSL Transformations (XSLT) Version 1.0: *http://www.w3.org/TR/xslt*

W3C XML Schemas Primer and Overview: *http://www.w3.org/TR/xmlschema-0/.*

Further Reading

Practical XML for the Web (Alex Shiell, et al., glasshaus, ISBN 1-904151-08-6)

Beginning XSLT (Jeni Tennison, Wrox Press, ISBN 1-86100-594-6)

XSLT Programmer's Reference (Michael Kay, Wrox Press, ISBN 1-86100-506-7)

6

- Level 0 DOM
- Intermediate DOMs of IE 4 and Netscape 4
- W3C DOM

Author: Peter-Paul Koch

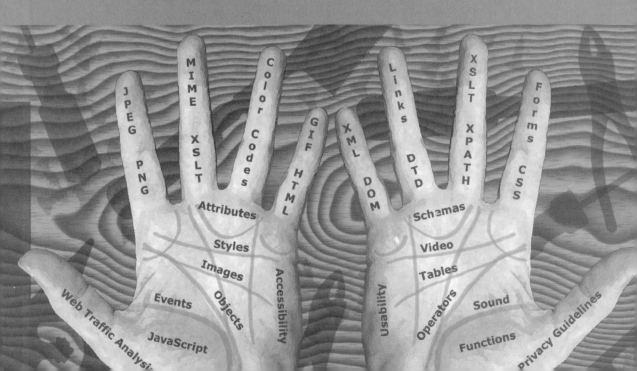

Document Object Models

When you use JavaScript, you often want to influence certain HTML elements. This may be as simple as retrieving the contents of a form field and validating it, or it can be as complex as removing certain paragraphs from the page and inserting images in their place. However, before you can do anything with an element, you must tell the browser exactly which element you want to manipulate. You must be very explicit in giving these commands: all browsers must understand which element you mean.

It's here that the **Document Object Model** or DOM comes into play. Each browser that supports JavaScript has some sort of DOM: some way of providing access to HTML elements. Of course, older browsers offer only limited access to elements, while modern browsers allow you to access any part of the HTML page.

There are no less than four "Document Object Models". This chapter deals with all of them.

DOM History

To understand why the DOMs are as they are and why there are four, it's best to start with a bit of browser history.

The Level 0 DOM

It was Netscape that invented JavaScript and incorporated it in the Netscape 2 browser. Right from the start, it was necessary to have some access to HTML elements, so Netscape was careful to add a DOM to its browser. Today, this DOM is known as the **Level 0 DOM**. It offers only very limited access to the HTML page: in Netscape 2 it was only possible to access form elements and hyperlinks. In Netscape 3, images were added to the list, making possible the famous rollover effect (of which we'll see an example later).

Competitors arrived. Microsoft, especially, was eager to promote its own IE as a viable alternative to Netscape. They were careful to copy the Level 0 DOM, and to make sure IE reacted to scripts in the same way as Netscape did. Unfortunately, IE 3 couldn't access images where Netscape 3 could, creating the first of the **cross-browser compatibility problems**.

Later, when other browsers like Opera came into play, they too carefully copied Netscape's Level 0 DOM. Even the version 5 or higher browsers still support it, since there are millions of web pages using the Level 0 DOM and any JavaScript browser must be able to execute these scripts. It has never been standardized by W3C, however. Instead, Netscape 3 remains the touchstone of Level 0 DOM-compatibility. Any newer JavaScript HTML browser should support everything that Netscape 3 supports.

> **If you use the Level 0 DOM you can be almost certain that your scripts will work in all JavaScript browsers. For optimal browser-compatibility of HTML pages, it's best to use the Level 0 DOM where possible.**

The Intermediate DOMs

Both Netscape 4 and IE 4 supported DHTML: the changing of element styles (like their position, their background color) and content through JavaScript. In order to make DHTML possible, the DOM of the browsers had to be upgraded. It now had to provide access not only to forms, links, and images, but also to other HTML elements.

Netscape assumed that, as before, other browsers would follow its lead. However, since Microsoft challenged Netscape's dominance on the browser market, it chose to develop its own DOM and to ignore that which the Netscape programmers were creating. This resulted in the two browsers each supporting its own DOM, these DOMs being completely incompatible. Thus came the era of the **Browser Wars**. While Netscape and Microsoft fought for dominance of the browser market, web developers were forced to write complicated cross-browser scripts and to work around the sometimes considerable differences between the two browsers.

In hindsight, the Microsoft DOM was seen as better, and is far closer to the eventual W3C DOM standards, than Netscape's. For this reason and others, IE continued to make inroads into the Netscape market share.

- The Netscape model (`document.layers`) is only supported by Netscape 4. When the new Mozilla code engine that drives Netscape 6 and higher was created, it was decided to completely remove the old layer-based DOM.

- The Microsoft model (`document.all`) is supported by IE 4 and higher, Opera 6 and higher, and some minor browsers like iCab and Omniweb.

The Level 1 DOM

Meanwhile the W3C had started the DOM standardization process. The result was an all-encompassing model that offers access to every single HTML element on a page. This was a big jump forward. Even better: all newer browsers support the Level 1 DOM. Microsoft implemented it from IE 5 onward, the Mozilla code engine implemented it, and browsers with a smaller market share, like Opera, iCab, and Konqueror, followed suit to a degree.

Although all these browsers support the Level 1 DOM, they do not support it in completely the same way. You'll still encounter some browser differences when you delve deeply into the DOM. Nonetheless the situation has again become manageable for web developers: all browsers at least make an effort to support the same DOM.

DOM	Used for	Netscape	IE	Opera	Other
Level 0 DOM	Form validation, image rollovers	From Netscape 2. Image rollovers added in Netscape 3	From IE 3. Image rollovers added in IE 4	From Opera 3	All JavaScript browsers
Netscape DOM: `document.layers`	DHTML	Netscape 4 only	none	none	Escape, Omniweb
IE DOM: `document.all`	DHTML	none	From IE 4	From Opera 6	iCab, Omniweb
Level 1 DOM (W3C)	DHTML and advanced W3C DOM scripting	From Netscape 6 (Mozilla)	From IE 5	DHTML from Opera 4. Full compatibility from Opera 7	iCab, Konqueror, Ice Browser

The Level 0 DOM

Recall that in *Chapter 4* we covered the `window` object. The Level 0 DOM is based around the most important child of the `window` object: the `document` object. Through this object, we can access forms, images, links, and a few more objects you'll hardly ever need.

♦ **forms** and their contained **form elements** can be accessed for form validation functions, and any other function that reads from or writes to a form field (a loan calculator, for instance).

♦ **images** are usually accessed to create the famous rollover effect.

♦ **links** can be accessed to add an event handler to each of them.

The core of the Level 0 DOM looks something like this:

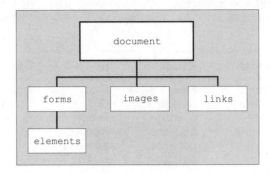

Not surprisingly, the root of the document is the document object. A DOM reference always starts at the document and then moves down the DOM tree. For instance:

```
document.forms['myform'].elements[1]
```

Here, we start at the document, then move to the form named 'myform', and then move to the second contained element. Once you've arrived there, you can ask the browser what the user has entered or enter your own text.

> *Though IE also accepts* myform.elements[1] *as a valid reference, the other browsers don't understand it and will give JavaScript errors. Therefore you must always start with the* document.

The document Object

Let's start with the document itself. It has a few properties of its own, which give access to old-fashioned attributes of the <body> tag, like fgColor (text color) or bgColor (background color). For instance, to make the background of the page red, use:

```
document.bgColor = '#cc0000'
```

Though old color properties like bgColor still work, it's better not to use them. Nowadays the colors of texts and links are usually set through CSS and should be changed through CSS or DHTML.

Property	Read/write	Description
alinkColor	read/write	Accesses the alink attribute of the <body> tag **Deprecated**
bgColor	read/write	Accesses the bgColor attribute of the <body> tag. **Deprecated**

Property	Read/write	Description
fgColor	read/write	Accesses the text attribute of the `<body>` tag. **Deprecated**
lastModified	read-only	Most web servers send the last modification date of the document in the HTTP header. This property gives the last modification date of the page as a string. If the web server doesn't support the sending of the last modification date, you'll see a date of 1 January 1970 (Netscape) or today (IE).
linkColor	read/write	Accesses the link attribute of the `<body>` tag. **Deprecated**
referrer	read-only	Gives the URL of the HTML page from which the current document was reached (for example, the page the user clicked a link on that brought them to this page). It should be empty if there is no referer, but there are some browser bugs.
title	read-only in older browsers, but from IE 5 and Netscape 6 onwards you can change the title of the page	Accesses the title of the page (in the `<title>` tag).
vlinkColor	read/write	Accesses the vlink attribute of the `<body>` tag **Deprecated**

Method	Description
open()	Opens the document to receive new input. In practice, this means it deletes the entire document and then allows you to use `document.write()` for generating new content. After the writing has been finished, you should use `document.close()` to end the input stream. Some browsers won't show the new page without this command. Don't confuse this with `window.open()`, which opens a new browser window. You can use `document.open()` and `document.write()` to write content into the new window.

Table continued on following page

Document Object Models

6

Method	Description
`close()`	Closes the input stream for the document (see above).

`write(`*script*`)`	Evaluates the script given as a parameter and then writes it to the page. For example:
	
	`document.write('Page last changed at ' +`
	`                    document.lastModified);`

`writeln(`*script*`)`	Does exactly the same as `write()`, except that it adds a newline character at the end of the output.

Apart from the above methods and properties, the `document` object also contains the `forms`, `images`, and `links` array objects as properties. Since you'll mostly work with these objects, we'll introduce them all.

The forms Object

The `document.forms[]` array object holds references to all the `<form>` elements in the page. To access a single form, you need to specify it in one of two ways:

♦ By giving the index number of the form. The first form in the page has index 0, the second form index 1, and so on.

♦ By giving the name of the form as specified in the `name` attribute. XHTML 1.0 Strict deprecates the `name` attribute of the `<form>` (though not of its contained elements). Instead the `id` attribute should be used, but older browsers can't handle this. When creating cross-browser sites, it's best to use the `name` attribute nonetheless.

For example, suppose you have two forms:

```
<form name="firstform">
  <input name="yourname" />
</form>

<form name="secondform">
  <input name="nickname" />
</form>
```

You can access the first form in two ways:

```
document.forms[0]
document.forms['firstform']
```

Similarly, these two DOM references access the second form:

```
document.forms[1]
document.forms['secondform']
```

You can even leave out the `forms[]` array entirely: `document.firstform` is a correct DOM reference and all browsers will access the form. The disadvantage is that your scripts become harder to read, which may be a problem when they need to be updated. It's better to fully write `document.forms['firstform']`.

IE even understands the call `firstform`, without any reference to the `document`. However, as we saw before, other browsers may have trouble with this syntax.

Here are some of the properties and methods of individual form objects.

Property	Read/write	Description
action	read/write	Accesses the `action` attribute of the form.
length	read-only	Gives the number of elements in the form.
method	read/write	Accesses the `method` attribute of the form.
name	read-only	Accesses the `name` attribute of the form.
target	read/write	Accesses the `target` attribute of the form.

Method	Description
reset()	Resets all elements of the form to their default values.
submit()	Submits the form. If you use this method, any `onsubmit` event handler is ignored.

For example, these properties and methods can be used to POST a form's data to `script2.pl`, like this:

```
document.forms['firstform'].method  = 'POST';
document.forms['firstform'].action = 'script2.pl'
document.forms['firstform'].submit()
```

The elements Object

When you access a form, you usually actually want to access one or more of its elements. In itself that's easy. Each form object has an `elements[]` array object as a property, which works in the same way as the `forms[]` array. Once again `document.forms[0].elements` is only an array – to actually access the element of your choice, you must specify it. For example, to access the input field named `input1` in the first form, we can use any of these four references:

```
document.forms['firstform'].elements[0]
document.forms['firstform'].elements['input1']
document.forms[0].elements[0]
document.forms[0].elements['input1']
```

Document Object Models

There are several types of form elements, and it's best to divide them into four groups:

- The text fields (text, textarea, hidden, and file). You may want to read out the data the user has entered or write new text to these elements.

- The checked elements (checkbox and radio). You may want to see if these are checked, or check/uncheck them yourself.

- The buttons (button, reset, and submit). You rarely want to do anything with these.

- The select element, which forms a group of its own. Each select box has one or more `options`. Select boxes have become powerful navigation tools and sometimes you want to change their options extensively.

These are some of the properties and methods of individual form element objects.

Property	Form Elements Applicable To	Read/write	Description
checked	Checked elements	read/write	Returns a Boolean that is `true` when the element is checked, and `false` when it isn't.
disabled	All elements, except hidden	read/write	Returns a Boolean. When set to `true`, the form field is disabled: the user cannot change anything. Supported by IE 4+, Netscape 6+, Opera 6+, iCab, and Konqueror.
form	All elements	read-only	Returns a reference to the form the element is a part of.
length	Select	read-only	Returns the number of options in the element
name	All elements	read-only	Accesses the `name` attribute of the element
selectedIndex	Select	read/write	Returns the index number of the currently selected option
type	All elements	read-only	Gives the type of the element. Its value is the same as the `type` attribute of the form field, except that: 1) `<select>` elements can be of two types: `select-one` (if attribute `multiple` is set to `false`) or `select-multiple` 2) A `<textarea>` element has type `textarea`

Property	Form Elements Applicable To	Read/write	Description
value	All elements	read/write. read-only for file upload fields	Accesses the value attribute of the element. If you set the content of a text element, it shows this value. Older browsers don't recognize the value of a select box.

Method	Form Elements Applicable To	Description
blur()	All elements, except hidden	Takes the focus away from the element.
click()	All elements except text	Simulates a mouse click on the element.
focus()	All elements, except hidden	Gives the element focus.
select()	Text elements, except hidden	Selects all text in the element.

Accessing Text Fields

The value attribute contains the value shown within a text field. You can read it out or write to it. For instance:

```
document.forms['firstform'].elements['input1'].value = 'Default user';
```

sets the text 'Default user' in the form field.

For security reasons web professionals are not allowed to set the value of a file upload field – only the user can do that. Thus malicious site owners cannot set the value to the user's password file and then upload it to their own server.

Accessing Checkboxes

When validating checkboxes and radiobuttons, you usually want to see if they're checked or not. This information is contained in the Boolean value of the checked property. For example, take this form:

```
<form name="firstform">
  <input type="checkbox" name="checkbox1" />Checkbox
  <input type="radio" name="radioarray" value="first" />First radio
  <input type="radio" name="radioarray" value="second" />Second radio
  <input type="radio" name="radioarray" value="third" />Third radio
</form>
```

If you want to know if the checkbox is checked, simply do:

```
if (document.forms['firstform'].elements['checkbox'].checked)
{
  // checkbox is checked; do something with this information
}
```

Note that the value of a checkbox without a `value` attribute is always `'on'`.

Accessing Radiobuttons

Radiobuttons are more complicated than checkboxes. Usually there are several radiobuttons which share one `name`. Only one of these radiobuttons can be checked at any time. If you use this DOM reference:

```
document.forms['firstform'].elements['radioarray']
```

then you access an array of all radiobuttons that share the name `"radioarray"`. In fact:

```
document.forms['firstform'].elements['radioarray'][0]
```

accesses the first radiobutton. To find out the value of the checked radiobutton, we use the following script to loop through all available radiobuttons and see if they have been checked:

```
var thevalue = '';
var x = document.forms['firstform'].elements['radioarray'];

for (var i=0; i<x.length; i++)
{
  if (x[i].checked)
  {
    thevalue = x[i].value;
    break;
  }
}

if (!thevalue)
{
  // No radiobutton is checked
  // Do something with this information
}
else
{
  // thevalue contains the value of the checked radiobutton
  // Do something with this information
}
```

Accessing Buttons

You'll rarely need to access buttons. The submit and reset elements have their own tasks, and the button element usually has an `onclick` event handler to make sure something happens when the user clicks the button.

However, sometimes you may want to change the text of the button.

```
<input type="button" name="example_button" value="Click me!" />
```

Changing the `value` property of the button gives it new text:

```
document.forms['firstform'].elements['example_button'].value = 'Don\'t click me!';
```

Accessing Selects and the Selected Option

Select boxes have drifted considerably from their original purpose. Nowadays select boxes are more important as navigation tools than as simple form fields. The `onchange` event handler allows you to monitor user actions quite precisely, so that you can immediately react when the user selects an option. The most common effect is to send the user to the selected page.

```
<form name="firstform" onchange="doSomething()">
  <select name="testselect">
    <option value="first">First option</option>
    <option value="second">Second option</option>
    <option value="third">Third option</option>
  </select>
</form>
```

Both for navigation purposes and for form validation, you usually want to know which option the user has selected.

Every select box object has an `options[]` array object as a property, which contains all the options. Note that these options are only accessible by index numbers, not by names, since options don't have names. To get the value of the first option, use:

```
document.forms['firstform'].elements['testselect'].options[0].value
```

However, we only want to know the value of the option that the user has selected. The `selectedIndex` property of the select box contains index number of the selected option. (In the case of a multiple selection within a select box, it gives the index of the *first* selected option.) We can read out the value of this option using the syntax:

```
var x = document.forms['firstform'].elements['testselect'];
var thevalue = x.options[x.selectedIndex].value;
```

Now `thevalue` contains the value of the option that is selected by the user.

> In Version 5 and higher browsers the value of the selected option is copied to the value of the select box itself, so that
>
> ```
> document.forms['firstform'].elements['testselect'].value
> ```
>
> gives the desired information. In older browsers, however, the select box itself has no value.

Common Tasks with Forms

Now that you know how to access all form elements, you can start writing scripts for forms to make them more responsive and dynamic. We'll show you three example scripts:

♦   The basics of form validation

♦   Using a select box as a navigation tool

♦   Changing the options in a select box

Form Validation

When your users fill in a form, it's always very important to validate the data first. After all, server-side database applications may become terribly confused if they are given a string when expecting a numeric quantity. Therefore, you should check whether the quantity field truly holds a quantity before putting the data in the database.

There are two ways of validating forms: client-side (for example, in JavaScript) and server-side (for instance, in Perl or ASP). In general, it's best to use both ways. Server-side form validation is absolutely safe since it always takes place, while client-side validation doesn't work if the user has JavaScript disabled. On the other hand, client-side validation is much quicker and saves the server some work, since the form is checked before it's sent.

JavaScript form validation starts with registering your validation function to the `onsubmit` event handler of the form. Thus, when the user submits the form, your script is executed first and validates the form data according to your criteria. Whenever it finds a mistake it alerts the user and cancels the submission of the form. Only when all form fields are validated correctly is the form sent to the server.

The basic syntax is:

```
<form name="myform" onsubmit="return validateForm(this)">
  // form elements
</form>
```

```
function validateForm(obj)
{
  // obj contains the relevant form element
  // Now check whatever you want to check
  if (data is incorrect)
  {
    // alert the user and then cancel form submission
    return false;
  }

  // If the script makes it to this line everything is OK,
  // so the form can be submitted
  return true;
}
```

Let's validate an example form.

```html
<form name="myform" action="somescript.pl" onsubmit="return validateForm(this)">
  <input type="text" name="Name" />Name<br />
  <input type="text" name="Address" />Address<br />
  <input type="text" name="Country" />Country<br />
  <input type="text" name="Email" />Email<br />
  <input type="radio" name="test" value="1" />1
  <input type="radio" name="test" value="2" />2
  <input type="radio" name="test" value="3" />3
  <input type="radio" name="test" value="4" />4<br />
  <input type="checkbox" name="check_1" value="1" />1
  <input type="checkbox" name="check_2" value="2" />2
  <input type="checkbox" name="check_3" value="3" />3
  <input type="checkbox" name="check_4" value="4" />4<br />
  <input type="submit" value="Submit form" />
</form>
```

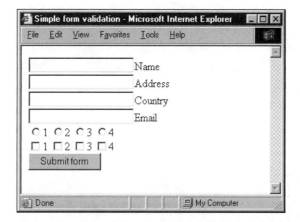

We take a simple case: all four text fields are required and at least one of the checkboxes and one of the radiobuttons must be checked.

Now let's build the validation script. We create two variables for keeping track of the radiobuttons and checkboxes. Initially these variables are `false`. As soon as we encounter a radiobutton or checkbox that is checked, we set the correct variable to `true`.

```
function validateForm(obj)
{
  var radioChecked = false;
  var checkboxChecked = false;
```

We then enter a `for` loop and go through the form elements in the order they appear in the sourcecode. First we create a short name for the current element, to avoid writing `obj.elements[i]` half a dozen times. Because the three types of form elements have to be validated in their own way, we read out the `type` of the form field.

```
for (var i=0; i<obj.elements.length;i++)
{
  var currentElement = obj.elements[i];
  var currentType = currentElement.type;
```

Next we test the current form element. If it's a text field, it should have a value (any value will do in this simple example). So we check if the `value` property has any value at all. If it doesn't, we do three things:

♦ We alert the user of the mistake. Since the user can understand the `name`s of the form elements, we use these names to indicate the faulty field.

♦ When the user closes the alert, we put the focus on the correct form field. Thus the user can start typing immediately.

♦ Finally, we return `false` to cancel the form submission.

```
if (currentType == 'text')
{
  if (!obj.elements[i].value)
  {
    alert('You must fill in your ' + currentElement.name + '!');
    currentElement.focus();
    return false;
  }
}
```

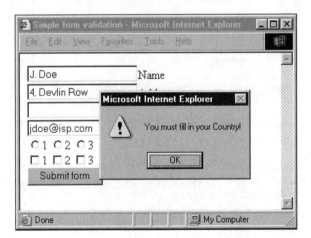

Validating radiobuttons and checkboxes requires the same code, but they are monitored by different variables. So we give radiobuttons and checkboxes separate code branches. If the element is checked we set the correct variable to `true`.

```
if (currentType == 'checkbox' && currentElement.checked)
{
  checkboxChecked = true;
```

```
    }
    if (currentType == 'radio' && currentElement.checked)
    {
       radioChecked = true;
    }
}
```

Now we have gone through all form elements and done what we needed to do. We haven't finished with the radiobuttons and checkboxes, though. The next step is to see whether checkboxChecked and radioChecked are still false. If so, we once again alert the user and cancel the form submission.

```
if (!radioChecked)
{
   alert('You should check at least one radiobutton');
   return false;
}
if (!checkboxChecked)
{
   alert('You should check at least one checkbox');
   return false;
}
return true;
}
```

Only when the form has passed this last test, do we return true to indicate that the form submission can proceed: all data is valid.

Select Box Navigation

JavaScript has made select boxes into powerful navigation tools. At its simplest, you give your users some navigational options in a select box. When the user selects an option, you immediately send them to the correct page.

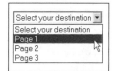

Creating such an effect is very easy. Put the destination of the option in its `value` attribute. Then add an `onchange` event handler, which will be executed when the user selects a new option.

```
<form>
  <select onchange="goTo(this)">
    <option>Select your destination</option>
    <option value="page1.html">Page 1</option>
    <option value="page2.html">Page 2</option>
    <option value="page3.html">Page 3</option>
  </select>
</form>
```

Within the `goto()` function, `obj` is a reference to the select box. The function first reads out the value of the selected option, and then checks if there is any destination. If the user inadvertently selects the ornamental option *Select your destination*, which has no `value`, nothing should happen. If there is a destination, load the new page.

```
function goTo(obj)
{
  var destination = obj.options[obj.selectedIndex].value;
  if (destination)
  {
    location.href = destination;
  }
}
```

Of course, some users have JavaScript disabled and cannot use this type of navigation. Make sure that there is another, non-JavaScript way of navigating to these pages, like a list of hyperlinks.

Changing Options in a Select Box

A more interesting application is a context-sensitive navigation. In this example the user states their preferences by checking a select box. A script then kicks in that removes all options from the select box and writes new options to it.

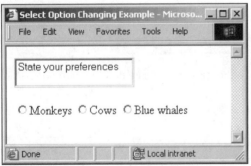 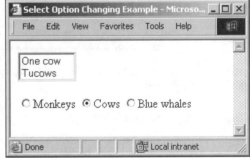

First, we need to discuss the syntax for adding and removing options. As we saw before, each select object has an `options[]` array object property, which contains all options. To remove an option from this array, simply make it `null`:

274

```
document.forms['firstform'].elements['testselect'].options[1] = null;
```

To add an option to the select box, create a new `Option` object and assign it to the correct option in the array. The argument `text` is the text seen by the user, and `value` is the value of the new option.

```
var newOpt = new Option('text','value');
document.forms['firstform'].elements['testselect'].options[1] = newOpt;
```

There's one important catch, though. As soon as you add or remove an option, the index numbering of the other options changes immediately. At the moment, `options[1]` accesses the second option, say Page 1. When you remove this option, Page 1 is removed and `options[1]` now refers to Page 2, which has become the second option. When you add a new option in `options[1]`, Page 2 moves back to `options[2]`.

Fortunately to remove all options, you just have to make the `length` of the `options` array 0:

```
var x = document.forms['firstform'].elements['testselect'].options
x.length=0
```

> **Browser compatibility notes:**
> If you add or remove options to a select, this select must have a `size` attribute larger than 1, or Netscape and IE each develop their own bugs.
>
> Netscape 4 and its predecessors can't resize a select box: it always keeps its initial width. Therefore you should make the initial value long enough to stretch the select box to hold the longest text you wish to insert.

So, let's write the script to change options. First of all, here's the HTML:

```
<form name="myform">
  <select size="2" onChange="goTo(this)" name="navigation">
    <option>State your preferences</option>
  </select>
  <br /><br />
  <input type="radio" name="prefs" value="monkeys"
         onclick="repopulate(this)" />Monkeys
  <input type="radio" name="prefs" value="cows"
         onclick="repopulate(this)" />Cows
  <input type="radio" name="prefs" value="blue_whales"
         onclick="repopulate(this)" />Blue whales
</form>
```

Now for the script. We create some data arrays containing the new options, making sure the name of the arrays correspond to the value of the radiobuttons. We then put all the arrays in an object called `data`. Note that the arrays hold text/value pairs for each option: first the text the user sees, and then the page it leads to.

```
var data = new Object();
data['monkeys'] = new Array(
  'Chimps','chimps.html',
  'Gorillas','gorillas.html');
data['cows'] = new Array(
  'One cow','cow.html',
  'Tucows','http://www.tucows.com');
data['blue_whales'] = new Array(
  'Blue whales in the sea','sea.html',
  'Blue whales elsewhere','elsewhere.html');
```

When the user clicks on a radiobutton, the function `repopulate()` is called. This function repopulates the select box with the correct options. We start by removing the current options by setting the `length` of the `options` array to 0:

```
function repopulate(obj)
{
  var select = document.forms['myform'].elements['navigation'];
  select.options.length = 0;
```

Now we take the array with the same name as the value of the radiobutton. We iterate through the array, increasing the array index by 2 each time, since each option consists of two elements: text and value. For each text/value pair we create one new option with the correct text and value. Finally, we insert this new option at the end of the select box.

```
  var newOptions = data[obj.value];
  for (var i=0;i<newOptions.length;i+=2)
  {
    var newOpt = new Option(newOptions[i],newOptions[i+1]);
    select.options[select.options.length] = newOpt;
  }
}
```

Finally, remember to add the `goTo()` function we created in the earlier select box example, so that the user moves to one of the option pages on clicking on an option.

The images Object

The `images` object is similar to the `forms` object. The array `document.images[]` holds all images in the page, and again you can access them either by name or by index number.

> *document.images is not supported by Netscape 2 and IE 3. In fact, this was the very first JavaScript browser-compatibility problem. The solution is given in the example script below.*

The most important feature of an individual `image` object is that you can change its `src` property. The browser shows the new image, downloading it when necessary. A now-forgotten genius used this behavior to create the image rollover effect.

Put an image in a link. When the user rolls the mouse over the link, a new image is loaded and displayed; when the user removes the mouse, the old image is restored. If the images are designed correctly, this will give a nice effect. Although rollovers are the oldest examples of (very simple) interactivity and have been used in millions of sites, the effect is still interesting. Even more important: users have come to expect rollovers. You'll find an example of such a script later in this chapter.

Accessing the `width` and `height` of the image can occasionally be useful (for instance when the image is shown in a pop-up and you want to size the pop-up according to the image size). But except for this and the rollover effect, there aren't many more common effects with the `images` object.

Property	Read/write	Description
height	read only	The height of the image, as specified by the `height` attribute or the actual height if this isn't specified.
name	read-only	The name of the image, as defined by the `name` attribute.
src	read/write	The source file of the image. Setting this property causes the browser to download the image file from the server.
width	read-only	The width of the image, as specified by the `width` attribute or the actual width if this isn't specified.

Creating Image Objects

It is possible to create your own image objects. For example:

```
var x = new Image();
x.src = 'pix/theNewImage.gif';
```

Here we have created an image object and assigned a file to its `src` property. The browser will start downloading the file, but the image isn't yet shown in the page. The advantage is that the browser **preloads** the image files. When the image is needed, the user doesn't have to wait for it to download: it shows up immediately. We'll use this technique in the rollover script below.

> *Preloading doesn't work in early releases of Netscape 6. This bug has been solved in later releases.*

Rollovers

In the years since the rollover effect was invented, many dozens of rollover scripts have been written. Some are good, some are ugly, and some are far too complex. The script below is one of the simplest and most powerful ones. It uses a strict system of naming. The normal image and the rollover image names should both start with the value of the `name` attribute of the corresponding `<img>` tag. For instance, in our example, we have a 'home' image and a 'place' image with the following names:

<img> element's name attribute	Normal Image	Rollover Image
home	home.gif	home_omo.gif
place	place.gif	place_omo.gif

If you use such a naming system, it's very easy to find out which image files you need for which <img> tags.

We start our script by declaring some variables. One points to the directory the image files are in, two are new arrays to hold all normal and all rollover images, and the important array stuff lists the names of all images with rollover effects within the document.

```
var base= "pix/"
var nrm = new Array();
var omo = new Array();
var stuff = new Array('home','place');
```

We now do some object detection. Does the browser support the document.images[] array? If not we shouldn't execute the script because it would only lead to error messages.

```
if (document.images)
{
```

Only when the browser supports document.images[] do we continue through the array stuff. Here we find the names of all images that should have a rollover effect. We go through them one by one and preload both the normal and the rollover images. These images are stored in the arrays nrm[] (normal images) and omo[] (onmouseover images).

```
for (i=0;i<stuff.length;i++)
{
  nrm[i] = new Image;
  nrm[i].src = base + stuff[i] + ".gif"
  omo[i] = new Image;
  omo[i].src = base + stuff[i] + "_omo.gif";
}
}
```

Now all is set up for the rollover effects. We write two functions: one to load the new image when the mouse rolls over the image and one to restore the old one when the mouse rolls off the image. Of course, in both functions we first check if document.images[] is supported. If it isn't we do nothing.

The over() function receives the index in the stuff array for the appropriate image name as a parameter and stores it in variable no. We find the name of the <img> tag through the array stuff[] and the src of the correct rollover image in the array omo[] under the same index number. We then change the src of the <img> tag to the newly found src.

```
function over(no)
{
  if (document.images)
  {
    document.images[stuff[no]].src = omo[no].src
  }
}
```

The out() function is exactly the same, except that it searches for the correct normal image in the nrm[] array.

```
function out(no)
{
  if (document.images)
  {
    document.images[stuff[no]].src = nrm[no].src
  }
}
```

Now to the HTML. You should assign `onmouseover` and `onmouseout` event handlers to the link around the image.

```
<a href="home.html" onmouseover="over(0)" onmouseout="out(0)">
  <img src="pix/home.gif" name="home" /></a>

<a href="place.html" onmouseover="over(1)" onMouseOut="out(1)">
  <img src="pix/place.gif" name="place" /></a>
```

> From IE 4 and Netscape 6 onwards browsers also accept event handlers on other tags than `<a>`, so you can register the event handlers on the `<img>` itself.

Note that it is possible to change the order of the `<img>` tags without breaking the page.

The links Object

Finally, the Level 0 DOM also has a `links` array object. Not surprisingly, it contains all the hyperlinks (`<a href="">`) in the document. You rarely need access to the links, but sometimes it's useful to set event handlers for all the links through a JavaScript function instead of hardcoding each one in the HTML. For example:

```
var x = document.links;
for (var i=0; i<x.length; i++)
{
  x[i].onclick = someFunction;
}
```

Property	Read/write	Description
href	read/write	Accesses the `href` attribute of the link. (You can also read out parts of the URL with the properties `hash`, `host`, `hostname`, `pathname`, `port`, `protocol`, and `search`).
text	read-only	The text (if any) between the `<a>` and the `</a>`. Only supported by Netscape 4+ and Opera. In IE you can use `innerText` or `innerHTML`, but these aren't part of DOM Level 0.

The `document` object has a similar property array called `document.anchors[]`, which contains all anchors (`<a name="">`) in the document. However, you hardly ever need it.

The Intermediate DOMs

Both Netscape and Microsoft updated their DOMs to allow access to element styles, when they introduced DHTML. Since they were also struggling for control of the browser market, the two companies produced radically different, completely incompatible DOMs. Since then, these two intermediate DOMs have been superseded by the W3C DOM. Nonetheless you will occasionally need them to write DHTML for the version 4 browsers.

DHTML

First, let's take a look at what DHTML actually is. "**Dynamic HTML**" is not a standard: it's a catch-phrase invented long ago to promote the version 4 browsers. Meanwhile it has become a basic tool for web developers.

Part of DHTML involves changing the styles of HTML elements without reloading the page. The trick is that, when you change a style, the browser immediately shows this change, without reloading the page. If you choose your effects wisely, DHTML can be a very valuable addition to any web site.

As an example, take this HTML

```
<div id="testdiv" style="
    position: absolute;
    top: 50px;
    left: 50px;
    font: 12px verdana;
    border: 1px solid #000000;">
  This is the test div<br />
  <a href="javascript:changeIt()">Change</a> its position
</div>
```

Using some script, we change the `<div>`'s styles extensively. The browser immediately reacts:

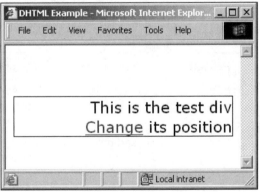

280

In the W3C DOM, which we'll look at shortly, the script would be as follows:

```
function changeIt() // W3C DOM
{
  document.getElementById('testdiv').style.left = 0;
  document.getElementById('testdiv').style.position = 'relative';
  document.getElementById('testdiv').style.font = '20px verdana,arial,helvetica';
  document.getElementById('testdiv').style.textAlign =  'right';
}
```

You access an HTML element, go to its `style` property, access a CSS property, and change it.

> *In JavaScript the dash (-) is a minus sign and cannot be used for style names. To translate the CSS property* `text-align`, *remove the dash and make the next character uppercase. Now it becomes the property* `textAlign`. *Similarly, CSS* `z-index` *becomes the script property* `zIndex`, *and CSS* `margin-left` *becomes the script property* `marginLeft`.

These changes are immediately visible. In our example, the test `<div>` changes its position from absolute to relative, its font size is enlarged, and the text is aligned right. If these changes make sense to your users, they will appreciate the extra effects in your site.

To execute such a script correctly, the browser has to be able to actually change the style. In modern browsers it should be possible to change any style, but you'll nonetheless find some browser-compatibility problems. IE 5 on Mac, for instance, doesn't support the changing of `fontSize` or `fontFamily`. There's nothing you can do about this sort of compatibility problem.

In the code example above we access the HTML element through the W3C DOM. Browsers that don't support this DOM will give error messages for this code. So, we need the Microsoft and Netscape DOMs to make our script cross-browser compatible.

Microsoft DOM

The Microsoft DOM, first supported by IE 4, was curiously ahead of its time. Although it doesn't offer access to text nodes, it is nonetheless much closer to the eventual W3C specification than Netscape's.

> **The Microsoft DOM is supported by IE 4+, Opera 7, iCab, and Omniweb. Opera 6 supports it, too, but only when the user selects "Identify as MSIE 5.0" in File > Preferences > Network > Browser identification.**

The most important feature of the Microsoft DOM is the `all[]` collection property of the `document` object. As its name indicates, this `all[]` collection collects all elements on the page. You can specify the `id` or `name` of an object between the square brackets and immediately access the correct element.

For our simple DHTML effect discussed above, we enter the `id` of the element and once again change the value of its styles.

```
function changeIt() // Microsoft DOM
{
  document.all['testdiv'].style.left = 0;
  document.all['testdiv'].style.position = 'relative';
  document.all['testdiv'].style.font = '20px verdana,arial,helvetica';
  document.all['testdiv'].style.textAlign = 'right';
}
```

Note that the changing of position *does not work in IE 4.*

The document.all[] collection can be used to access any HTML element in the page. For instance, to access the test form we used earlier, we can use this DOM reference:

```
document.all['firstform']
```

An HTML element in the page can also have an all[] collection property. For instance:

```
document.all['firstform'].all['navigation']
```

This accesses the form element with name="navigation" within the <form> called firstform.

The document.all[] collection includes the following properties:

Property	Description
children[]	An array with all HTML tags that are children of the selected element. For example: document.all['myName'].children[0] is the first child element of the element with name myName.
length	The number of elements in the all[] collection. For example: document.all['myName'].length tells you the number of elements in the document with name myName.
tags[]	An array with all tags of one kind. For example: document.all.tags['a'] gives an array of all <a> tags in the document.

The Microsoft DOM contains other interesting properties that we don't look at here, including the innerHTML property, which is explained below in the W3C DOM section.

282

Netscape DOM

While Microsoft's DOM is progressive and fairly easy to use, the Netscape DOM isn't. It's a very complicated set of rules and, even when you apply them perfectly, you can still encounter weird problems.

> The Netscape DOM is supported by Netscape 4. However, the Mozilla project, which produces the code engine for Netscape 6+, has decided to completely remove the Netscape DOM since it was unworkable. Escape and Omniweb also support the Netscape DOM.

The Netscape DOM is founded on the `layer` object. A layer is a separate part of an HTML page that sometimes acts as a separate page altogether. You can change a few of its styles, notably for moving the layer or making it invisible. It's also possible to load a separate HTML page into a layer, though this is rarely done.

Netscape 4 also introduced a `<layer>` tag, but using it is not a very good idea. No other browser supports it: not even Netscape 6. Besides, using this tag is not necessary, since `layer` objects are also created by elements that have their `position` set to `absolute` or `relative`.

Let's take our DHTML example code from above:

```
<div id="testdiv" style="
    position: absolute;
    top: 50px;
    left: 50px;
    font: 12px verdana;
    border: 1px solid #000000;">
  This is the test DIV<br />
  <a href="javascript:changeIt()">Change</a> its position
</div>
```

Since this `<div>` is positioned absolutely, Netscape 4 counts it as a layer. It's then possible to move it, just like we did in the other DOMs. We can get the layer by `id` and then change its `left` property. Note however, that the Netscape DOM doesn't know the `style` property.

Theoretically, our code would become:

```
function changeIt() // Netscape DOM
{
  document.layers['testdiv'].left = 0;
  document.layers['testdiv'].position = 'relative';
  document.layers['testdiv'].font = '20px verdana,arial,helvetica';
  document.layers['testdiv'].textAlign =  'right';
}
```

However, if you try this you'll immediately notice that Netscape 4 only executes the changing of the `left` style. All other style changes are ignored. Netscape 4 simply can't handle them.

Property	Read/write	Description
`background.src`	read/write	The source of the background image.
`bgColor`	read/write	The background color.
`clip`	read/write	The clipping of the layer. Contains `clip.top`, `clip.bottom`, `clip.left`, `clip.right`, `clip.height`, and `clip.width`.
`document`	read-only	The document inside the layer. This is necessary whenever you want to access an HTML element within the layer (a form or an image, for instance).
`left`	read/write	The left position of the layer.
`src`	read/write	The source of the layer. By changing this property, you can load another page into the layer.
`top`	read/write	The top position of the layer
`visibility`	read/write	The visibility of the layer. This takes four values: `show` and `hide` or, equivalently, `visible` and `hidden`. When reading out the `visibility` value, Netscape 4 always returns `show` or `hide`.
`zIndex`	read/write	The z-index of the layer.

These properties are the only style properties that can be changed in Netscape 4. Changing any other style simply won't work. Even when you change the properties mentioned in this table, you may find that the effect sometimes won't work or works strangely.

Layers as Separate Documents

Netscape 4 treats layers as separate documents. So, to access elements inside a layer, you must first access the layer object itself. For instance, to access the link in the `<div>`, a simple reference to:

```
document.links[0]
```

should be enough. After all, it is the first (and only) link in the document. But in Netscape 4, this DOM reference doesn't work. It considers the link to be inside the layer. Therefore you must access it as the first link in the `document` in the `layer` with `id="testdiv"`. Thus, to access the link, you need this code:

```
document.layers['testdiv'].document.links[0]
```

This also goes for images and forms, and even for other layers.

DHTML micro-API

Now we know how to perform our DHTML magic in three DOMs: the W3C DOM (which will be discussed in more detail below), the Microsoft DOM, and the Netscape DOM. Let's repeat the code. In the W3C DOM, you should use:

```
function changeIt() // W3C DOM
{
  document.getElementById('testdiv').style.left = 0;
  document.getElementById('testdiv').style.position = 'relative';
  document.getElementById('testdiv').style.font = '20px verdana,arial,helvetica';
  document.getElementById('testdiv').style.textAlign = 'right';
}
```

For IE 4's sake, you should use:

```
function changeIt() // Microsoft DOM
{
  document.all['testdiv'].style.left = 0;
  document.all['testdiv'].style.position = 'relative';
  document.all['testdiv'].style.font = '20px verdana,arial,helvetica';
  document.all['testdiv'].style.textAlign = 'right';
}
```

And for Netscape 4's sake you should use:

```
function changeIt() // Netscape DOM
{
  document.layers['testdiv'].left = 0;
}
```

How do we merge these various ways of accessing the correct elements into one script? What we need to know is which DOM the browser supports. Then we can offer it some lines of code that make use of this DOM. How do we find out which DOM a browser supports?

The worst possible solution is a **browser detect** or **browser sniffing**. Although a browser detect will work for all browsers that the writer of the script knows about, it won't work for any other browsers. Any browser should have the chance to execute the script, unless it doesn't support a DHTML-capable DOM. If the Konqueror browser, which has excellent W3C DOM support, isn't allowed to execute the script for the silly reason that it isn't Netscape or IE, your script is badly written.

Solving the problem is easier than it seems. The main problem is accessing the correct <div> element. As soon as we get there, we only need to change its style properties, and this works in nearly the same way in all browsers. Accessing the correct <div> can be done in many ways. One of them is the following.

The function changeIt(), attached to the href attribute of the link in the HTML, just asks for the element with id="testdiv" and changes its styles. Actually getting the correct element is the task of another function, getObj().

```
function changeIt()
{
  var x = new getObj('testdiv');
  x.style.left = 0;
  x.style.position = 'relative';
  x.style.font = '20px verdana,arial,helvetica';
  x.style.textAlign = 'right';
}
```

The `getObj()` function is passed the `id` of the element that it needs to find. Then it starts detecting DOMs. If the W3C DOM is supported (in particular, if `document.getElementById` is supported), the W3C DOM code is executed. If it isn't supported, we look for the Microsoft DOM (in particular, `document.all`). If that isn't supported, we check for the Netscape DOM (in particular, `document.layers`).

```
function getObj(name)
{
  if (document.getElementById)
  {
    // W3C DOM code
  }
  else if (document.all)
  {
    // Microsoft DOM code
  }
  else if (document.layers)
  {
    // Netscape DOM code
  }
}
```

If the function has found a DOM the browser supports, it sets two properties: `style` and `obj`. The syntax of the W3C DOMS is very much like Microsoft's:

```
if (document.getElementById)
{
  this.obj = document.getElementById(name);
  this.style = document.getElementById(name).style;
}
else if (document.all)
{
  this.obj = document.all[name];
  this.style = document.all[name].style;
}
```

The Netscape DOM is different, though. Layers have no `style` property, so `style` and `obj` should both refer to the layer itself.

```
else if (document.layers)
{
  this.obj = document.layers[name];
  this.style = this.obj;
}
```

In the function that actually changes the styles (`changeIt()`), the `style` and `obj` properties are assigned to the "object" `x`. Now we can change the `style.left` of `x` without compatibility problems.

This simple function solves most DHTML browser incompatibilities, except for the most important one: some browsers simply don't support the changing of certain styles.

In Netscape 4, though, there's one more problem concerning nested layers. For more information on this, see the text document and example in the code download.

The W3C DOM

The W3C DOM has been created for accessing or changing any aspect of an XML or HTML document: tags, text, attributes, and even comments. It's far more versatile than DHTML. It's actually split into modules: in Chapter 5 we gave an overview of the Core and XML modules, but here we'll concentrate exclusively on the use of the W3C DOM in (X)HTML pages.

> **The W3C DOM is supported by IE 5+, Mozilla (which powers Netscape 6+), and Konqueror. Opera 4 and iCab implemented a small part of the W3C DOM. Complete support for the W3C DOM Level 1 of HTML is only available in Opera 7+. Of course there are still some browser-incompatibilities. For an overview of browser support for the W3C DOM, see http://www.xs4all.nl/~ppk/js/ under 'W3C DOM Compatibility Table'.**

To understand the differences between the W3C DOM and the older DOMs, let's take this bit of HTML:

```
<p id="w3cdomtest">
  The <a href="http://www.w3.org/DOM/">W3C DOM</a> offers Web developers access to
  <em>all elements</em> in an HTML page.<br /> Thus it is the most complete DOM
  available
</p>
```

Of course, it looks like this:

With the older DOMs, you can access only some parts of this paragraph:

◆ The Level 0 DOM only allows you to access the link through `document.links[0]`.

◆ In the Netscape DOM, the paragraph is not a layer because it doesn't have a relative or absolute position set. Therefore, Netscape 4 can't access it.

◆ The Microsoft DOM allows you to access the paragraph itself by `document.all.tags['p'][0]` and the `<a>` and `<em>` tags through its `children[]` array. The text can be accessed through the `innerText` property. However, it is not easy to manipulate the text and elements in order to move their position within the HTML document.

- The W3C DOM allows you to access any part of this HTML, and to easily manipulate it. For example, to move or delete elements or text from within the HTML document.

The W3C DOM creates a tree structure for this paragraph that looks like this:

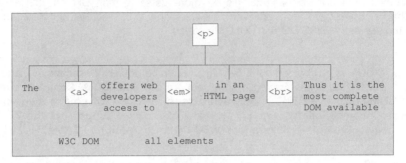

The `<p>`, `<a>`, `<em>`, and `<br>` tags are **element nodes**, and all texts are **text nodes**. Finally, there are some **attribute nodes** (not shown in the diagram): the `href` attribute of the `<a>` and the `id` attribute of the `<p>`.

The W3C DOM is all about manipulating these nodes. For instance, you can remove an element node or a text node; you can change the value of an attribute node or a text node; you can move a node from one position to another. In all these cases the browser immediately shows the result: it immediately updates the DOM tree and thus the page as shown in the browser.

Walking Through the DOM Tree

The W3C DOM offers several properties, such as `parentNode` and `firstChild`, that allow you to access parents, siblings, or children of a node.

Let's take another look at part of the DOM tree of our example page and take the `<a>` element as our starting point. Its `parentNode` is the `<p>` element; its `previousSibling` is the text node 'The'; its `nextSibling` is the text node 'offers Web developers access to'. As for child nodes, since the `<a>` element has only one (the text node 'W3C DOM'), the properties `firstChild`, `lastChild`, and `childNodes[0]` all three relate to this single node.

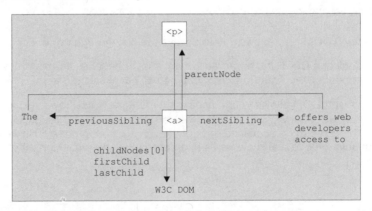

You can make the DOM references as complicated as you like:

```
document.lastChild.childNodes[1].nextSibling.firstChild
```

is perfectly valid code. Nonetheless this sort of coding will quickly lead to problems. First of all it's not quite clear to which element this line refers, which may become a problem when updating the code. Secondly, the W3C DOM is meant to make changes in the document structure. After a few changes, the line above might refer to an element different from the one you originally meant.

Here are the DOM properties that can be used for navigating the tree. In all examples, `x` is a reference to the `<a>` element from the HTML example above.

Property	Description	Example
childNodes[]	Returns an array with all child nodes of the element	x.childNodes[0] is the text child node "W3C DOM"
firstChild	Accesses the first child of the element, in document order	x.firstChild is also the text node "W3C DOM"
lastChild	Accesses the last child of the element, in document order	x.lastChild is once again the text node "W3C DOM", since x doesn't have any other children
nextSibling	Accesses the next sibling of the element, in document order	x.nextSibling is the text node "offers...to"
previousSibling	Accesses the previous sibling of the element, in document order	x.previousSibling is the text node "The"
parentNode	Accesses the parent of the element	x.parentNode is the `<p>` element

Accessing an Element

The W3C DOM offers two important methods for immediately gaining access to the element you need. The first and most important one is the `getElementById()` method that we already used in our previous DHTML example.

```
document.getElementById('w3cdomtest')
```

This accesses the element with `id` attribute `"w3cdomtest"`. The position of this element in the DOM tree doesn't matter, so you are absolutely certain to reach the element (so long as it exists), wherever it currently is.

Another useful method is `getElementsByTagName()`. This returns an array of the elements with the tag name you ask for.

```
var x = document.getElementsByTagName('em');
```

After this script statement, x is an array holding all `<em>` elements in the document. Since there is only one `<em>` in our example, `x[0]` is the only available element in this array.

The `getElementsByTagName()` method can be used on element nodes as well as the `document` node. For instance:

```
document.getElementById('w3cdomtest').getElementsByTagName('em')
```

creates an array of all `<em>` elements that are descendants of the element with `id` attribute `"w3cdomtest"`.

Method	Description
`getElementById('w3cdomtest')`	Accesses the element with `id` attribute `"w3cdomtest"`.
`getElementsByTagName('em')`	Returns an array containing all `<em>` elements that are descendants of the current `document` or element node.
	`document.getElementsByTagName('*')` returns an array containing all elements in the document.
	Not supported by IE 5 and 5.5 on Windows.

Adding and Removing Nodes

The reason for accessing a certain element is usually that you want to change, move, clone, or delete the element. The following example script allows the user to add sets of form fields in a CD review form, or to delete them.

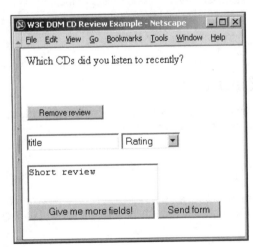

Initially there's only enough room for reviewing one CD…

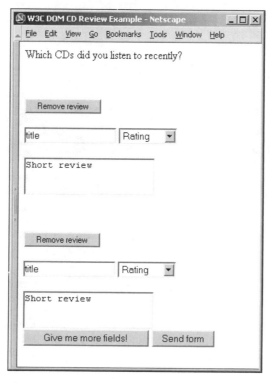

…but when the user clicks the 'Give me more fields!' button, a new set of form fields appears. Attached to the button is a script that copies a template of the set of form fields and adds this copy to the document. The browser immediately reacts by showing it. When the 'Remove review' button is clicked, a script similarly removes the set of form fields from the document.

First of all, let's take a look at the HTML. The form itself is plain and simple. However, there are two extra elements in it.

- The set of fields that will contain one CD review is placed in a `<div>` with id attribute "readroot". This `<div>` is hidden from view by the display:none CSS declaration. This is our template and it should retain its default values – the user is only allowed to enter data in the clones of this template.

- There is one empty `<span>` near the end of the form. This is a marker: the script will add the new form fields just above this span.

```
<div id="readroot" style="display: none">
  <p class="hr"> </p>
  <input type="button" value="Remove review" style="font-size: 10px"
         onClick="this.parentNode.parentNode.removeChild(this.parentNode);" />
  <br /><br />
  <input name="cd_1" value="title" />
```

```
    <select name="rankingsel_1">
      <option>Rating</option>
      <option value="excellent">Excellent</option>
      <option value="good">Good</option>
      <option value="ok">OK</option>
      <option value="poor">Poor</option>
      <option value="bad">Bad</option>
    </select>
    <br /><br />
    <textarea name="review_1">Short review</textarea>
  </div>

  <form action="storereviews.pl">
    <span id="writeroot"></span>
    <input type="button" value="Give me more fields!" onClick="moreFields()" />
    <input type="button" value="Send form" onClick="alert('Fake submit')" />
  </form>
```

Now for the actual script. We first set a variable `counter`, which will count the number of clones made. After all, each form field should have a unique name. By appending the value of `counter` to the default names of the fields, we make sure that each name is unique.

```
var counter = 0;
```

Next we have the function that clones the set of form fields and adds the clone to the document. It first checks whether the W3C DOM is supported by seeing if the browser understands `getElementById()` and `insertBefore()`. If it doesn't, it ends the function by a `return`. If it does, then we make a new set of the form fields, so we increase `counter` by one.

```
function moreFields()
{
  if (!document.getElementById && !document.insertBefore)
  {
    return;
  }
  counter++;
```

We take the element with `id` attribute `"readroot"` and clone it using the `cloneNode()` method. We reset its `id` value (an `id` should be unique, after all) and set its `display` style to `block` so that it will be visible.

```
var newFields = document.getElementById('readroot').cloneNode(true);
newFields.id = 'clone' + counter;
newFields.style.display = 'block';
```

Having cloned the set of form fields, we now make sure that each field has a unique name. We go through all children of the cloned `<div>`. Every form field has a name, so we see if the current child node has a `name` attribute. If it has, we remove the last character of its name (the number) and add the current value of `counter`. Now the form field has a unique name.

```
var newField = newFields.childNodes;
for (var i=0;i<newField.length;i++)
{
  var theName = newField[i].name
  if (theName)
  {
    newField[i].name = theName.substring(0,theName.length-1) + counter;
  }
}
```

The set of form fields is now ready to be inserted. We insert it just before the `<span>` with `id` attribute `"writeroot"`.

```
var insertHere = document.getElementById('writeroot');
insertHere.parentNode.insertBefore(newFields,insertHere);
}
```

In the final part of the script, we call this function once the page has loaded, so that the user will initially see one set of form fields.

```
window.onload = moreFields;
```

Remember from the HTML that each set of form fields has its own "Remove review" button:

```
<input type="button" value="Remove review" style="font-size: 10px"
       onClick="this.parentNode.parentNode.removeChild(this.parentNode);" />
```

When it is clicked, the button's parent node (the `<div>`) is removed from its own parent node (the `<form>`). Thus the review disappears completely from the document and cannot be retrieved. As a summary, here are the W3C DOM methods that help to add and remove nodes:

Method	Description	Example
appendChild()	Append a node to another node as its last child node. If the element is already in the document, it is removed from its previous position. Use insertBefore() to append a node in another position than as the last child.	x.appendChild(y): Append node y as the last child of node x.
cloneNode()	Clone a node. If an argument of true is passed, its descendants are also cloned. If an argument of false is given, no descendent nodes are cloned.	var x = y.cloneNode(true): Clone node y, including its children, and temporarily store the clone in x. (Later x can be added to the node tree.)

Table continued on following page

Method	Description	Example
createElement()	Create a new element.	`var x = document.createElement('p');` Create a new `<p>` tag and temporarily store it in x. (Later, x can be added to the node tree.)
createTextNode()	Create a new text node.	`var x = document.createTextNode('text');` Create a new text node with value text and temporarily store it in x. (Later, x can be added to the node tree.)
insertBefore()	Insert a node into the document tree as a child node, before the existing child node specified.	`x.insertBefore(y,z);` Insert node y into the document as a child of node x, just before node z.
removeChild()	Remove a child node from the node tree.	`x.removeChild(y):` Remove child node y of node x.
replaceChild()	Replace a child node with another node.	`x.replaceChild(y,z):` Replace node z, a child of node x, by node y.
setAttribute()	Set the value of an attribute. There are several serious browser-compatibility problems with this method, so don't use it unless there is no other way to set an attribute. In the next table you'll find code to set the most common attributes of an element (id, class, and title).	`x.setAttribute('align','right'):` Set the align attribute of node x to 'right'.

Information About Nodes

Property	Read/write	Description
className	read/write	Accesses the class attribute of an HTML element node. `x.className = 'newClass'`: Changes the class of node x. If the new class has associated styles, these styles are immediately applied.

Property	Read/write	Description
id	read/write	Accesses the `id` attribute of an HTML element node. `x.id = 'newID'`: Changes the `id` of node `x`. Here, too, the browser immediately applies the styling of `#newID`, if it exists.
innerHTML	read/write	Accesses the HTML contained by a node. This is originally a Microsoft property, not a W3C one, but it's so useful that all browsers have copied it. `x.innerHTML = 'A <b>new</b> HTML!'`: Changes the content of node `x` to 'A new HTML!'.
nodeType	read-only	Provides the type of a node. The `x.ELEMENT_NODE` syntax, which is recommended by W3C, is not supported by IE on Windows. `var x = y.nodeType`: `x` takes a numeric value depending on the node type of `y`. For example, `x=1` if `y` is an element node, `x=2` if `y` is an attribute, and `x=3` if `y` is a text node.
nodeValue	read/write	Accesses the value of an attribute node or text node. `var x = y.nodeValue`: If `y` is a text node, `x` contains the text. If `y` is an attribute node, `x` contains the value of the attribute. `x.nodeValue = 'New value'`: Sets the value of node `x`.
tagName	read-only	Provides the tag name of an element node. `var x = y.tagName`: `x` is now the tag name of node `y` (For example, `'P'` or `'A'`).
title	read/write	Accesses the `title` attribute of a node. `x.title = 'New title'`: Sets the `title` of node `x`. The new title is immediately visible when the mouse hovers over node `x`.

Method	Description
getAttribute()	Gets the value of an attribute. `x.getAttribute('align')`: Gets the value of the `align` attribute of node `x`.

Document Object Models

6

Method	Description
hasChildNodes()	Tells us whether the node has child nodes. `var x = y.hasChildNodes():` If node y has child nodes x becomes `true`; if it hasn't, x becomes `false`.

Using the W3C DOM

The main challenge of the W3C DOM is that it's still fairly new. We haven't yet caught up with the exciting possibilities it offers. The CD review script we saw earlier was only a small example of the way the W3C DOM may revolutionize interactive design. We can offer our users pages they can customize completely without reloading the page. This is useful for large forms (insurance, bank loans), and it may be useful for many more web applications.

The ideal way of using the W3C DOM hasn't been invented yet, however. Programmers and designers will create new concepts, new ways of interacting with their users, and the Web will be changed by these ideas. Besides, there are still some browser incompatibilities to solve.

All this means that if you create a really good application, which uses the W3C DOM to its maximum potential and serves to give your users more power over their environment, you could take a leading part in this quiet revolution.

The W3C DOM is waiting to be discovered.

Summary

In this chapter we've introduced the four Document Object Models that you need for writing cross-browser JavaScript code. We've seen that the Level 0 DOM only offers access to forms, images, and links, but is supported by nearly all browsers. The two Intermediate DOMs, `document.layers` (Netscape) and `document.all` (IE) enjoy only a limited browser support, but are necessary for cross-browser DHTML. The W3C DOM is the most complete of all available DOMs and is supported by all version 5 and higher browsers. It allows you to completely rewrite a page, or to change any aspect of a page you like.

Bookmarks

DOM Level 0 description – http://developer.netscape.com/docs/manuals/js/client/jsref/index.htm. This contains a description of JavaScript as implemented in Netscape 2, 3, and 4. Any object, method, or property supported by Netscape 3 is part of the Level 0 DOM.

Netscape DOM – Same resource. Any object, method, or property supported by Netscape 4, but not by Netscape 3, is part of the Netscape DOM.

IE 4 DOM – http://msdn.microsoft.com/library/default.asp?url=/workshop/author/om/doc_object.asp. Confusingly, MSDN calls the IE 4 DOM the 'DHTML Object Model'.

W3C DOM level 1, 2, and 3 – http://www.w3.org/DOM/DOMTR gives a list of all W3C DOM specifications.

W3C DOM Compatibility Table – http://www.xs4all.nl/~ppk/js/.

7

- GIF, JPEG, and PNG file formats

- Typography: the use of text

Author: Adrian Roselli with contribution from Dave Gibbons

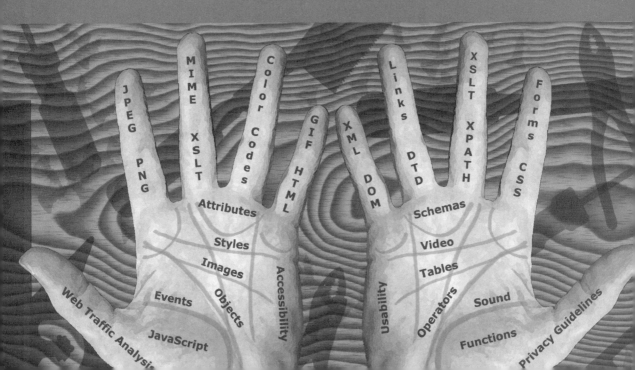

Web Graphics

This chapter will focus on graphics formats for the web, but primarily raster formats (yes, we'll even tell you what that means). It will also help you consider when the right image format is actually **no** image at all. Finally, we'll touch on typography from a design perspective. The chapter will break down into:

◆   Raster vs. vector graphics

◆   GIF, JPEG, and PNG

◆   Screen and print resolution issues (DPI, PPI)

◆   Text on the Web

Raster vs. Vector Graphics

Traditional web graphics formats, such as GIF, JPEG, and PNG, are **raster** formats (also called **bitmap** formats), which as you probably know means they are made up of pixels ("picture elements", which essentially means colored dots). Every pixel is assigned a specific color and position, so when they are assembled they create an image. As such, information for every pixel must be stored within the file. Scaling the file to larger or smaller sizes means some pixels need to be ignored or combined, or some pixels need to be expanded across multiple pixels, and perhaps combined with other new pixels. This type of file is ideal for representing something like a photograph as an image, but not ideal for line drawings and non-photographic pictures. It can also result in larger file sizes for relatively simple images, and can have problems with scaling.

By contrast, **vector** graphic formats, like SVG (Scalable Vector Graphics, a W3C Recommendation for describing two-dimensional vector and mixed vector/raster graphics in XML) and Flash, are made up of mathematical *instructions* instead of *pixels*. With a vector format you can draw a large circle on the screen with just a few instructions to the rendering software (how big the circle is, where it is positioned on the screen, the width of the line, and any color instructions), and therefore just a few bytes of information.

The same large circle in a bitmap format would include pixels for each point in the circle and more pixels for colors inside or outside the circle – potentially a huge amount of data for the same effect on the screen. If the vector-based circle got bigger, the file size would stay pretty much the same, since you'd only be changing the single instruction that told the browser its size. If the bitmap circle grew, though, so would the file size because you'd be adding more and more pixels. However, vector graphics are not such a good choice for photographic images, or anything that requires complex color gradients.

All graphical browsers support GIF and JPEG image formats, and the more recent browsers tend to support at least some of the features of PNG. While there are literally dozens of graphics formats we could discuss here, most notably a newer raster format called PNG ("ping"), GIF and JPEG are the foundations of web graphical presentation today.

Not all browsers or user agents support SVG, and Flash is supported through a third-party plugin (available for Internet Explorer and Netscape and compatible browsers). There are also times where your vector image can get so complex that your file size might even be comparable to, or higher than, the same image represented as a GIF or JPEG at a particular size.

It's important to note that sometimes image formats that you think are ideal for one image can actually be the less suitable when you consider file size, color palette, or other features. See also *http://www.w3.org/Graphics/SVG/Overview.htm8* for more details on SVG, and *http://www.macromedia.com/software/flash/* for more on Flash.

Raster	Vector
At least two formats supported in all graphical browsers.	Requires a plugin to be viewed in a browser.
Most appropriate for photos and graphics that won't change size.	Most appropriate for line-art, flat color, and images that will need to change size.
Smaller file sizes for very complex images.	Smaller file sizes for most art.
Made up of pixels.	Made up of mathematical instructions.
Does not scale size up or down well.	Scales size up and down very well.

GIF, JPEG, and PNG

Let's move on to discuss the three primary raster formats in common use on the Web today. We'll examine what they're good for, what they're not so good for, and show you some examples of why this is the case. We'll also look a new option, MNG. Here's the running order:

- ♦ File Sizes and Compression
- ♦ JPEG
- ♦ GIF
- ♦ PNG
- ♦ MNG

First, though, a word about the size of your graphics files.

300

File Sizes and Compression

File size is one of the major considerations in creating a web site. Most projects require you to consider users able to download data at consumer modem speeds of 56Kbps (although there are a few still surfing at 14.4Kbps). For example, a 200Kb graphic that takes a second or two to show up with your broadband connection would take about 30 seconds to download on a 56Kbps connection. It's important to establish a maximum page load time early in a project and target that when creating the HTML and graphics for the page. 30 seconds on a 56Kbps connection is generally unacceptable. A handy rule of thumb is no more than eight seconds, which works out to roughly 24Kb on a 56Kbps connection for the entire page (all graphics and the HTML). Clearly this will vary from project to project, but knowing that number upfront helps you make decisions later on when optimizing graphics for quality and file size.

The following table shows guidelines for how long different file sizes will take to download on different Internet connections:

File size	500Kbps speed (broadband)	56Kbps modem	28Kbps modem
1 Mb (medium-sized Flash animation)	16 seconds	146 seconds	286 seconds
200 Kb (very large graphic)	3 seconds	29 seconds	57 seconds
20 Kb (standard-size graphic)	<1 second	3 seconds	6 seconds

GIF, JPEG, and PNG use different compression mechanisms that cut down file size. GIF and JPEG are universally supported bitmap formats, and PNG has growing support. So why choose one over the other? Because even though they're technically similar, they're designed for very different applications. The following table illustrates the principal differences between JPEG, GIF, and PNG:

	Color palette	Compression	Animation	Transparency
JPEG	Virtually unlimited (24-bit is supported by most browsers)	Lossy; highly customizable	None	None
GIF	Limited to 256 colors (8-bit)	Lossless; simple run-length encoding	Handled by embedding multiple pictures into one file	Available by setting a transparent color
PNG	8-bit to 48-bit, including 16-bit grayscale	Lossless; highly customizable	Only via its cousin, MNG	Alpha transparency (256 levels)

We'll explain what lossy and lossless compressions are when we look at examples of them in action.

JPEG

Conventional wisdom says JPEG is exclusively for photos and GIF is for everything else. The "Joint Photographic Experts Group" designed the JPEG format, hence its name. Digitizing photographs is a significantly different process from digitizing words or line drawings. Photographs are usually made up of continuous tones without very sharp distinctions between objects. The flow of color change across shadows in grass, for example, is not a perfect outline of each blade. As you see in the example below, you can blur much of the information in a photograph and still recognize the image:

JPEG compression is very flexible. These JPEGs look very similar at first glance, but the one on the left is 185Kb while the one on the right is 15Kb. You can also set your JPEG images to "progressive" display, which means the image displays a blurry version of itself when it starts downloading, and gets progressively sharper as it loads the rest of the image file. Depending on the image, you should see a negligible impact on image size, and it doesn't impact the quality of the compression.

JPEG's approach is called "lossy" compression, because you literally lose some of the picture's information when you compress it with JPEG. Don't panic when you hear that the compression is lossy, though. What you lose is minute variations in color and tone, which are replaced with colors that meet somewhere between the original colors. As you see in the example, the tightly compressed version on the right loses only a bit of detail in very busy elements, like the grass and the shadows in the trees. The more you compress the image, the more information you lose, and unlike file compression utilities such as GZip or WinZIP, you'll never get it back if you save the compressed file. It's always worth keeping the uncompressed original if you can.

The following close-ups on the same part of the image illustrate the difference in quality as we zoom in:

Words, like the ones you're reading now at 1270 dots per inch (dpi) or those you see on your monitor at something like 96 ppi (pixels per inch) on Windows or 72 on Mac, require sharp boundaries and little or no loss. You can do simple edge smoothing on text (**anti-aliasing**, which blurs the text a bit to softly transition to the background color), but you can't compromise more than a pixel or two along the edges of the letters without the effect becoming very noticeable. If you compress a paragraph of text with JPEG, it usually becomes unreadable:

Nonummy Lipsum

Elit nulla eum modo, olim, ut ideo, mara vindico virtus suscipit in minim ut blandit. Tego sed, imputo vel, dignissim exerci fatua dolore aliquip foras sed dolore quibus. Letalis vulputate, nisl accumsan abbas feugiat praemitto, proprius quod, iusto dolore pertineo nibh. Regula vulpes tincidunt importunus camur sed pecus augue luctus. Vereor nostrud utrum ea, capto tation vereor zelus quidem. Vero sed modo ea comis at duis os tincidunt verto.

Nonummy, ideo, vel neque ut usitas, tation, praemitto. Nostrud melior, vulputate conventio aptent verto duis ut pertineo vulputate, qui nunc dignissim letatio adipiscing. Refoveo valde nulla, wisi acsi valde eum, odio, luptatum. Zelus si si ille haero mauris eu suscipere iusto occuro suscipere. Damnum luptatum loquor vulpes eros voco in, fere haero usitas facilisi blandit vindico.

Quidem eros quidne letatio reprobo tation. Occuro suscipit neque facilisi, valetudo appellatio tristique odio blandit consequat nulla euismod.

In this example, the original graphic only had black pixels and white pixels, with very sharp edges. As we mentioned before, JPEG compression smoothes out very busy objects and hard edges, so it tries to blend the hard edges of the black letters into the white background. The result, as you see, is as muddy as a page that has been photocopied too many times. As a rule of thumb, JPEG is great for pictures, but not good at all for text, line-art, flat color, and other graphics that require hard edges.

Enter GIF, a format that uses "lossless" compression.

GIF

Here's that same text, saved as a GIF instead of a JPEG:

Nonummy Lipsum

Elit nulla eum modo, olim, ut ideo, mara vindico virtus suscipit in minim ut blandit. Tego sed, imputo vel, dignissim exerci fatua dolore aliquip foras sed dolore quibus. Letalis vulputate, nisl accumsan abbas feugiat praemitto, proprius quod, iusto dolore pertineo nibh. Regula vulpes tincidunt importunus camur sed pecus augue luctus. Vereor nostrud utrum ea, capto tation vereor zelus quidem. Vero sed modo ea comis at duis os tincidunt verto.

Nonummy, ideo, vel neque ut usitas, tation, praemitto. Nostrud melior, vulputate conventio aptent verto duis ut pertineo vulputate, qui nunc dignissim letatio adipiscing. Refoveo valde nulla, wisi acsi valde eum, odio, luptatum. Zelus si si ille haero mauris eu suscipere iusto occuro suscipere. Damnum luptatum loquor vulpes eros voco in, fere haero usitas facilisi blandit vindico.

Quidem eros quidne letatio reprobo tation. Occuro suscipit neque facilisi, valetudo appellatio tristique odio blandit consequat nulla euismod.

Interestingly, the JPEG image of the text takes up 24KB, while the GIF (Graphics Interchange Format) image is only 14KB, so as well as being clearer it is also smaller and naturally a quicker download; an example of the right image format for the right purpose. Well, almost. You shouldn't be setting this text as an image if you want people to be able to read it; it should be in HTML.

For any image that requires clearly defined boundaries and flat color, including text, cartoons, drawings, screenshots, and computer-generated graphics, GIF is a natural choice, up to a point. GIF has its limitations as well, particularly in that it can only display images that contain 256 colors or less, because it only stores 8 bits of information for each pixel. Compare this with JPEG, which stores up to 24 bits per pixel. This is why GIF isn't the best choice for photographs, even though it's capable of storing photographs. Still, it's rare that a graphic on the Web (apart from a photograph) requires anything near 256 discrete colors – at least for now. If you've created an intricate computer graphic with a thousand discrete colors, you have two choices: make it a JPEG, or use the "dithering" feature in your graphics software to cut down the colors to a GIF-safe 256.

Dithering reduces the number of colors in a graphic by picking dominant colors and filling pixels that have similar tones with those colors. For example, if you have a smooth gradient fill from red to blue, you'll have some pixels in the middle that are 50% red/50% blue (standard purple), while all the intervening steps are odd numbers like 21% red/79% blue. Depending on how you dither the picture, you might see bands of different colors (red, maroon, purple, indigo, blue), no change at all, or anything in between.

So, what if you want to use a photograph with a GIF-specific feature like animation or transparency? You'll have to use your graphics software to dither the photo down to 256 colors or fewer, but that should be acceptable for most photos after a bit of experimentation:

The GIF on the right uses a standard ordered palette, resulting in a very messy image, particularly the sky, and the file is still larger than the JPEG we saw earlier; 44KB in this example. The one on the left uses "optimized" dithering, giving us a reasonably clean picture but a much larger file; 81KB in this example. Compare this to the compressed JPEG we saw earlier, which was 15KB. Below we see the two GIF images zoomed in – as with the JPEG, the lower-quality image is on the right.

Clearly at the size we've been using for these images, roughly 600x600 pixels, you're going to get large file sizes. As you cut the file width and height down, you will obviously shrink the file size as well.

The GIF format, like JPEG's progressive display option, has an interlacing option. This also allows the image to start to display a low-quality image that refines itself with more and more detail as it downloads. This also usually causes a negligible increase in file size.

GIF allows for transparency, but only single-bit transparency. A pixel is either transparent, or it's a color; there's nothing in between. You can create this transparency from an alpha channel, a path, a color, or whatever your image-editing package supports, but in the end, a pixel has to be on or off. This can make it hard to make GIFs with soft transitions to a background color or texture without integrating it into the image itself.

PNG ("ping")

Seemingly sitting on the sideline for a few years now is a format that was designed to address the strengths and weaknesses of both GIF and JPEG. This format, known as Portable Network Graphic, or PNG, has sadly not been as widely adopted among browsers as it could. PNG is similar to GIF in that it offers lossless compression, animation, and transparency, but PNG does each better, much better (it was, after all, designed to replace the GIF format). PNG offers the following features:

- **Progressive display**, which means a graphic can be shown in layers or increasing clarity, starting with a general idea of the final picture and gradually adding more layers of detail (this feature is also available in GIF, where it is known as interlacing, and is also found in JPEGs as progressive JPEGs). PNG uses two-dimensional interlacing, meaning instead of line-by-line increases in clarity, the entire image quality improves as it downloads.

- **Advanced transparency options** that don't rely on the GIF technique of "erasing" specific colors. This is a major problem with transparent GIF files. If you set white as your transparent color in a GIF file, for example, you might end up with a person with transparent eyes or seemingly random bits of transparency where individual white pixels become transparent. With PNG, however, you can define a region as transparent regardless of what colors would be "erased" by this process. This transparency is known as "alpha transparency" and simply means that a single pixel can have up to 256-levels of transparency via an 8-bit alpha channel.

- **Lossless compression**, unlike JPEG's loss of quality every time the image is saved.

- **Very good compression** that can be up to twice as good as GIF. It does not, however, compete well with JPEG for photographic image compression.

- **Virtually unlimited colors**; up to 48-bit color, as well as support for up to 16-bit grayscale.

- **Built-in gamma correction**, to help control cross-platform image brightness (since images generally appear much lighter on Macintosh computers than on Windows computers).

The main attraction of PNG for designers is probably the nearly unlimited color palette (up to 48-bit color), knocking down one of the main drawbacks of GIF and positioning PNG as a reasonable replacement for both GIF and JPEG. The consensus in the industry is that PNG is a natural successor to GIF, but that JPEG's natural kinship with photographs will keep it in the web design arena.

At the time of this writing, Internet Explorer 6, Opera 6, and Netscape 6 support PNG to varying degrees, with full support expected in the near future. Older browsers, like Internet Explorer 4, can't display PNG at all, while even IE 6 can't display many PNG images with complex transparency. This means virtually none of your users will be able to see advanced PNG images in their browsers, although they should be able to see basic PNG images. Most bitmap graphics applications, however, can already open, manipulate, and create PNG files, though you'll have to check the application's documentation to see if it supports all of PNG's more advanced features. In practical terms, this means you should be prepared to incorporate PNG into your graphics repertoire, and you can probably start playing with it using the graphics application you already own, but it may be a few years before the majority of web users have browsers that are fully compatible with PNG.

You can find out more about PNG at *http://www.libpng.org/*. Read about browser support at *http://www.libpng.org/pub/png/pngapbr.html*.

MNG ("ming")

Come on, you didn't think it would stop there, did you? Well, you're right. MNG stands for Multiple-image Network Graphics, and is an outgrowth of the PNG project. The idea was to create a similar format that supports multiple images, animation, and transparent JPEG (which will later be known as JNG, believe it or not).

While MNG has been around for nearly as long as PNG, the final MNG specification wasn't released until the end of January 2001. Browser support is even less available than for PNG, although it has been integrated into Mozilla and Mozilla-based Netscape browsers, is available as a library for Konqueror, and can be added as an ActiveX plugin for Internet Explorer for Windows. Each has varying support for the features of MNG (and JNG ["jinh"]), but you can stay on top of that support at *http://www.libpng.org/pub/mng/mngapbr.html* as well as more browser-support tracking at *http://libmng.sourceforge.net/downloadbrowsers.html*. You can read more about the MNG specification at *http://www.libpng.org/pub/mng/*.

DPI?

When working with graphics for the Web, people need to keep in mind two issues of resolution (commonly expressed as **dpi** or **dots per inch**). The first issue is the resolution of the source graphic. The second is the size you want it to appear on the screen. Both factors are commonly misunderstood.

The digital camera, graphics, or scanning program you use to create or manipulate the graphic controls the resolution of the source graphic. For the sake of illustration, we'll assume you have a new 1200 dpi scanner and you want the best possible picture it can deliver, which you will then publish to the Web. Even though it sounds counterintuitive, the best picture you can create with this scanner is not 1200 dpi – at least not for web delivery. For the Web, you'll probably want to scan any picture you use at 100dpi or so. Here's an example of why scanning at a very high resolution is counterproductive:

In this example, let's say you scan a 2-inch (~5 cm) square at 1200 dpi. Mathematics tells us the resulting graphic contains 5,760,000 pixels (although compression can make it seem like less, but we're considering the worst-case scenario).

That's 1200 x 1200 for one inch-square, 1,440,000 pixels, times by four because we've got four inch-squares. Each of those pixels could be anything from 1 bit black-and-white (720,000 bytes) at one extreme to 48-bit color (34,560,000 bytes) at the other, or even higher. What happens when we display those graphics in a web browser? In addition to having to wait forever to download them (even the small example is a very large file at 720K, and 34.5MB for the 48-bit color file is ridiculous), we get another surprise: we don't see a 2-inch square graphic any more. Now we see our graphic exploded to 24 inches or so, depending on the resolution of the monitor:

What went wrong? We told the browser to show our 2-inch square, right? Well, no. There are two rules to keep in mind when putting bitmap graphics online.

Rule #1: Monitors (and, by extension, browsers) don't know anything about dots per inch, they only know about pixels. They are classified as having a resolution in dots per inch, but each dot is in fact a pixel.

If you put a 2400-pixel-wide picture on a 100 dpi monitor, for example, the monitor will show you one of its pixels for each dot in the original, therefore the picture shows at 24 inches across. What you really want is not a 2400-pixel-wide graphic, then. You really want one that is maybe 200 pixels wide (assuming 100 dpi in this case). You can shrink your graphic in a graphics program or use a more efficient resolution in the scanning software, but whatever method you choose, you'll want to make the source file **as close as possible to the desired output size**.

In addition to controlling the size of the original graphic, we need to decide how big we want the graphic to display in the browser. Here, you use the `<img>` tag in the HTML:

```
<img src="location/filename" width="X pixels" height="Y pixels"
    alt="one of my pictures" />
```

The most important thing to keep in mind here is:

Rule #2: The width and height factors in the `<img>` tag are **screen pixels**, not pixels in the original graphic.

With our example, now that we've got a 200-pixel graphic instead of the 2400-pixel monstrosity, if we wanted a 1-to-1 relationship between pixels in the new graphic file and pixels on the screen we'd use this tag:

```
<img src="location/filename" width="200" height="200"
    alt="one of my pictures" />
```

Will this give us a 2-inch graphic on the screen? Probably not, but it will be close enough for most desktop monitors. Screen sizes vary widely, from the 2-inch quarter-VGA screens on PDAs to giant 38-inch conference room monitors and beyond in both directions, and most can be set to different resolutions. On some monitors, each horizontal inch shows 60 pixels, some 70, 80, 96, 100, 125, or just about any other number. 2 inches, then, could be 120 pixels or 250 pixels, or something else. Can we ask for 2 inches of screen real estate? No (at least, not until we get into some more advanced CSS). Remember Rule #1: Monitors (and, by extension, browsers) don't know about dpi, they only know about pixels. We can ask for a certain number of pixels, but not a certain amount of space.

So, remembering Rule #2, we need to set up our `<img>` tag to show the appropriate amount of screen space, regardless of the original image's resolution. These values should match but they don't necessarily *have* to match. You could go wild and squeeze that earlier 24-inch-wide example into a 2-inch space, but that would be a huge waste of space and bandwidth, and would probably look horrible to boot. You can also ask a browser to stretch a small graphic to fill a larger area, but this will also often look horrible. It's not just bandwidth that suffers, either: asking the browser to resize images means they will take longer to render.

Using our 200-by-200-pixel image and the corresponding 200-by-200-pixel image tag, we see what we intended: a roughly two-inch square.

Choose Wisely

At the beginning of this chapter, we discussed some of the disadvantages of using bitmap graphics compared with vector graphics; primarily size, but also quality. When the computer is figuring out how to draw a line or a letter rather than using a pre-drawn bitmap, the quality is often noticeably better.

For text, use bitmaps sparingly if at all. Your company logo is probably a bitmap, which is natural, but unless you have some particularly earth-shattering effects to apply to headings and menus, stick with plain text. In fact, you can apply some pretty earth-shattering effects (including simple things like shadows and fonts) using CSS.

Two other areas where bitmaps can frequently be replaced are in animation and mouseover effects. CSS is an excellent option for mousover effects, as is JavaScript. If you're animating something that has to be a bitmap, like a photograph, Flash won't save you any space and may even add overhead, but for most other applications it offers more flexibility than script languages for similar bandwidth. Of course, adding proprietary content to a site introduces the problem of users who don't have the right plugin for their browser, so in the end you will probably be better served by sticking to open standards like CSS and JavaScript rather than adding Flash.

Text on the Web

We've touched on text just a little bit above when talking about the right image format, or when to even use an image for text, but since text is usually the meat of your web page, we'll talk just a bit about how to make copy that communicates your intentions and ideas clearly and effectively (assuming your words can do that, too).

General Typography Rules

Many of the rules I'm going to go over here only apply to when you'll be setting type in images, primarily because there is such varied support for text styling via CSS, at least as far as traditional print typography goes. I'm hitting some very general rules, partly because we're only talking about the Web, and partly because there are some things that you just cannot do on the Web (whether using images or not). I'd always suggest a book for typography over surfing web sites primarily because of the nature of the medium – books are a great opportunity to see type in its natural environment, and a good book for that is *The Elements of Typographic Style* by Robert Bringhurst, Hartley & Marks, ISBN 0-88179-132-6.

- ♦ You'll hear the words **serif** and **sans-serif** bandied about a lot, and since those are CSS keywords, you should have an idea of what they are. Letters that are serifs essentially have little tails on them, while sans-serif letters don't. An example of a serif typeface with which we should all be familiar would be Times New Roman. An example of a sans-serif typeface would be Arial. Hundreds of years of print typography say serif faces are easier to read in print; a shorter period of screen typography says sans-serif faces are easier to read on-screen.

- It's usually a good idea to get a feel for the nature of the text before you start choosing typefaces. The text should have some relationship not just between the copy and logos, but also with the other design elements on the screen: photos, captions, notes, pull-quotes, etc. If your logo is completely handled in a high-tech-style typeface, pairing it with a script face might not look very cohesive, for example.

- Will the page have a footer with links to disclaimers and copyright information? Will the navigation be text-based or image-based? Will there be special characters used in the copy? Perhaps you need a typeface that has all the extended characters known to man, perhaps you just want one that is legible on the screen and matches your logo.

- Start the project with a single type family. From there, see if you need to include others to handle different types of content. This doesn't mean you have to find a clone for headers and pull-quotes. You simply need to find a comfortable match. The fewer type families you use, the less disjointed your test will appear.

- When you do mix serif and sans serif typefaces, look to the weight and shape of the letters when making your decision. Ideally, you'd like them to be similar. If you expect to need to use many typefaces or match yours to other alphabets, plan this out from the start so there are no surprises.

- When setting type in images, consider the space between letters, words, and lines of text. If the text is too bunched together, it can not only be hard to read, but also feel stuffy to a reader, or perhaps convey tension you don't want.

- The space between words needs to tell the reader where one word ends and another begins. The space between lines of text is also important to help readers move from the end of one line to the beginning of the next. Too close, and the reader may re-read the same line over and over. Too far, and the reader has to hunt for the next line of text.

- The number of words per line is also important for legibility. Generally 45 to 75 characters per line are considered satisfactory for a single-column page. 66 characters are often considered ideal. With users able to control their own window sizes or font settings, however, it's hard to know what the user may see. You can be almost certain that it won't be what you see.

- Choosing to center your page content, make it left justified, right justified, or fully justified (left- and right-aligned) is a challenge many designers face. For the most part, left justified will be your best bet until setting fully justified text becomes something browsers can do well. The copy on a page should never be centered without very good reasons.

- Once you're in an illustration or photo manipulation package like FreeHand or Photoshop, you may have the urge to start stretching or squishing letters. Adjusting the shape of the letterform may impede readability, so be very careful.

- When setting abbreviations or acronyms in your text, use what are called small caps if available in the typeface you've chosen. They look very much like the capital letters of the typeface, but smaller.

- When setting content apart on the page, for example when you want to emphasize or stress a particular word or phrase in your copy, only change one parameter at a time. Make the text either bold or italic, for example, but not both.

- Avoid using underlines. On the Web underlines imply a link.

- Page headings and subheads (`<h1>` through `<h6>`) need not be extremely large. Often, setting them the same size as the type on the page is ideal, depending on the site. If you want very large headings, consider making them a light gray or other light color to help reduce the weight they have on the page. CSS is great for exercising this kind of control.

Don't let the earlier part of this list put you off using CSS, though: it's still your best option since it controls text, not images. XHTML text styled with CSS is far more usable and accessible than the most perfectly crafted typography set in an image.

Using Text or Images

So you've figured out what typefaces you want to use, and you think you're ready to start stuffing them into words. Before you do that, you need to decide if that headline is going to be inserted as an image, or if it's going to be drawn by the browser and CSS.

The first thing you need to consider is how the words will be used. Is it navigation, a header, body copy, a pull quote, a footer, or something else? Here are some other issues to think about when choosing to use an image for text.

First Impressions

Don't forget that if your text is set as an image, the user has to wait for it to download before it can be seen and read. We'll just assume that all your users have their browsers set to display images, although it is possible they don't have them set, may be browsing offline, or just may have a slow and unreliable connection. Either way, if you want to impress a user on their first visit to your site with fancy type images, you may have the opposite effect simply because they may have to wait for the images to download before they can even tell what the site is about or even if it's useful.

Maintainability

If you choose to use images in place of text, every time you need to change a line of text, fix a spelling error, or even adjust things like color or weight, you have to edit the image. This means opening the source file in an application such as Photoshop, making the necessary changes, and then exporting the image into the desired format. The frequency that text will need to be changed is a good indicator of whether or not it is worthwhile using an image instead. If you're using SVG for the words, it will be easier to change than, say, a GIF, but still not as easy as letting XHTML and CSS do the work.

Localization

Often when words are translated into other languages, they become much longer. This can result in images that can no longer hold the text once translated without scaling it to an illegible size. As such, you need to consider this localization bloat if your site has an audience, now or in the future, that speaks more than your native tongue.

Content Management Systems

If you're designing a site to be powered by a content management system (CMS), then you need to determine what that CMS can affect. Does it create the navigation dynamically? The headings and subheads? Footer information? If it does, using images to drive any of that will be pretty much impossible, or at least render the CMS impotent to do its day-to-day job.

Accessibility

Don't forget that not all of your audience may be as sharp-eyed as you are. Clearly, one concern is users who are visually impaired. If you use images, as long as you include appropriate text in your `alt` attributes, you should be fine. If you use text, then you're often in better good shape for addressing users who are blind. For users with vision impairments (color-blind, low vision, etc.), it's not quite as easy a fix. You need to ensure the images and text you create are large enough to be seen, have enough contrast against the background, and don't use colors that, when paired, can make the text invisible or hard to see for users who are color blind.

Let's not forget search engines, which are more likely to use plain text and structural markup when it comes to weighing the content of a page. If all your copy or keywords are hidden in images, then the search engine spider cannot get to them. Using `alt` attributes can certainly help, but they usually don't carry the weight plain text does to a search engine spider.

Identity

Is the format for the copy, text, or images, appropriate to maintain the identity of the project? Sometimes you absolutely have to have a particular typeface somewhere on the page to maintain the logo or other identity of the project. You'll need to weigh this decision early on to be certain you get off on the right foot when creating images and templates.

Screen-Friendly Fonts

There are many other fonts out there that are optimized for screen viewing, including "pixel" fonts, which are designed for screen only, and usually for very small sizes. In general it's a good idea to find a font that displays well on screen, whether it will be used in an image, or rendered as HTML. By default, most Macintosh and Windows systems have Verdana, Trebuchet, Georgia, and other typefaces already installed. These typefaces are optimized for on-screen use, and a sample image is included below so you can see how they would look on screen. You'll want to specify a number of options in your CSS, so that people without these fonts (people on Linux systems, for example) will get the general impression you're trying to give.

If you don't have these typefaces, you can download them from the Microsoft site at *http://microsoft.com/typography/*. The Apple Internet Developer site has a great resource of some of these typefaces and how they render on Macintosh and Windows systems at the same point size at *http://developer.apple.com/internet/fonts/fonts_gallery_verd_px.html*.

Summary

GIF, JPEG, and PNG are the staples of web graphics, but they're not for all applications. JPEG is excellent for photographs; GIF and PNG for just about everything else. All types of bitmaps are notoriously susceptible to bloating, which adversely affects the download speed of your pages.

When you use bitmaps, remember that the concept of "dots per inch" has a unique meaning in the browser world. Browsers don't know the original size of the source graphic, they only understand the instructions in the `<img>` tag, or the actual pixel size of the file. They display graphics to the specifications of the `<img>` tag, even if it tells the browser to stretch or squeeze the graphic. This behavior can be exploited, stretching single-pixel graphics into lines, bars, and rectangles. There are other strategies for reducing bandwidth, including replacing bitmaps with text and CSS, or with Flash or other vector graphics.

We've also touched on some of the factors that contribute to typography on your pages. It's important to know the ultimate goal of the text, who will be reading it, and how much you'll need to have. Once you have that planned, you can apply some time-honored rules of typography to help make your content a little easier to read and a little more professional looking.

8

- Using multimedia within your HTML

Author: Robert Goodyear

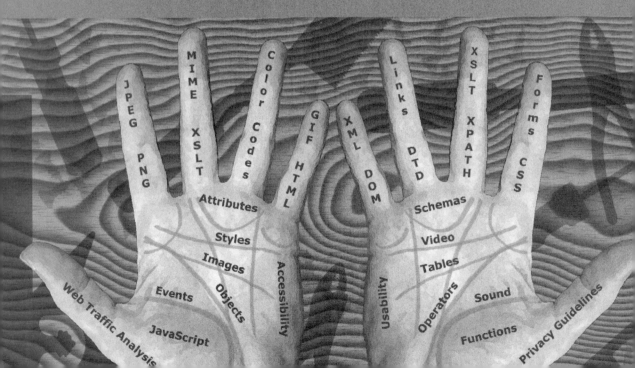

Introduction to Multimedia

In this chapter, we're going to run through some of the options currently available when it comes to web content other than text and static images. Multimedia takes in the spectrum of animation, video, and audio.

Here we will look at some of the basics of multimedia:

♦ The history

♦ Basic concepts and terminology

♦ A brief nod towards emerging multimedia technologies

> For a more detailed examination of streaming media and the future of multimedia, see the *Supplement* to this chapter, which can be downloaded from the glasshaus site: *http://www.glasshaus.com*.

History of Multimedia on the Web

In the beginning there was text. SGML's concept of transportable, structurally reproducible documents created a fantastic platform for moving information across the wire and to the researcher's desktop. Then our friends at the University of Illinois came along and, with the help of HTML, put some images inline with the text and linked content together across multiple documents. While HTML was never envisioned as such, the standard has evolved to embrace the concept of self-describing syntax with the recently approved XHTML standards. The rest, as they say, is history, and there's no turning back now; we're on an exponential ride up the bandwidth curve with no end in sight. Even wireless devices are evolving from sluggish 9.6kbps data transfer to the "Wireless Broadband" promise of 172kbps via GPRS (General Packet Radio Service).

The convergence of the PC and the home entertainment system is near, and in many ways is already in place with digital cable television, network-enabled games consoles like Sony's PlayStation 2 and Microsoft's Xbox, and DirecTV's use of MPEG-2 for picture delivery, interactive menus, and on-demand pay-per-view fulfillment. Even Microsoft is releasing a new version of Windows XP (called Media Center Edition) that promises to blend all your entertainment needs with your computing platform.

In the meantime, however, we've got to make the most of the varied connection speeds our users are limited to with clever encoding, caching, predictive preloading, and fallback, which we'll address later. Fortunately, one thing we can count on is the continuous acceleration of processor speeds. Whether we have software makers to thank for extremely aggressive system requirements or consumer needs for speed, the user base out there is keeping up quite nicely with the Joneses. What this means to us is that we can rely on the computational power on the receiving end to decode, process, animate, and display our rich, exciting content no matter how small we squeeze it down. But first it's time for a little reality check. **Just because you can doesn't always mean you should**. Let's take a look at the multimedia formats (sometimes called Rich Media formats), and what they're best suited for.

Animated GIFs and WAV Files – Non-interactive

One of the earliest forms of multimedia was the animated GIF. Through the clever use of hyperlinked pages, the user could experience a flipbook- or cartoon-style animation that responded to events (the click of a mouse on an imagemap or control, be it text or graphic) from page to page. Playing WAV or AU files teased us with a little bit of audio feedback to complete the illusion. However, we've seen the problem with GIFs in *Chapter 7*: Their very limited 256-color palette and inefficient compression of continuous-tone images wreaks havoc on photographs and is not suited to delivering the rapid frame rates necessary for a true multimedia experience. Even modern navigational structures are employing more elegant movements and transitions than the animated GIF is appropriate for.

Early Flash, Macromedia Generator – Responsive

The evolution of MacroMind Director to its Internet sibling, Flash, brought a much more efficient animation platform online: vector images. By using mathematical formulae to describe shapes and attributes, plus the addition of a truly choreographed timeline, Flash introduced a huge surge in cartoon-like animation, beautiful graphic effects, mouseover events, smooth transitions, and object interaction. The server-side complement to Flash, called Generator, allowed the dynamic creation of SWF content, so we could finally create customized animations based on database feeds, user input, randomness, or just about any variable you could throw at it, so long as your audience took a moment to install the Flash plugin.

DHTML – Pseudo-Responsive

Dynamic HTML, in cooperation with our friend JavaScript (including DOM manipulation), allowed the user to interact with their browser's state and, through cause-and-effect conditional programming, manipulate the structure of the HTML document. In fact, one of the greatest features of the DOM and DHTML is the ability to manipulate the content of a document that's *already* in the browser from the actions taken in another document, a pop-up for example. The pop-up could be developed to act as a remote control or preferences panel. DHTML provides some extremely powerful animation tools such as the ability to show and hide layers, much like animation cells, atop one another. For example, a few years ago, to make a logo bounce, you'd have to animate all the frames of the bounce effect and compress them into one animated GIF. With DHTML, a single GIF image can be moved, revealed, replaced, and hidden by dynamically controlling these attributes through a client-side language like JavaScript.

A major consideration of DHTML-dependent development, however, is the extremely inconsistent implementation of the DOM by different browsers. Until all software developers agree to conform to W3C DOM standards, we're in for a rough ride. In fact, the first thing many developers do when venturing into the world of DHTML is find a really good browser-detection script, so the different quirks in DOM-compatibility can be addressed. This inevitably leads to a lot of bloated code and in most cases, even with the best workarounds, inconsistent results across the different popular browsers.

Flash, QuickTime, SVG – Truly Interactive

Modern multimedia formats are now taking advantage of the truly two-way communications analogy that is the Internet. Flash has evolved its ActionScript language to provide a robust data gathering framework with the ability to fire JavaScript events, interact with the DOM, and deliver most graphic formats in its own shell. This is a good thing because just about everyone on the planet has some form of the Flash plugin, unless their computer has been in cold storage since 1995. A particularly nice function of Flash is its future-proofing, in that it does a great job of handling its own upgrades without a lot of user interaction. At the same time, I see a lot of poor implementations of the Flash detection routines, and as such, many Macintosh users will be fooled into thinking they're using an inferior computer because "Fred's Snake Supply dot com" says it can't find the Flash plugin. Please do yourself a favor and use a well-coded Flash detect as provided in the Macromedia Flash Deployment Kit.

Although not known for vector animation until recently, QuickTime 6 also provides a robust scripting environment as well as support for MPEG-4 video, Flash 5, and many other content formats like AAC audio, an aggressive compression codec that rivals MP3 in quality and size. Several years ago, QuickTimeVR introduced the world to three-dimensional imagery with panoramic photography and the ability to move through nodes in 3D space to view objects from multiple angles by navigating on hyperlinks within the Virtual Reality movie. QuickTime also allows a fully scriptable and customizable interface, so the branding possibilities are huge, compared with being forced to see Microsoft's Windows Media Player logos and controls in all your WMP files.

SVG, or Scalable Vector Graphics, is a competitive answer to Flash. Unfortunately, no browser currently supports SVG natively in its stock trim. Downloading the SVG plugin can work around this, but at 1.6 Mb for the Mac version and 2.5 Mb for Windows, the size of this plugin is much larger than that needed for Flash, and the development for multi-platforms has lagged behind what was seen for Flash. As we saw in *Chapter 5*, however, SVG is an application of XML, and as such all its objects and attributes can be generated using just about any programming language and data source.

VRML, Viewpoint – Too Ambitious?

A few years back, Virtual Reality Markup Language (VRML) was making waves as the next best thing. VRML does for 3D graphics what HTML did for documents on the Web. By describing objects in the three axes of space and a handful of properties like lighting, surface characteristics, and atmospheric conditions, VRML generates the 3D scene in conjunction with standard HTML. Outside the movie *Disclosure*, though, nobody could think of anything useful to do with it. Perhaps VRML was a few years ahead of its time and should have waited for broadband, as is currently the issue with Viewpoint's huge plugin that allows the user to manipulate a 3D wireframe in real time. Viewpoint's shading engine makes good use of the client-side processor power to render the object, but unfortunately, the wireframes themselves are quite large and cumbersome.

Introduction to Multimedia

Rationale

So we know about our options, but how can we choose the right one?

How Much Is Too Much?

Extreme caution and good judgment should be exercised in choosing how to convey our multimedia experiences to the end user. As content developers we must take a ruthless editorial eye to everything we put forward to ensure that we're neither excluding a large portion of our audience because of technical loftiness nor applying interactivity for the sake of the "wow factor" alone. On the content development end, we're accustomed to fast computers, current operating systems, and up-to-date browser plugins. Always keep an eye on contemporary trends to keep yourself and your development team on the cutting edge, but not the bleeding edge.

But Not Too Little...

Jakob Nielsen, the usability expert, has many intelligent insights into web usability, navigation, and information architecture in general, most of which center around his plea for text-only web sites with a search box near the top of the page. Generally, his concept is a sound way of hammering home the point that we always over-design web sites with the consumer's best interest nowhere in sight. The Internet, however, has evolved so far beyond a vehicle for hyperlinked text documents that we have to understand our audience's needs from a visual and aural perspective, not simply from an information-gathering standpoint. Comparing the original intent of the Internet to that of another medium, it could be argued that television should be tuned to news channels 24 hours a day with no commercials nor sponsorship of any kind. Yet cartoons, sitcoms, and soap operas were some of the first things to grace the airwaves, and they're not going away anytime soon. The point here is that there's a reason and rationale behind what we do and how we do it. We're out to catch and hold the attention of our audience, and we absolutely must embrace the available senses to do so.

Accessibility, Usability, and Navigational Common Sense

We can have all the eye candy, motion graphics, rollovers, dissolves, and sound effects we want, without making a web site inaccessible, unusable, or confusing. These properties aren't mutually exclusive. Granted, we've got to take some extra steps in creating a good site with such effects, but that's all part of the fun, right? In brief, think of your audience when you plan a site, and consider the potential effects of developing a site with technical requirements that could exclude your core audience. At the most basic level, a public-facing site that endeavors to serve the widest audience should consider:

- Static assets for non-Flash viewers. Provide GIF images with hyperlinks in place of Flash-enabled navigation as a fallback for visitors who don't use Flash. Even if your fluid-motion, timeline-enabled, draggable navigation bar is the best way to display information, you'll still need a way for non-Flash folks to move around your site.

- Proper `alt` attributes for all `<img>` tags and `summary` attributes for all `<table>` tags, as described in *Chapter 10, Accessibility*. This includes any and all GIF images you use as fallbacks for people not using Flash.

- Static HTML functions for non-JavaScript-enabled browsers: Using JavaScript to submit forms or for navigation can help improve the quality of your data capture with error trapping, but be sure to expose standard HTML elements if they don't have JavaScript enabled (you could do this by setting a session variable or a cookie, then branching your server-side code as needed).

If you spend enough time in pre-production thinking about the small amount of time necessary to address backward-compatibility, you'll find yourself spending a lot less time defending the reasons why your site's navigation doesn't work on the CEO's home computer. A prime example is the clever pull-down `select` navigation element that became so popular a few years ago. While the `onchange` function in JavaScript makes the site seem so smart and responsive to the user, those of us who relied on this functionality without a standard HTML submit button accompanying the `select` found out the hard way that we made our sites unusable for those who disable JavaScript to avoid pop-ups.

Graceful Degradation

It should be noted that we're seeing increasing assortments of user agents (browsers, but from a more platform-agnostic standpoint) that will introduce bandwidth limitations and display quirks beyond comprehension. Already, Mobile Internet, WAP, GPRS, PocketPC, iMode, SMS, MMS, Bluetooth, WiFi, and other non-traditional platforms and protocols are being rolled out worldwide that enable every piece of consumer electronics you can think of to talk to one another, share data, and access the Internet for us.

These developments are pushing needs in the opposite direction of high-bandwidth multimedia, and you should keep this in mind and plan a low-bandwidth version of your content. With XHTML, XML, XSLT, and stricter adherence to DOM standards, you can minimize the impact of supporting many devices by separating content from display rules on the server-side and delivering an appropriate stylesheet for your target device. One of the great side-affects of DOM-compliance is that your web pages tend to degrade (that is, display all your information rather than suppress some of it) nicely across less-capable browsers. It may not look pretty, but delivering plain text to a cellular phone is far better than sending a complex graphic that won't be displayed at all.

Principal Formats to Use

Let's take a look at the distribution of the principal formats to use for adding multimedia to your web page.

Vector-based Formats

Currently, SWF (Shockwave Flash) is the most widely supported vector art format on the Internet. The SVG format, as supported by the Adobe plugin, is gaining popularity, but native browser support is lacking. Embedding a SWF object into a new HTML page can be accomplished inside Flash MX when authoring your animation, and just about every WYSIWYG web-authoring package out there recognizes SWF files and properly places them into your code.

Introduction to Multimedia

Bitmap-based Formats

All graphical browsers support the GIF and JPEG formats, and you can be 99% certain that everyone out there can read these file types. Use caution with GIF89a (basically, GIF that adds support for transparency) as some people still set their browser's background color manually. For years, Netscape used a gray background and IE a white background, so that nice headshot of your CEO that was supposed to float in a sea of white may end up with an odd color poking through the transparent parts. While most modern browsers support animated GIFs, they don't support JPEG2000. This format introduces a frame-based animation technique to JPEG-compressed images, but a plugin is required to display them at this time. PNG is increasingly well supported, but its more advanced features still don't work on major browsers.

Movie Formats

Great advances in MPEG (Motion Picture Expert Group) compression formats have delivered great quality movie formats to the desktop in recent years. The current specification, MPEG-4, provides some of the smartest algorithms around and can intelligently adjust frame rates, compression levels, alpha channel matting, and appropriate delivery, based on bandwidth, to various user agents from cell phones all the way up to satellite-delivered HDTV streams.

Streaming protocols (most notably Apple QuickTime, RealMedia, and Windows Media) deliver content in real-time directly to the player. While this provides a slightly higher level of control over your content by bypassing the media download, you might find that for anything that doesn't require streaming a *live* source video, progressive download is better. Progressive download allows the client to begin playing the content as soon as it thinks it's received enough of a buffer (as determined by throughput, processor speed, and video encoding scheme) to begin the video. Most end users will appreciate the perception – or rather the near-instant gratification – of streaming video without the server overhead required to support true streaming. In short, to stream live content, you'll need a fairly robust server farm, since each user stream creates a *state* or session on the server that manages the throttling and error correction of the video being served. For each streaming media server, assuming your upstream connection can handle the massive bandwidth requirements; count on a theoretical maximum of 1,000 simultaneous streams.

Flash MX can handle contemporary video formats by embedding them in the SWF movie, but for delivering standalone content you're better off settling for more easily-recognized formats to accommodate a wider range of client-side players, media bins, and asset organization utilities. The standalone players leading the pack are Microsoft Windows Media and Apple QuickTime, and their many associated formats. For many years RealMedia was very popular with the dial-up crowd, but Microsoft and Apple have both enhanced their media products with streaming support, progressive download, and a wide range of encoding formats for all content types.

Audio Formats

Everyone's heard of MP3, right? Well, that doesn't mean MPEG-3: MP3 is really MPEG-1, layer 3. It just gets more confusing from here... MACE, IMA 4:1, MPEG-4, uLaw, and more. Fortunately we can focus on the formats that best suit the content itself. A wide variety of codecs (enCOder/DECoders) are available for the most popular players, and since we will usually need a delivery platform for the browser to understand, we can rely on our friends at Apple (QuickTime), Macromedia (Flash), and Microsoft (Windows Media) to support whatever we throw at them. MP3 or AAC is good for full-range audio such as music or high-quality sound effects: use MP3 for MPEG-1 and MPEG-2 video, use AAC (Advanced Audio Coding – see the *Supplement* to this chapter for more detail) if you're using MPEG-4.

More efficient (but lossy) codecs are available for special-purpose recording, like Qualcomm's PureVoice for spoken-word audio that covers a fairly narrow dynamic range and can reproduce speech reasonably well at extremely low bit-rates.

Emerging Formats – SMIL

There are a number of emerging formats for including multimedia elements in a web page. We discussed SVG earlier, but we must also make a note of SMIL.

SMIL (Synchronized Multimedia Integration Language) promises to coordinate and synchronize all the content in an HTML page. Rather than rendering large vector-based animations or bitmapped effects, the movements and transitions of page elements can be choreographed against a timeline. Versions of IE since 5.5 have begun to recognize the specification, and now dependencies between animations can be staged so that, for example, an MPEG video would end with a screen fade and the appearance of new text in its place, or a slide show can step through images every five seconds. This provides a very simple and lightweight alternative to Flash or QuickTime, with the added benefit that a very junior programmer could modify a presentation in minutes.

Native Support: Embedding, Applets, and Objects

Modern browsers already support GIF, JPG, SWF, and a host of other basic formats by default. Just send the media format to the browser and the browser displays it; display a link to it and the browser will play, display, save, or send the item to an external program when clicked. However, we're not quite able to point a browser at some new media and expect it to figure out what to do with it on its own, so how do we point it in the right direction?

MIME Type Support

What happens when a media format is released that your browser doesn't (yet) understand? If you're managing an intranet and need to deliver a proprietary file type via the browser, you can associate a MIME (Multipurpose Internet Mail Extension) type with the file, which will force the browser to handle the file with a client-side application or plugin that you know is compatible with your media type. MIME types can be declared either through server configuration or programmatically by server-side code, like ASP or PHP. Of course, this still assumes your new file type can be handled with an existing MIME association built into the browser or operating system by default.

If it's a new media type not already supported by the browser, you'll have to ask the end user to manually set a custom MIME type to handle your file. (This is not recommended unless you're guaranteed to be working in a very controlled environment.) In just about every browser's preferences settings, you'll find a table of MIME types and rules telling the browser what to do with them, with the exception of IE. For IE, file associations are set via the operating system and are generally based on the file extension.

The syntax of a MIME type is a two-part description: TYPE and SUBTYPE, separated by a slash. For example, by default an HTML page is delivered with a MIME type of text/html, which tells the browser that the data it's about to receive is text and should be treated as HTML. To deliver a Microsoft Word document, you would set the MIME type to application/msword. A list of common MIME types is given in Appendix C.

Embedding

Beyond MIME type, Netscape introduced the `<embed>` tag, which allowed the browser to handle a file referenced in the document's body with the help of a plugin. Remember how trendy it was to have those WAV or MIDI tunes play when you loaded a web site in the late 90s? Thank the `<embed>` tag for that. However, the `<embed>` tag is not valid HTML or XHTML as recognized by the W3C, and as such, you can't assume a browser will handle the file at all. An easy workaround is to wrap the embedded item in the `<object>` tag, which provides a safe way for browsers to interpret your intent while ignoring the deprecated tag. In fact, beginning with IE 5.5SP2, Microsoft has removed all support for the `<embed>` tag entirely in favor of objects.

Applets

The `<applet>` tag, much like `<embed>`, has also been deprecated in favor of `<object>`. Applets, as their name suggests, are small applications written in Java that are intended to load and run within the web page. For the same reasons that led to the demise of `<embed>`, referencing an applet with the `<object>` tag opens up a much wider range of possibilities given the `<object>` tag's flexibility. For example, `<applet>` only supported Java-based applications, whereas `<object>` can deliver functionality in any programming language supported by the browser, like VBScript on Internet Explorer for Windows.

Objects

Objects are a much more scalable and future-proof method of specifying an entity within an HTML page. They are designed to enable an object of any type to be added to your XHTML, and allow the developer to force the browser to use an external application to handle the asset if needed, rather than the browser itself.

As well as its own attributes, which can be used to describe the type of object and source of the object to display or play, it also has the ability to pass parameters to the object through the use of `<param>` elements that it contains. (For detail on the attributes of `<object>` and `<param>`, see Chapter 1.)

It's actually possible to use the `<object>` tag to place an image in a page. Unlike the `<img>` tag, the `<object>` tag has the ability to specify parameters about the object or pass values to the object.

```
<object codebase="myPhoto.jpg" height="100" width="100">
  <param name="alt" value="Photo Alt Text">
  <param name="src" value="images/myPhoto.jpg">
</object>
```

As another example of using the `<param>` tags, you could tell a QuickTime movie to play immediately and loop forever. Alternatively, you could fire an event in JavaScript that plays the object by changing the values of the `<param>` tags.

The syntax of the `<object>` element is extensive, but in summary, provides the following unique and powerful functions:

♦ References a URL to retrieve the plugin or application to handle the media type

♦ References an external file containing data or executable script

- Allows fallback media types, to be used if the browser can't handle the specified media

- Provides alternative text to describe an object

- Allows the MIME type to be declared within the tag, not by the web server or application

Here are a few examples of using `<object>` to reference a variety of media types. First, a Flash movie:

```
<object classid="clsid:D27CDB6E-AE6D-11cf-96B8-444553540000"
        codebase="http://download.macromedia.com/pub/shockwave/cabs/flash/
                                      swflash.cab#version=6,0,0,0"
        height="100" width="100" name="It's my Flash movie!">
  <param name="scale" value="exactfit">
  <param name="movie" value="myFlash.swf">
  <param name="quality" value="best">
  <param name="play" value="true">
  <embed height="100" name="It's my Flash movie!"
         pluginspage="http://www.macromedia.com/go/getflashplayer"
         src="myFlash.swf" type="application/x-shockwave-flash"
         width="100" quality="best" play="true" scale="exactfit">
</object>
```

Here's a QuickTime movie:

```
<object classid="clsid:02BF25D5-8C17-4B23-BC80-D3488ABDDC6B"
        codebase="http://www.apple.com/qtactivex/qtplugin.cab"
        height="116" width="100" name="It's my QuickTime movie!">
  <param name="cache" value="true">
  <param name="src" value="myQT.mov">
  <param name="autoplay" value="false">
  <param name="controller" value="true">
  <embed height="116" name="It's my QuickTime movie!"
         pluginspage="http://www.apple.com/quicktime/download/"
         src="myQT.mov" type="video/quicktime" width="100"
         controller="true" autoplay="false" cache="true">
</object>
```

And finally, here's some music to go with it all:

```
<object classid="clsid:CFCDAA03-8BE4-11cf-B84B-0020AFBBCCFA"
        height="100" width="100" name="It's my Music!">
  <param name="autostart" value="true">
  <param name="src" value="myMusic.rm">
  <param name="controls" value="controlpanel">
  <embed height="100" name="It's my Music!" src="myMusic.rm"
         type="audio/x-pn-realaudio-plugin" width="100" autostart="true"
         controls="controlpanel">
</object>
```

Summary

In this chapter we've briefly looked at where multimedia on the Web has come from, where it is now, and where it's going. Remember that you'll find more detail on streaming media and the future of multimedia in the downloadable *Supplement* to this chapter.

9

- Audio and video media standards
- Server architectures for streaming media

Author: Cliff Wootton

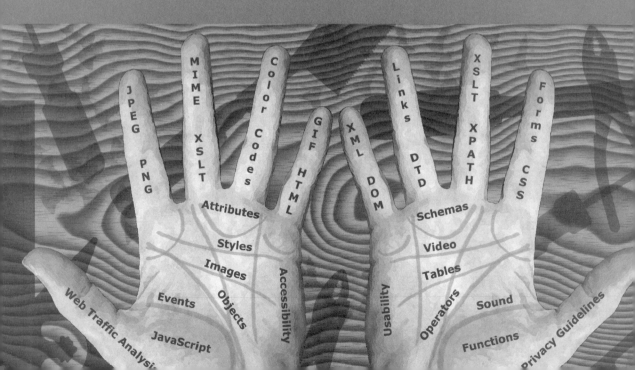

Principles of Usability

Usability is often relegated to being an afterthought in web projects. The design, branding, or marketing message of the site, as well as the whims of the client, can often make for a confusing experience for your users. Only after users complain do many developers get called in to apply abbreviated usability "fixes" to a site to address specific complaints.

This, of course, is the worst way to try to make a site more usable. Instead, it should be considered at the start. From the very moment design prototypes are built, there should be consideration of the usability of the design. From the moment the site structure is conceived, or the features for the site are considered, usability should be a factor weighing on the minds of the decision-makers.

As you go through this chapter, you'll see references to traditional user interface design, as well as usability aspects unique to the Web. This is because the Web is a blend of both worlds: the traditional application world and the traditional marketing world. Merging the two will always be tricky, but hopefully this chapter can make it a little bit easier.

We'll be dividing this chapter into sections that cover:

- General principles of usability

- Different styles of layout

- Web forms, their elements, attributes, and layout

- Scripting and whether server-side is more usable than client-side

- Navigation (making it easy to find your way)

- Multi-purpose elements and attributes

- Presenting text on the page

General Principles

As with most things that involve people, there are many different responses possible to any given experience. Despite this, there are some principles that can be applied to designing elements of a web page in order to make it more usable.

Fitts' Law

In interface design there is a general principle (not really a law) that was originally composed as a rule for interface design of operating systems and applications. It states that the time to acquire a target is a function of the distance to and size of the target.

Sure, you don't need to be a genius to intuit this concept, but it is often missed by interface designers and web developers. A further principle of this law is that the corners of the screen are the easiest for the user to target with the mouse cursor, and the screen edges are next easiest. This is because a user can quickly move the mouse to the edges or corners with any "speed" or "force" and the cursor will stop at the edge. In an operating system, this makes for an ideal place to put control elements (not that many operating systems make use of this, and when they do, they often add a border requiring the user to move the mouse up from the edge). In a web page, it rarely extends to the very edge of the screen, mostly because of the windowing state of GUIs – there is always chrome at the very edge of the screen.

In general, this "law" has translated to the Web in the form of hit areas. Generally, it's easier to hit a larger space with a mouse click than it is to hit a smaller space. It's also a good idea to have some dead space between active areas so the user can see the cursor arrow reappear, indicating a change from one active area to the next. A row of text links with no space between them, for instance, would require the user to roll over every word and watch the browser status bar in order to know where each previous hyperlink ended and the next one began. This is also analogous to an image map with no dead space between each active area, making it harder for a user to know when he or she has rolled the mouse over a fuzzy border and invisible demarcation.

Of course, there are exceptions. Having too large a hit area or too much space between active elements can make it harder for users to accurately or quickly (or both) select the element they want.

Feedback

Of course, this careful consideration of the placement of elements is all moot if the user has no idea that he or she is holding the mouse cursor over an active area of the page. Think about when you hover over a hyperlink. The cursor generally changes from a pointer to a hand. This kind of feedback tells the user that there is a hyperlink there, regardless of the color of the link or even lack of underlines. This same principle holds true for image rollovers, which are simply a JavaScript-driven method of indicating to the user over which image the mouse cursor is hovering.

The blinking cursor in a textbox is another cue to the user to indicate that he or she may start typing. The "I-beam" cursor over text on the page similarly tells the user that it is plain text, and may be selected and even copied.

Finding ways to reformat this interface feedback can prove problematic. For instance, if you remove underlines from hyperlinks, you have forced the user to rely on color alone to detect a hyperlink without the use of the mouse. If the color does not provide enough contrast, it may be impossible for a user to find the hyperlink.

Using CSS to change the mouse cursor over other elements of a page can also introduce problems. For instance, changing the "I-beam" cursor to an arrow over a text input box doesn't imply to the user that he or she can type in that space; the trick is to know if that is your goal.

User Goals

Ultimately, these and other interface considerations are in place for one purpose: to allow the user to move to their destination as quickly and efficiently as possible, even if they don't yet know their destination. Granted, there are sites whose sole purpose is to allow the user to wander, to explore something new, but knowing good interface design principles is an even more effective way to know how to subvert these same principles when creating these experimental sites. There are some methods involved in finding the goals of users.

The first thing you can do to determine what your users want is to ask them. Use traditional market research techniques to determine who will use the site. If you know this, you can find out how they think, what they expect from sites, and what content or features make them come back. Focus groups with new and existing users can give you even more insight, like telling you if your homepage is effectively addressing their interests, if the branding is clear, what features and content are doing their job, and even shortcomings of the interface and design of your site.

Different from focus groups in this context are user groups. Watching your users as they use your existing site will tell you *how* they use it. These user groups can tell you about content they can't find, useless error messages, failed navigation models, inappropriate metaphors, and all sorts of other things on which you thought you maybe had a handle.

Make sure the layout of your site addresses your users' goals. Use design to emphasize important content, make the site meaningful to the type of user you expect, and consider placement on the page. Users tend to equate content on the left or in the center and "above the fold" as important. Anything that fits into their window without vertically scrolling is considered to be "above the fold." Anything below that point is considered much less important. Content that is roughly ad banner-shaped, has a strong advertising feel (logos, branding, etc.), is near an ad banner, or lives on the far right of the page tends to be ignored by users.

Consider how users read on the Web. Make sure your text is clear and concise, since for the most part users don't read unless they absolutely have to. Often users scan the page for keywords, pausing to look for hyperlinks, a bold word, or even an image that might match their goal. Users won't read the instructions you post for them, so consider placing them inline with each step. Be careful how literal you are in your instructions, as some users may actually look for a key on their keyboard labeled "any." Write as if you were a newspaper reporter: starting with the conclusion, and working your way backward to the original ideas. Bullet lists will prove more effective than long paragraphs of copy, but if you do use paragraphs, keep them short and simple.

Finally, consider the all-important search feature of a site. So many users go straight to the search box on a page that it is often more used than the navigation itself. Make sure you offer instructions on how to search, but don't require a degree in logic or knowledge of SQL from your users. Consider simple searches and offer a more detailed search screen with the results. If your search is in any way restricted (for example, to a particular product class or to one sub-site), make sure it's clear upfront. Finally, remember that not all users are great spellers, typists, or use the same words you do. Make sure your search can show results for spelling errors or alternative words (I may not call a pair of denim jeans "dungarees," but an entire generation before mine often does).

Know Your Medium, Your Users, and Your Favorite Color

It's important to keep in mind from the very beginning that you are building a web site: not a Windows application, not a printed brochure, not a CD-ROM, and not a VCR interface. It's a new(ish) medium that owes a lot of its current standards (de facto and formal) to existing media. As such, it behooves a good developer to note when they are wandering into the domain of other media. For instance: yes, CSS allows a modicum of typographical control over the text on the page, but you just aren't going to get the wonderful ligatures and careful kerning that you will with a page layout application. Yes, you can embed Flash movies and PowerPoint presentations, but don't expect your users to be satisfied when roped into a linear "previous/next" walk through your site. And don't be surprised when more advanced users who've disabled plug-ins or scripting just leave the site when navigation or understanding is reliant on those technologies.

Instead, you have to factor in all sorts of other variables you wouldn't worry about in any other medium:

- Bit depth (browser-safe is, after all, only a 22-color palette
- Screen resolution (never make a window larger than this)
- Window size (not the same as screen resolution, since the size of a window includes pixels for 'chrome' such as the frame of the window and any scroll bars)
- Browser (there are, after all, well over a hundred browsers, not counting each version)
- Browser configuration (JavaScript-enabled? cookies? integrated mail client?)
- Operating system (not just MacOS and MS Windows)
- Connection speed (lots of people still use modems)
- User expectations (are underlines always links on your site?)
- User capability (including users who are color blind, blind, physically handicapped, or otherwise inhibited)
- User system (flat panel display? 486SX-25 with 4MB of RAM?)

It's almost always a good idea to know the typical values of all these for users before you build a site for them. It's also good to know the extremes on the edges of those bell curves. Of course, you need to make sure that the statistics you gather aren't tainted from an existing implementation. For instance, if the current site that you hope to replace is only viewable in IE 5.5 on Windows, the logs will show just that. Sure, there will be the occasional Navigator hit, but that user won't be coming back, and so the site has fulfilled its goal of only catering to one browser. Using those numbers to determine the audience of the new site may cause you to relive the same problems you hope to fix with the new build. For more on analyzing your server logs, see *Practical Web Traffic Analysis*, by Peter Fletcher et al, glasshaus, ISBN 1-904151-18-3.

Bit Depth

Are your users surfing your site at 256 colors, and do you even know? If you design sites on your 24- or 32-bit system without ever previewing them at 8- or 16-bit, you may be in for a surprise as your designs shift and dither into completely unexpected colors. It is possible that colors that are the same RGB value in your images as those in your HTML won't even match up next to one another if you haven't considered lower bit-depths. The browser-safe palette is, after all, only 22 colors when you factor 16-bit systems into the mix. You can read about this revised palette in *Death of the Websafe Color Palette?* at *http://webmonkey.com/00/37/index2a.html*.

Screen Resolution and Window Size

Building pages that are larger than the user's window size can make for a very frustrating experience for your visitors. If the user needs to scroll right-to-left-right in order to read every line of text on your site, you've done them a disservice. Keep in mind that screen resolution is not the same as window size. Not all users surf full-screen, and all browsers have some chrome on the screen to include buttons, scroll bars, status bars, and even the logo of the browser.

You can find out what space you have available in your users' windows with some client-side and server-side combined scripting power. Numbers gathered by these means suggest that at 640x480 resolution, you have about 620x304 pixels to play with in the browser window; at 800x600 resolution, you have about 779x420 pixels; at 1,024x768, you have about 918x579 pixels; and at 1,280x1,024 you have about 932x755 pixels. Clearly these numbers can vary across audiences.

Browsers

You don't really think that Netscape Navigator and Microsoft Internet Explorer make up all the browsers on the market, do you? What about the fact that similar versions of Internet Explorer on Macintosh and Windows don't render content in exactly the same way? Or that Netscape Navigator and the new AOL Netscape browser run on completely different rendering engines? And of course we have other popular browsers out there like Opera or iCab, all of which have differing levels of support for all the web technologies we want to use on our sites.

For a humbling view of how many browsers are available to users, visit the *evolt.org* Browser Archive at *http://browsers.evolt.org/* and take a look at all the different browsers, and versions, available.

Browser Configuration

Not every user leaves the browser in its default configuration. Power users, parents of power users, neighbors of power users, people subject to the whims of their help desk power users, and even average users sometimes take a few minutes to explore their browser options.

Sometimes they kick their default font sizes up or down, or turn off Flash because it slows their system, or turn off JavaScript because they heard it was bad, or otherwise disable or modify features of the browser on which you as a developer would like to rely.

These users are out there, and when they encounter a site that doesn't perform under their configuration, they (rightly) assume that it's the site's fault, and move on, never to return.

Operating Systems

Believe it or not, those people on Unix or Amiga machines do find a way to get online, and do spend a good deal of time surfing. Sometimes they even help their friends on terribly old Windows 3.1 or MacOS machines get online as well. This means they may not have the typefaces you specify, or can't download a PowerPoint file you post, or maybe even can't get an up-to-date browser. Leaving these users out in the cold is all too common, but giving them a place they can surf without problems can make them loyal users.

Connection Speed

Despite the proliferation of cheaper broadband consumer access, many users are still on old 56k (or less) modems. Some broadband users even experience speeds as low as 56k modem users when they sign on right after dinner. If your site requires broadband access but caters to home users, you may need to reconsider your page weight. For some users who pay per minute, this kind of site can be an infuriating site to surf, and you can expect them to disable images and plugins in order to quickly make their way around the Web.

User Expectations

An underline is a link. If you underline a regular block of text, expect a user to hover on it for a moment to see where it goes. This is why the underline element was deprecated. Conversely, a link with no underline that is too similar to the color or style of the rest of the text on the page may never be found by your users.

This sort of user expectation permeates all the sites we build. Rightly or wrongly, users have come to expect what they've seen on *Amazon.com*, *CNN.com*, *Google.com*, and dozens of other high-traffic sites. Keep these expectations in mind when building your site.

User Capability

It should be assumed that, if a user is online, they can click a link. This doesn't mean they know how to search, or how to operate DHTML menus. If your audience is young, you can probably assume that they are quite capable users. If it is elderly, you might want to rethink how you let them re-sort columns on data tables or add items to a cart.

This includes users who are color blind, otherwise visually impaired, or even physically handicapped but can still surf. It may take them so long to use or even find elements on a page that the entire site is worthless to them. This subtopic of usability is called **accessibility**, and is covered in detail in *Chapter 10*.

User System

Believe it or not, there are plenty of machines on the Web that are as old as the Web itself. If it got online when the Web first started, it could still be online now. That Centris 610 or 486SX25 might still be chugging away, desperately trying to crunch that Flash movie, or generate the JavaScript menu system you've built. Those CPU cycles are valuable to that user, so spending them without concern can result in a grumpy user.

This also includes your laptop users who may need more contrast in order to see the content on your page thanks to their LCD screen and bad lighting conditions. Users with touchpads instead of mice might also have trouble getting their cursors onto your 12x12-pixel navigation icons.

General Layout

Taking everything we know about our users and combining it with the most basic elements of a page is where the rubber meets the road. We want to be certain the user is comfortable and familiar with the elements of the page, even if they are part of a unique design.

The header generally holds the logo and branding or marketing message of the site. It frequently holds the primary navigation as well. You can expect to see ad banners in here on commercial sites.

The footer appears at the bottom of every page, and often has links to site maps, contact pages, disclaimers, and even links back to the top of the page. Often the branding is reinforced here. This is another popular location for ad banners.

Between these two is the page content area, which is often divided into a number of sections itself. Sub-navigation generally appears on the left, but some sites place it on the right, or integrate it into the header. The right side of the page often holds related links, pull quotes, ad banners, or other related content. Between these is where the content generally lives.

We talk more about specific elements of the page throughout this chapter. The following two images are from two web sites with very different audiences, yet they share a lot of common elements:

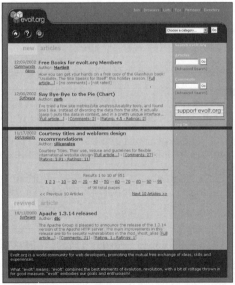

Both pages have a header, which contains the logo and primary navigation, and even an ad banner. Each page has a footer with links to related content or meta content about the site. While *CNN.com* puts its additional navigation down the left side of the page, the *evolt.org* site uses the right side to offer search options and links to additional content on the site. Both rely on the bulk of the center of the page to present summaries of the content on the site.

Liquid vs. Fixed-Width Pages

With so many users who leave their screen resolution at the factory default, users who cannot change resolutions due to hardware limitations, and those who run at the highest resolution possible, there are a number of variations out there. Couple that with the fact that not everyone surfs full-screen, and most users have toolbars of some sort taking up space that could otherwise be used for web page display, and you've got an almost infinite number of possible dimensions in browser windows.

Instead of leaving users at low resolutions with a scroll bar at the bottom of their screen (requiring them to constantly scroll left-to-right-to-left to read content or see ads), or leaving users at high resolutions with large amounts of whitespace outside of your content, consider building pages that scale to fit the user. There are many advantages to this "liquid" design approach.

By allowing a page to scale up to any resolution, as well as down to nearly any resolution, you can ensure the user determines some very important aspects of the page: the readability of the content (characters per line), the ability to print pages regardless of the user's window size, the bandwidth constraints (since images are often tiled, reused, or skipped in favor of colored table cells), and compatibility (if you design it correctly, you could even accommodate users on palm-top browsers).

One of the first decisions you'll need to make, even before creating a design, is what is the minimum resolution you are prepared to support. Will 640x480 be your minimum target? Do you expect WebTV traffic? If so, then perhaps 540 pixels in width would be best. What about palm-top users? Do you see Pocket IE or Windows CE (as an example) in your logs often?

The next thing you'll need to decide is how far back in the Navigator and Internet Explorer version history and what other browsers you plan to support. If you can get away with supporting Navigator 4.x and higher, you'll have more options available to you via CSS. If you have to support versions of Navigator in the 3.0 and below range, you'll find that you may want to skip some CSS in order to provide a more consistent experience for all your users.

There are some issues with building liquid pages you'll need to keep in mind when designing your pages.

- Ideally, a good template has some flat color or simple tiling somewhere within it to allow its width to expand without it looking like an afterthought. Plan for this in the design phase.

- It is also a good idea to set some parts of the design apart, almost as if there were a horizontal line dividing sections. This allows you to make only parts of the page liquid.

- The design should not rely on the proximity of elements to one another. For instance, if the logo is in the upper-left, it can get very far from a search box in the upper right, so don't slice images to line up between the two.

- Navigation elements, however, should have consistency from page to page, and they should also easily fit within the smallest possible size the design will accommodate.

- Choose background image tiles wisely. If the image is too large, the entire image may be lost to some users; if too small, a repeating pattern can be very busy and distracting. Generally, the less obtrusive the part of the page that expands, the better.

- When working up a design, consider what elements you can reuse. The more you can reuse images, the lower the overall weight of the page will be. Using areas of flat color is also a good idea, allowing you to use HTML to color areas of the layout instead of tiling images.

Just because you may like the way a page looks at a particular resolution (whether it's low or high), that doesn't mean others will find your hard-coded decision easy to use. This also doesn't mean that every site you build needs to be liquid. There are some very well-known and good sites out there that sit at a rock-solid 600 pixels in width, and just float to the center of the browser window.

Web Forms

Your average web-based form is intended to gather information from customers, potential customers, clients, or other people that generally you would like to keep happy. So you want to make the form as easy to use and friendly as possible. This means not only a clear, simple design, but also useful, user-friendly error messages. The information we gather in a form can be as simple as a search query, or as complicated as a user's personal details for registration, payment, or goods delivery.

We will now look at some sample elements and attributes that benefit the users when correctly employed.

Elements

The first thing to use to achieve these goals is the very markup that you are using to build the page. There are some very useful elements introduced in HTML 4.0 that help web-based forms mimic those on the user's operating system. Since XHTML 1.0 is simply HTML 4.01 reformulated in XML 1.0, most of the attributes are the same, with only minor syntax differences.

<label>

The `<label>` element provides a way to associate the name of a form field with the form field itself via the `id` attribute of the form field. If a user were to click on the text label of a field, the browser should put the cursor in the appropriate form field. In the case of radiobuttons and checkboxes, the browser should toggle the form element when its associated text is clicked.

Earlier builds of Mozilla were buggy in their display of `<label>`, as well as their ability to attach styles, but that has been fixed in later builds (specifically Mozilla 0.9.4, although it made it into nightly builds before that) and in Netscape 6 and 7. Internet Explorer 4.0 and up support `<label>`, as well as Opera 6 and above, and any other browser that follows the HTML 4 specifications.

The `<label>` element has two optional attributes:

- `for`
  matches "`id`" of associated form element

- `accesskey`
  method to select element with keyboard shortcut (we'll see this in the *Accesskey* section)

```
<label for="strMonkey">Monkey</label>
<input type="checkbox" id="strMonkey">
```

Other attributes are allowed on this element as well, such as event handlers, `title`, `style`, and `lang`. Using it as a style anchor is a good way to apply general styles to your forms. Given that `<label>` has so few bugs associated with it, and that it degrades well (if a browser doesn't support it, it just ignores the tag), there is no good reason not to use it, and it should be considered required for all forms you build. It is also a checkpoint (specifically 12.4) for the Web Content Accessibility Guidelines (WCAG), and is required for level A compliance: *http://www.w3.org/TR/WAI-WEBCONTENT-TECHS/#tech-associate-labels*.

It is also legal to encode the text label and the corresponding form element within the same `<label>` element. At this point, the `for` attribute is unnecessary:

```
<label>Monkey <input type="text" id="strMonkey"></label>
```

<fieldset> and <legend>

Two other underused form elements are `<fieldset>` and `<legend>`. Together, they can be a powerful way to semantically and structurally group form elements. The fact that there's a visual representation is, of course, a nice perk. These elements will help satisfy Checkpoint 13.6 of the WCAG, which is a priority 3 checkpoint. It states that developers should group related links, and these elements used in conjunction do just that. You can read more about the checkpoint at: *http://www.w3.org/TR/WCAG10/wai-pageauth.html#tech-group-links*.

Use `<fieldset>` to group a related collection of elements, such as a group of radiobuttons, and use `<legend>` to give that group a name or caption.

```
<fieldset>
<legend>Animals</legend>
<input type="radio" id="strLions"> <label for="strLions">Lions</label><br>
<input type="radio" id="strTigers"> <label for="strTigers">Tigers</label><br>
<input type="radio" id="strBears"> <label for="strBears">Bears</label><br>
</fieldset>
```

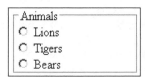

`<fieldset>`	form control group. Takes the following optional attributes:	
	style	Allows you to insert inline CSS styles
	lang	Defines the language for the collection of elements

`<legend>`	fieldset caption	
	style	Allows you to insert inline CSS styles
	lang	Defines the language for the collection of elements

Browser support includes Internet Explorer 4.0 and above, Netscape 6 and above, and Opera 6 and above. For a full list of the other attributes these elements take, including those that aren't so related to usability, see: *http://www.w3.org/TR/html401/interact/forms.html#h-17.10*.

Attributes

In addition to the underused elements above, there are many attributes that are not used as often as they should be. Often this is a result of the developer not knowing they are available because they use a WYSIWYG editor that doesn't provide these options, or even a lack of concern on the developer's part. Below are some of them, which I've chosen as the few that are most often missed, but can bring the most value to a site when used properly. There are, of course, many other attributes in HTML and XHTML that may prove useful to you and your users. You can see the full list of attributes for each at: *http://www.w3.org/TR/html4/ index/attributes.html*.

accesskey

The `accesskey` attribute provides a method for users to select elements on a page with a keyboard shortcut. The single letter in the `accesskey` attribute is the letter needed to activate it. So with `accesskey="f"`, the user would need to press the letter "*f*" on the keyboard, usually along with a qualifier key (*alt+f* on MS Windows, *command+f* on the Macintosh, for example).

It is worth noting that this may cause problems for some users on the MS Windows platform. For instance, *alt+f* is a keyboard shortcut on most Windows applications that opens the file menu. However, in many browsers (such as Internet Explorer), hitting *alt+f* while an element on the page has an `accesskey` of "*f*" will prevent the file menu from opening, and will instead result in the element receiving the focus. Currently, no user agents render the letter associated with the `accesskey` in any way different from the rest of the text, making it difficult to tell users what key to use without embedding styles.

The following elements are allowed to use the `accesskey` attribute:

`<a>`	`<label>`
`<area>`	`<legend>`
`<button>`	`<textarea>`
`<input>`	

Depending on the element, different things may happen when it's given focus with the `accesskey`. A hyperlink with an `accesskey` will follow the link when it receives focus from the `accesskey`. A radiobutton or checkbox will toggle. A textbox will receive focus by placing the cursor within the element. You can find `accesskey` in the W3C specifications at: *http://www.w3.org/TR/html401/interact /forms.html#adef-accesskey*.

9

Principals of Usability

tabindex

The `tabindex` attribute tells the browser in what order to allow a user to tab through the elements of a page with the keyboard. Much as `accesskey` allows direct access to a field, this element allows you to place it within the tabbing flow at a specific point. Valid numbers range from 0 to 32,767, and browsers should strip leading zeroes.

Beware that assigning a `tabindex` can prove problematic should you need to later rearrange elements on the page. `tabindex` is most useful to allow users to tab between elements that aren't immediately following one another in the code (such as form elements across columns). Otherwise, `tabindex` may be unnecessary if your form or other elements are linear on both the page and in the code.

The flow through the elements of a page when tabbing proceeds as follows:

1. Elements that support `tabindex` and have a positive value assigned are navigated first, from the lowest `tabindex` value to the highest. `tabindex` values need not be sequential, nor do they need to start at a specific value. Elements that have the same value will be navigated in the order they appear in the code.

2. Elements that do not support `tabindex`, or have a value of zero, are navigated next, in the order in which they appear in the code.

3. Elements with the `disabled` attribute are not factored into the tabbing order.

The following elements accept the `tabindex` attribute:

`<a>`	`<object>`
`<area>`	`<select>`
`<button>`	`<textarea>`
`<input>`	

The use of `tabindex` is a method to satisfy a priority 3 checkpoint in the WCAG, namely the use of a logical flow in the page. You can read about it at: *http://www.w3.org/TR/WCAG10/wai-pageauth .html#tech-tab-order*.

When to Use id or name

The `name` attribute was deprecated in XHTML 1.0 in favor of the `id` attribute. Originally, HTML 4.0 removed the `name` attribute until it was recognized that nearly every page on the web would not validate. Since so many image rollovers, anchors, and other features on web pages relied on the `name` attribute, it was impractical to expect developers to rebuild all their sites. Coupled with the fact that few browsers supported all the features of the `id` attribute, the `name` attribute was added back into the HTML 4.01 specification as a deprecated attribute. As such, it still appears in the XHTML 1.0 specification (as deprecated), but has been removed from the XHTML 1.1 specification.

Unless you are building a site to be XHTML 1.1 compliant, you should consider using `name` and `id` together for anchor links to account for support issues. Until such time as you can safely replace all instances of the `name` attribute with `id` on all your forms, I recommend that your `name` and `id` values match whenever possible:

```
<input name="strAardvark" id="strAardvark">
```

Keep in mind that each `id` on a page must have a unique value. The trick above can prove problematic when applying it to radiobuttons or checkboxes, since each radiobutton or checkbox in a group will share the same name. This can make it very hard to apply `<label>` elements.

For a quick shortcut, consider merging the `name` and the `value`, or even just its numeric position in the collection:

```
<input type="radio" name="strAnimal" value="Lemur" id="strAnimal_Lemur">
<input type="radio" name="strAnimal" value="Tamandua" id="strAnimal_Tamandua">
<input type="radio" name="strAnimal" value="Oso Hormiguero"
       id="strAnimal_Oso_Hormiguero">
```

or:

```
<input type="radio" name="strAnimal" value="Lemur" id="strAnimal_1">
<input type="radio" name="strAnimal" value="Tamandua" id="strAnimal_2">
<input type="radio" name="strAnimal" value="Oso Hormiguero" id="strAnimal_3">
```

maxlength

This may sound completely trivial, but don't underestimate the value of this attribute. Just as the length of a form field should be a clue to users about how much text can be entered, the `maxlength` attribute should be the first step for form validation. Sure, a user who really wants to can find a way around it, but its better purpose is to tell a user when he or she has entered too much text (it will cause the browser to throw an event, usually resulting in a noise being made by the system, typically a beep). It affords the user an immediate opportunity to reformat or modify the entry, as opposed to throwing an error from your application, or worse yet, trimming the data entered because there is no check for the length of the text (and it's longer than your data bucket will accept).

For example, if you have a form that asks for someone's last name, but your database will only accept 25 characters, then you would want your form field to have a `maxlength` of 25. Allowing more than that would return an error page (in a best case) or just cause the application to fail (in a worst case). The HTML 4.01 specifications briefly describe `maxlength`: *http://www.w3.org/TR/html401/interact/forms.html#adef-maxlength*.

Choosing the Right Element for the Job

There are many cases when creating a form that a developer struggles over what elements are most appropriate for the information to be gathered. For instance, is a `<select>` menu better than a set of radiobuttons, or a `<textarea>` better than a text `<input>` box under certain circumstances? You need to consider the user, the type of information, and what the field itself conveys.

For instance, if you were gathering the States in which your user lives (as opposed to another state to which your user may ship something), would you use a select menu pre-populated with the abbreviations of all 50 states, or would you have a two-character text input field? Consider the two-character field, as most users generally know their own state abbreviation and can type it fairly quickly. Using a select menu requires a user to open the menu, scroll to the state, and click it to select.

Even using the keyboard to quickly highlight a state might not guarantee the correct state (hitting "N" doesn't bring up "NY"). With proper server-side (or even additional client-side) validation, you can eliminate the worries of someone typing in an imaginary 51st state.

Visual Cues

Some simple questions can help you determine if your form conveys its purpose to the user effectively. Does it tell the user, just by looking, what is expected of them?

- Do the visual field lengths match the allowed character limit?

- Do the form elements convey the type of information required?

- Are checkboxes and radiobuttons being used appropriately?

- Do fields have examples where necessary to show formatting or type of data?

- Are all the fields on one screen, and if not, does the user know how many screens there are?

- Are enough options visible in a multiple select box?

- Are the fields grouped thematically?

- Are the mandatory fields really always required, and will they always be known?

<select> as Navigation

While this topic has been argued many times over, it's worth addressing it here in order to allow you to assess the value of using a `<select>` menu as a navigation item as opposed to a plain old list of links.

Consider the number of clicks involved. To see all the options, the user must click to open the menu just to see the options. If there are too many options to show without scrolling, the user may have to click to scroll. Then the user has to click to select an option. If the menu has a *Go* button, that's another click. This means that a user has to click at least twice just to choose an option, and perhaps four or more times depending on the number of options and the presence of a button. A list of text links, however, requires one click.

Also consider the user who clicks on the wrong option when the form is fired from a JavaScript function. Often an accidental click results in the user going to the wrong page altogether, even if they just wanted to look at the options. While a *Go* button makes the form more usable and accounts for users without JavaScript enabled, it does still introduce another click. Of course, there are users who prefer to open new pages in tabs or new windows. The select-menu navigation prevents such users from surfing the way they want to, which can contribute to an overall bad experience with the site.

Layout

The layout of the form on the screen tells the user a lot about what is expected. We've already touched on aspects of that above, but there are still some other basics to keep in mind.

Alignment

One of the simplest things you can do to make your forms look more professional (which is a good thing if you're trying to sell something online) is ensure that the elements and labels are aligned. The form overall should make a discrete box on the page, with each form element aligning beneath or next to one another, and the text consistently placed and aligned. Not only will your visitors find it easier to use, but also it will convey professionalism. Think about all the terrible forms you've ever seen, and you should note that alignment is one of the major problems they all have.

An example of alignment that's all over the place. The form doesn't look very cohesive:

An example of alignment that's clear and consistent, making the form look like a unified whole:

341

Flow

The flow of the form is important to guide the user. Multiple columns aren't always easy for users, and can sometimes create forms wider than the window. Forms with a clear progression (from top to bottom, start to finish) are best. The fields should build on one another, and make sense in their flow. For instance, asking for a credit card number before you've provided the total, including tax, shipping, and delivery date, is generally a bad way to build a form.

A form that shows good overall flow gives the user a good idea of what is expected. The progression is logical from top to bottom, it tells the user what page they are on out of the total number of steps, and it provides simple, contextual instructions:

Required Fields

Denote fields that are required in a clear, consistent manner. Don't rely on color alone. Consider using `<strong>` to embolden your fields, which may also be read by assistive technologies, such as screen readers. If you insist on using an asterisk, make sure you place it consistently and that its alignment is also consistent. Placing it before the field label text, if the label is to the left of the field, allows users to quickly see all required fields. Placing it after the text labels, which may all be different lengths, will only make it harder to quickly see which fields are required.

Using just emboldened text, it is possible to denote all required fields. This is a very simple way to render the page, and requires the user have a browser capable of either making text bold, or otherwise appropriately displaying the `<strong>` or `<b>` tag.

The same form also using color (which appears as very dark gray here, and perhaps to colorblind users) as well as bold text and an asterisk to denote required fields. Neither way is necessarily more correct than the other: they require testing with your audience to know which is the best fit:

Your feedback is very important to us. Please use this form to submit any specific questions or comments you may have. Fields in **bold blue** and marked with an * are required.

First Name*: [   ]
Last Name*: [   ]
Company/Organization: [   ]
Phone*: [   ]
555-555-5555
Email: [   ]
Questions/Comments*: [   ]

[Submit]

Client-side or Server-side

Since we can use JavaScript to accomplish many things that could be done on the server, there is a temptation to use it to do everything. This is clearly not a good idea, even if it does mean that the user doesn't have to wait for a connection to your web server. In this section we take a look at what and when to script on the server or the client.

Error Messages

Make your error messages useful and concise. Don't let a user submit a form and return a screen that just says "*There were errors on your form, hit the back button*". Instead, redraw the page with the errors, and note all the errors at the top of the page, telling the user specifically what is wrong. On top of that, highlight the erroneous fields for the user so they can quickly find them on the page (with color, an icon, or some cue to the user that the field needs to be corrected). The extra programming necessary to do this is usually minimal, and should be included.

Client-side validation, using JavaScript, for example, should be considered an add-on, and not the sole method of validating the form. It should not create more problems for the user (like errors, bad checks, and constant firing). It is also too easy to bypass client-side validation by simply disabling JavaScript on the browser, so it can't be the only method of validating your forms.

Use client-side validation to warn the user of missing or incorrect information. It can be used to tell the user they have entered too much text in a `<textarea>`. Be careful how you fire the validation, though. You can do it field-by-field, or you can do it on form submission, but test it to be sure you aren't breaking the form or otherwise throwing an error every time the user tries to do something unrelated.

Form Submission

Don't rely on JavaScript, or any other client-side script, to submit a form. Granted you may have specific cases where you control the audience and can get away with it, but for the most part relying on client-side script to submit a form will only create problems. Not only will it make a form unusable to a user without JavaScript enabled, but it can also break easily if the user's browser doesn't support that version of JavaScript or otherwise throws an error because of something else on the page.

HTML already provides an adequate means to submit forms through the `action` attribute on the `<form>` element. At this time, all browsers support this method, whether or not they have client-side scripting enabled. Set the `action` attribute to the server-side script that will process your form.

Some may argue that automatic submission from a select-menu navigation item is better than a button to do the job, but the argument is based on the flawed assumption that a select menu is appropriate for navigation.

Client-side Scripting

Just as we discussed with forms, we need to ensure that any client-side script on the page works for our users, including users who have it disabled. Sure, JavaScript is a great way to do image rollovers, and users without JavaScript enabled generally aren't penalized in those cases, but consider CSS methods to achieve the same effect, and consider how the scripts will fail for users with older JavaScript engines, or without JavaScript enabled.

Navigation

Obviously, all your work is moot if your users cannot use your navigation. You need to make sure that it not only makes sense, but that it can be found. It should provide appropriate clues to your users as well, allowing them to know what is navigation and what is not. Your navigation should also indicate to your users what page is being viewed at any given time, especially when many users may come in from somewhere other than the homepage.

Image or Text

Text is generally a more robust solution when building navigation. It's easy to change, it's more accessible, it can be localized/translated more quickly, it's easier to build dynamically from a content management system (CMS), it's possible to scale (if CSS is used appropriately), and it's faster. Images certainly provide more design control, but they are not as easy to modify, and can be harder on users who don't have as clear a vision as the designer.

Rollovers

Rollovers are a great method to indicate to users when their cursor is over a navigation link (which is obviously useful only in graphical browsers). With images, the traditional method has been JavaScript rollovers, provided the user has JavaScript enabled. With text, CSS can take the place of JavaScript. This also helps users know when they have their mouse over the correct element.

Using the same rollover color or image as you use to indicate the current page, is a lot less useful to users than having a unique style; so consider having three "states" for your rollovers. One inactive state, one state that accounts for the hover, and one state to tell the user that that option is already selected (the current page).

Placement on Page

Users have become accustomed to navigation existing in certain places on the page, generally the top, or left, or both. Placing your navigation in this location will capitalize on prior user experience. Also, being sure to place the navigation "above the fold" will help your users see all their options at once. "Above the fold" refers to the viewable space in the browser window that shows the top of the page without any scrolling. This size will likely be a little bit different for every user (see above on window sizes and screen resolution).

As we discussed earlier, since users tend to look to the left and center of the page, and see the top of the page first, placing your navigation in these high-priority locations is probably a better option than placing it on the right side of the page, where users expect to see ad banners. This may account for why so many sites have stuck with the 2-axis navigation with the primary site navigation across the top, and subsection and page navigation down the left side.

Site Maps

Site maps are a quick and easy way for users to see and understand the overall structure of your site. A simple bullet list can not only show the hierarchical structure, but also provide links to every page on the site. A more complex site map can be useful if you need to include summaries of the page or other notes as well. Providing a means to get to the site map from every page on the site can reduce the time to get to any page to just two clicks.

Search Forms

Users are quite accustomed to being able to search a site immediately, often instead of navigating it. Because of this, it is worth determining how your users rely on the search capability of your site, and placing the form appropriately on the page. If your users rely on the search almost exclusively, consider placing it near or above the primary navigation. If it's a rare use, consider placement lower on the page. Either way, allowing the user to have just a small search box and submit button is usually adequate, but linking to a page that offers more search options (when possible) can be a good way to reward your power users who are more familiar with searching or need more robust searches. In many sites, this is a button or text hyperlink for *Advanced Search*.

DHTML Menus

DHTML menus certainly have their advantages in that they can show the entire structure of a site with simply a mouse hover, as well as allowing links to any page on the site. Keep in mind, however, the users and their browsers. Given all the freely available (and not so free) scripts out there, finding and implementing one should be carefully done to ensure support for as many users as possible. Given all the versions of browsers on the Web, the varying existing support, and the potentially unique support in future browsers, maintaining such a script can take up a significant chunk of time. In addition, there absolutely should be traditional navigation for those users without JavaScript or DHTML capability.

Breadcrumbs

Breadcrumbs are a great way to show the user his or her place within the structure of the site at any time, and are sometimes referred to as "user trails" or "path." Instead of acting as an analog to the *back* button of the browser, breadcrumbs indicate site structure, allowing the user to move up the site tree as many levels as necessary to get to the root. Consider the breadcrumb as analogous to one branch from the site map.

A map in a shopping mall usually says, "You are here" but tells you nothing of how you got there. It still provides valuable information on how you can get out and where you can go from there. A breadcrumb serves the same purpose, without replicating existing back-button capability.

Other Elements and Attributes

There are other elements and attributes introduced in the HTML 4 specification that can enhance the usability of a site.

The alt Attribute

The `alt` attribute is used most commonly on images to display alternative text for users without image capability in their browser (using screen readers or having images turned off, for example). `alt` is required for the `<img>` and `<area>` tags, and optional for `<input>` and `<applet>` tags. `alt` should not be used to fill out the "ToolTip" boxes that appear when hovering over an image, Use the `title` attribute instead. `alt` should be a description of the image for those who cannot see it. The quickest way to test your images for appropriate `alt` attributes is to load up the page in the Lynx browser.

Use of this attribute is a priority 1 requirement for compliance with the WCAG, and is the first checkpoint. You can read the requirements at *http://www.w3.org/TR/WCAG10/wai-pageauth.html#gl-provide-equivalents*.

The longdesc Attribute

The `longdesc` attribute can be used in an `<img>` tag to provide a link to a long description of an image. While the description should supplement the text in the `alt` attribute, you can assume only those users who cannot see the image will actually read the long description associated with it.

Unfortunately, no browsers currently offer a way to access the URL specified in this attribute. In the interim, it has been suggested that you use a regular hyperlink around the letter "d" (or around "[d]"), next to the image, with the same URL as the `longdesc` so that users can still access the URL. Using a `title` attribute to tell the user what the link is would also be idea. Sample code follows:

```
<img src="chart1.gif" alt="Annual Water Use" longdesc="water_use_chart.html">
<a href="water_use_chart.html" title="Link to a description of this image">d</a>
```

Along with the `alt` attribute, use of `longdesc` is a priority 1 requirement for compliance with the WCAG, and is the first checkpoint. You can read the requirements at *http://www.w3.org/TR/WCAG10/wai-pageauth.html#gl-provide-equivalents*.

The title Attribute

The `title` attribute is a method to provide just what it implies, a title, to nearly every element on the page. Some browsers, such as browsers based on the Gecko engine (Mozilla, Netscape), Internet Explorer, or Opera, show titles as "ToolTips" when the user has their cursor over the element. Using a `title` on a link can be a useful to tell users more about the link without having to insert the text into the flow of the page content.

The following elements are the only ones that **do not** take a title attribute:

`<base>`	`<meta>`
`<basefont>`	`<param>`
`<head>`	`<script>`
`<html>`	`<title>`

\<abbr\> and \<acronym\>

These two tags provide a method to offer more information on an abbreviation (`<abbr>`) or an acronym (`<acronym>`). Using the `title` attribute, an author can specify what the full text might be:

```
<abbr title="Mister">Mr.</abbr>
<acronym title="World Wide Web">WWW</acronym>
```

Here's how the three main browsers render this text, first IE 6:

next Mozilla 1.0:

and Opera 6.01:

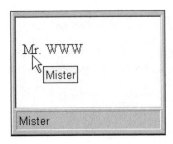 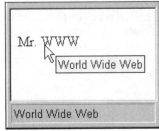

CSS for Everything But the Screen

Back in the golden days of the Web, authors would often create printable pages of their sites, allowing users to get a copy devoid of ad banners, navigation, and other page elements. Today, we can do that with CSS, assuming the user has a more recent browser (Opera 6+, Internet Explorer 5+, Netscape 6+). Thanks to media types in CSS, it is possible to have one CSS file applied only for one medium, such as print. This also allows the author to specify CSS for other media types, listed below:

Media Type	Suitability
all	Suitable for all devices.
aural	Intended for speech synthesizers. See the section on aural stylesheets for details.
braille	Intended for Braille tactile feedback devices.
embossed	Intended for paged Braille printers.
handheld	Intended for handheld devices (typically small screen, monochrome, limited bandwidth).
print	Intended for paged, opaque material and for documents viewed on screen in print preview mode. Please consult the section on paged media for information about formatting issues that are specific to paged media.
projection	Intended for projected presentations, for example projectors or print to transparencies. Please consult the section on paged media for information about formatting issues that are specific to paged media.
screen	Intended primarily for color computer screens.
tty	Intended for media using a fixed-pitch character grid, such as teletypes, terminals, or portable devices with limited display capabilities. Authors should not use pixel units with this media type.
tv	Intended for television-type devices (low resolution, color, limited-scrolling ability screens, sound available).

Support for media types other than print is still very shaky, but it does allow you to start building now for when the support is commonplace. Opera uses the projection media to deliver full-screen presentations, which means that you can create fully accessible slideshows in HTML, at least if your target audience uses Opera.

A common technique to hide the navigation bar from a printed page would be to set its `display` property to `none` in the CSS file:

```
#SubNavBar {display: none ; }
```

And you would call it like this:

```
<html>
<head>
<link rel="stylesheet" href="print.css" media="print" type="text/css">
</head>
<body>
<ul id="SubNavBar">
 <li>Navigation Item</li>
</ul>
</body>
</html>
```

Below are samples of a page rendered through the browser normally, and then in print preview mode, showing how the printed version will appear when elements like the above navigation bar are styled appropriately. As you can see, the background colors and images were removed, as well as all navigation. Now the user is presented with a page that makes the most use of the paper, and still keeps the branding in place.

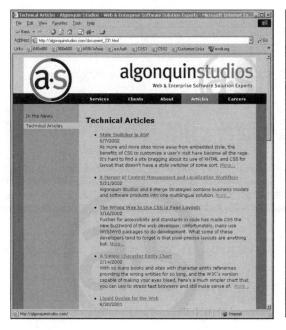
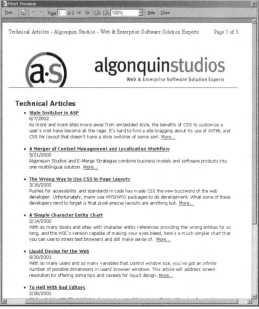

The Written Word

Usability is about more than just how the user navigates about a site, or how we display pages on different devices. As important is the general appearance of text on the page, as well obviously as how the text itself reads.

Typography

It is important to consider how text is flowed into the page. Text that is too short from line to line, or too long, can be much harder to read. Text that is bunched together can be hard to read, as well. Appropriate typefaces and colors need to be chosen to provide enough contrast and detail. Choose the typeface appropriately, ideally from a selection of screen-optimized fonts. While not all users will have the same typefaces, most Windows and Macintosh users will at least have Verdana (sans-serif), Georgia (serif), and Courier (monospace) installed, all of which are intended for on-screen reading.

As covered in *Chapter 7*, a serif is one of the little lines on the end of a letter, and they are designed to make the words more readable in print. A sans-serif font doesn't have any serifs, and is usually intended for easier reading on the screen. A monospace font is one where all the characters take up the same amount of space, be they an i or an m. Here is an example of three common fonts so you can see the differences:

Sans-serif
Arial

Serif
Times New Roman

Monospace
Courier

Setting type in images may provide for greater design freedom, but it can make the text inaccessible to some users. Instead, set the text in HTML using CSS to style it appropriately.

Use appropriate elements for your text. Use the `<h1>` through `<h6>` elements for headings, use `<p></p>` to enclose paragraphs, and use other elements as appropriate. Not only does it provide semantic and structural meaning to the page, but also those are all anchors to which you can attach CSS styles. Another book by glasshaus has an entire chapter devoted to the appropriate use of text on the Web: *Web Graphics for Non-Designers*, ISBN 1-904151-15-9.

Also, keep in mind how users read on the Web; they generally skim, quickly scanning the page looking for keywords, hyperlinks, or other areas of interest.

Text Size

Allowing the user to resize the text on the page is a good way to help prevent them from becoming frustrated with content that is too small. Ideally, letting the user's default font size control the font sizes of your page is best, but with most browsers set to display text at 16pt. on-screen, a designer will rarely want to let the text stand that large.

One method for giving the user control over the type size is with server-side scripting and a few preset options for users to choose from. While it requires an extra trip to the server, it doesn't rely solely on CSS to allow control and can work in any browser if coded well.

Even though most browsers support font sizing of some kind with a built-in widget, sometimes the CSS can override the options altogether. Internet Explorer for Windows has the unfortunate distinction of being one of the only browsers that won't resize type set in pixels via CSS. Other sizing units can work, but they each have their own caveats, many of which include browser bugs, differences in CSS interpretations, and too complex layouts. And so the debate continues on the best way to handle type size.

Summary

In this chapter we looked at general principles of designing a web page for usability. We also saw how to increase usability through layout, making forms more usable, and easing navigation. We covered some general-purpose attributes and elements, and looked at making text usable.

I've also tried to impress upon you as a reader that good usability comes from knowing your audience as much as from knowing the rules. There may be times when it is perfectly valid to ignore one of the rules above, and when those times come, you'll know what you're gaining and what you're losing.

In conjunction with the *Chapter 10* on *Accessibility* (which you will find overlaps usability in a number of places), you should be well on your way to understanding the basics. Staying on top of the latest writings and research from sites like those suggested on the links page for this chapter can also help keep your skills sharp as user behaviors and technologies continue to evolve.

10

- General principles of usability

- Usability of forms and navigation

Author: Adrian Roselli

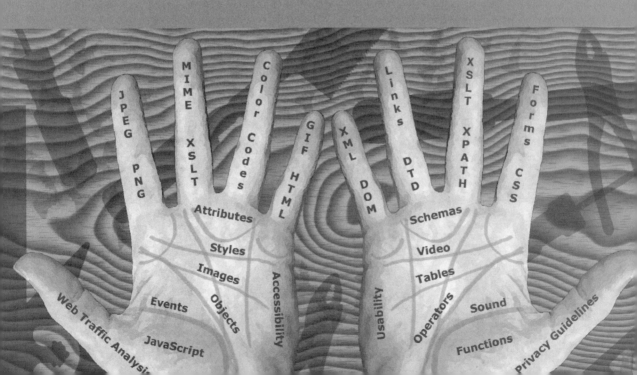

Accessibility

Creating accessible web pages has never been more important than it is today. With the recent adoption of accessibility standards in the United States, Canada, the European Union, Australia, Japan, and Brazil, it is mandatory for designers and developers to ensure that people with disabilities are able to access the contents of web sites and web applications.

In addition, ensuring that web sites are accessible to people with disabilities is simply the right thing to do. For people with disabilities, the Internet can be a tremendously valuable tool. It can provide access to the world around them, as well as a level of independence not previously possible.

Imagine a task as simple as reading the newspaper. Prior to the Internet, a blind person who wanted to read the paper had two choices. They could get a Braille version of the paper, which was expensive and often hard to find, or could ask someone to read the paper to them. Today, they are able to use software called a screen reader to read the news to him from a web site each day. Dependence on others is eliminated.

Now, imagine a person with a disability writing a memo to a colleague, or applying for a promotion, or taking a course at a university. For many people with disabilities, accessibility is about much more than convenience. It is about access to employment, education, and the community. It's about being able to lead a normal life.

This chapter provides a brief overview of both the issues faced by people with disabilities and the relevant accessibility policies and standards aimed at alleviating them – as well as a look at some important techniques developers can use for achieving accessibility. The discussion begins with a look at the challenges presented to users with disabilities and the assistive technologies used to meet those challenges. From there, an examination of the accessibility standards will help connect the various policies in effect around the world. Finally, this chapter will examine the W3C web content accessibility standards in greater detail.

This is not intended to provide a comprehensive look at the issue of accessibility and the related standards, policies, and design techniques. For a more detailed discussion of accessibility, *Constructing Accessible Web Sites* (Thatcher, et al, glasshaus, ISBN 1-904151-00-0) is a tremendous resource.

Accessibility Overview

In general terms, accessibility describes how well web sites work for people with disabilities. An accessible site is one in which design elements such as color, font size, or layout do not obscure the site's content. An accessible web site is also compatible with the assistive technologies used by people with disabilities.

More specifically, policies such as **Section 508** of the US Rehabilitation Act (*http://www.section508.gov/*) and guidelines such as the **Web Accessibility Initiative**, specify what constitutes an accessible site with a series of checkpoints. Each checkpoint addresses issues for specific disabilities and technologies.

This section provides a more complete definition of accessibility in terms of the range of disabilities commonly found among web users, the assistive technologies used, and the policies governing web accessibility. Finally, we review a number of reasons for incorporating accessibility into web site design.

Defining Disabilities

A 1997 report by the US Census Bureau categorizes 19.6 percent of the United States population as having some sort of disability. This percentage is generally considered to be consistent with worldwide statistics. Within the broader category of disability are the following:

- Visual impairments
- Hearing impairments
- Motor impairments
- Cognitive impairments

Each of these categories includes a range of conditions. For example, visual impairments include low vision, color blindness, and blindness. The tools and techniques addressing issues for people who are blind are very different from those that address issues for people who are color blind. Perhaps the most diverse category is that of cognitive impairments. This group includes people with seizure disorders, as well as people with learning or developmental disabilities. Building sites that are accessible to people with cognitive disabilities can be a complex task as the obstacles to comprehension often lie in the content as well as in the page design. Below is a brief description of some common challenges facing each of these groups.

Visual Impairments
For people who are blind, it is worth mentioning two significant challenges presented by the Web (though there are many more). First, an accessible site should provide text descriptions of visual elements, such as images. Blind web users have no means of interpreting images if the designer does not provide a text description. Second, an accessible site is well structured. Listening to a page using a screen reader has been compared to reading a page through a soda straw. You can only see one word at a time and you can't see anything else around it. Using heading elements and being thoughtful about the text used as a hyperlink are two important ways designers can help users more easily make sense of the page.

For people with low vision, it is important to use text on the page, rather than images of text. This makes it easier for users with low vision to increase the font size on the page. Designers often use images to control the formatting of the text. However, Cascading Style Sheets can be used to help control formatting and still allow users to modify text to meet their specific needs.

Hearing Impairments

For users with hearing impairments, auditory content needs to be provided as text. Most people are familiar with captioning. This is often seen as the text of the audio that appears at the bottom of the television screen. With the growing availability of video on the Web, there is surprisingly little of this content that is captioned. This severely restricts the ability of people with hearing impairments to take advantage of video delivered over the Web.

Motor Impairments

This category includes people with limited or no use of their hands. In these cases, people will rely on the keyboard or alternative pointing devices to interact with the computer. For a person with limited use of their hands due to carpal tunnel syndrome, they may simply rely on the keyboard rather than use the mouse to interact with the page. People with no use of their hands may also use the keyboard, but in conjunction with a tool such as a mouthstick to press keys. For these individuals, it is not possible to press more than one key at a time. They will use a mode in the operating system know as "sticky keys", which allows the user to press a modifier key (such as the shift key) once, and for it to continue to be regarded as depressed by the operating system until after the next key is pressed.

Cognitive Impairments

Cognitive impairments are perhaps the most diverse and the largest category of disabilities. They include issues such as seizure disorders, learning disabilities, and developmental disabilities. In these cases, pages made up of long blocks of unbroken text may be difficult to read. Blinking or animated elements should be avoided, to make the contents easier to read. In addition, it is often helpful to people with cognitive disabilities if we provide illustrations or animations of central concepts to enhance understanding.

Disability categories can overlap and might also include temporary disabilities. One group that is often overlooked is the deaf-blind community. For people who are deaf and blind, the Internet can be an immensely important means of communicating with others. In addition, any one of us may find ourselves temporarily disabled. Someone with a broken wrist may have difficulty using a mouse but still need access to the Web to meet day-to-day job requirements.

At the same time, it is important to keep in mind that as people get older, most face a disability of some kind. While only 20 percent of the total US population has a disability, the proportion of people with disabilities grows higher with increasing age (see table, overleaf – source: http://www.census.gov/hhes/www/disable/sipp/disab97/ds97t1.html). In fact, almost 75 percent of the people over the age of 80 has a disability. Thus, accessibility is not just about opening doors; it is about keeping them open. Accessibility allows people to maintain a level of independence that age might otherwise make difficult.

10

Accessibility

	Total Number	With Disability	Percent with Disability
All Ages	267,665,000	52,596,000	19.7%
Under 15 years	59,606,000	4,661,000	7.8%
15 to 24 years	36,897,000	3,961,000	10.7%
25 to 44 years	83,887,000	11,200,000	13.4%
45 to 54 years	33,620,000	7,585,000	22.6%
55 to 64 years	21,591,000	7,708,000	35.7%
65 years and over	32,064,000	17,480,000	54.5%

Assistive Technologies

Users with disabilities frequently rely on hardware and software to access web content. These tools, known as assistive technologies, range from screen readers to touch screens and head pointers.

Users of the Web who are blind frequently use software called a screen reader to read the contents of a web page out loud. Two common screen readers, already mentioned above, are JAWS, from Freedom Scientific (*http://www.freedomscientific.com/fs_products/software_jaws.asp*), and Window-Eyes, from GW Micro (*http://www.gwmicro.com/windoweyes/windoweyes.htm*). Screen readers enable users to hear, rather than read, the contents of a web page. However, a screen reader can read only text, not images or animations. It is essential, therefore, that images and animations be assigned text descriptions that screen readers can read. These text descriptions are called alternative text, or alt text.

Users with impaired mobility may rely on the keyboard instead of the mouse to navigate web pages. For individuals with nerve damage, arthritis, or repetitive motion injuries, use of the mouse may not be comfortable or possible. Using only *Tab* and *Enter* on the keyboard, it is possible for these individuals to negotiate a properly designed page with ease. Many users of the Internet have this capability and are simply unaware of it. In Internet Explorer, pressing *Tab* moves the focus of the browser among all available links or form elements on a page. The dotted lines around links in IE lets the user know where the current focus of the browser is positioned. Pressing *Enter* activates whatever page element currently has focus, giving the same effect as clicking (and releasing) a mouse. In the next screenshot, notice the dotted lines around the word "*Search*" on the *Search* button of the form:

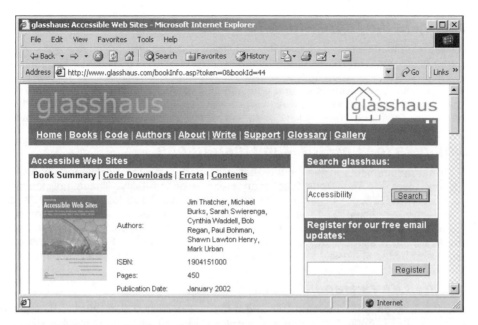

In some cases, users may employ touch screens, head pointers, or other assistive devices. A touch screen allows an individual to navigate the page using their hands without the fine motor control required by the mouse. A head pointer is simply a stick placed in a person's mouth or mounted on a head strap that the person uses to interact with a keyboard or a touch screen.

In these cases, it is very important that essential components of the page work without a mouse. Rollovers, drop-down lists, and interactive simulations are all examples of elements that typically depend on the mouse for user interaction. The designer or developer of these elements must ensure that keyboard-defined events are included along with mouse-defined events. A quick test using the keystrokes available in IE can provide a valuable glimpse of the difficulties a web page may present for users who cannot use a mouse. For example, a user can move to any focusable object including links, form controls, and embedded objects by pressing the *Tab* key and pressing the *Enter* key will activate selected links. Pressing *Ctrl* and *Tab* moves between frames.

Why Is Accessibility Important?

For most people, the reasons for creating an accessible web site are simple: it is the right thing to do and it is the law. It is often helpful, however, to point out the additional benefits of creating an accessible web site. The following is a list of reasons many find compelling:

- ◆ Accessibility is the right thing to do
- ◆ Accessibility is the law for many institutions
- ◆ Accessibility offers benefits for **all** users, not just those with disabilities
- ◆ Accessibility uses innovative technology
- ◆ Accessibility creates market opportunity

Accessibility Is the Right Thing to Do

Accessibility represents an important step toward independence for individuals with disabilities. Accessible web pages provide access to fundamental government services and information such as tax forms, social programs, and legislative representatives. Accessible web pages also make possible a broader range of employment and educational opportunities by providing added means of communication. In addition, accessibility allows users with disabilities to participate in day-to-day activities many of us take for granted, such as reading a newspaper or buying a gift for a loved one.

Accessibility Is the Law for Many Institutions

With new national requirements in the United States, Canada, and the European Union, Australia, and Hong Kong, there are numerous legal mandates for accessibility. These policies will likely expand in scope. In the US, for instance, Section 508 sets standards for web pages designed or maintained by federal agencies. State and local governments as well as educational and non-profit institutions around the US are considering their own accessibility policies. For example, earlier this year the University of Wisconsin at Madison adopted an Accessibility Policy requiring all pages published or hosted by the university to conform to all WCAG Priority 1 and 2 checkpoints.

Accessibility Offers Benefits for All Users

As with many improvements intended for individuals with disabilities, the enhancements of accessible design offer benefits for all users of the Web. Anyone who has pushed a shopping cart out of a grocery store can attest to the value of automatic doors and ramps cut into curbs. Similarly, accessible web pages are often easier to read, easier to navigate, faster to download, and are more readily indexed by search engines, as they are optimized for ease of use and don't tend to contain so many of the page elements (such as Flash movies, and large images) that are the culprits of large and slow-loading sites.

Accessibility Uses Innovative Technology

Accessible design is based on the premise that web pages must work with a range of browsers that includes more than just Netscape and Internet Explorer. A page must be accessible whether using a screen reader, a refreshable Braille display, or a head pointer. Making pages work with non-standard browsers often makes them available to other consumer Internet devices, such as WAP-enabled phones or handheld Personal Digital Assistants (PDAs).

The techniques of accessibility are based on recent technologies and design strategies. Older, static HTML designs often intermix content with formatting on web pages. Accessibility guidelines encourage the separation of formatting from content through the use of Cascading Style Sheets (CSS) to allow more flexible use of content and easier implementation of more powerful dynamic models. For more on the use of CSS for accessibility, refer back to *Chapter 2* of this book.

Accessibility Creates Market Opportunity

Accessibility offers potential for organizations and businesses to reach new customers and new markets. As additional policies are adopted, the need among government and educational institutions for goods and services that support an accessibility policy is growing. In the US, businesses providing goods and services to the government via the Web or other information technology should understand Section 508. Businesses that understand accessibility issues and comply with Section 508 have a strong market advantage. This advantage is multiplied as local governments implement new policies.

Accessibility Standards

Accessibility policies vary from country to country, but many countries, including the United States, Australia, Canada, the European Union, and Japan have adopted policies based on standards developed by the **World Wide Web Consortium** (**W3C**). In 1994, the W3C began investigating accessibility issues that might be encountered by people with disabilities on the new emerging World Wide Web. This group led to the formation of the Web Accessibility Initiative (WAI). The WAI consists of several efforts to improve the accessibility of the Web. Perhaps the most widely used document is the **Web Content Accessibility Guidelines** (**WCAG**).

For each of the fourteen guidelines that constitute the WCAG, there are a series of checkpoints rated as Priority 1, Priority 2, or Priority 3:

- Priority 1 checkpoints are the actions designers *must* take to make a site accessible

- Priority 2 checkpoints are the actions designers *should* take to make a site accessible

- Priority 3 checkpoints are the actions a designer *might* take to improve the accessibility of a site

The Priority 1 checkpoints of the WCAG serve as the basis of accessibility standards in almost every country where a formal policy has been adopted. The exceptions are Canada and Germany, where web site designers for the national governments are required to follow the Priority 1 and Priority 2 checkpoints of the WCAG.

In the United States, the law governing web accessibility is commonly referred to as Section 508. Section 508 of the US Rehabilitation Act prohibits federal agencies from buying, developing, maintaining, or using electronic and information technology that is inaccessible to people with disabilities. Originally enacted in 1988, Section 508 made little progress until Congress passed the Workforce Investment Act ten years later. This amendment to Section 508 mandated standards for accessibility and, what is more, gave members of the public and government employees with disabilities the right to sue agencies in federal court and file administrative complaints for non-compliance.

As of June 21 2002, all federal web sites are expected to comply with the standards mandated under Section 508. These standards are based on the Priority 1 checkpoints of the WCAG, with one Priority 3 checkpoint thrown in for good measure. Section 508 does not make any provision for Priority 2 checkpoints of the WCAG.

The difference between Section 508 and the WCAG is subtle but important. Section 508 was intended to define when a problem became severe enough to serve as the basis of a lawsuit. The WCAG defines a set of goals for accessible design. As a result, the Section 508 standards were designed to be evaluated more easily. This has made the Section 508 standards a popular basis for accessibility policies at the state, local, and institutional level. Designers and developers in these settings are often under no federal mandate to follow the Section 508 standards. Instead, their state-, local-, or institutional-level accessibility policy may require use of these standards. This distinction can be confusing but important. The consequences for non-compliance may vary significantly from place to place.

W3C Web Content Accessibility Guidelines

To present a clear picture of what is expected of an accessible web site, the following section discusses Priority 1 checkpoints of the Web Content Accessibility Guidelines (WCAG, often pronounced, "wick-ag"). This discussion should only serve as a brief discussion of the issues of accessible design, but will provide designers and developers alike with a solid basis for understanding common issues.

WCAG Checkpoint 1.1

> **Provide a text equivalent for every non-text element (for example, via "alt", "longdesc", or in element content). This includes: images, graphical representations of text (including symbols), image map regions, animations (for example animated GIFs), applets and programmatic objects, ASCII art, frames, scripts, images used as list bullets, spacers, graphical buttons, sounds (played with or without user interaction), stand-alone audio files, audio tracks of video, and video.**

Checkpoint 1.1 covers a wide range of media used on the Web and an even greater number of associated techniques. The issues and techniques related to several different types of content commonly found on the Web will now be considered separately.

Text equivalents for images and graphical buttons.

When a web page is read with a screen reader, the contents of the page are read aloud to the user. Since screen readers are not able to 'read' the individual pixels that make up the image to 'see' its contents, it is up to the designer to leave in some text, describing the image. This text alternative (commonly referred to as 'alt text') is hidden in the HTML for the screen reader to read.

An important issue related to the use of alt text is deciding what the alt text should say. In most cases, a generic, one-word explanation such as, "picture" will not suffice. This provides no information to a user who cannot see the image itself. On the other hand, too much information is not helpful either.

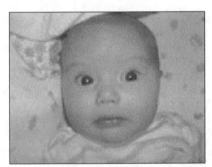

For example, the image here is taken from a child health web site. It is used primarily for decorative purposes, not to convey information about a specific issue. Thus, the alt text should be short. An inappropriate use of alt text for this image in this context would read "*Baby with wide-eyed expression wearing white shirt with blue stripes*". This presents more detail than is relevant. More practically, it forces the screen reader user to listen to this explanation each time the page is visited. The sample code actually used in this example is shown below.

```
<img src="baby.jpg" alt="Baby">
```

A second means of presenting an alternative representation of an image is through the use of the `longdesc` (long description) attribute. For images requiring a description longer than 50 characters, the long description attribute provides a link to a separate page. On that page, the user would find a longer description of the image. It is important to note that the long description is intended to be used in conjunction with the `alt` attribute, not in place of it. Alt text must be provided for every image.

In the example below, a graph is placed on a page. The alt text for the chart reads, "*Group Comparison*". The long description, on a separate page, lists a qualitative description of the data used to construct the graph as well as the data in table form. There is an important downside to the `longdesc` attribute, however. Though it has been in existence since December 1999, it is still poorly supported by browsers and screen readers, as well as web-authoring tools.

```
<img src="pop.gif" width="284" height="196"
     alt="United States Population 1970-2000" longdesc="population.htm">
```

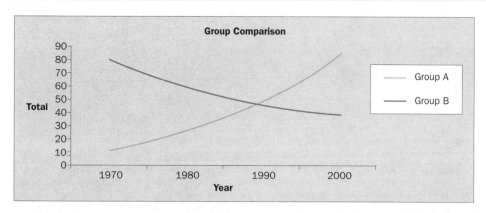

A text equivalent for graphical representations of text (including symbols).
Text is frequently included in images. This technique provides designers more control over the font, spacing, and layout. However, screen readers have no way of reading the text in an image. Consequently, all text included in an image should also be included in the alt text. As an additional problem, people with low vision often increase their text size to make the page more readable. Text within an image cannot be adjusted in this way (except in some less common browsers, such as Opera). Thus, accessible design discourages the use of images to represent text.

In addition, this checkpoint is intended to address the use of mathematical symbols and equations on the Web. To control the layout of symbols in mathematical symbols and equations, many designers draw them in a graphics program and then export the equation as an image. Again, this prevents users who are blind or have visual impairments from accessing the contents of the equation. The WCAG recommends designers instead use appropriate markup languages such as MathML to present equations. However, to date support for MathML in visual browsers as well as screen readers is poor to non-existent. As a result, many designers of math content have relied on the use of alt text to describe math equations. An informal standard known as 'mathspeak' was developed by a blind mathematician to facilitate consistent description of mathematical expressions. For more info on mathspeak, see *http://www.nfbcal.org/s_e/list/0033.html*.

A text equivalent for images used as "spacers".

Images are frequently used in web pages to help organize the page visually. In HTML, pages are often arranged visually using tables. Each column of these tables expands to accommodate the contents of the cells. Since text sizes can vary from computer to computer, images are often used to hold cells open to a specific width. These images, called spacer images, are often placed in either the top or bottom row of the table. Since they convey no content, the appropriate alt text is either `alt=""` or `alt=" "`. I have frequently encountered instances where well-intentioned designers will assign the alt text `"spacer image"` to these cases. The result in a screen reader can be that the words "spacer image" are read twenty to thirty times in a row at the beginning of each page. Using the space character or an empty string has the effect of telling the screen reader to skip over these images to the content.

A text equivalent for image map regions.

Image maps are single images that link to more than one location. The links are defined on areas called 'hotspots' and each hotspot may link to a different location. In order to make the target of the link clear to a screen reader user, alt text must be defined for each hotspot. The alt text typically reflects the image text contained within the boundaries of the hotspot. Note this sample HTML code for a small image map. It includes the `alt` attribute to represent the text equivalent of each hotspot area.

```
<map name="Map">
 <area shape="rect" coords="8,7,60,30" href="index.htm" alt="home">
 <area shape="rect" coords="265,7,97,30" href="link.htm" alt="Links">
 <area shape="rect" coords="86,7,139,30" href="news.htm" alt="news">
</map>
```

Text equivalent for animations (for example, animated GIFs).

Animations are commonly used on the Web as decorative, instructional, or entertaining elements on the page. They are frequently presented using either animated GIFs or Macromedia Flash. An animated GIF is a series of images that displays in a sequence to provide the illusion of a moving image. Animated GIFs were particularly popular in the early days of the Web, since no additional software is required to run them in a browser. A screen reader reads alt text for an animated GIF in the very same way it does for an image. The user is not provided with any clue that the text equivalent is for an animation rather than an image. Sample code is shown below.

```
<img src="dancing_baby.jpg" alt="Dancing Baby">
```

A second common form of animation is created using Macromedia Flash. Flash can be used to create a lot of different types of files, but it got its start as an animation tool. Files created in Flash require a separate piece of software, called the Flash Player, to run. The Flash Player is free and a relatively small application. However, until Flash MX was released in March of 2002, the Flash Player did not work with assistive technologies of any kind. Screen readers were able to view neither the images nor any text contained within a Flash animation. Moreover, the HTML used to connect Flash files to the page did not allow any means of providing a text equivalent. Thus, not only were the contents of a Flash file inaccessible, there was no way to provide a text equivalent. Text equivalents and other accessibility considerations for Flash content must be taken into account as the files are being designed. For more information on designing accessible Flash content, see the Macromedia Accessibility Resource Center, *http://www.macromedia.com/accessibility*.

WCAG Checkpoint 1.2

> **Provide redundant text links for each active region of a server-side image map.**

As was mentioned earlier, an image map is a single image that links to more than one page. Image maps may be generated in one of two ways. A server-side image map does not send all of the information to the user's machine. This is an older way of creating image maps that helped to keep files sizes of web pages small. Since support for server-side image maps is poor among some assistive technologies, this checkpoint encourages designers to place redundant text links for each hotspot of an image map somewhere on the page. However, use of server-side image maps is very rare today.

WCAG Checkpoint 1.3

> **Until user agents can automatically read aloud the text equivalent of a visual track, provide an auditory description of the important information of the visual track of a multimedia presentation.**

The use of video on the Web has become increasingly popular. The availability of software such as iMovie (*http://www.apple.com/imovie/*) has significantly lowered the cost of producing video and moving this video to the Web. However as with images and animations, content conveyed using video is not available to people with visual disabilities. This checkpoint encourages designers to provide equivalents for video using audio descriptions of the visual content. This audio is stored in a separate track that the user can turn on and off. Using a free tool created by the National Center for Accessible Media, called MAGpie (*http://ncam.wgbh.org/webaccess/magpie/*), audio descriptions may easily be added to existing files.

WCAG Checkpoint 1.4

> **For any time-based multimedia presentation (for example, a movie or animation), synchronize equivalent alternatives (for example, captions or auditory descriptions of the visual track) with the presentation.**

As mentioned in the previous checkpoint, the availability of production tools has made the use of video on the Web increasingly popular. As with any instance of video, it is important to provide a text equivalent, or caption, for the audio used. Captioning is one of the oldest and most familiar of assistive technologies. Ironically, few video production tools available today include a means for providing captions. Again, using a tool such as MAGpie, captions may be quickly and easily added to existing video files.

WCAG Checkpoint 2.1

> **Ensure that all information conveyed with color is also available without color, for example from context or markup.**

10

Accessibility

This checkpoint discourages the use of color alone to convey information. For example, it is common in charts to distinguish between portions of a graph using color alone. For people who are color blind, this can make it very difficult to understand the information being presented. As an example, consider the two charts below. The first was actually designed as a color chart, with a legend that indicates the data for Group A in green and Group B in red. If you can see these colors, then the chart very clearly shows Group A with an upward trend and group B with a downward trend. However, since this book is printed in black and white, it is very difficult to differentiate between these two groups, just as it would be for people with particular forms of color blindness.

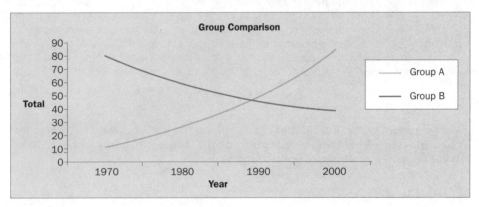

This checkpoint does not prohibit the use of color. Instead, designers need to ensure there is an alternative means of accessing the information. Continuing the example above, in the next chart, the data for Group B is shown via a red dotted line, while A is shown as a green solid line. This provides a clear means of distinguishing data from Group A and Group B for people who are color blind.

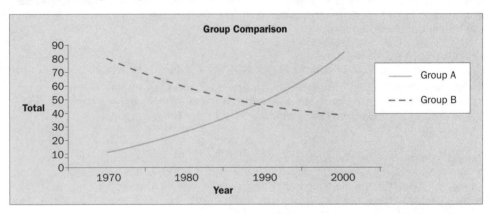

WCAG Checkpoint 4.1

> **Clearly identify changes in the natural language of a document's text and any text equivalents (for example, captions).**

Screen readers are capable of reading pages using a variety of voices. Each voice is designed to read a specific language. Reading a page that is written in English with a French voice can make for a page that is very hard to understand. In cases where the language changes within a page, this checkpoint encourages designers to mark up these changes so that screen readers can change voices accordingly. In the example below, notice that the language changes from English to French. Notice that the `<span>` element around the sentence in French has the attribute `lang` with the assigned value `"fr"` for French.

```
<p>The class has been asked to read <span lang="fr">Les Fleurs des Mals</span>
this week.</p>
```

WCAG Checkpoint 5.1

> **For data tables, identify row, and column headers**

Tables are used in one of two ways. First, tables are commonly used to control the layout of a page. Using tables for layout designers place the contents of the page into different cells in the table to create visual relationships between the parts of the page. While this practice is acceptable under Section 508 and WCAG Priority 1-based policies, it is discouraged under stronger policies based on WCAG priority 2 checkpoints. Those policies encourage the use of CSS for positioning as opposed to tables.

In cases where table are used for layout, it is important to ensure that the content makes sense in the order it is read by a screen reader. A screen reader will read the contents of a table based on the order it is encountered in the HTML. Visually, this roughly equates to the screen reader reading each row, left to right, from top to bottom.

Secondly, and this is perhaps more familiar to non-designers, tables are used to present and organize data. For screen reader users, tables can be very difficult to keep track of unless they are properly marked up. Take the simple example below of a bus schedule taken from my local bus line.

South Transfer Point	Park & Haywood	West Johnson & Park	Main & Carroll	Jennifer & Ingersoll	Winnbago & Atwood	Oa & E. Washington	North Transfer Point
8:00a	8:08a	8:16a	8:25a	8:31a	8:35a	8:39a	8:47a
8:30a	8:38a	8:45a	9:00a	9:07a	9:11a	9:15a	9:23a
9:00a	9:08a	9:15a	9:30a	9:37a	9:41a	9:45a	9:53a
9:30a	9:38a	9:45a	10:00a	10:07a	10:11a	10:15a	10:23a
10:00a	10:08a	10:15a	10:30a	10:37a	10:41a	10:45a	10:53a
10:30a	10:38a	10:45a	11:00a	11:07a	11:11a	11:15a	11:23a
11:00a	11:08a	11:15a	11:30a	11:37a	11:41a	11:45a	11:53a
11:30a	11:38a	11:45a	12:00p	12:07p	12:11p	12:15p	12:23p

A screen reader will read this table row by row, from left to right. The first three rows would be read: *South Transfer Point, Park & Haywood, West Johnson & Park, Main & Carroll, Jennifer & Ingersoll, Winnbago & Atwood, Oak & E. Washington, North Transfer Point, 8:00a, 8:08a, 8:16a, 8:25a, 8:31a, 8:35a, 8:39a, 8:47a, 8:30a, 8:38a, 8:45a, 9:00a, 9:07a, 9:11a, 9:15a, 9:23a.*

Since I live just past the stop at Park & Haywood, I would need to remember that the second point in the list is the one for my stop. After that, every eighth point in the list refers to my stop. After a couple of rows, this gets rather difficult to remember.

To make working with tables easier, screen readers can associate the headers in the top row with the data presented in the following rows. This often requires two steps. First the headers need to be identified. In HTML, table headers are distinguished from data cells using the `<th>` element. Second, the data cells need to be associated with the headers. This can be done in HTML by using the `scope` attribute for the `<th>` element to identify whether the header modifies a column or a row.

If the table is marked up in this way, the screen reader is able to read the contents of the table as follows: *South Transfer Point, 8:00a, Park & Haywood, 8:08a, West Johnson & Park, 8:16a, Main & Carroll, 8:25a, Jennifer & Ingersoll, 8:31a, Winnbago & Atwood, 8:35a, Oak & E. Washington, 8:39a, North Transfer Point, 8:47a, South Transfer Point, 8:30a, Park & Haywood, 8:38a, West Johnson & Park, 8:45a, Main & Carroll, 9:00a, Jennifer & Ingersoll, 9:07a, Winnbago & Atwood, 9:11a, Oak & E. Washington, 9:15a, North Transfer Point, 9:23a.*

This makes it much easier to keep track of the times and the stops to which they correspond. The code for the first three rows of this table would read like this.

```
<table>
  <tr>
    <th scope="col">South Transfer Point </th>
    <th scope="col">Park &amp; Haywood </th>
    <th scope="col">West Johnson &amp; Park </th>
    <th scope="col">Main &amp; Carroll </th>
    <th scope="col">Jennifer &amp; Ingersoll </th>
    <th scope="col">Winnbago &amp; Atwood </th>
    <th scope="col">Oak &amp; E. Washington </th>
    <th scope="col">North Transfer Point </th>
  </tr>
  <tr>
    <td>8:00a </td>
    <td>8:08a </td>
    <td>8:16a </td>
    <td>8:25a </td>
    <td>8:31a </td>
    <td>8:35a </td>
    <td>8:39a </td>
    <td>8:47a </td>
  </tr>
  <tr>
    <td>8:30a </td>
    <td>8:38a </td>
    <td>8:45a </td>
    <td>9:00a </td>
```

```
      <td>9:07a </td>
      <td>9:11a </td>
      <td>9:15a </td>
      <td>9:23a </td>
    </tr>
  ...
  </table>
```

WCAG Checkpoint 5.2

> **For data tables that have two or more logical levels of row or column headers, use markup to associate data cells and header cells.**

For more complex tables, those with more than two levels of headers, an alternative method of marking up tables is preferred. This method uses the `headers` and `id` attributes. Each header is assigned a unique `id` attribute. Each data cell references that `id` using the `headers` attribute. Note that in the table below, there are three headers modifying each cell.

		Woodland Tour Guide	**Marshland Tour Guide**
Saturday			
	Morning	David	Susan
	Afternoon	Tenesha	Luis
Sunday			
	Morning	David	Tenesha
	Afternoon	Luis	Susan

The code for this table is listed below. Notice that in each `headers` attribute, the list is delimited by a space. For this reason, it is important to ensure that `id` attribute values do not include spaces.

```
<table>
  <tr>
    <td></td>
    <td></td>
    <th id="woodland">Woodland Tour Guide</th>
    <th id="marshland">Marshland Tour Guide</th>
  </tr>
  <tr>
```

```
      <th id="saturday">Saturday</th>
      <td></td>
      <td></td>
      <td></td>
    </tr>
    <tr>
      <td></td>
      <th id="morning">Morning</th>
      <td headers="woodland saturday morning">David</td>
      <td headers="marshland saturday morning">Susan</td>
    </tr>
    <tr>
      <td></td>
      <th id="afternoon">Afternoon</th>
      <td headers="woodland saturday afternoon">Tenesha</td>
      <td headers="marshland saturday afternoon">Luis</td>
    </tr>
    <tr>
      <th id="sunday">Sunday</th>
      <td></td>
      <td></td>
      <td></td>
    </tr>
    <tr>
      <td></td>
      <th id="morning">Morning</th>
      <td headers="woodland sunday morning">David</td>
      <td headers="marshland sunday morning">Tenesha</td>
    </tr>
    <tr>
      <td></td>
      <th id="afternoon">Afternoon</th>
      <td headers="woodland sunday afternoon">Luis</td>
      <td headers="marshland sunday afternoon">Susan</td>
    </tr>
  </table>
```

WCAG Checkpoint 6.1

> **Organize documents so they may be read without stylesheets. For example, when an HTML document is rendered without associated stylesheets, it must still be possible to read the document.**

Screen readers will read the contents of a web page from the HTML file directly. Thus it is very important, particularly when CSS is used for positioning, that attention is paid to the order of the content on the document itself. Using CSS, the content may be ordered visually to be coherent but not affect the order of content in the HTML itself.

WCAG Checkpoint 6.2

> **Ensure that equivalents for dynamic content are updated when the dynamic content changes.**

Web sites are not always static documents. Web designers will often design pages to change, depending on the date, the user, or other variables. In cases where the content is dynamic, it is important that text equivalents for content are updated at the same time.

WCAG Checkpoint 6.3

> **Ensure that pages are usable when scripts, applets, or other programmatic objects are turned off or not supported. If this is not possible, provide equivalent information on an alternative accessible page.**

As mentioned above, the use of plugin technologies can often introduce their own accessibility issues. For this reason, this checkpoint encourages designs that are not dependent on plugins. Use of plugins on pages should be done with great attention to how people without support for those plugins may reach the same content. This does not prohibit designers from using third party plugin technologies. Instead, it encourages a more thoughtful use of these tools.

WCAG Checkpoint 7.1

> **Until user agents allow users to control flickering, avoid causing the screen to flicker.**

A screen flicker of a specific rate can trigger seizures in people with epilepsy. The WCAG cites rates between, "4 to 59 flashes per second". Since flicker rates can be affected by a variety of factors on the end user's machine (such as the memory and speed) it can be very hard for designers to determine if a flicker rate is too high or too low. One approach to this issue is to ensure that all motion and blinking on the page come to a stop after a few seconds.

WCAG Checkpoint 9.1

> **Provide client-side image maps instead of server-side image maps except where the regions cannot be defined with an available geometric shape.**

As was mention in Checkpoint 1.1, an image map is a single image that links to multiple sites. There are two types of image maps. A client-side image map moves all information to the user's machine. A server-side image map leaves some information on the web server. Client-side image maps allow the designer to provide text equivalents for each link, or hotspot and for each link to be activated using the keyboard. Since not all server-side image maps allow this, client-side image maps are preferred.

Title each frame to facilitate frame identification and navigation.

Frames are used to divide the contents of a screen. Each part or frame displays a separate web page. A common use for frames is to isolate elements used consistently throughout a site, such as a navigation bar. This allows a designer to display the same navigation bar across an entire site. When the navigation page is changed, it may be changed across the entire site all at once rather than changing it page by page, which may be rather time consuming.

Frames pose three particular issues when it comes to accessibility, yet only one is addressed in the guidelines. First, older browsers and screen readers may not support frames. To address this problem, the W3C includes a `<noframes>` element in HTML. This tag is intended to contain all of the same content, only without the use of frames. Notice that in the example listed below, the `noframes` content follows the frameset.

```
<frameset rows="80,*">
  <frame src="top.htm" title="banner">
  <frame src="content.htm" title="content">
</frameset>
<noframes>
<body>
Place site contents here
</body>
</noframes>
```

Second, when a screen reader user comes to a page with frames, most screen readers will notify the user of the total number of frames and which frame they are currently in. Next, the screen reader will read the name assigned for that frame. This checkpoint encourages designers to assign a title that helps provide a cue to screen reader users as to the purpose of that frame. Simple titles, such as `"banner"` or `"content"`, can help to orient a user significantly. However, it is very common for designers to forget or neglect to assign these names. In these cases, the user will simply be given the name `'untitled'`. Notice the use of the `title` attribute in the previous example.

A third problem related to the use of frames emerges when there is a complex or large number of frames. Although such designs are generally an inherently bad idea anyway in terms of performance and layout, theW3C does not prohibit such usage, or prescribe how frames should be used. In these cases, the W3C simply recommends the use of the `longdesc` attribute of the `<frameset>` element to explain the relationship between various frames.

WCAG Checkpoint 14.1

Use the clearest and simplest language appropriate for a site's content.

As a web design instructor, I noticed that many of my students found this checkpoint to be one of the most disconcerting. After all, the University of Wisconsin is a prestigious institution where faculty have trained long and hard in learning how *not* to be clear or simple!

All kidding aside, this checkpoint is intended to address the needs of those with cognitive or learning disabilities. Use of jargon, slang, or complex language can reduce one's access to the content. In many academic contexts, there is simply no way to accomplish this: to change the language is to change the ideas. However, attention can be paid to the language used explaining how to navigate the site. This checkpoint encourages the use of clear and simple explanations wherever possible to help improve understanding.

Summary

This chapter has outlined the accessibility issues facing designers. As a quick reference, here is a list of issues to keep in mind.

♦ Provide text descriptions for images and other non-text elements

♦ Don't use color as the only means to convey information

♦ For data tables, identify table headers

♦ Ensure pages can be read without stylesheets

♦ Provide meaningful titles for frames

♦ Use the simplest language appropriate for your site

For more information on national accessibility policies referenced in this chapter, please refer to the web page for this book on the glasshaus web site for a list of links to online documentation.

11

- Overview of accessibility

- WCAG Checkpoints: principles of accessible design

Authors: Alan Foley and Bob Regan

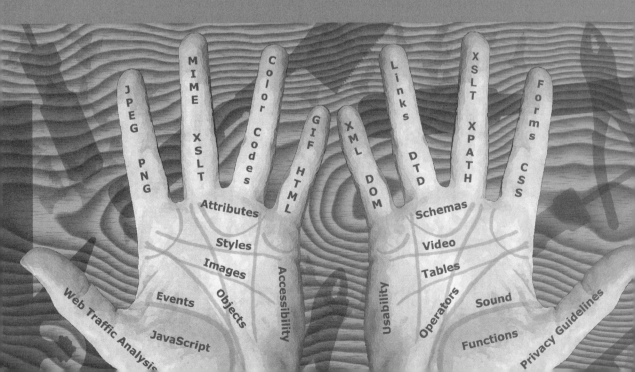

Web Traffic Analysis

Knowing how many people are using our web site, and where they are coming from, is one of the most important questions asked of a web professional, as the answers impact budgeting, marketing, advertising, and sales, as well as the continuous development of the site itself. This chapter will give clear and definitive solutions for web developers and webmasters charged with delivering meaningful figures about web traffic which they can stand by and discuss with confidence.

Whilst there are many competing methods for analyzing web traffic, with varying price tags accompanying them, we will focus on the most popular and potentially the most straightforward to implement: analyzing the data contained in the web server log files. We will begin by looking at what data is contained within most log files, and discuss how useful this can be, as well as highlighting the information that is either not included, or potentially misleading. We will then take a detailed look at how to analyze the log files themselves with the aid of the most widely used (and free) tool, Analog (*http://www.analog.cx/*). Once we have established how to analyze log files, we will discuss some of the problems that this process throws up, and how the adoption of current standards can help to clarify these issues. Finally, we suggest some rules to bear in mind when planning the analysis of traffic on your web site.

At the end of this chapter, you will know how to extract essential and meaningful data from your log files easily and efficiently, and then be able to present this information in a manner consistent with current standards, and justify the decisions that you have made. As ever, we are focusing on practical labor-saving solutions for web professionals. In this spirit, let's get down to business.

Analyzing Log Files with Analog

In this section, we will look at what is usually contained in a log file, what this can tell us, and what it is not possible to deduce from this data. Then we will look at what is probably the most widely used log file analysis tool, Analog, and examine how it takes a skeptical, though accurate and brilliantly efficient, view of what the log file is telling us. Finally, we will look at cookies: how they constitute a widely used attempt to add some detail to server log analysis, and try to determine the extent to which they are useful.

Log Files

Firstly, exactly what is a log file? A web server, such as Apache or Microsoft's IIS, can be configured by the system administrator to record all requests received, including both information received in the HTTP request itself and information generated by the server (for example, file size, and the status of the request, such as success or failure). This information is then recorded in a plain text format, and stored as a file on the server. It is usual for a new file to be generated for each 24 hour period that the server is running, that is a new file for each day. The format of the data in the file can be configured in a variety of ways, depending on the web server being used. Furthermore, the web server administrator and the site manager (who might be the same person) can configure the web server to record information about each request received, based on the data that they deem to be relevant. In the example in this chapter, we have made a typical selection, based on a judgment as to what is useful for the purposes of analyzing user behavior on a site, as well as some common log file elements. It is worth taking time now to go through this selection and explain what each element tells us.

date time

As it sounds, this indicates the time and date of the request. This is set to the time and date on the server hosting the site, which is likely to be the local time, UTC, or GMT – make sure you know which.

c-ip

This is the IP address of the computer – the client – making the request. However, this is not necessarily the IP address of the end user's computer, and it is likely to be a company or ISP proxy server. There are a number of issues with making assumptions about the client IP address, which we discuss later.

s-ip

Here we have the IP address of the server receiving the request. Hopefully this will come as no surprise, but it is included here as it is a default entry in many log files. Also, depending on the architecture of the hosting system, several different servers may be used, and this field is helpful to determine which one this log file belongs to. Each web server produces its own log file, so load-balanced installations generate several files which need to be collated.

s-port

This is the port through which the request was received. Standard HTTP requests are typically received on port 80.

cs-method

Here's the method of the request. Most HTTP requests are made using the GET method, but they can also be made using POST (typically for web form data), or various less common methods.

cs-uri-stem

The part of the URI requested after the domain name. For example, a request for the glasshaus web site homepage: *http://www.glasshaus.com/default.asp* would appear as *"/default.asp"*.

cs-uri-query

The querystring data from the requested URI.

sc-status

The response status of the request, for example, whether it succeeded, was refused, the file could not be found, and so on. For the purposes of traffic analysis, it is advisable to ignore log entries with certain status codes. We will discuss this in more detail later.

cs(User-Agent)

This is effectively the type of browser used to make the request, though this would also include automated systems such as search engine robots. The following line is typical, indicating that the user agent was a Mozilla 4.0+ compatible browser (in fact Internet Explorer 6.0) running on Windows NT 5.0 (or Windows 2000, as it is known to its friends):

```
Mozilla/4.0+(compatible;+MSIE+6.0;+Windows+NT+5.0)
```

A word of warning here: a user agent can claim to be whatever it likes, and this is not "verified" by the server. For example, some browsers claim to be Internet Explorer, because some web pages have been designed to vet the browsers that are accessing them, in order to ensure that they have the sufficient functionality to render the page according to the web designer's vision (using tables or CSS). Some of these designers can become over-zealous, and construct the page so as to not deliver the full content to a browser that is not recognized, sometimes simply returning a message advising the user to "update your browser". By simply presenting itself as a well-known browser type, such as Internet Explorer 6, this problem is averted by the less common browser. It does mean, however, that these browsers can be undercounted in the logs, something which might itself assist in perpetuating this practice amongst web designers.

cs(Cookie)

Any cookie data that is included in the request. We will be taking an in-depth look at how cookies can be useful to us later on in this chapter.

cs(Referer)

If the request was initiated by clicking on a link from a source which has a URI, then that URI appears here as the "referer". Amusingly, this misspelling (it should be "referrer") was included in the original HTTP specification, and has remained there ever since.

Usually, the vast majority of referers in the log will be from the web site itself, indicating that users are accessing pages using the web site's own internal linking. Due to caching and other effects, it is unsafe to assume that this represents a reliable "click-stream" (sequential flow of pages as requested by the user), but this field is potentially interesting as an indication of which external sites are driving our traffic. The URI is recorded in full, including the querystring data, which is useful as it indicates the search terms used when the referer is a search engine.

Web Traffic Analysis

For a full list of the HTTP methods, visit *http://www.w3.org/Protocols/HTTP/Methods.html*.
The W3C has a full list of status codes here: *http://www.w3.org/Protocols/rfc2616/rfc2616-sec10.html*.

More information is available on HTTP referer here: *http://www.w3.org/Protocols/rfc2616/rfc2616-sec14.html#sec14.36*.

What Does the Log Not Tell Us?

The temptation, with so rich a source of data as a log file, is to read too much into it, but the information in a log file is likely to be incomplete and misleading. We will examine here the skeptical case against making assumptions based on the data in a log file. Later in this chapter we look at the case in favor of intelligent assumptions, and in particular the advocacy of standards for web traffic analysis. First, we need to understand exactly where the traps are.

Users in the Log File Are Anonymous

HTTP is an anonymous and stateless protocol. This means that users are not individually identifiable, and each request made is independent and not explicitly connected to other requests by the same user (unless the web site requires a password login, for example, or uses some other method of state-management, such as cookies). The server does know the IP address of the computer making the request (so that it knows where to send the response back), but this IP address does not necessarily relate to the actual user who initiated the request, for two reasons:

 ♦ Firstly, ISP, university, or company proxy servers or firewalls will often use a single IP address to represent several users.

 ♦ Secondly, some ISPs can allocate a different IP address to a user for each request.

It is difficult to find a foolproof way out of this predicament of over- and under-counting. IP addresses remain interesting, since they give an impression of which types of organization are accessing your web site, but for identifying individual users they can be highly misleading.

This means that we cannot deduce exactly how many unique users we have had with reference to IP addresses. It also means that we cannot deduce how many "visits" we have had. A "visit" or "session" is often used to describe a connected sequence of requests from a single unique user. Clearly, as it is not possible to determine unique users from the IP address alone, attaching requests to them and compiling them into a single session is also a meaningless activity. Cookies are often cited as a realistic way to get around the problem of identifying users, but they introduce difficulties of their own, and we cannot always assume that they provide a foolproof system of user identification. They are very extensively deployed, however, and can be effective if the potential problems are suitably handled, so we will look at them in detail later in this chapter.

Assuming that in certain cases this was possible, how do we define a distinct visit? What length of gap between page requests can we reasonably assume constitutes a new visit: ten minutes, thirty, an hour, twenty-four hours? In practice, visits vary in length. Sometimes users will not request a page for a long time, but will still consider themselves to be visiting the site. Perhaps they have taken time out to answer an e-mail or the telephone, or fix a snack?

They may even be paying close attention to the site all along, reading a longer article in detail. (This is also a problem for those trying to solve the "visit" question by enforcing a login system: how long do we allow our visitors to remain on the site without making a request before we "time them out" and force them to log in again?) Add to this the problem that not all requests actually get logged in the first place (due to the intervention of a cache, as detailed below), and we can see that allocating a meaningful "timeout" period for the purposes of defining visits is almost impossible.

Log File Data Is Incomplete

The server can only record the requests that it receives. When a user clicks on a link to request a page from our web site, that request may never reach the server, as the files requested might be cached by the browser, or the proxy server of the user's ISP or company. This has a number of effects. The log will be undercounting the "real" number of page impressions that our site is generating, and this will generally penalize the more popular pages on the site, as these are the ones most likely to be cached.

The fact that the log is incomplete makes assuming things about the actual route the user took through the site highly problematic (even presuming that we can identify individual users). It is common practice to use the *Back* button to navigate around a site: viewing a page, and then going back a step, perhaps to an index, and then viewing another page. By using the *Back* button – incidentally an excellent usability tool – in this way, popular pages, and in particular "*index*" pages which contain navigational links, will often be undercounted, thereby presenting us with a false "click-stream". Nevertheless, much analysis of log files incorrectly assumes that they contain a complete picture of user activity. There are products and services available, at a cost, which claim to track user behavior more accurately, in particular by placing script "tags" on the web page itself. A more detailed account of these products however, is outside the scope of this chapter, as we are focused on generating meaningful information without unduly adding to our cost or workload.

It is possible to design a web site that contains pages that instruct client machines not to cache them, and this is sometimes advocated as a potential solution to the problem of incomplete log data. This is, however, probably not advisable. Caching is there for a reason: to improve the user experience by speeding up download times, and to reduce strain on the web server. While there are legitimate reasons why a designer might wish a web page not to be cached (for example on the homepage of a frequently updated news site), collecting traffic data is probably not one of them, and in any case, due to sophisticated caching techniques by ISPs, the data collected would still most likely be partly incomplete. It is better to know that the data is incomplete, and handle it accordingly, than to incorrectly assume that it is authoritative.

What Else Don't We Know?

Log files will not tell us how long a user has spent on the web site, or how long they spent viewing each page. Certainly we know the time of each request logged, but as we now realize, this is an incomplete picture of their route through the site. Even if it were possible to assume that the log recorded all requests, it cannot record the time at which the user stopped looking at the last page, or left the site for another.

The server is unable to log where the user goes after leaving the site, as by definition that request is sent to a different server. Time spent on the last page of the visit is unknown, and therefore the total time spent on the site cannot be determined. The possibility that the last page viewed might well be the one that held the attention of the user the longest can only add to this uncertainty.

Certain sites, such as online banks, enforce a session login/logoff, but this does not tell us how long the final page was truly viewed for, as commonly users will allow the last page to time out, or simply close down the browser window. In any case, this solution is not appropriate for most sites.

There are many commercial web analysis tools on the market that generate information on visits, unique users, time spent on each page, and so on. The problem with using one of these "off-the-peg" tools is that, without knowing how they work out these figures, and what assumptions they have made, it is difficult to lend any credibility to their results. Skeptical analysts are therefore suspicious of tools that claim to know too much, as they may be misleading at best, and at worst, plain wrong.

What Can We Say for Certain?

The skeptical view presented here may appear somewhat negative: if there are so many difficulties and ambiguities, why bother to analyze server logs at all? The answer is that, if we define exactly the boundaries of what we know, then we can also define what we do not know, and that information becomes all the more valuable as a result. We will now look at the positive side to server log analysis, and determine what we can safely deduce, using the popular log analysis tool Analog.

Analog

Analog is an excellent tool for analysis for a number of reasons:

♦ It is open source, free software. This means that it is free of charge, and free to use commercially. Any organization, large or small, rich or poor, can download and use it.

♦ As open source software, more experienced developers can examine how it works, verifying its methodology, and adding extensions or adaptations.

♦ There are versions that run on most platforms, including Windows, Mac, Linux, and Unix.

♦ It has built-in support for a wide variety of languages including English, Portuguese, French, German, Swedish, Czech, Slovak, Slovene, Romanian, and Hungarian.

For more details about how this works in practice, and any restrictions of reuse, refer to the license that is included in the standard Analog download, or on the Web here: http://www.analog.cx/docs/Licence.txt.

♦ The documentation is very explicit about what it does and does not do. The definition of the skeptical analyst viewpoint specified above has, in part, been derived from the rules to which Analog adheres. It doesn't make assumptions about the data that it collects: it merely reports the facts as it finds them.

♦ The program is very efficient, and can process a large amount of data in a short period of time. Analog's creator, Stephen Turner (http://homepage.ntlworld.com/adelie/stephen/), claims that it can process 28 million lines in 20 minutes, on a 266MHz chip (equivalent to 1Gb of data in a little over five minutes). This makes Analog a practical application for even the highest volume sites. **BBC News Online**, (http://news.bbc.co.uk/) a very popular web site with massive log files – containing over 300 million page views in the average month – uses Analog to produce its audited traffic figures.

As Analog is so strict in terms of what it allows into its reports, it also makes an excellent tool for understanding the mechanics of log files themselves. To web developers who are used to using sophisticated GUI tools for creating web sites (which is, let's face it, most of us), Analog's text interface can seem intimidating and austere at first. We should not be put off by this, however, because it is in fact very straightforward to set up and operate, and once the basic rules of the configuration file are established, it is very easy to customize it to your own requirements.

The latest copy of Analog, with full documentation, can be downloaded from the Analog web site, at *http://www.analog.cx/download.html*. The download contains a copy of the program, which is ready to run and does not require any setup or installation. All that is required is that the configuration file, `analog.cfg`, has all the details entered into it, including the location of the log files to be analyzed. These files must be on the same computer that is running Analog, and so may need to be downloaded from the web server and placed in a suitable location. In practice, many of these administration functions can be run automatically (for example using a scheduled script) but, for clarity, here we will step through the process manually.

We can now take a look at how Analog can be used to analyze a log file, and examine what it claims to do.

Configuring Analog involves editing a simple text file, a version of which is included in the Analog download. First, we need to specify where the log file to be analyzed is located:

```
LOGFILE C:\analog\logfiles\logfile.log
```

We do not need to specify each file specifically by name, but can use wildcards to indicate to Analog that any number of files in a given directory, are to be processed:

```
LOGFILE C:\analog\logfiles\*
```

Analog returns the output in an HTML file, so we need to specify what we want this to be called, using the OUTFILE command. We can choose to insert the name of the site (or part of the site) being analyzed using HOSTNAME:

```
OUTFILE report.html
HOSTNAME "My Website"
```

Analog counts all requests that have valid status codes. As far as Analog is concerned, this means codes in the 200's range, and code 304 (a file is requested, but the file is not physically served, as the client already has a copy which has not been altered since it was previously cached). Full explanations for the decisions that Analog makes here are included in the supporting documentation, but in summary, it only counts genuine successful requests.

Unless we specify otherwise, Analog will count all files as requests, including images, stylesheets, and so on. This is fine so far as it goes, but we also need to know how many "pages" were downloaded. To do this, we need to tell Analog what we consider to be a viewable "page", as opposed to a file. We can do this either by listing all the URIs for the pages that we want included, or by using wildcards to indicate the form that our pages take. The simplest way to do this is to specify which file types to include. For example:

```
PAGEINCLUDE *.asp
PAGEINCLUDE *.pdf
PAGEINCLUDE *.htm
```

These lines indicate that all files with suffixes `.asp`, `.pdf`, and `.htm` should be considered pages. Similarly, we can specify pages by directory. Any number of lines can be added to specify exactly what should be considered a page:

```
PAGEINCLUDE /articles/*
PAGEINCLUDE /default.asp
```

Pages specified in this way can be interpreted as "Page Impressions" in the sense defined later in the chapter, when we discuss standards and definitions.

Analog uses this information to generate the general summary at the top of the report:

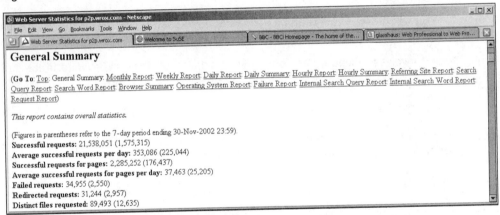

It also uses it to generate a more detailed breakdown of the pages requested:

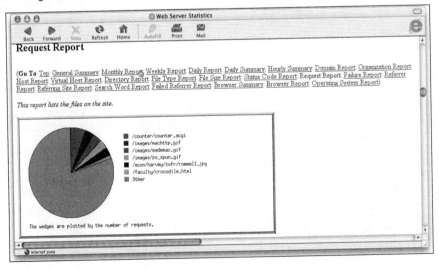

We can tell Analog which user agents we want to exclude, robots for example. Any requests from a robot in this list will then not be counted as either a request, or a page. Telling Analog about robots is very straightforward:

```
ROBOTINCLUDE REGEXPI:robot
ROBOTINCLUDE REGEXPI:spider
ROBOTINCLUDE REGEXPI:crawler

ROBOTINCLUDE Googlebot*
ROBOTINCLUDE Infoseek*
ROBOTINCLUDE Scooter*
ROBOTINCLUDE Slurp*
ROBOTINCLUDE Ultraseek*
```

The first three lines above give Analog a regular expression instruction, essentially saying "anything that says it is a robot or a spider or a crawler should be excluded". The other five lines name the specific known robots that we wish to exclude. Note that these instructions do not remove the relevant lines entirely, as we are interested in robot activity: we want to know what devices are accessing the site, but we don't want to confuse them with "genuine" page views.

Following on from this, we also want to tell Analog what we believe to be a search engine, so that it can report on the search words most commonly used to direct users to the site. Again, we can give Analog a named list:

```
SEARCHENGINE http://*altavista.*/* q
SEARCHENGINE http://*yahoo.*/* p
SEARCHENGINE http://*google.*/* q
SEARCHENGINE http://*lycos.*/* query
SEARCHENGINE http://*aol.*/* query
```

The first part of the line tells Analog that this is a search engine, the second part defines how to identify a referral from that search engine – basically the URL with wildcards – and the final part tells Analog how that particular site denotes the search words in its querystring.

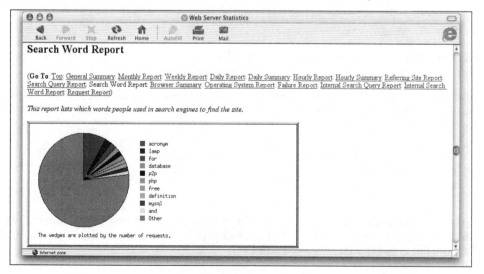

It is possible to turn the reporting of various elements on and off. For example, we can ask Analog to tell us about the referrers (referers) that have directed traffic to the site:

```
REFERRER ON
REFSITE ON
```

These two reports tell us which web pages have referred the most people to us, and which sites have referred the most, respectively:

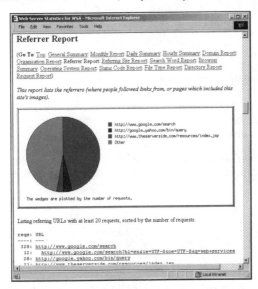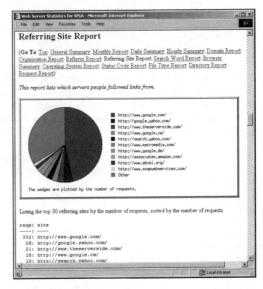

It is a good option, if using the referrer reports, to exclude "internal" referrals, that is those from pages on our own site:

```
REFREPEXCLUDE http://www.MyWebsite.com/*
REFSITEEXCLUDE http://www.MyWebsite.com/
```

The first command refers to the referring *page* report, and the second to the referring *site* report, as above. Note that the wildcard character – * – is not required in the case of the site report.

Another useful report is the browser summary, which is not included by default. As with many of the reports that Analog produces, there is an optional chart, but the basic report must be included for the chart to be displayed:

```
BROWSERSUM ON
BROWSUMCHART ON

SUBBROW */*
```

The last line here tells Analog to include a breakdown of each type of browser by version, which is rather useful, to avoid all versions of Internet Explorer from being grouped together, for example. The output from the browser summary looks like this:

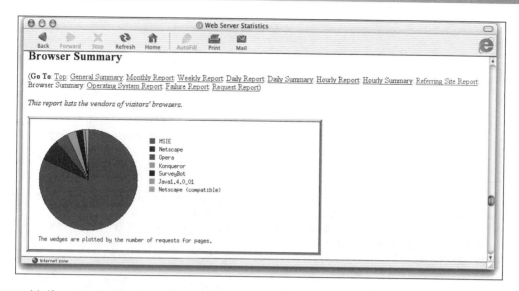

We could, if we wanted to, turn the BOTINCLUDE functionality we looked at earlier on its head, and use it to filter out regular browsers, leaving only bots. This would let us see what robot activity our site was receiving. They would be displayed as browsers, of course.

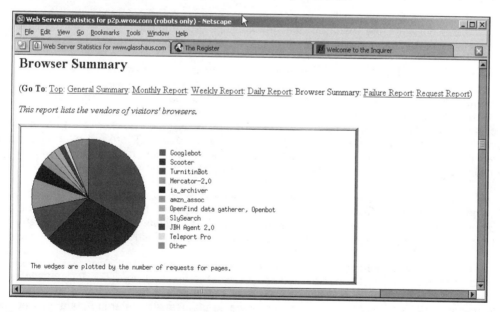

The final element to note in the basic configuration file is the ability to create aliases for file extensions: essentially saying "anything that ends with .htm is a HTML page, anything that ends .jpg is a JPEG, and so on:

```
TYPEALIAS .html     ".html [Hypertext Markup Language]"
TYPEALIAS .htm      ".htm [Hypertext Markup Language]"
TYPEALIAS .jpg      ".jpg [JPEG graphics]"
TYPEALIAS .jpeg     ".jpeg [JPEG graphics]"
```

It is also possible to configure Analog to do a DNS lookup on the IP addresses in the log file, in other words turning `204.148.170.150` into *glasshaus.com*. This is useful for working out which organizations are accessing your site, and potentially also from which geographical location. Instructing Analog to perform a DNS lookup is easy: simply include the following command:

```
DNS WRITE
```

This instructs Analog to perform a DNS lookup of all the IP addresses in the logs being processed, and write a file called `dnscache`, which records details of the resolved addresses, for use next time. While Analog is running, it will also create a file called `dnslock`, which is there to prevent another copy of Analog running simultaneously from overwriting the information. `dnslock` is deleted once the processing is complete. There are three other types of DNS command, which will not look up any IP addresses:

♦ `DNS NONE`, which instructs Analog not to convert any IP addresses

♦ `DNS READ`, which only looks in the cache file, and does not perform any new lookups

♦ `DNS LOOKUP`, which will both perform new lookups, and reference the `dnscache`, but does not write the results of the new lookups into the cache file – this is used if `DNS WRITE` fails, for example if the `dnscache` file is locked by `dnslock`

It is important to note that this is an extremely long process, particularly compared with Analog's normal speed of operation. As an anecdotal illustration of the time involved, one of our log files which would normally be processed in less than 1 second, took 39 minutes to complete the first time that `DNS WRITE` was set, because a new lookup had to be performed for all of the IP addresses in the file (over 600). The second time it was run, however, was much quicker, as it could use the information in the cache file, and again completed in under a second. There are other applications, however, that are optimized to perform DNS lookups in a more timely manner, and some of these are helpfully referenced in Analog's *Helper Applications* page: *http://www.analog.cx/helpers/*.

A word of caution here, however: as we have seen before, IP addresses conceal as much as they reveal, and it is dangerous to trust them too much. Many log files, for example, will reveal that a large proportion of users appear to be accessing a site from Virginia, USA, but only because AOL hosts most of their proxy servers in that state. The actual users are distributed all over the country.

In summary, Analog is a great tool for conducting "skeptical analysis". It does not "interpret" the results that it finds in the logs, it parses and reports what is there. It does this very efficiently and accurately, and it is free software, which means that, not only is it free of charge, but the source code is available for us to check and reconfigure if we so choose. As a starting point for web traffic analysis, Analog has a lot to recommend it: it does its job without any fuss, and reminds us what information we know that we know, and what information is the result of interpretation – valid or otherwise.

Cookies

As we have seen, ambiguities caused by the fact that HTTP is an anonymous and stateless protocol make it impossible to make reliable or accurate conclusions about unique users and visits. For many web developers, the solution to this problem is the cookie. Now this humble confection has caused quite a bit of controversy recently, although privacy concerns are slowly being dampened. Both users and legislators are becoming more aware that browsers now allow a good deal of control over what we allow sites to do, and web sites themselves are realizing the importance of publishing an explicit privacy policy, and sticking to it. For the moment then, we need to establish exactly what cookies can tell us, and, as before, where the dangers in interpretation lie.

We have separated the discussion of cookies from that of how Analog acts as skeptical analyst. Though it is possible to include cookie data in the server logs, Analog does not explicitly have a report for this field, because cookies fail its test of reliability when it comes to interpreting the data. To understand why, we need to review how cookies work, how they can be used, and what assumptions we can make about the data they provide.

A cookie is a small alphanumeric string, which is sent by the web server as part of the HTTP response. The cookie is stored by the user agent – in practice, the browser – as a simple text file, and its contents are returned to the web server that sent it every time a new request is made to that server. There are various rules and security measures that accompany the use of cookies by the browser:

- The cookie data can only be returned to the server with the same domain that sent the original cookie. For example, the BBC can use a single cookie for all web sites that are part of the *bbc.co.uk* domain, including *www.bbc.co.uk* and *news.bbc.co.uk*.

- Cookies can have an expiry date, which can be set well into the future. If no expiry date is set, then the cookie expires once the user closes down their browser. Cookies with expiry dates are sometimes referred to as "permanent cookies", and those without are referred to as "session cookies" or "transient cookies".

- The browser should allow the user to configure it to reject cookies, or regulate their acceptance, for example by warning when a site is offering to set a cookie.

Cookies therefore allow web developers and site administrators to place small quantities of data on the browser, which can be retrieved and used on future requests. This data is often designed to enhance seamlessly the user's experience, for example by recording preference settings that the user has opted for on a previous visit. Perhaps the most common use of a cookie, however, is to send a "token": a long randomly generated character string designed to uniquely identify that particular cookie, and by extension, that user. Each time the user makes a request to the web server, the token is sent, and this same token is returned in the cookie as part of the response.

This is an attempt to overcome the stateless nature of HTTP, as it effectively links all requests made by the same browser. It is possible to record the contents of the cookie in the log file or a database and count the number of distinct tokens, generating a figure for unique users of the web site. It is also possible to cross-reference all requests made with the same token, and construct data concerning visits. So why does Analog's documentation caution against counting cookies?

The answer is that, while it is possible to record and count this data, many assumptions have to be made to go from "I have *x* number of distinct tokens in the log file" to "I have *x* number of unique users":

Web Traffic Analysis

- Users can opt to reject cookies altogether. In this case, the browser will never send cookie data back to the server. Users that opt to do this are therefore invisible to this analysis.

- Cookies are set on browser instances, not people. It is possible, even likely, that a single individual might be represented by several different tokens for a given web site. For example, if they have two different types of browser on their machine (Netscape and Internet Explorer, say), and they use both browsers to visit the web site over a period of time, then they will appear in the web site's analysis as two different individuals. Similarly, if someone visits a web site from two different machines, one at home and one at work, for example, then again, they will appear as two unique users (or more, if they have several different browsers on each machine, and several individuals might share the same computer...).

- It is possible for the user to delete the cookies on a browser from time to time (and more common among the more technically literate – or suspicious – audiences). This effectively destroys the unique user from the perspective of the web site, and creates a new one when the user next visits. Over time, this will inflate the number of unique users visiting the web site.

Perhaps all of these factors, some under-counting, some over-counting, will cancel each other out, leaving us with a fairly reliable idea of our user numbers. Or perhaps not. The fact remains that all of these unknowables, compounded together, make the assumption that tokens in cookies represent actual unique individuals unreliable at best, and at worst, completely misleading.

In the face of such strong evidence against the use of cookies to represent identity, should anyone still be using them to track users? From the standpoint of the strict skeptical analyst, clearly not, but this is not the end of the story. In the next section, we will examine how the adoption of common standards for web traffic analysis is an attempt to overcome the problems detailed so far, and draw the boundaries inside which we can make some assumptions about our user behavior.

Analog does not normally count cookies in one of its standard reports, but it does allow cookies to be counted by using what the documentation refers to as a "kludge" (it works though...). The procedure for this is not difficult, but a little longwinded.

Use the `LOGFORMAT` command to specify explicitly the format of the log files being analyzed, and thereby tell Analog about the `cs(Cookie)` field, which it would ordinarily ignore. We need to specify each field in order, as found in the log file. For example, a log file with the following format:

```
date time c-ip cs-username s-ip s-port cs-method cs-uri-stem cs-uri-query sc-
status cs(User-Agent) cs(Cookie) cs(Referer)
```

would be represented as follows:

```
LOGFORMAT (%Y-%m-%d %h:%n:%j %s %j %j %j %j %r %q %c %A %u %f)
```

The `cs(Cookie)` ID is represented by the `%u` symbol, which tells Analog that this is a "User" field, and will be reported accordingly. The `%j` symbol means "ignore this field", and must be used to represent any field Analog will not report, such as the `s-ip` – the server address.

The date and time fields are a little tricky, as each part has to be specified individually, and in order, so in this case year (in four digits)–month–day etc., with hyphens or colons as delimiters, as appropriate. The other important thing to remember is that the LOGFORMAT command must come before the LOGFILE command which tells Analog where to find the file(s) in question. It is possible to specify as many different LOGFORMATs as necessary, so long as the format is always specified before the path to the file(s) to which it refers.

Having specified the format of the log file, and made Analog aware of the cookie data, the next step is to tell Analog to report it. This is more straightforward, and is activated by the following command:

```
USER ON
```

Easy enough. This will produce a report which details, by default, the top 50 users by number of requests, and then summarizes the rest, with a line such as:

```
[not listed: 867 users]
```

This is fine as far as it goes, as we can add the "others" number to the 50 listed, to determine that we had 917 users, or unique cookie IDs, in this period. To refine the report slightly, we can set a FLOOR which tells Analog to only explicitly list those users that meet certain criteria. For example, we could say, "list the top 5 users by number of requests":

```
USER ON
USERFLOOR -5r
```

or "only list those users with more than 1000 requests":

```
USER ON
USERFLOOR 1000r
```

If this latter number is set sufficiently high, then no users might meet the criterion, and therefore Analog will only report the summary data, effectively telling us straightaway how many unique cookie IDs it has counted:

```
[not listed: 867 users]
```

Standards for Web Traffic Analysis

This subject is clearly fraught with confusion and competing claims, ideas, and definitions. Different methods for analyzing traffic give us different perspectives on user behavior, but disagreements persist as to what we can or cannot know. Should we even try to measure anything except the strain on our web server to cope with demand? Well, there are ways of making sense of this apparently daunting confusion of information. In this section we will look at the standards that are being developed, and discuss what they are designed to achieve.

There is a movement to promote standards for web measurement led by organizations with responsibility for auditing companies' circulation, originally in an offline advertising context but increasingly in the digital arena. In particular, the International Federation of Audit Bureaux of Circulations (IFABC – *http://www.ifabc.org/*) has established a Web Measurement Committee, currently chaired by the UK, which has drawn up a set of standard definitions. The IFABC was founded in Sweden in 1996, and currently represents 36 Audit Bureaux in 32 countries.

We should now examine the standards recommended by this committee in a little detail. Once we have established the suggested terms and definitions, we can examine how and why these were chosen, what purpose they are designed to serve, and the extent to which they answer the objections of the skeptical analyst.

Metrics

The committee has a whole range of different metrics and measurements, many related to the auditing of advertising, and also to other digital areas, such as e-mail or WAP access, but the measurements that are most relevant to our discussion are summarized below. The following are the IFABC's agreed definitions:

♦ **Hits**

This is a highly ambiguous term. Originally, "hits" referred to the number of files downloaded from the web server – equivalent to Analog's use of the term "requests". Over time, however, the use of the term has mutated, and many people seem to use it to mean what we would normally refer to as page views or impressions. Due to this ambiguity, the term "hits" is rejected as a standard measure.

♦ **Page Impression**

This is sometimes referred to as "page view", though "impression" is adopted as the standard term. A page impression is a single file, or collection of related files, sent by the web server to the user as a result of a single request made by that user. The important point here is that only one page impression can be counted for each single user-initiated request. For example, if the user clicks on a link and requests a page, and that page contains several image files which the browser also requests from the server, then this counts as a single page impression. Images are not the only factor to filter out here (CSS files, for instance). The more obscure consequence of this definition concerns pages that include frames, which in turn display several (HTML) files. There is one page impression per user-initiated request, no matter what the type of file.

♦ **Unique Host**

A host is represented in the log file by the client computer's IP address. A unique host is therefore a unique IP address in the log.

♦ **Unique User**

This is intended to identify an end user, as opposed to a host, which can in practice represent several unique users. The unique user is defined as a cookie ID or token, a registration ID, or a unique combination of client IP address and some other identifying factor such as the user agent (effectively the browser-Operating System combination).

- **Single and Repeat Unique Users**

  A single unique user is a unique user that has only made one visit to the site, and a repeat unique user is one who has visited the site more than once. Both of these measures are expressed as a percentage of total unique users.

- **Visit**

  A visit is defined as a sequence of page impressions requested by a single unique user before any gap of 30 minutes between requests by that unique user. This is similar to a "user session".

- **Visit Duration**

  This is a calculation of the average length of a visit on the site, defined by the total amount of time for all visits of more than one page impression, divided by the total number of visits of more than one page impression. This is measured in seconds.

- **Unique Visit Duration**

  This is a calculation of the average total length of time that unique users spend on the site over a given period. It is defined by the total amount of time for all visits, divided by the total number of unique users for the given period, and again is measured in seconds.

Some of these standard measurements are clearly useful, and others appear more controversial. Rejecting the term "hits", for example, will come as a great relief to everyone, as the term has long since ceased to hold any real meaning, and yet its continued use has a degrading effect on attempts to conduct sensible web traffic analysis. Likewise, nailing down a definition of page impressions to replace what some people might previously have referred to as hits, is a positive move: the hit is dead, long live the page impression. Some other measurements, however, seem to break all the rules established by the skeptical analyst.

Take the definition of unique users, for example. We have seen that using the IP address as a representation of actual individuals is highly misleading, hence the requirement to combine IP address with user agent. But is this enough? After all, combining one flawed measure with another flawed measure surely just produced a combined flawed measure of indeterminate value?

Imagine a typical user, behind a company firewall, and with Netscape and Internet Explorer on their PC. If they use both browsers to look at your web site, then this user will still appear as two unique users, with one user agent/IP address combination for each browser. If cookies are used, this individual will still be double counted, as each browser would have its own cookie anyway. On the other hand, two different individuals in the same company are more likely to have the same user agent identity, as many corporations will have universal IT policies which coordinate the upgrade of their systems. If cookies are not accepted by these two users, they will appear as a single unique user to the web site.

Combining two uncertainties does not necessarily cancel out uncertainty, but rather compounds it. In practice, we would have no idea of the extent to which the over-counting/under-counting is resolving itself, and we cannot safely draw conclusions about actual numbers of unique users on this basis.

We have also discussed the dangers of calculating time spent on our web site by using the timings of requests, as the time spent on the final page is not accessible to us. Again what we see represented by these standard definitions is an attempt to analyze the unknowable.

Web Traffic Analysis

So, other than replacing hits with page impressions as a standard unit of measurement, are these definitions of any use at all? The answer is that they are, but only if we know exactly what we are doing with them, and where the line between usability and confusion should be drawn.

It is important to understand what these organizations are trying to achieve by setting these standards, as this gives us an important guide to why and how the decisions were made. The standards are drawn up by organizations with experience of and responsibility for auditing circulation figures. So what is the purpose of auditing in this context? Fundamentally, the goal of the audit is to allow the companies, or third parties, to review the audited figures and make comparisons as a result. It is this principle of comparability that is at the heart of the standards that are being devised, and perhaps rightly so.

We have seen that it is extremely difficult, not to say impossible, to determine exact numbers in web traffic analysis. In attempting to set the standards, therefore, this is not the goal. The purpose of defining standards is essentially twofold:

- Firstly, to establish a common vocabulary, so that everyone can discuss the topic and understand what everyone else is talking about, remove misleading terms, and so on.

- Secondly, to establish auditable rules that will allow web sites and third parties to assume with a fair degree of confidence that they can compare one site's figures with another.

Once we reject the idea that audited web traffic measures tell us the absolute truth about a web site's world and accept them rather as a way to talk sensibly about how one web site can be compared to another, then the standards defined above start to make more sense.

Take the example of the definition of a unique user, by combining the IP address with the user agent. Now in reality, this is not a measure of unique users, but it is possible to compare the unique user number from site A with that of site B, if the measure was determined using the same criteria, with some qualifications. Two very different sites, let's say a news site and a toy retailer, might have difficulties in comparing figures, because the types of user accessing the site (including home users, children, workers in large corporations) are themselves very different. In other words, there is more uncertainty, and inaccuracies will most likely be exaggerated. In practice, however, we want to compare sites that are very alike, with similar demographic profiles, and so these inaccuracies will be reduced.

The same principle can be applied across the other measures being standardized. In the case of timings of visits, if we effectively ignore the time on that last page we reject the idea of "what really happened", and replace it with "what can we measure consistently across other similar sites", then the standards start to make more sense. In fact, the argument that scientists often reject "reality" in favor of "what can I measure", is one that has been debated by philosophers for a long time now (but perhaps that is another story).

Different measuring techniques will give different figures for the same standard measure on the same site. If we calculate our unique users by counting distinct IP/user agent combinations, and then recalculate it using cookie tokens, we will almost certainly produce two quite different totals (excepting a rather bizarre coincidence, or a site with a very small number of unique users). In effect, we have a single definition of each element, but several variants of that element, depending on the method used for producing the data.

The role of the auditor is crucial to the accreditation of the audited figures, as they will ensure that the rules have been followed in a consistent manner. The auditor will first of all verify that the raw data was collected in an acceptable way, and that the necessary exclusions have been made (removing robot traffic from page impressions, for example). Secondly they will check that the measures reliant on the standards (the skeptical analyst might refer to these as "assumptions") have been calculated correctly. And finally, the auditor must release the verified information in the right context. In other words, ensure that when we are comparing traffic numbers, we are genuinely comparing like with like: cookies with cookies, and user agents with user agents.

One final warning. The auditors are the referees in the process; they check that everyone has followed the rules, and they make decisions and clarifications. They make it possible for those of us who understand the rules (why they exist, and the extent of their limitations) to make educated judgments about the information as it is presented. The danger of well-audited traffic data is that there is a great temptation, albeit amongst those less well-versed in the complexities of web traffic analysis, to read more into the numbers than is reasonable. Auditors diligently point out that measures arrived at through different means cannot be compared, but it is likely that many people casting a more casual eye on the audited figures might well miss this distinction. "An audited number is an audited number, is it not?" Well, no. It is a starting point for examination, not a conclusion.

In a world in which it is difficult to stop people talking randomly about hits, how much more difficult will it be to convince people of the fine distinctions between user agents and cookie tokens when calculating unique users? For many, standards, definitions, and auditors are there to remove the "well, it depends" from the debate. Yet the important fine distinctions remain, and can make all the difference. This is why it is crucial that, while we may adopt the standards that are being proposed, and indeed benefit greatly from so doing, we do not forget the purpose for which they were devised, and the scope within which they can be usefully applied. Applying standards and employing auditors is not a replacement for proper intelligent interrogation of the data that is being presented.

Summary

We have found that the process of accurate data collection and interpretation is somewhat complex, and that standards go some way to ironing out the confusion, but also introduce potential misunderstandings of their own. It is important at all times to be very aware of what it is that is being analyzed, where the data came from, and the ultimate purpose of the analysis.

The first rule of web traffic analysis is that any measure or metric produced is extremely context-sensitive. The adoption of standards allows us to compare apples with apples, and oranges with oranges, but make sure you are not carrying a sack full of bananas, as you will be sure to slip on some of their skins. In fact, this applies not only to statistical measures, but to all elements of web traffic analysis.

Web sites are constructed for any number of different reasons, and audiences. So not only do we have news sites and toy retailers, we also have auction sites, sites with information aimed at the working professional, the professional at leisure, children, retired people, pet lovers, religious people, extreme sports enthusiasts, and women called Susan. Some sites are free of charge, others are subscription only, some are funded by advertisers, others by government agencies, and so on. All users of these sites have subtle (and sometimes not so subtle) differences in their expectations, needs, and tolerances.

The second rule of web traffic analysis, therefore, is that the user should be at the center of any analysis that is undertaken. As the owner or administrator of the web site, you know your business, and your customer, better than anyone else. If they want lots of personalization, and you need to track them in great detail in order to customize their options, then you know that. If you are providing an online financial services application in which confidentiality and discretion are the prime drivers of your business, then the moment you so much as wave a cookie in your customers' general direction, you might see your profits crumble into dust. And no level of intelligent tracking and analysis will bring them back.

Web Traffic Analysis

Appendices

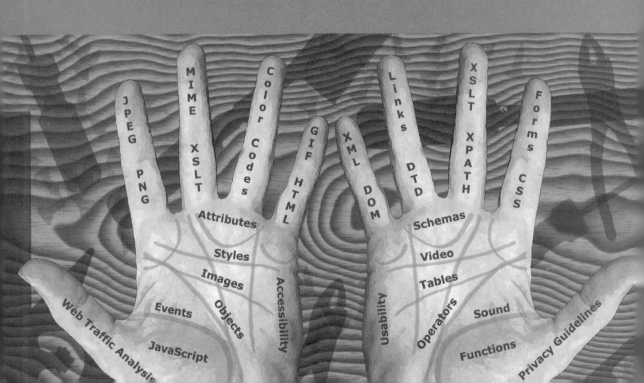

Appendix A
Color Names

Here we present two tables of color names, one that contains those color names and their values that are valid for HTML 4/CSS2, and a second, larger table of those that work in IE 6 and other browsers.

First, those color names that are valid for HTML 4 with CSS2:

Name	Value		Name	Value
Black	#000000		Green	#008000
Silver	#C0C0C0		Lime	#00FF00
Gray	#808080		Olive	#808000
White	#FFFFFF		Yellow	#FFFF00
Maroon	#800000		Navy	#000080
Red	#FF0000		Blue	#0000FF
Purple	#800080		Teal	#008080
Fuchsia	#FF00FF		Aqua	#00FFFF

And now the larger list, those color names that the major browsers recognize, and the hex value they are rendered as:

Name	Value	Name	Value
AliceBlue	#F0F8FF	DarkOrchid	#9932CC
AntiqueWhite	#FAEBD7	DarkRed	#8B0000
Aqua	#00FFFF	DarkSalmon	#E9967A

Table continued on following page

Name	Value	Name	Value
Aquamarine	#7FFFD4	DarkSeaGreen	#8FBC8F
Azure	#F0FFFF	DarkSlateBlue	#483D8B
Beige	#F5F5DC	DarkSlateGray	#2F4F4F
Bisque	#FFE4C4	DarkTurquoise	#00CED1
Black	#000000	DarkViolet	#9400D3
BlanchedAlmond	#FFEBCD	DeepPink	#FF1493
Blue	#0000FF	DeepSkyBlue	#00BFFF
BlueViolet	#8A2BE2	DimGray	#696969
Brown	#A52A2A	DodgerBlue	#1E90FF
BurleyWood (not Opera)	#DEB887	Firebrick	#B22222
CadetBlue	#5F9EA0	FloralWhite	#FFFAF0
Chartreuse	#7FFF00	ForestGreen	#228B22
Chocolate	#D2691E	Fuchsia	#FF00FF
Coral	#FF7F50	Gainsboro	#DCDCDC
CornFlowerBlue	#6495ED	GhostWhite	#F8F8FF
CornSilk	#FFF8DC	Gold	#FFD700
Crimson	#DC143C	Goldenrod	#DAA520
Cyan	#00FFFF	Gray	#808080
DarkBlue	#00008B	Green	#008000
DarkCyan	#008B8B	GreenYellow	#ADFF2F
DarkGoldenrod	#B8860B	Honeydew	#F0FFF0
DarkGray	#A9A9A9	HotPink	#FF69B4
DarkGreen	#006400	IndianRed	#CD5C5C
DarkKhaki	#BDB76B	Indigo	#4B0082
DarkMagenta	#8B008B	Ivory	#FFFFF0
DarkOliveGreen	#556B2F	Khaki	#F0E68C
DarkOrange	#FF8C00	Lavender	#E6E6FA
LavenderBlush	#FFF0F5	MistyRose	#FFE4E1
LawnGreen	#7CFC00	Moccasin	#FFE4B5
LemonChiffon	#FFFACD	NavajoWhite	#FFDEAD
LightBlue	#ADD8E6	Navy	#000080

Name	Value	Name	Value
LightCoral	#F08080	OldLace	#FDF5E6
LightCyan	#E0FFFF	Olive	#808000
LightGoldenrodYellow	#FAFAD2	OliveDrab	#6B8E23
LightGrey	#D3D3D3	Orange	#FFA500
LightGreen	#90EE90	OrangeRed	#FF4500
LightPink	#FFB6C1	Orchid	#DA70D6
LightSalmon	#FFA07A	PaleGoldenrod	#EEE8AA
LightSeaGreen	#20B2AA	PaleGreen	#98FB98
LightSkyBlue	#87CEFA	PaleTurquoise	#AFEEEE
LightSlateGray	#778899	PaleVioletRed	#DB7093
LightSteelBlue	#B0C4DE	PapayaWhip	#FFEFD5
LightYellow	#FFFFE0	PeachPuff	#FFDAB9
Lime	#00FF00	Peru	#CD853F
LimeGreen	#32CD32	Pink	#FFC0CB
Linen	#FAF0E6	Plum	#DDA0DD
Magenta	#FF00FF	PowderBlue	#B0E0E6
Maroon	#800000	Purple	#800080
MediumAquamarine	#66CDAA	Red	#FF0000
MediumBlue	#0000CD	RosyBrown	#BC8F8F
MediumOrchid	#BA55D3	RoyalBlue	#4169E1
MediumPurple	#9370DB	SaddleBrown	#8B4513
MediumSeaGreen	#3CB371	Salmon	#FA8072
MediumSlateBlue	#7B68EE	SandyBrown	#F4A460
MediumSpringGreen	#00FA9A	SeaGreen	#2E8B57
MediumTurquoise	#48D1CC	SeaShell	#FFF5EE
MediumVioletRed	#C71585	Sienna	#A0522D
MidnightBlue	#191970	Silver	#C0C0C0
MintCream	#F5FFFA	SkyBlue	#87CEEB
SlateBlue	#6A5ACD	Tomato	#FF6347
SlateGray	#708090	Turquoise	#40E0D0

Table continued on following page

Colour Names

A

Name	Value	Name	Value
Snow	#FFFAFA	Violet	#EE82EE
SpringGreen	#00FF7F	Wheat	#F5DEB3
SteelBlue	#4682B4	White	#FFFFFF
Tan	#D2B48C	WhiteSmoke	#F5F5F5
Teal	#008080	Yellow	#FFFF00
Thistle	#D8BFD8	YellowGreen	#9ACD32

Appendix B
HTML Character Entities

Numeric	Named	Description	Netscape Mozilla 1.0	IE 6	Opera 6.01
&#001;		Undefined			
&#002;		Undefined			
&#003;		Undefined			
&#004;		Undefined			
&#005;		Undefined			
&#006;		Undefined			
&#007;		Undefined			
&#008;		Undefined			
			Horizontal tab	Space, or tab if in `<pre></pre>`		

		Line feed	Space, or a new line if in `<pre></pre>`		

&#011;		Undefined		Space, or if in `<pre></pre>`	
		Undefined		Space, or if in `<pre></pre>`	
		Carriage return	Space, or carriage return if in `<pre></pre>`		
&#014;		Undefined			

Table continued on following page

Numeric	Named	Description	Netscape Mozilla 1.0	IE 6	Opera 6.01
&#015;		Undefined			
&#016;		Undefined			
&#017;		Undefined			
&#018;		Undefined			
&#019;		Undefined			
&#020;		Undefined			
&#021;		Undefined			
&#022;		Undefined			
&#023;		Undefined			
&#024;		Undefined			
&#025;		Undefined			
&#026;		Undefined			
&#027;		Undefined			
&#028;		Undefined			
&#029;		Undefined			
&#030;		Undefined			
&#031;		Undefined			
&#032;		Space	Space	Space	Space
&#033;		Exclamation mark	!	!	!
&#034;	&quot;	Double quote	"	"	"
&#035;		Hash	#	#	#
&#036;		Dollar	$	$	$
&#037;		Percent	%	%	%
&#038;	&amp;	Ampersand	&	&	&
&#039;		Apostrophe/Single quote	'	'	'

Numeric	Named	Description	Netscape Mozilla	IE 6	Opera 6.01
(		Left parenthesis	(	(	(
)		Right parenthesis	)	)	)
*		Asterisk	*	*	*
+		Plus	+	+	+
,		Comma	,	,	,
-		Hyphen	-	-	-
.		Period	.	.	.
/		Slash	/	/	/
0		Digit 0	0	0	0
1		Digit 1	1	1	1
2		Digit 2	2	2	2
3		Digit 3	3	3	3
4		Digit 4	4	4	4
5		Digit 5	5	5	5
6		Digit 6	6	6	6
7		Digit 7	7	7	7
8		Digit 8	8	8	8
9		Digit 9	9	9	9
:		Colon	:	:	:
;		Semicolon	;	;	;
<	<	Less than	<	<	<
=		Equals	=	=	=
>	>	Greater than	>	>	>
?		Question mark	?	?	?
@		At sign	@	@	@

Table continued on following page

Numeric	Named	Description	Netscape Mozilla 1.0	IE 6	Opera 6.01
&#065;		Uppercase letter A	A	A	A
&#066;		Uppercase letter B	B	B	B
&#067;		Uppercase letter C	C	C	C
&#068;		Uppercase letter D	D	D	D
&#069;		Uppercase letter E	E	E	E
&#070;		Uppercase letter F	F	F	F
&#071;		Uppercase letter G	G	G	G
&#072;		Uppercase letter H	H	H	H
&#073;		Uppercase letter I	I	I	I
&#074;		Uppercase letter J	J	J	J
&#075;		Uppercase letter K	K	K	K
&#076;		Uppercase letter L	L	L	L
&#077;		Uppercase letter M	M	M	M
&#078;		Uppercase letter N	N	N	N
&#079;		Uppercase letter O	O	O	O
&#080;		Uppercase letter P	P	P	P
&#081;		Uppercase letter Q	Q	Q	Q
&#082;		Uppercase letter R	R	R	R
&#083;		Uppercase letter S	S	S	S
&#084;		Uppercase letter T	T	T	T
&#085;		Uppercase letter U	U	U	U
&#086;		Uppercase letter V	V	V	V
&#087;		Uppercase letter W	W	W	W
&#088;		Uppercase letter X	X	X	X
&#089;		Uppercase letter Y	Y	Y	Y
&#090;		Uppercase letter Z	Z	Z	Z
&#091;		Left square bracket	[	[	[

Numeric	Named	Description	Netscape Mozilla 1.0	IE 6	Opera 6.01
&#092;		Backslash	\	\	\
&#093;		Right square bracket	]	]	]
&#094;		Caret	^	^	^
&#095;		Underscore	_	_	_
&#096;		Grave accent	`	`	`
&#097;		Lowercase letter a	a	a	a
&#098;		Lowercase letter b	b	b	b
&#099;		Lowercase letter c	c	c	c
&#100;		Lowercase letter d	d	d	d
&#101;		Lowercase letter e	e	e	e
&#102;		Lowercase letter f	f	f	f
&#103;		Lowercase letter g	g	g	g
&#104;		Lowercase letter h	h	h	h
&#105;		Lowercase letter i	I	I	I
&#106;		Lowercase letter j	j	j	j
&#107;		Lowercase letter k	k	k	k
&#108;		Lowercase letter l	l	l	l
&#109;		Lowercase letter m	m	m	m
&#110;		Lowercase letter n	n	n	n
&#111;		Lowercase letter o	o	o	o
&#112;		Lowercase letter p	p	p	p
&#113;		Lowercase letter q	q	q	q
&#114;		Lowercase letter r	r	r	r
&#115;		Lowercase letter s	s	s	s
&#116;		Lowercase letter t	t	t	t
&#117;		Lowercase letter u	u	u	u

Table continued on following page

HTML Character Entities

B

Numeric	Named	Description	Netscape Mozilla 1.0	IE 6	Opera 6.01
&#118;		Lowercase letter v	v	v	v
&#119;		Lowercase letter w	w	w	w
&#120;		Lowercase letter x	x	x	x
&#121;		Lowercase letter y	y	y	y
&#122;		Lowercase letter z	z	z	z
&#123;		Left curly brace	{	{	{
|		Vertical bar	|	|	|
&#125;		Right curly brace	}	}	}
&#126;		Tilde	~	~	~
&#127;		Undefined			
&#128;	&euro;	Euro money symbol	•	•	•
&#129;		Undefined	?		
&#130;		Comma	‚	‚	‚
&#131;		Florin, or function sign	ƒ	ƒ	$\int$
&#132;		Right double quote low	„	„	„
&#133;		Ellipsis	…	…	…
&#134;		Dagger	†	†	†
&#135;		Double dagger	‡	‡	‡
&#136;		Circumflex	ˆ	ˆ	ˆ
&#137;		Permil	‰	‰	‰
&#138;		Undefined	Š	Š	Š
&#139;		Less than	‹	‹	‹
&#140;		Capital OE ligature	Œ	Œ	Œ
&#141;		Undefined	?		

Numeric	Named	Description	Netscape Mozilla 1.0	IE 6	Opera 6.01
&#142;		Undefined	Ž	Ž	Ž
&#143;		Undefined	?		
&#144;		Undefined	?		
&#145;		Left single quote	'	'	'
&#146;		Right single quote	'	'	'
&#147;		Left double quote	"	"	"
&#148;		Right double quote	"	"	"
&#149;		Bullet	•	•	•
&#150;		En-dash	–	–	–
&#151;		Em-dash	—	—	—
&#152;		Tilde	˜	˜	˜
&#153;		Trademark symbol	™	™	™
&#154;		Undefined	š	š	š
&#155;		Greater than	›	›	›
&#156;		Small oe ligature	œ	œ	œ
&#157;		Undefined	?		
&#158;		Undefined	ž	ž	ž
&#159;		Capital Y umlaut	Ÿ	Ÿ	Ÿ
		Non-breaking space	a non-breakin g space	a non-breaking space	a non-breakin g space
&#161;	&iexcl;	Inverted exclamation	¡	¡	¡
&#162;	&cent;	Cent sign	¢	¢	¢

Table continued on following page

Numeric	Named	Description	Netscape Mozilla 1.0	IE 6	Opera 6.01
£	£	Pound sign	£	£	£
¤	¤	General currency symbol	¤	¤	¤
¥	¥	Yen sign	¥	¥	¥
¦	¦	Broken vertical bar	¦	¦	¦
§	§	Section sign	§	§	§
¨	¨	Umlaut	¨	¨	¨
©	©	Copyright	©	©	©
ª	ª	Feminine ordinal	ª	ª	ª
«	«	Left angle quote	«	«	«
¬	¬	Not sign	¬	¬	¬
­	­	Soft hyphen	nothing	- if required, nothing if in <pre></pre>	nothing
®	®	Registered trademark	®	®	®
¯	¯	Macron accent	¯	¯	¯
°	°	Degree sign	°	°	°
±	±	Plus or minus	±	±	±
²	²	Superscripted 2	^{2}	^{2}	^{2}
³	³	Superscripted 3	^{3}	^{3}	^{3}
´	´	Acute accent	´	´	´
µ	µ	Micro sign	µ	µ	µ

Numeric	Named	Description	Netscape Mozilla 1.0	IE 6	Opera 6.01
¶	¶	Paragraph	¶	¶	¶
·	·	Middle dot	·	·	·
¸	¸	Cedilla	¸	¸	¸
¹	¹	Superscripted 1	¹	¹	¹
º	º	Masculine ordinal	º	º	º
»	»	Right angle quote	»	»	»
¼	¼	One quarter	¼	¼	¼
½	½	One half	½	½	½
¾	¾	Three quarters	¾	¾	¾
¿	¿	Inverted question mark	¿	¿	¿
À	À	Capital A grave	À	À	À
Á	Á	Capital A acute	Á	Á	Á
Â	Â	Capital A circumflex	Â	Â	Â
Ã	Ã	Capital A tilde	Ã	Ã	Ã
Ä	Ä	Capital A umlaut	Ä	Ä	Ä
Å	Å	Capital A ring	Å	Å	Å
Æ	Æ	Capital AE ligature	Æ	Æ	Æ
Ç	Ç	Capital C cedilla	Ç	Ç	Ç
È	È	Capital E grave	È	È	È
É	É	Capital E acute	É	É	É
Ê	Ê	Capital E circumflex	Ê	Ê	Ê

Table continued on following page

HTML Character Entities

B

Numeric	Named	Description	Netscape Mozilla 1.0	IE 6	Opera 6.01
&#203;	&Euml;	Capital E umlaut	Ë	Ë	Ë
&#204;	&Igrave;	Capital I grave	Ì	Ì	Ì
&#205;	&Iacute;	Capital I acute	Í	Í	Í
&#206;	&Icirc;	Capital I circumflex	Î	Î	Î
&#207;	&Iuml;	Capital I umlaut	Ï	Ï	Ï
&#208;	&ETH;	Capital eth	Ð	Ð	Ð
&#209;	&Ntilde;	Capital N tilde	Ñ	Ñ	Ñ
&#210;	&Ograve;	Capital O grave	Ò	Ò	Ò
&#211;	&Oacute;	Capital O acute	Ó	Ó	Ó
&#212;	&Ocirc;	Capital O circumflex	Ô	Ô	Ô
&#213;	&Otilde;	Capital O tilde	Õ	Õ	Õ
&#214;	&Ouml;	Capital O umlaut	Ö	Ö	Ö
&#215;	&times;	Multiply	×	×	×
&#216;	&Oslash;	Capital O slash	Ø	Ø	Ø
&#217;	&Ugrave;	Capital U grave	Ù	Ù	Ù
&#218;	&Uacute;	Capital U acute	Ú	Ú	Ú
&#219;	&Ucirc;	Capital U circumflex	Û	Û	Û
&#220;	&Uuml;	Capital U umlaut	Ü	Ü	Ü
&#221;	&Yacute;	Capital Y acute	Ý	Ý	Ý
&#222;	&THORN;	Capital thorn	Þ	Þ	Þ
&#223;	&szlig;	Small sz ligature	ß	ß	ß
&#224;	&agrave;	Small a grave	à	à	à

Numeric	Named	Description	Netscape Mozilla 1.0	IE 6	Opera 6.01
á	á	Small a acute	á	á	á
â	â	Small a circumflex	â	â	â
ã	ã	Small a tilde	ã	ã	ã
ä	ä	Small a umlaut	ä	ä	ä
å	å	Small a ring	å	å	å
æ	æ	Small ae ligature	æ	æ	æ
ç	ç	Small c cedilla	ç	ç	ç
è	è	Small e grave	è	è	è
é	é	Small e acute	é	é	é
ê	ê	Small e circumflex	ê	ê	ê
ë	ë	Small e umlaut	ë	ë	ë
ì	ì	Small i grave	ì	ì	ì
í	í	Small i acute	í	í	í
î	î	Small i circumflex	î	î	î
ï	ï	Small i umlaut	ï	ï	ï
ð	ð	Small eth	ð	ð	ð
ñ	ñ	Small n tilde	ñ	ñ	ñ
ò	ò	Small o grave	ò	ò	ò
ó	ó	Small o acute	ó	ó	ó
ô	ô	Small o circumflex	ô	ô	ô
õ	õ	Small o tilde	õ	õ	õ
ö	ö	Small o umlaut	ö	ö	ö
÷	÷	Divide	÷	÷	÷

Table continued on following page

HTML Character Entities

B

409

Numeric	Named	Description	Netscape Mozilla 1.0	IE 6	Opera 6.01
&#248;	&oslash;	Small o slash	ø	ø	ø
&#249;	&ugrave;	Small u grave	ù	ù	ù
&#250;	&uacute;	Small u acute	ú	ú	ú
&#251;	&ucirc;	Small u circumflex	û	û	û
&#252;	&uuml;	Small u umlaut	ü	ü	ü
&#253;	&yacute;	Small y acute	ý	ý	ý
&#254;	&thorn;	Small thorn	þ	þ	þ
&#255;	&yuml;	Small y umlaut	ÿ	ÿ	ÿ

Appendix C
MIME Types

MIMEType	Description
*	Wildcard match everything
/	Wild card match both parts separately
application/binary	Application Binary Data
application/gzip	GZIP archive
application/HexEdit	Untyped Binary Data
application/java-archive	Java Archive
application/JPEGView	OS/2 Bitmap
application/mac-binhex40	Binhex File
application/macbinary	MacBinary
application/MacBooz	Zoo Archive
application/MacLHA	LHArc Archive
application/MoviePlayer	DV Video
application/octet-stream	Binary Executable
application/pdf	PDF File
application/Photoshop	Photoshop Document
application/PictureViewer	OS/2 Bitmap
application/postscript	PostScript File

Table continued on following page

MIMEType	Description
application/QuarkXpress	QuarkXpress Document
application/self-extracting	Self-Extracting Archive
application/Self_Extracting_Archive	Self-Extracting Archive
application/smil	SMIL Document
application/SunTar	Unix BAR Archive
application/vnd.rn-realmedia	RealMedia File
application/vnd.rn-realplayer	RealPlayer File
application/x-compress	Unix Compressed (.z) Files
application/x-cpio	Unix CPIO Archive
application/x-director	Shockwave
application/x-gtar	GNU Tape Archive
application/x-gzip	GZIP File
application/x-hdf	HDF Data File
application/x-javascript	JavaScript Program
application/x-javascript-config	JavaScript Config
application/x-javascript-config	JavaScript Config
application/x-macbinary	MacBinary File
application/x-perl	Perl Program
application/x-pkcs7-crl	Certificate Revocation List
application/x-pkcs7-mime	PKCS7 Encrypted Data
application/x-pkcs7-signature	PKCS7 Signature
application/x-rtsp	Real Time Streaming Protocol
application/x-sgml	SGML Document
application/x-shockwave-flash	Shockwave Flash
application/x-tar	TAR Archive
application/x-zip-compressed	ZIP Compressed Data
application/xhtml+xml	XHTML documents
application/xml	XML Document
application/zip	ZIP Archives

MIMEType	Description
audio/aiff	AIFF Audio
audio/basic	AU Audio
audio/mid	MIDI
audio/midi	MIDI
audio/mp3	MPEG Movie
audio/mpeg	MPEG audio stream
audio/mpegurl	MP3 PlayLists (.m3u, .pls)
audio/mpg	MP3 Audio
audio/rmf	audio/rmf
audio/scpls	MP3 PlayLists (.m3u, .pls)
audio/vnd.qcelp	QCP Audio
audio/vnd.rn-realaudio	RealAudio Clip
audio/wav	WAV Audio
audio/x-aiff	AIFF Audio
audio/x-midi	MIDI
audio/x-mp3	MPEG Movie
audio/x-mpeg	MPEG audio stream
audio/x-mpegurl	MP3 PlayLists (.m3u, .pls)
audio/x-mpg	MP3 Audio
audio/x-pn-realaudio	RealAudio
audio/x-pn-realaudio-plugin	RealPlayer Plugin
audio/x-rmf	audio/x-rmf
audio/x-scpls	MP3 PlayLists (.m3u, .pls)
audio/x-wav	WAV Audio
image/gif	GIF Image
image/ief	IEF image
image/jpeg	JPEG Image
image/pict	PICT Image

Table continued on following page

Mime Types

C

MIMEType	Description
image/png	PNG Image
image/svg+xml	SVG Image
image/tiff	TIFF Image
image/vnd.rn-realflash	RealFlash Clip
image/vnd.rn-realpix	RealPix Clip
image/x-bmp	Windows BMP Image
image/x-cmu-raster	CMU Raster Image
image/x-fits	Flexible Image Transport
image/x-macpaint	MacPaint Image
image/x-macpict	PICT Picture
image/x-MS-bmp	Windows Bitmap
image/x-pbm	Portable Bitmap
image/x-pgm	Portable Graymap
image/x-photo-cd	PhotoCD Image
image/x-photoshop	Photoshop Image
image/x-pict	PICT Image
image/x-png	PNG Image
image/x-portable-anymap	PBM Image
image/x-portable-bitmap	Portable Bitmap
image/x-portable-graymap	Portable Graymap
image/x-portable-pixmap	Portable Pixmap
image/x-ppm	Portable Pixmap
image/x-quicktime	QuickTime Image
image/x-rgb	SGI Image
image/x-sgi	SGI Image
image/x-targa	Targa Truevision Image
image/x-tiff	TIFF Image
image/x-xbitmap	X Bitmap Image
image/x-xbm	X-Windows Bitmap

MIMEType	Description
image/x-xpixmap	X-Windows Pixmap
image/x-xpm	X-Windows Pixmap
image/x-xwd	X-Windows Dump
image/x-xwindowdump	X Window Dump Image
image/xbitmap	X Bitmap Image
image/xbm	X Bitmap Image
message/external-body	URL Bookmark
text/css	CSS File
text/html	An HTML document.
text/JavaScript	Text-formatted JavaScript sourcecode inside a `<script>` block
text/Jscript	Text-formatted JScript sourcecode inside a `<script>` block
text/plain	Form content and other plain text documents
text/url	URL File
text/vbs	Text-formatted VBScript sourcecode inside a `<script>` block
text/vbscript	Text-formatted VBScript sourcecode inside a `<script>` block
text/vnd.rn-realtext	RealText Clip
text/x-cdf	Channels
text/x-vcard	Visiting Card
text/xml	XML Document
undefined	UU-Encoded Data
video/avi	Microsoft Video
video/flc	FLC Animation
video/mpeg	MPEG video/audio stream
video/msvideo	Microsoft Video
video/quicktime	QuickTime Movie

Table continued on following page

Mime Types

C

MIMEType	Description
`video/vnd.rn-realvideo`	RealVideo Clip
`video/x-mpeg`	MPEG video/audio stream
`video/x-mpeg2`	MPEG2 Video
`video/x-msvideo`	Microsoft Video
`video/x-qtc`	video/x-qtc
`x-world/x-3dmf`	QuickDraw 3D File
`x-world/x-vrml`	VRML File

Index

A Guide to the Index

The index is arranged in word-by-word order with preceding symbols ignored and numbers treated as though spelled out (so New York would appear before Newark, the :lang pseudo-class under 'lang' and 3D graphics at 'three'). Unmodified headings indicate main treatments and acronyms have been preferred to their expansions as main entries because they are easier to recall or to work out. Comments specifically about the index would be welcome at *billj@glasshaus.com*

Notes

Notes

glasshaus

web professional to web professional

glasshaus writes books for you. Any suggestions, or ideas about how you want information given in your ideal book will be studied by our team. Your comments are always valued at glasshaus.

Free phone in USA 800-873 9769
Fax (312) 893 8001

UK Tel.: (0121) 687 4100   Fax: (0121) 687 4101

Registration Code: | 1221H80AKGIH5301

Web Professionals Handbook – Registration Card

Name _____

Address _____

_____

_____

City _____ State/Region _____

Country _____ Postcode/Zip _____

E-Mail _____

Occupation _____

How did you hear about this book?

❏ Book review (name) _____

❏ Advertisement (name) _____

❏ Recommendation _____

❏ Catalog _____

❏ Other _____

Where did you buy this book?

❏ Bookstore (name) _____ City _____

❏ Computer store (name) _____

❏ Mail order _____

❏ Other

What influenced you in the purchase of this book?

❏ Cover Design ❏ Contents ❏ Other (please specify):

_____

How did you rate the overall content of this book?

❏ Excellent ❏ Good ❏ Average ❏ Poor

What did you find most useful about this book? _____

_____

What did you find least useful about this book? _____

_____

Please add any additional comments. _____

_____

What other subjects will you buy a computer book on soon?

_____

What is the best computer book you have used this year?

Note: This information will only be used to keep you updated about new glasshaus titles and will not be used for any other purpose or passed to any other third party.

Check here if you DO NOT want to receive support for this book ❏

glasshaus

web professional to web professional

Note: If you post the bounce back card below in the UK, please send it to:

glasshaus, Arden House, 1102 Warwick Road,
Acocks Green, Birmingham B27 6HB. UK.

Computer Book Publishers